"It is widely recognized that 'salvation' tends to serve as the comprehensive label, gathering up all the other categories: justification, election, redemption, regeneration, sanctification, and so forth. This excellent volume, grounded in responsible exegesis and wise theological reflection and synthesis, fills in the connections, and thus succeeds in painting an edifying and holistic picture of salvation. This work deserves wide circulation."

—**D. A. Carson**, emeritus professor of New Testament
at Trinity Evangelical Divinity School

"Morgan and Schreiner have produced an enjoyable and comprehensive work on salvation. This volume will serve as an ideal textbook for whoever wants to know what God revealed about salvation in Scripture and how the people of God have historically understood salvation. I highly recommend this work for students of theology, preachers, and Bible teachers."

—**Dongsun Cho**, associate professor, Korea Baptist
Theological University and Seminary

"This book on salvation by Morgan and Schreiner is first rate: clearly written, thoughtfully organized, and informed by close attention to the biblical text and the biblical plotline, but also engaged with past and contemporary debates. Union in Christ insightfully colors the work which treats all the important doctrinal topics from election to the glory of God in salvation. This book is to be savored."

—**Graham Cole**, dean emeritus and professor of biblical and
systematic theology, Trinity Evangelical Divinity School

"In this hefty book, Morgan and Schreiner take on the impressive task of making accessible the complex conversations around the topic of salvation. They do not shy away from disagreements but helpfully bring in voices and texts from traditions they differ from, showing how various conclusions are reached but making clear their logic. Most helpfully, they provide systematic summaries at the end of each chapter to help the reader bring everything together by the end of the book. This is an engaging read on an important subject."

— **Mariam Kovalishyn**, associate professor of
New Testament studies, Regent College

"From the fall to redemption and consummation, Morgan and Schreiner provide an in-depth look at a biblical theology of salvation, including a definition and pastoral application of the Bible's vocabulary of salvation. A must read for every pastor and seminary student who wants to understand the depths of God's grace in salvation for all nations through Christ and in the Holy Spirit."

—**John Massey**, associate professor of missions and Charles F. Stanley Chair for the Advancement of Global Christianity, Southwestern Baptist Theological Seminary

"What a treasure this volume is, filled to the brim with the promises of God by which we're saved from our sins and given new life in Christ by the Spirit. It is comprehensively biblical, systematically arranged, centered on the person and work of Christ on our behalf, and laid out by two faithful, learned, godly theologians. This work deserves a wide reading among all those who want to know what God has revealed about the way of salvation."

—**Douglas A. Sweeney**, dean and professor of divinity, Beeson Divinity School

SALVATION

THEOLOGY *for the* PEOPLE *of* GOD

SALVATION

Christopher W. Morgan & Thomas R. Schreiner

EDITORS

David S. Dockery | *Nathan A. Finn* | *Christopher W. Morgan*

B&H
ACADEMIC
BRENTWOOD, TENNESSEE

Dedication

To Shelley and Chelsey, I am beyond blessed to
be Shelley's husband and Chelsey's dad.
Chris

To my wife Diane, my greatest earthly gift!
Tom

ACKNOWLEDGMENTS

From Chris:

Dr. Robert Peterson, for your collaboration, theological insight, and terrific research and writing assistance. Thank you for strengthening, deepening, and clarifying this whole volume.

President Ron Ellis, Provost Chuck Sands, the administration, and trustees at California Baptist University, for your vision and leadership.

Gary McDonald, for joyfully participating in life together, believing in my writing, and excelling in grace and generosity.

Dr. Tony Chute, for sharing life, ministry, leadership, administration, and theology together.

Maigen Turner, for your friendship, skillfulness, and assistance.

CBU's School of Christian Ministries' faculty and students, for your friendship and resolve to exalt the Lord, serve churches, and invest in people.

Immanuel Baptist Church in Highland, for sharing life together.

Julie Tilman, for your friendship and readiness to help.

SoCal Baptist Ministries and the Baptist Foundation of California, for your encouragement and support.

Dr. Milton Higgins, for your friendship, love, prayers, and support.

Elliott Pinegar, for your quality editorial help.

Madison Trammell, Michael McEwen, Audrey Greeson, and the B&H Academic team, for your encouragement, service, and commitment to serve the church.

Tom Schreiner, for your example, scholarship, and friendship.

From Tom:

President Albert J. Mohler and Vice President and Provost Matthew J. Hall, for their encouragement and support for writing.

Southern Baptists, who contribute to the Cooperative Program, which provides enough funding to free up time to work on projects such as this.

Chris Morgan, for joining me in this volume. His partnership and friendship have been a gift to me.

CONTENTS

ABBREVIATIONS

AB	Anchor Bible
ATS	Africa Theology Series
BECNT	Baker Exegetical Commentary on the New Testament
CCT	Contours of Christian Theology
cf.	(Lat.) confer, compare
chap.	chapter
CSB	Christian Standard Bible
DPL	*Dictionary of Paul and His Letters*
EBT	Explorations in Biblical Theology
ed.	editor; edition; edited by
EDNT	*Exegetical Dictionary of the New Testament*
ESV	English Standard Version
FET	Foundations of Evangelical Theology
HALOT	*Hebrew and Aramaic Lexicon of the Old Testament*
IVPNTC	InterVarsity Press New Testament Commentary
JETS	*Journal of the Evangelical Theological Society*
JTS	*Journal of Theological Studies*
KJV	King James Version
LNTS	Library of New Testament Studies
LXX	Septuagint
n.	note
NASB	New American Standard Bible
NET	New English Translation
NICNT	New International Commentary on the New Testament
NICOT	New International Commentary on the Old Testament

NIDNTTE	*New International Dictionary of New Testament Theology and Exegesis*
NIGTC	New International Greek Testament Commentary
NIV	New International Version
no.	number
NSBT	New Studies in Biblical Theology
NT	New Testament
NTC	New Testament Commentary
OT	Old Testament
par.	parallel
PNTC	Pelican New Testament Commentaries
repr.	reprint
rev. ed.	revised edition
SJT	*Scottish Journal of Theology*
TOTC	Tyndale Old Testament Commentaries
TPG	Theology for the People of God
WBC	Word Biblical Commentary
WTJ	*Westminster Theological Journal*
WUNT	Wissenschaftliche Untersuchungen zum Neuen Testament

INTRODUCTION

"For God so loved the world, that he gave his only
Son, that whoever believes in him should not perish but have eternal life." (John 3:16 ESV)

John 3:16 has helped millions around the globe understand salvation. In one verse we learn many truths. We read of God's love as the motivation for our salvation: "God so loved the world." We discover the ground of salvation: the coming of the Son of God, who died and rose for us. We see a major aspect of our salvation: eternal life. We find our responsibility concerning salvation: to trust in Christ alone to save us. We also delight in the universal offer of salvation: because God loves the world, he invites all to come and receive the blessing of salvation ("whoever believes"). That includes us, and thankfully so, since the surrounding verses reveal that we all need this salvation. No one will see or enter the kingdom of God without being born again, which is to receive new spiritual life from God (vv. 3–5). Indeed, all of us are already condemned (v. 18), live presently under the wrath of God (v. 36), and need the salvation found only in Jesus (vv. 12–18).

The Bible abounds with such teachings on salvation. By God's grace and through our faith in Christ, we have a new identity. We are included in this salvation, chosen, and called by God. We have spiritual vitality, having been joined to Christ and having received new life in him. We believe, turning from our sin and trusting Christ. We are accepted, declared righteous by God because of Christ. We are family, adopted as God's sons and daughters. We are saints, being transformed into holy people. We are glorious, being changed from glory to glory. Our salvation changes everything: how we relate to and view God, ourselves, other believers, and those without Christ. This volume aims to unpack these life-changing teachings on salvation, but first we will treat some preliminaries.

Biblical Words for Salvation

The verb "save" and the noun "salvation" are common in both the OT and the NT.[1] The verb "save" in English versions most often translates the Hebrew verb *yāša'* and the Greek verb *sōzō*. The noun "salvation" usually stems from the Hebrew nouns *yešû'â*, *tešû'â*, and sometimes *peletâ*. In Greek we find the noun *sōtēria*, while "Savior" derives from *sōtēr*.

Physical Preservation

Often the different terms translated "save" and "salvation" refer to physical deliverance. The angels tell Lot to leave Sodom to save his life (Gen 19:17). In Isaiah the Lord pledges to save Jerusalem from the Assyrians (Isa 31:5). It is the same in the NT. The disciples implore Jesus to save them from death when a tempest engulfs the Sea of Galilee (Matt 8:25). The woman who stretches out her hand and touches Jesus's robe is delivered from her physical ailment (9:21).

The noun "salvation" often denotes physical deliverance too. The Lord saves and delivers Israelites by parting the sea so that they walk on dry land, but he destroys the Egyptians when they enter the sea (Exod 14:13). The common OT reference to physical deliverance is less common in the NT. Paul assures those on the ship with him during the storm that everything that happens will be for their salvation, their physical preservation (Acts 27:34).

Spiritual Deliverance

Most OT texts using these terms refer to physical deliverance, while some also speak of spiritual salvation. But the NT often presents the idea of

---

[1] For a helpful survey of the meaning of the word in Greek literature, Jewish literature, and in the NT, see "*Sōzō*," *NIDNTTE*, 4:420–35. Cf. also W. Radl, "*Sōzō*," *EDNT*, 3:319–21.

spiritual salvation. This occurs in Acts 4:12, for example, where Peter proclaims concerning Jesus Christ, "There is salvation in no one else." Paul declares that salvation is open to every person who believes, from both the Jews and the Gentiles (Rom 1:16). The sinful woman whose tears bathed Jesus's feet and who wiped them off with her hair was saved and forgiven of her sins by virtue of her faith (Luke 7:50). Believers are also saved, spiritually rescued, by Jesus's blood (Rom 5:9) and his resurrection (v. 10). Hebrews declares that Jesus, as our Melchizedekian priest, "is able to save completely those who come to God through him" (Heb 7:25).

God as Savior

The use of "Savior" for God and Christ stands out in the Pastorals, where Paul refers to God as Savior ten times while using the term only twice elsewhere (Eph 5:23; Phil 3:20).[2] Six times in the Pastorals God is identified as Savior (1 Tim 1:1; 2:3; 4:10; Titus 1:3; 2:10; 3:4) and four times Jesus Christ is Savior (2 Tim 1:10; Titus 1:4; 2:13; 3:6), which shows that both share deity.[3] Paul emphasizes God's role as Savior (1 Tim 2:3) in the same context where he says that God "wants everyone to be saved and to come to the knowledge of the truth" (2:4). God as Savior in the Pastorals is linked with his longing for all to be saved and his provision of Jesus to make this a reality.

The Time of Salvation

To think of salvation as focused on the past is appropriate, but salvation is richer than this. In fact, we should think of every aspect of our great salvation as eschatological, for the end times have arrived in Jesus Christ. Paul tells the Corinthians that "the ends of the ages have come" (1 Cor 10:11). Hebrews affirms that "in these last days, [God] has spoken to us by his Son" (Heb 1:2).

---

[2] See the essay by J. A. Fitzmyer, "The Savior God: The Pastoral Epistles," in *The Forgotten God: Perspectives in Biblical Theology*, ed. A. A. Das and F. J. Matera (Louisville: Westminster John Knox, 2002), 181–96.

[3] We note Richard Bauckham's impressive work showing that second temple Judaism thought in terms of God's identity and that from the earliest days Christians included Jesus in the unique identity of Israel's one God: *Jesus and the God of Israel* (Grand Rapids: Eerdmans, 2008).

The word "salvation" means that we are rescued or delivered, and the concept isn't restricted to the words "Savior," "save," and "salvation." For example, Paul tells of salvation when he says Jesus "gave himself for our sins to rescue us from this present evil age" (Gal 1:4).

A feature of NT eschatology is the already-but-not-yet character of God's redeeming work.[4] The end times have been inaugurated but not consummated. So, even when salvation is spoken of as a past event, it still has an eschatological character. Jesus has already rescued believers from their sins: "By grace you have been saved through faith. And this is not your own doing; it is the gift of God" (Eph 2:8 ESV). Some texts speak of believers in the process of being saved: "The word of the cross is foolishness to those who are perishing, but it is the power of God to us who are being saved" (1 Cor 1:18). The participle "being saved" is progressive, for Paul contrasts those who are being saved with "those who are perishing" (cf. 2 Cor 2:15).

Salvation isn't only past and present but is also future. The end-time nature of justification is apparent in Paul's earliest letter, where he speaks of the Jesus "who rescues [ryomenon] us from the coming wrath" (1 Thess 1:10; cf. 5:9). Paul shares a similar idea in Rom 5:9: "How much more then, since we have now been justified by his blood, will we be saved through him from wrath" (cf. v. 10). As Heb 9:28 says, Christ "will appear a second time . . . to bring salvation to those who are waiting for him" (cf. Rev 12:10). Peter also regards salvation as eschatological, for he tells of "a salvation that is ready to be revealed in the last time" (1 Pet 1:5).

Preliminary Exegetical Reflections

Scripture emblazons the truth that salvation is of the Lord. Jonah famously sums up this theme inside the great fish: "Salvation belongs to the Lord" (Jonah 2:9). The psalmist exclaims, "The Lord is my light and my salvation—whom should I fear?" (Ps 27:1). Salvation is found *only* in the Lord, and humans can't accomplish it but must depend entirely upon God. When Egypt's army thundered toward Israel at the Red Sea, Moses did not

---

[4] Many have argued this point. Perhaps George Ladd has influenced evangelicals on this matter more than anyone else. See George Eldon Ladd, *The Presence of the Future*, rev. ed. (Grand Rapids: Eerdmans, 1996).

summon Israel to battle. Rather, he exclaimed, "Stand firm and see the LORD's salvation that he will accomplish for you today" (Exod 14:13). The OT is replete with God's people calling upon him to save them, for they realize that there is no help anywhere else (e.g., Pss 22:21; 28:9; 31:1, 16; 54:14; 80:7).

This theme appears also in the NT: "The Son of Man has come to seek and to save the lost" (Luke 19:10). The hope for spiritual deliverance originates not with humans but with God, who chooses people for salvation (2 Thess 2:13; cf. 2 Tim 2:9–10). Salvation is of the Lord and can't be accomplished by humans because of our sin, and thus God's grace shines when "Christ Jesus [comes] into the world to save sinners" (1 Tim 1:15) through his death and resurrection.

This great salvation isn't limited to Jews but is extended to all people everywhere (Isa 45:22; 49:6; Acts 28:28). Both Testaments declare: "Everyone who calls on the name of the LORD will be saved" (Joel 2:32; cf. Acts 2:21; Rom 10:13). Salvation means confessing that Jesus is Lord and believing that God raised him from the dead (vv. 9–10).

Saving faith includes repentance (2 Cor 7:10), for there is no true faith without turning to the Lord and a change in life. God's saving work includes perseverance, for Jesus says that "the one who endures to the end will be saved" (Matt 10:22). Indeed, if people refuse to continue in belief, they won't be saved (Heb 2:3; 10:39). Saving faith produces good works (Jas 2:14), which aren't the basis of salvation but its necessary fruit.

Salvation and the Biblical Story[5]

Before we zoom in on various aspects of the doctrine of salvation in subsequent chapters, we zoom out to view the Scriptures with a wide-angle lens. Conrad Mbewe of Zambia helpfully observes:

> As you read the Bible from Genesis to Revelation, you will notice
> that there is a coherent story line that holds it all together: the

---

[5] Much of what follows depends on Christopher W. Morgan, with Robert A. Peterson, *Christian Theology: The Biblical Story and Our Faith* (Nashville: B&H Academic, 2020), 3–34, 325–92. For a more thorough treatment of how the biblical story frames theology, see D. A. Carson, *The Gagging of God: Christianity Confronts Pluralism* (Grand Rapids: Zondervan, 1996), 193–345.

themes of this story line are creation, the fall, redemption, and restoration. These are not equal themes in the way the Bible treats them. Most of the Bible is given to unfolding the third of these, the great drama of redemption through Jesus Christ. But this redemption is set against the backdrop of creation and the fall, and this redemption will find its final completion in restoration and final judgment, when the original creation is restored to what it was originally intended to be. The Old Testament develops this story line, preparing for Jesus, and the New Testament fulfills this story line, portraying Jesus. The person and work of Christ, therefore, is what unites the entire Bible. As we read both Old and New Testaments through the lens of redemption in Christ, we will understand the whole Bible the way God wants us to understand it.[6]

Creation

"In the beginning God created the heavens and the earth" (Gen 1:1). Already in existence prior to matter, space, or time, the eternal, self-existent God creates the universe and all that exists. Bruce Waltke introduces Gen 1:1–2:3: "The creation account is a highly sophisticated presentation, designed to emphasize the sublimity (power, majesty, and wisdom) of the Creator God and to lay the foundation for the worldview of the covenant community."[7]

As the chief character in Genesis 1, God "creates, says, sees, separates, names, makes, appoints, blesses, finishes, makes holy, and rests."[8] God is not the sky, sun, moon, water, trees, animals, or anything else created; God creates them, and they are subject to him. The creation is neither God nor a part of God; he is absolute and has independent existence, whereas creation has derived existence from him and continually depends on him as its sustainer (cf. Acts 17:25–28). Christina Gonet puts it well: "God created the

---

[6] Conrad Mbewe, "How to Read and Understand the Bible," in *ESV Global Study Bible* (Wheaton: Crossway, 2012), 1866.

[7] Bruce K. Waltke, with Cathi J. Fredricks, *Genesis: A Commentary* (Grand Rapids: Zondervan, 2001), 56.

[8] C. John Collins, *Genesis 1–4: A Linguistic, Literary, and Theological Commentary* (Phillipsburg, NJ: P&R, 2006), 71.

heavens and earth *ex nihilo*, and all things depend on him for their existence and happiness."[9]

The transcendent Creator is sovereign, with amazing authority and power. Like a king, he effects his will by his word, bringing things into being out of nothing (Gen 1:3; Heb 11:3). He further displays his authority over all creation by calling and naming the things he has created (Gen 1:5).

The transcendent, sovereign Creator is also personal. On each day of creation God is personally involved in every detail, crafting his world in a way that pleases him and benefits his creatures. In dramatic fashion, on the sixth day he personally creates man in his own image, breathing life into him. The personal God has made humans personal as well, with the ability to relate to him, live in community, and have dominion over creation. As D. A. Carson reminds, "We are accorded an astonishing dignity" and have "implanted within us a profound capacity for knowing God intimately."[10] By making us in his image, God distinguishes us from the rest of creation and establishes that he is distinct from us—we are not gods but creatures made in his image.

God is also good, which is reflected in the goodness of his creation and reinforced in the steady refrain, "And God saw that it was good" (1:4, 10, 12, 18, 21, 25). On the sixth day creation is even described as "very good" (v. 31). The inherent goodness of creation leaves no room for a fundamental dualism between spirit and matter, such that spirit is good and matter is evil. Indeed, material creation reflects God's goodness, which is evident also in his generous provision of light, land, vegetation, animals, and creeping, crawling things. These are blessings given for humanity's benefit, as are the ability to relate to God, fertility to procreate, and authority to use the earth's abundant provisions for man's good. Although creation reaches its summit in God's creating man in his image, Gen 1:1–2:3 culminates in the rest of God. By the seventh day God finishes his creative work, rests, and blesses and sanctifies the day as holy, as a Sabbath to be kept. In doing so God displays his joy and

---

[9] Christina Gonet, "The Narrative of Salvation in Anselm of Canterbury's *Cur Deus homo*: Extracting and Explicating the Story Embedded in the Text" (PhD diss., Gateway Seminary, 2022), 131.

[10] Carson, *The Gagging of God*, 205.

satisfaction in his creation and his celebration of completion, and he com-
memorates this special event.[11]

God provides the garden of Eden as a place in which man and woman
may live and work.[12] God "forms the man, plants the garden, transports man
there, sets up the terms of a relationship with man, and searches for a helper
fit for the man, which culminates in the woman."[13] Man is formed from the
dust of the ground but is more than dust; his life comes directly from the
very breath of God (2:7). In planting the garden and moving man there,
the Creator and covenant Lord provides a delightful and sacred space in
which humans can enjoy a harmonious relationship with him, each other, the
animals, and the land. Waltke observes, "The Garden of Eden is a temple-
garden, represented later in the tabernacle."[14] As such the garden highlights
God's presence with man.

So God creates Adam and Eve in his image as good and with wonderful
privileges and significant responsibilities in the garden of Eden. They experience an unhindered relationship with God, intimate enjoyment of each
other, and delegated authority over creation. God establishes the terms for
living in his presence and graciously puts forward only one prohibition: they
must not eat of the tree of the knowledge of good and evil.

Fall

Foolishly, Adam and Eve do not obey God's command but fall (Genesis 3).
This account begins with a Tempter who calls into question God's truthful-
ness, sovereignty, and goodness. The Tempter is "cunning" and deflects the
woman's attention from the covenantal relationship God has established. In
verses 6–8 the central scene in the story of the fall reaches its climax. The
fatal sequence is described rapidly in 3:6: she saw, she took, she ate, and
she gave, culminating in "he ate." Wenham observes that the midpoint of
verses 6–8, "and he ate," employs the key verb of the narrative—"eat"—and is

---

[11] Allen P. Ross, *Creation and Blessing: A Guide to the Study and Exposition of Genesis* (Grand Rapids: Baker, 1996), 114.

[12] Collins, *Genesis 1–4*, 39, 101.

[13] Collins, 132.

[14] Waltke, *Genesis*, 85.

placed between the woman's inflated expectations in eating (the fruit is good to eat, is a delight to the eyes, and gives insight) and its actual effects: their eyes are opened, they know they are nude, and they hide in the trees.[15] The contrast is striking: the forbidden fruit does not deliver what the Tempter has promised but brings dark new realities warned of by the good and truthful covenant Lord.

This initial act of human rebellion brings divine justice: "They sinned by eating, and so would suffer to eat; she led her husband to sin, and so would be mastered by him; they brought pain into the world by their disobedience, and so would have painful toil in their respective lives."[16] The consequences of their sin are fitting and devastating. The couple immediately feels shame, realizing they are naked (3:7). They sense their estrangement from God, even foolishly trying to hide from him (vv. 8–10). They are afraid of God and how he might respond (vv. 9–10). Their alienation from each other also emerges as the woman blames the serpent, while the man blames the woman and by intimation even God (vv. 10–13). Pain and sorrow also ensue. The woman experiences greater pain in childbirth; the man toils in trying to grow food in a land with pests and weeds; both discover dissonance in their relationship (vv. 15–19). Even worse, the couple is banished from Eden and from God's glorious presence (vv. 22–24).

How they surely wish they had listened to God's warning: If you eat of the tree of the knowledge of good and evil, "you will certainly die" (2:17). Upon eating the forbidden fruit, they do not immediately fall over and die from something like cardiac arrest. But they do die. They die spiritually, and their bodies also begin to experience the gradual decay that leads ultimately to their physical deaths (3:19).

Most devastating is that these consequences do not befall only Adam and Eve but extend to their descendants as well. Sin has entered the picture and has brought disruption and alienation in each human relationship—with God, oneself, one another, and creation. The immediate context and storyline of Genesis 4–11 underline this gloomy new reality. In Gen 4:7 God warns Cain that sin is "crouching at the door" and that its "desire is for you,

---

[15] Gordon J. Wenham, *Genesis 1–15*, WBC (Waco: Word, 1987), 75.
[16] Ross, *Creation and Blessing*, 148.

but you must rule over it." Sadly, Cain refuses to heed the advice and kills his brother, Abel. Cain is consequently cursed by God, alienated from the earth, and banished from God's presence (vv. 10–16).

Genesis 5 reminds us that God has created humans in his image and blessed them; the chapter offers hope through mention of Enoch and Noah but soberly underlines the domain of death with the refrain "then he died" eight times. Genesis 6 clarifies the extension and intensification of sin, which is portrayed as massive, pervasive, continual, and characteristic (6:5–11). God graciously establishes a covenant with Noah and appropriately judges humanity with the flood (Genesis 6–9). After the flood God reemphasizes the creational blessing and mandate and offers a covenant promise (9:1–17). Genesis then recounts the history of the Tower of Babel, at which God judges proud, self-seeking humans who attempt to make a name for themselves and to multiply their influence rather than serving as God's image-bearers and advancing his name (11:1–9).

Redemption

Thankfully, God does not completely eradicate humanity for such cosmic treason but graciously begins a restoration project instead. He begins the process of redeeming humanity and the cosmos, particularly restoring humans as full image-bearers so that we can participate in and reflect the glory, identity, and mission that we have longed for the whole time.

God calls Abraham from a family of idol-worshipers and enters into a covenant with him, promising to be God to him and his descendants (Gen 12:1–3; 17:7). God promises to give Abraham a land, to make him into a great nation, and through him to bless all peoples (12:3). From Abraham come Isaac and Jacob, whose name God changes to Israel and from whom God brings twelve tribes of his people. The rest of the Old Testament concerns God's dealings with the twelve tribes of Israel.

Through Moses, great plagues, and a dramatic exodus, God calls Israel out of Egyptian bondage to be his people. He gives them the Ten Commandments, promises to be their God, and claims them as his own. He promises to be with them and gives them the Promised Land, which they occupy under Joshua's leadership after defeating the Canaanites.

After Joshua dies, judges such as Gideon, Deborah, and Samson become leaders of the people.[17] History repeats itself, as generation after generation experiences peace, then rebels, then receives God's judgment, then cries out to God, and then experiences peace once again.

God gives his people a king, first Saul, then David, then Solomon. Under David, a man after God's own heart, the kingdom grows significantly, Jerusalem becomes the capital, and God renews his covenant promise with his people. God promises to make David's descendants into a dynasty and to establish the throne of one of them forever. God uses David's son Solomon to build a temple, where God's covenant presence is manifest. Solomon does much right but also disobeys God in major ways, and this leads to the kingdom's splitting into northern (Israel) and southern (Judah) kingdoms.

God sends many prophets to call the people to covenant faithfulness. They warn his people of the judgment that will come if they do not repent of their sins and turn to the Lord. Nevertheless, the people repeatedly rebel against him and his prophets. In response he sends the northern kingdom of ten tribes into captivity in Assyria in 722 BC and the southern kingdom of two tribes, Judah and Benjamin, into captivity in Babylon in 586 BC. Through the prophets God also promises to send a deliverer (Isa 9:6–7; 52:13–53:12).

God promises to restore his people to their land from Babylonian captivity after seventy years (Jer 25:11–12), and he brings this about under Ezra and Nehemiah. The people rebuild the walls of Jerusalem and build a second temple. Yet the Old Testament ends with God's people continuing to turn away from him (Malachi).

After four hundred years God sends his Son as the promised Messiah, Suffering Servant, King of Israel, and Savior of the world. The Son of God is conceived of a virgin and becomes fully human. In time Jesus is baptized, successfully defeats Satan's temptation in the wilderness, and is declared to be the Messiah. Jesus chooses and invests in twelve disciples as new leaders of his messianic community. He teaches about the kingdom of God, that God's rule has come in Jesus the Messiah. Jesus displays this by casting out demons, performing miracles, and preaching the good news to the poor.

---

[17] Preben Vang and Terry G. Carter, *Telling God's Story: The Biblical Narrative from Beginning to End*, 2nd ed. (Nashville: B&H Academic, 2013), 1–9.

Jesus completely follows the will and plan of God, even without sin. He is loved by many but opposed by Jewish religious and political leaders. Not only does he not fit their conception of a Messiah, but he also undercuts their pride, beliefs, and traditions. The opposition increases, as the Jewish Sanhedrin condemns Jesus in an illegal trial. Because the nation is occupied by the Roman Empire, the leaders must send Jesus to their staunch enemy, Pontius Pilate, who finds Jesus innocent. Under pressure from the Jewish leaders and crowds, however, Pilate crucifies Jesus anyway. Jesus the innocent one, the righteous one, dies on the cross. From a human vantage point, Jesus dies as a victim in this despicably evil act. Yet the biblical story highlights that this death is part of God's eternal plan to save sinners. Jesus's mission is to seek and save the lost, and he does not fail to do so. Jesus saves sinners as their substitute, victor, sacrifice, new Adam, redeemer, and peacemaker.

Incredibly, Jesus not only bears the sin of the world on the cross but also is raised from the dead three days later. In a variety of places, situations, and groups, over five hundred people witness the resurrected Jesus. Through his resurrection he confirms his identity, defeats sin and death, gives new life to his people, and provides a foretaste of his people's future resurrection.

Jesus directs his disciples to take the gospel to all nations to fulfill God's promise to Abraham to bless all peoples through him. His disciples are to make disciples of others, who will then make disciples of still others. On the day of Pentecost, Jesus sends his Spirit, who forms the church as the New Testament people of God. The Spirit empowers the church to bear witness to Christ among the nations.

The early church "devote[s] themselves to the apostles' teaching, to the fellowship, to the breaking of bread, and to prayer" (2:42). The early church is involved in evangelism (vv. 38–41), sharing the gospel with those who do not know Christ as the means of salvation. The church is committed to discipleship, instructing believers in how to follow Jesus as a way of life. The church is devoted to fellowship (vv. 42–47), sharing life together, knowing one another, loving one another. The church is also involved in ministry (vv. 42–46), praying for one another, giving to one another, meeting each other's needs. The church is active in worship (v. 46), praising God, publicly meeting together, and privately teaching, praying, giving, and partaking together. The church grows and faces persecution, but the gospel keeps moving on. Some Jews and many Gentiles trust Christ, churches are planted, and the cycle continues. Along the way, the churches teach sound doctrine, correct error, and call believers to live in love, unity, holiness, and truth.

Apostles such as Paul and Peter also teach about salvation. The Father has planned salvation, the Son accomplishes it, and the Spirit applies it to all who believe in Christ. God chooses, calls, and gives new life in Christ to believers. God forgives, declares righteous, and adopts into his family all who have faith in Christ. God is making his people holy in Christ and will finally glorify all who know him. God saves out of his generous love and for his glory.

Consummation

Jesus will finish what he has started. He will return to reign as king, bringing justice, peace, delight, and victory. The kingdom is God's reign over his people through King Jesus. The kingdom is both a present reality and a future promise tied to Christ's second coming. Jesus brings the kingdom in phases. It is inaugurated in his public ministry, as he teaches, performs miracles, and casts out demons (Matt 13:1–50; 12:28). When Jesus ascends to God's right hand, the place of greatest power, the kingdom expands (Eph 1:20–21) and thousands enter it through the apostles' preaching (Acts 2:41, 47). The fullness of the kingdom awaits Christ's return, when he will sit on his glorious throne (Matt 25:31). Jesus will judge the world, inviting believers into the final stage of the kingdom while banishing unbelievers to hell (25:34, 41).

The classic passage depicting the consummation and related truths is Revelation 20–22. Just as Genesis 1–2 reveals that the biblical story begins with God's creation of the heavens and the earth, Revelation 20–22 shows that it ends with God's creation of a new heavens and a new earth. The story begins with the goodness of creation and ends with the goodness of the new creation. The story begins with God's dwelling with his people in a garden-temple and ends with God's dwelling with his covenant people in heaven, a new earth-city-garden-temple.

Once and for all God's victory is consummated. God's judgment is final, sin is vanquished, justice prevails, holiness predominates, God's glory is unobstructed, and the kingdom is realized. God's eternal plan of cosmic reconciliation in Christ is actualized, and God is "all in all" (1 Cor 15:28).

As a part of his victory, God casts the devil and his demons into the lake of fire, where they are not consumed but are "tormented day and night forever and ever" (Rev 20:10). Satan and the demons thus receive their due punishment, that will know no end. Then God judges everyone: those whom the world deems important, those whom the world never notices, and everyone in between. "Anyone whose name was not found written in the book of life was thrown into the lake of fire" (v. 15). God does not send only the ruthless Roman emperors to hell (which we might expect); he consigns to hell all who are not the people of Jesus (cf. Dan 12:1; Rev 13:8; 21:8, 27).

Magnificently, the new heavens and new earth arrive, and God dwells with his covenant people (Rev 21:3, 7), brings comfort to them (there is no more pain, death, etc.; v. 4), makes all things new (v. 5), and proclaims, "It is done!" (v. 6). Heaven is then depicted as a perfect temple, glorious, multinational, and holy (vv. 9–27). The people of God rightly bear God's image: serving him, reigning with him, encountering him directly, and worshipping him (22:1–5). God receives the worship he is due, and humans are blessed beyond description, finally living to the fullest the realities of being created in his image.[18]

This is the essence of the biblical story, and it is also the story of salvation. Indeed, if we know Christ, it is our story too. Before creation, God the Father plans our salvation. In space and time two thousand years ago, Jesus comes and does the work necessary to save us. And ever since, the Holy Spirit brings God's grace to bear on our lives as we trust Christ. Notice how the Bible describes our salvation not only in black and white but in technicolor. The apostles paint many pictures to teach that God rescues us when we could not free ourselves. The overarching picture is union with Christ, God's joining believers to his Son by grace through faith so that all of his saving benefits become ours. When the Holy Spirit unites us spiritually to Christ, we receive many other benefits as well. The Father effectively summons us to Christ through the gospel (calling). The Spirit makes us alive spiritually (regeneration). He turns us from sin (repentance) and to Christ (faith) as he is offered in the gospel (conversion). The Father declares us righteous in his sight because of Christ's righteousness (justification). He places us into his family as his children (adoption). The Spirit purifies us, setting us apart from

---

[18] For a clear and edifying overview of the biblical story, framed with the doctrine of God, see D. A. Carson, *The God Who Is There: Finding Your Place in God's Story* (Grand Rapids: Baker, 2010).

sin unto holiness once and for all and progressively working holiness into us (sanctification). God keeps us (preservation) so we continue to walk with him (perseverance) and do not turn away from Christ (apostasy). Because God chose us in Christ (election) and Christ died and rose to save us, God will share his glory with us on the last day (glorification).

A Roadmap

In this volume we will study the doctrine of salvation, and we will look at each identity-forming and life-changing aspect of our salvation:

- We are in Christ (union with Christ).
- We are chosen in Christ (election).
- We are called to Christ (calling).
- We are alive in Christ (regeneration).
- We believe in Christ (conversion).
- We are righteous in Christ (justification).
- We are adopted in Christ (adoption).
- We are holy in Christ (sanctification).
- We are kept in Christ (perseverance).
- We are glorious in Christ (glorification).

We will then connect the dots. We will examine how each part of our salvation is not only for our good but also for God's glory. We will see how the doctrine of salvation relates to other key theological themes and how the doctrine of salvation functions in the Christian life.

1

Union with Christ

A wide-angle view of salvation includes God's planning, accomplish-ing, and applying our salvation. God planned salvation before creation when he chose a people for himself. He accomplished salvation through Jesus's life, death, resurrection, ascension, and session in the first century. God applies salvation to believers when he grants them saving grace so that they come to know him. Theologians call this the application of salvation, or union with Christ, the means by which God grants all the other blessings of salvation to believers. Because we belong to Christ, we are saved, elected, jus-tified, adopted, reconciled, redeemed, sanctified, and glorified. Calvin aptly described union with Christ:

> As long as Christ remains outside of us, and we are separated from him, all that he has suffered and done for the salvation of the human race remains useless and of no value for us. Therefore, to share with us what he has received from the Father, he had to become ours and to dwell within us. For this reason, he is called "our Head" [Eph 4:15], and "the first-born among many brethren" [Rom 8:29]. We also, in turn, are said to be "engrafted into him" [Rom 11:17], and to "put on Christ" [Gal 3:17].[1]

The OT doesn't speak directly of being united to Christ but contains the categories the NT employs. For instance, Adam is the head of the human

---

[1] John Calvin, *Institutes of the Christian Religion*, ed. John T. McNeill, trans. Ford Lewis Battles, 2 vols. (Philadelphia: Westminster, 1960), 3:1.1; 1:537.

race, and all human beings are united to him. Our organic unity with Adam is clear since we all come from him: "From one man [God] has made every nationality to live over the whole earth" (Acts 17:26). We see the unity of the human race when all human beings enter the world as sinners who will die by virtue of their union with Adam (Rom 5:12–19). On the other hand, those who belong to Christ enjoy life and righteousness by virtue of their union with him. Paul sums up his understanding of the roles of Adam and Christ in 1 Cor 15:21–22: "Since death came through a man, the resurrection of the dead also comes through a man. For just as in Adam all die, so also in Christ all will be made alive." All human beings will die by virtue of their union with Adam, but those united with Christ will enjoy resurrection life forever.

Exegetical Foundations

Abraham

The father of the Jewish people is Abraham (Josh 24:3; Luke 1:73). Isaiah says to Israel, "Look to Abraham your father" (Isa 51:2; cf. Acts 7:2), and Israel is designated as his "offspring" (Ps 105:6; Isa 41:8). An individual Israelite may be described as a "daughter of Abraham" (Luke 13:16) or as his son (19:9). Abraham is also described as "the rock from which you were cut, and . . . the quarry from which you were dug" (Isa 51:1). Israel was tempted to think that they would be safe from judgment simply because they were physical descendants of Abraham (Matt 3:7–10; Luke 3:7–9; John 8:33–42; Rom 9:6–9). Those who truly belong to the Lord are the children of Abraham (4:9–12; Gal 3:6–9). Paul argues in Galatians that Jesus is the true offspring of Abraham (3:16), and thus those who are Abraham's offspring put their trust in Jesus Christ (v. 29). We see, then, that one must be a child of Abraham to belong to the people of God, and only those who believe in Jesus, who are united with him, are truly the children of Abraham.

When we call Jesus the true seed of Abraham, this is another way of saying that Jesus is the true Israel, the true Son of God. In the OT Israel is described as God's vineyard (Ps 80:8, 14; Isa 5:1–7; 27:2–3; Jer 2:21; 12:10; Ezek 15:2, 6; 19:10; Hos 10:1). Many of these verses lament that Israel has become an unfruitful vine, a degenerate vine. It is highly significant, then, that Jesus is "the true vine," and those who belong to Jesus, those who are part of the true Israel, are branches united with the true vine (John 15:1–2, 4–5).

Moses

When we think of Moses, we think of the person who brought the law to Israel, and in that sense he functioned as an intermediary between the Lord and the people of Israel (Gal 3:19). When Israel sinned so blatantly against the Lord by making a golden calf, the covenant between the Lord and Israel was broken, symbolized by Moses's breaking the tablets of the law (Exod 32:19). Moses interceded with the Lord, and the Lord did not destroy Israel but forgave them and restored the covenant with them so he could dwell in their midst (vv. 7–14, 31–32; 33:12–34:17). Moses's intercession for Israel also spared them from destruction when they failed to obey the Lord and enter the land of promise (Num 14:11–25; cf. 16:20–24).

Moses was also conceived of as the human agent of Israel's liberation, Israel's redemption, along with Aaron: "The LORD . . . appointed Moses and Aaron . . . who brought your ancestors up from the land of Egypt" (1 Sam 12:6; cf. v. 8). Moses's role as a leader is evident, since Joshua was installed in place of Moses as leader of the people (Num 27:15–23). Joshua is described as a "shepherd" (v. 17), which signifies his leadership role. This means that Moses is also conceived of as the shepherd of God's people, since the authority Moses enjoyed is granted to Joshua (v. 20). We also see from Ps 77:20 that Moses and Aaron were viewed as shepherds: "You led your people like a flock by the hand of Moses and Aaron." They were also both understood to be priests (99:6).

There is a sense in which all of Israel was incorporated into Moses: "All were baptized into Moses in the cloud and in the sea" (1 Cor 10:2). Israel was, so to speak, plunged into Moses, united with Moses, their shepherd, their leader, their deliverer, their prophet, and their priest. But Jesus is greater than Moses. Moses predicted a prophet like him would arise (Deut 18:15), and that prophet is clearly Jesus Christ (cf. Matt 17:5; Luke 9:35; John 1:45; Acts 3:22–23; 7:37). Still, Jesus is greater than Moses, for Moses was a servant while Jesus is God's Son (Heb 3:1–6). Believers are incorporated into Jesus by baptism (Rom 6:3–4; Gal 3:27), and thus they belong to the one who is the final revelation of God (Heb 1:2), the good shepherd of the flock

(John 10:11) who has delivered his people with a greater salvation than that accomplished under Moses.

Leaders and Kings

Those who are identified as judges in the book of Judges delivered and saved the people (Judg 2:16, 18; 3:9; 10:12). The word for "judge" (*šāpaṭ*) is used to describe both the *person* and the *activity* of the judges in the book (2:16, 17, 18, 19; 3:10; 4:4; 10:2, 3; 12:7, 8, 9, 11, 13, 14; 15:30; 16:31). The word "judge" to English ears points to a person who makes legal decisions, but in Judges it has the idea of restoring peace "to a community after it has been disturbed."[2] The judges, then, were leaders, restorers, and deliverers.

The notion of leadership develops further with the institution of the kingdom, especially with David's rule, since the Lord made a covenant with David that promised that his dynasty would never end (2 Sam 7; 1 Chr 17; Pss 89, 132). The king represents the nation, as is clear in 1–2 Kings, for the state of the nation in both Israel and Judah depends upon the spiritual state of the king. It is remarkable that 1–2 Kings tell us very little about what is happening in individual lives; one of the points of the story is that the lives of the people are summed up in the behavior of the king. Both the southern and the northern kingdoms are represented by the king. Since the Lord promised that a Davidic king would reign on the throne, it was intended that a king from David's line would represent the people. Such a promise is fulfilled in Jesus the Christ, and as the King, as the Messiah, he represents his people. The NT picks up this concept when it speaks of believers being in Christ. Those who are "in Christ" are represented by their king.

Son of Man

Daniel had a remarkably strange dream in which he saw four beasts representing kingdoms (Babylon, Medo-Persia, Greece, and Rome; Dan 7:1–8). After seeing such ferocious beasts—and they are beasts because their rule

---

[2] "*šāpaṭ*,"in L. Koehler, W. Baumgartner, and J. J. Stamm, *The Hebrew and Aramaic Lexicon of the Old Testament*, trans. and ed. M. E. J. Richardson (Leiden: Brill, 1999), 4:1622.

ravages and destroys—Daniel had a vision of God's throne room and the Ancient of Days (vv. 9–14). During the vision "one like a son of man" came "with the clouds of heaven" into the presence of "the Ancient of Days" (v. 13). "He was given dominion, and glory, and a kingdom; so that those of every people, nation, and language should serve him. His dominion is an everlasting dominion that will not pass away, and his kingdom is one that will not be destroyed" (v. 14). Clearly the Son of Man in Daniel 7 receives the kingdom, but who is this Son of Man? We note that the kingdom is given to a human being (that is what "Son of Man" means) instead of to an animal. The kingdom given to the Son of Man is humane, just, righteous, and peaceable. The vision is interpreted for Daniel immediately after he sees it (vv. 15–28). We are told three times who will receive the kingdom.

> "But *the holy ones* of the Most High will receive the kingdom and possess it forever, yes, forever and ever." (Dan 7:18)[3]

> "As I was watching, this horn waged war against *the holy ones* and was prevailing over them until the Ancient of Days arrived and a judgment was given in favor of *the holy ones* of the Most High, for the time had come, and *the holy ones* took possession of the kingdom." (vv. 21–22)

> "But the court will convene, and his dominion will be taken away, to be completely destroyed forever. The kingdom, dominion, and greatness of the kingdoms under all of heaven will be given *to the people, the holy ones* of the Most High. His kingdom will be an everlasting kingdom, and all rulers will serve and obey him." (vv. 26–27)

Those who receive the kingdom are identified as "the holy ones" (Dan 7:18), "the holy ones" again (v. 22), and then "the people, the holy ones of the Most High" (v. 27). The last reference demonstrates that the holy ones are human beings and not angels, since they are called "people." When the vision is explained, the "Son of Man" of the vision is identified with the holy ones, and the people of the holy ones. The son of man, then, refers to the people of Israel, to those who belong to God. The kingdom promised to Israel will be granted to them. Despite all the twists and turns of history, despite the

---

[3] All italics in Scripture are ours.

ferocious and ungodly rule of these beasts, the kingdom will come! Still, it is too simplistic to limit the rule to the people of Israel. The kingdoms are represented by ferocious beasts, but the kingdoms were also represented by a king. Indeed, the vision given of the Son of Man suggests he is an individual.

When we come to the NT, repeatedly Jesus identifies himself as the Son of Man. The title was chosen carefully, since the meaning of son of man in Daniel 7 wasn't immediately clear. Jesus, by appropriating this title, identifies himself as the king, as the representative of the holy ones of Daniel. Jesus as the Son of Man is the corporate representative of the holy ones, so that all those who belong to him, all those who are united to the Son of Man, belong to the people of God.[4] They are part of the true Israel because they belong to Jesus, the Son of Man.

Servant of the Lord

We see something quite similar to the Son of Man when it comes to the servant of the Lord in Isaiah. Israel is often identified as the servant:

> But you, Israel, my servant, Jacob, whom I have chosen, descendant of Abraham, my friend—I brought you from the ends of the earth and called you from its farthest corners. I said to you: You are my servant; I have chosen you; I haven't rejected you. (Isa 41:8–9)

> "Who is blind but my servant, or deaf like my messenger I am sending? Who is blind like my dedicated one, or blind like the servant of the LORD?" (42:19)

> "You are my witnesses"—this is the LORD's declaration—"and my servant whom I have chosen, so that you may know and believe me and understand that I am he. No god was formed before me, and there will be none after me." (43:10)

> "And now listen, Jacob my servant, Israel whom I have chosen. This is the word of the LORD your Maker, the one who formed you from

---

[4] Oscar Cullmann argues that the Son of Man could function representatively for the saints. *The Christology of the New Testament*, rev. ed., trans. S. C. Guthrie and C. A. M. Hall (Philadelphia: Westminster, 1963), 138–40.

the womb: He will help you. Do not fear, Jacob my servant, Jeshurun whom I have chosen." (44:1–2)

"Remember these things, Jacob, and Israel, for you are my servant; I formed you, you are my servant; Israel, you will never be forgotten by me." (44:21)

"I call you by your name, for the sake of my servant Jacob and Israel my chosen one. I give a name to you, though you do not know me." (45:4)

"Leave Babylon, flee from the Chaldeans! Declare with a shout of joy, proclaim this, let it go out to the end of the earth; announce, 'The Lord has redeemed his servant Jacob!'" (48:20)

He said to me, "You are my servant, Israel, in whom I will be glorified." (49:3)

Israel was God's chosen servant and his beloved, but the people were exiled to Babylon because they had sinned and forsaken the way of the Lord. The Lord promised to redeem and deliver them as his servant. At the same time, it becomes apparent as Isaiah continues that the servant goes beyond Israel. The servant "will bring justice to the nations" (Isa 42:1) and be "a light to the nations" (v. 6). Isaiah could possibly have Israel in mind here and be envisioning Israel's spiritual turnaround and its corresponding influence to the ends of the earth. But at 49:5 such a reading goes astray, for there it says that a servant will raise "up the tribes of Jacob" and restore "the protected ones of Israel," as well as being a light for the nations (v. 6). The servant can't be coterminous with Israel if he restores Israel. Israel can't restore itself, and thus we have a distinction within Israel, an Israel within Israel—a servant who is the true servant. Furthermore, the servant is teachable, is obedient, and suffers despite his innocence (50:4–10), but this stands in contrast to Israel, which was in exile because of its sins and plagued with ungodliness (40:2; 42:18–25; 43:24–28; 44:22; 50:1). Finally, the servant dies for the sins of his people (53:4–6, 10–12), even though he was innocent and without sin (v. 9).

When we turn to the NT, Jesus is identified as the servant of the Lord (Matt 20:28; Mark 10:45; Acts 8:30–35; Rom 4:25; 1 Pet 2:22–25). He dies as the servant of the Lord to bring forgiveness to Israel, to fulfill covenant promises, and to bring salvation to the ends of the earth. We could say that Jesus is the true Israelite, the only true servant of the Lord, who always obeys the Lord. As the representative of Israel, he brings Israel (and the Gentiles) back to God through his atoning death. All those who belong to the Servant, all those who are united with Christ, are members of his people.

"In Christ"

The notion of union with Christ plays a significant role in Paul's thought. Union with Christ in Paul is found regularly with the expression "in Christ."[5] But the concept cannot be confined to the places where "in Christ" itself occurs. For example, Eph 1:3–14 speaks of being "in Christ" (vv. 3, 10, 12), "in him" (vv. 4, 9, 10), "in the Beloved" (v. 6), and "in whom" (vv. 7, 11, 13, KJV). The diversity of expressions to describe being in Christ in this one long sentence (vv. 3–14) is astonishing, and the sheer repetition of the formula indicates that it is crucial in Pauline thought. Some scholars have even maintained that the mystical doctrine of being in Christ or participation in Christ is the center of Pauline theology.[6] Certainly participation in Christ, or union with Christ, is of tremendous importance in Paul's thinking, but it isn't clear that the theme is the center of Paul's thought or the most important truth for understanding his theology.

Some use the word *mystical* to describe Paul's in Christ theology, but the term does not provide the best inroad for understanding Paul's "in Christ" theology. Since mystical is a vague term with a diversity of connotations, it is too imprecise to prove useful in defining Paul's theology. In particular, during the course of NT scholarship some have attempted to forge a connection between Paul and the mystery religions of his day. Paul's indebtedness to the mystery religions was forcefully argued for in the earlier part of the twentieth

---

[5] The material here comes from my Pauline theology with some changes. See Thomas R. Schreiner, *Paul, Apostle of God's Glory in Christ: A Pauline Theology*, 2nd ed. (Downers Grove: IVP Academic, 2020).

[6] See Albert Schweitzer, *The Mysticism of Paul the Apostle* (New York: Henry Holt, 1931), 219–26; and E. P. Sanders, *Paul and Palestinian Judaism: A Comparison of Patterns of Religion* (Philadelphia: Fortress, 1977).

century.[7] Few scholars today would accept such a thesis. The evidence has been carefully sifted through, and most have rightly concluded that the parallels between Paul and the mystery religions are superficial.[8] Some scholars uncritically used sources later than the Pauline writings and then proceeded to argue that Paul borrowed from the latter. Paul's faith is rooted in historical events—the death and resurrection of Jesus the Messiah. This is a far cry from the ahistorical and experiential character of the mystery religions. Paul's theology is rooted in and reflects upon the OT Scriptures, not pagan mystery religions, which Paul would have dismissed as idolatrous and part of the elements of the world. For this reason alone, the term "mystical" should be avoided as misleading in explaining Paul's use of the phrase "in Christ." Others have taken the phrase "in Christ" too literally, even to the point of understanding Christ to be akin to a fluid that permeates our existence. This conception, advocated by Adolf Deissmann among others, has been vigorously challenged, and most scholars now doubt its accuracy.[9]

It is fruitful to explore Paul's use of the term "in Christ" by beginning with Adam Christology. Paul does not use the phrases "in Christ," "in Christ Jesus," or "in the Lord" in only one fashion. The expression oscillates between the ideas of manner, locality, and instrumentality.[10] Sometimes the idea of manner seems prominent: "I speak the truth in Christ" (Rom 9:1). In many

---

[7] The influence of mystery religions on Paul was advocated by Richard Reitzenstein, *Hellenistic Mystery-Religions: Their Basic Ideas and Significance* (Pittsburgh: Pickwick, 1978); cf. Wilhelm Bousset, *Kyrios Christos: A History of the Belief in Christ from the Beginnings of Christianity to Irenaeus* (Nashville: Abingdon, 1970). Few scholars today would accept such a thesis. For example, those studying the history of religions were disposed to think that the Pauline doctrine of baptism was influenced by the mystery religions.

[8] For a decisive and careful refutation of this notion, see A. J. M. Wedderburn, *Baptism and Resurrection: Studies in Pauline Theology Against Its Graeco-Roman Background*, WUNT 44 (Tübingen: J. C. B. Mohr, 1987); cf. Günter Wagner, *Pauline Baptism and the Pagan Mysteries: The Problem of the Pauline Doctrine of Baptism in Romans VI.1–11 in the Light of Its Religio-Historical "Parallels"* (Edinburgh: Oliver & Boyd, 1967).

[9] G. Adolf Deissmann, *Paul: A Study in Social and Religious History* (New York: George H. Doran, 1927), 135–57, esp. 138–42; cf. Bousset, *Kyrios Christos*, 154–63.

[10] For a thorough study, see Constantine R. Campbell, *Paul and Union with Christ: An Exegetical and Theological Study* (Grand Rapids: Zondervan, 2012). But see Mark A. Seifrid's penetrating review, http://themelios.thegospelcoalition.org/review/paul

instances "in Christ" denotes both means and locality. Both of these notions fit under the rubric of Adam Christology, though we must be careful not to force every use of the phrase into this category.

We have observed earlier that in Paul's thought all people are either in Adam or in Christ. Adam and Christ are the two representative heads for humanity. When Paul says believers are "in Christ," he means that they are incorporated in Christ rather than in Adam. Christ is now their representative and head rather than Adam. Some scholars raise doubts about whether such representative or corporate Christology can be sustained by examining the evidence. They object that the whole notion of "corporate personality" is imposed upon the evidence instead of being vindicated by careful study.[11] Doubtless some go too far when they speak of corporate personality. But the contrast between Adam and Christ supports the representative character of Paul's Christology, and it is clear that these two are the heads of humanity. Such an idea is found also in the OT, as we have seen that the king functions as the representative of his people (e.g., 2 Sam 19:40–43; 20:1), and the Son of Man and the Servant of the Lord represent Israel.

Those who are in Adam experience all the liabilities of being descended from him. Similarly, those who are in Christ experience all the blessings of being united to him. Every spiritual blessing belongs to believers in Christ (Eph 1:3). Those who are in Christ are a new creation (2 Cor 5:17), redeemed (Rom 3:24; Eph 1:7), and sons of God (Gal 3:26). What marks out Christian communities or assemblies, then, is that they are in Christ (1:22; Col 1:2; cf. 1 Thess 1:1). Both Jews and Gentiles have been brought near to God in Christ (Eph 2:13). God has reconciled the world in Christ (2 Cor 5:19). The blessing of Abraham is available to Jews and Gentiles in Christ (Gal 3:14). Thus, believers from every social class and ethnic group—both males and females—are one in Christ Jesus (v. 28). Believers have been chosen before the world began in Christ (Eph 1:4), and it is only by virtue of God's work that they are in Christ (1 Cor 1:30). There is no condemnation for those

---

-and-union-with-christ-an-exegetical-and-theological-study, accessed December 28, 2017. See also Mark Seifrid, "In Christ" *DPL*, 433–36.

[11] See John W. Rogerson, "The Hebrew Conception of Corporate Personality: A Re-examination," *JTS* 21 (1970): 1–16; Stanley E. Porter, "Two Myths: Corporate Personality and Language/Mentality Determinism," *SJT* 43 (1990): 289–307.

in Christ (Rom 8:1), and believers are alive to God in Christ Jesus (6:11). Believers are seated in the heavenlies with Christ (Eph 2:6) and experience freedom in him (Gal 2:4). When we see the comprehensive blessings that belong to those in Christ, it is clear that the promise to reclaim the world for God is inaugurated through him. The church is a new society that expresses in part what God intended when he made Adam and Eve. The saving promises made to Abraham are becoming a reality in Christ, since he reverses the curse and devastation imposed upon the world through the first Adam.

Since the apostles John and Paul are the two chief biblical teachers of union with Christ, we will examine key passages in John's Gospel and Paul's Epistles before we seek to correlate their teachings into a systematic theology of union.

John 17:20–26

The traditional division of Jesus's great prayer is correct. He prays first for himself (John 17:1–5), next for his disciples (vv. 6–19), and then for the world (vv. 20–26). In the last seven verses he prays for those who will believe through the apostles' preaching (and writing). He prays for the unity of his church according to this remarkable standard: "as you, Father, are in me and I am in you" (v. 21). The Father and the Son (along with the Holy Spirit) share the divine nature and therefore mutually indwell one another.

Jesus goes further, praying, "[Father,] may they also be in us, so that the world may believe you sent me" (v. 21). Astonishingly, Jesus prays that believers will be in the Father and the Son! So the Father, the Son, the Spirit, and believers will indwell one another.

Jesus goes further still, asking the Father to bring believers to heaven to see Jesus's glory (v. 24). (Although Jesus had not yet gone to the cross, he is so determined to go that he prays this prayer as if he had already returned to his Father in heaven [vv. 4–5, 11, 24].) Jesus's last words in the prayer speak of divine indwelling: "I made your name known to them and will continue to make it known, so that the love you have loved me with may be in them and I may be in them" (v. 26). Jesus has revealed the Father to the disciples so that Jesus's love and he himself might indwell them. Present union with Christ overlaps with God's indwelling his people. Though evangelicals correctly teach that the Spirit indwells them (Rom 5:5; 8:9–11; 1 Cor 3:16; 6:19–20;

2 Cor 1:21–22; Gal 3:13–14; 4:6; 1 Thess 4:8; 2 Tim 1:14), Scripture teaches that the Father (2 Cor 6:16; Eph 2:22) and Son (Rom 8:10; 2 Cor 13:5; Gal 2:20; Eph 3:17; Col 1:27; 3:11) indwell them too.

John teaches much about union with Christ. We can summarize his teaching in three points. First, the Father and the Son indwell one another (John 10:38; 14:10–11; 17:21). Theologians call this *perichoresis*. Though John does not systematize and include the Holy Spirit, taking all Scripture into account we do include him and say that the three trinitarian persons indwell one another. Second, the Father, the Son, and the Spirit will indwell believers (14:20, 23; 17:22–23, 26). Third, the Father, the Son (and the Spirit), and believers will indwell one another (14:17, 20; 6:55–56; 15:4–5; 17:21).

Romans 5:12–19

As we have seen, John has amazing things to say about union with Christ, but Paul is rightly recognized as the Bible's premier theologian of union. Although he does not use "in Christ" language here or say that believers shared in Jesus's saving events (e.g., died and rose with him), this passage offers a big-picture presentation of union with Christ. Paul presents a meta-biblical theology involving the two Adams as heads of their respective people. The first man Adam represented the human race when he sinned in the garden of Eden. Through his primal sin, sin and death entered the world of humanity (Rom 5:12). Paul begins a comparison between Adam and Christ but leaves it incomplete. Paul next seems to appeal to Adam's original sin to explain why death *reigned* from the time of Adam to the time of Moses's giving the law, even over people who did not break a divine command as Adam did (vv. 13–14). Paul adds, "He is a type of the Coming One" (v. 14), laying the foundation for the thoughts he will develop in verses 18–19. Adam is an Old Testament prefiguring of Christ, the second and last Adam. There is thus similarity between them.

Instead of immediately developing this similarity, Paul shows in verses 15–17 how the two Adams are dissimilar. Adam's sin brought death to many people, but Christ's grace brought abundant grace, justification, and eternal life to many (v. 15). Adam's one sin brought condemnation to the human race, but God's grace brought justification and with it the forgiveness of many sins (v. 16). Death reigned through Adam's sin, but those who accept grace and free justification will reign in eternal life through Christ (v. 17).

Finally, in verses 18–19 Paul completes the unfinished comparison of verse 12 in light of the similarity of the two Adams hinted at in verse 14. Paul had written, "Therefore, just as sin entered the world through one man, and death through sin, in this way death spread to all people, because all sinned" (v. 12). Now he completes that thought:

> So then, as through one trespass there is condemnation for every-one, so also through one righteous act there is justification leading to life for everyone. For just as through one man's disobedience the many were made sinners, so also through the one man's obedience the many will be made righteous. (vv. 18–19)

Adam's primal sin resulted in condemnation for all those in union with him: the human race. In a similar way, Christ's "one righteous act" of dying on the cross resulted in justification to eternal life for all those in union with him: the race of the redeemed (v. 18). Verse 19 recapitulates verse 18: just as Adam's disobedience to God made sinners out of all whom he represented before God, so Christ's obedience "to the point of death—even to death on a cross" (Phil 2:8) will make righteous all whom he represented before God.

To summarize: In Rom 5:12–19 Paul views the history of humankind in terms of the two Adams. Their respective acts had catastrophic consequences for the people they represent. All whom Adam represents find death and condemnation in union with him. All whom Christ represents find justification and eternal life in union with him.

Romans 6:1–14

In one of Scripture's most important passages on the Christian life, Paul is once more under attack. His opponents accuse him again of antinomian-ism (see Rom 2:7–8): "What should we say then? Should we continue in sin so that grace may multiply?" (6:1). As before, this slander provokes him: "Absolutely not! How can we who died to sin still live in it?" (v. 2). If we ask when we died to sin, the apostle has a ready reply: "Are you unaware that all of us who were baptized into Christ Jesus were baptized into his death?"

(v. 3). Baptism signifies union with Christ in his death and resurrection. When believers are baptized, they are spiritually joined to Christ's death. This means that through union with Christ they have died to sin. It has no more right to dominate their lives. Paul explains further, "For we know that our old self was crucified with him so that the body ruled by sin might be rendered powerless so that we may no longer be enslaved to sin" (v. 6).

Jesus's death and resurrection are the only antidotes to the poison of sin. They saved us once and for all from sin's penalty (Rom 8:1). When Christ returns, his death and resurrection will save us from sin's very presence (v. 5; 1 Thess 5:19–20). In this life, Jesus's death and resurrection save us from sin's power, and they do so by virtue of our union with Christ. We died with him to sin's dominion, and we are raised with him to live "in newness of life" (Rom 6:4).

Jesus's saving work empowers the Christian life, but believers are not inactive. Paul urges them to put into practice what they know: "So, you too consider yourselves dead to sin and alive to God in Christ Jesus" (v. 11). The words "in Christ Jesus" here signify union with Christ. Once more Paul expands his teaching:

> Therefore do not let sin reign in your mortal body, so that you obey its desires. And do not offer any parts of it to sin as weapons for unrighteousness. But as those who are alive from the dead, offer yourselves to God, and all the parts of yourselves to God as weapons for righteousness. For sin will not rule over you, because you are not under the law but under grace. (vv. 12–14)

Union with Christ, then, is indispensable for successful Christian living. God calls us to walk with Christ step by step, trusting the Holy Spirit to apply Jesus's death and resurrection to us again and again. Sin is no longer our master, but Christ is. We trust his atoning death to have set us free from sin's cruel domination. We trust his mighty resurrection to empower us for a new life that pleases God and blesses us.

Ephesians 1:1–14

Union with Christ pervades this passage as perhaps no other in Scripture. Paul even mentions union in his salutation to the epistle, addressing his readers as "the faithful saints *in Christ Jesus*" (v. 1). He begins his introduction with praise to God the Father for blessing the people of God with all spiritual blessings in union with the Son (v. 3). He then mentions one particular spiritual blessing from the Father: election, for God chose us "in" Christ (v. 4). The Father predestined us to adoption into his family, and with adoption comes an inheritance that is "in [Christ]" (v. 11).

Paul mentions the Son's role in salvation: "In him we have redemption through his blood" (v. 7), where "in him" refers to union with Christ. God has a grand plan of salvation, a "mystery," a truth contained in the Old Testament but revealed fully only in the New. God made known to the apostles this plan "according to his good pleasure that he purposed in Christ" (v. 9). Even God's eternal plan was formulated in view of uniting his people savingly to Jesus. God's goal? "To bring everything together in Christ, both things in heaven and things on earth in him" (v. 10). God will not only rescue all of his people but will deliver his creation from the curse (Rom 8:19–22; Rev 22:3) and bring about a "new heaven and a new earth" (21:1). And all of this will take place "in Christ," "in him" (Eph 1:10).

In this passage Paul has spoken of the Father's election and the Son's redemption as being "in Christ." It comes as no surprise, then, that the Holy Spirit's work of applying salvation to God's people is also in union with the Savior. When we believed the gospel, God the Father sealed us "in [Christ] . . . with the promised Holy Spirit" (v. 13). The Spirit thus serves as "the down payment of our inheritance, until the redemption of the possession, to the praise of his glory" (v. 14). The Spirit is thus seal and down payment, guaranteeing that God will keep us to the end (cf. 4:30).

Eph 1:1–14, therefore, is replete with references to union with Christ and our salvation. Union permeates the passage from beginning (v. 1) to end (v. 13). Union pertains to the roles of the trinitarian persons in salvation: Father (vv. 3–4), Son (v. 7), and Spirit (v. 13). Union crisscrosses election (v. 4), redemption (v. 7), God's plan to deliver heaven and earth (v. 10), adoption (v. 11), and sealing (v. 13). Indeed, our great God "has blessed us with every spiritual blessing in the heavens in Christ" (v. 3).

Ephesians 2:1–7

Few texts show our need for salvation as clearly as this one. We were besieged by the world (v. 2), the flesh (v. 3), and the devil (v. 2). We were spiritually devoid of eternal life (vv. 1, 5), sinning in desire, thought (v. 3), and deed (vv. 2–3). Worst of all, "We were by nature children under wrath" (v. 3). If God were to repay us as our sins deserved, we would perish forever. Thankfully, however, Paul writes, "But God, who is rich in mercy, because of his great love that he had for us . . . saved [us] by grace!" (vv. 4–5).

What follows does not speak of God's planning salvation before creation, as Eph 1:4 did. It does not recount Christ's making atonement, as Eph 1:7 did. Rather, it treats the application of salvation, that is, union with Christ. One way Paul communicates union is by teaching that by grace believers participate in Christ's narrative. So it is here. The apostle says that God

> made us alive with Christ (Eph 2:5),
> raised us up with him (v. 6),
> and seated us with him in the heavens in Christ Jesus (v. 6).

The first two clauses are complementary. God united us to Christ in his resurrection—he "raised us up with him" (v. 6) and in that way "made us alive with Christ" (v. 5). In joining us to the risen Christ, God regenerated us now and will raise us from the dead to eternal life on the last day.

Uniquely in all of Scripture, verse 6 says that God "seated us with him in the heavens in Christ Jesus." God graciously applies salvation to believers by spiritually linking them to Jesus's death, resurrection, ascension, and here even his session, his sitting at God's right hand! We have sat down with the Son of God in heaven. Revelation 3:21 portrays this as a future event: "To the one who conquers I will give the right to sit with me on my throne, just as I also conquered and sat down with my Father on his throne." But Paul here portrays it as a present one. Like other aspects of salvation, it is both already and not yet. This is one way God ministers his preservation to us. We—with all our temptations, struggles, and sins—are as good as in heaven now, seated with Christ! By God's matchless grace he joins us to Christ permanently. Surely this is a grand motivation to love, serve, and live for God all our days.

God's purpose in uniting us to his Son in this passage is cosmic and eternal: he did this "so that in the coming ages he might display the immeasurable riches of his grace through his kindness to us in Christ Jesus" (Eph 2:7). God will put us, his church, on display to the universe to magnify his amazing grace, mercy, and kindness!

Ephesians 3:1–10

As he had done previously in Eph 2:11, Paul speaks directly to Gentile believers in Ephesus in 3:1: "I, Paul, the prisoner of Christ Jesus on behalf of you Gentiles. . . ."[12] Paul tells about "the administration of God's grace that he gave me for you" (3:2). God made this administration known to Paul by revelation. Paul also refers to it as "the mystery of Christ" (v. 4). It was a mystery because, although the Old Testament predicted it, it was not realized until the coming of Christ in the New Testament. Jesus gave the Holy Spirit to the "apostles and prophets" that they might broadcast the mystery (v. 5).

Paul explains the content of the mystery of Christ: "The Gentiles are coheirs, members of the same body, and partners in the promise in Christ Jesus through the gospel" (v. 6). Paul had previously described the pitiable situation in which the Gentiles had found themselves before they believed in Christ: "At that time you were without Christ, excluded from the citizenship of Israel, and foreigners to the covenants of promise, without hope and without God in the world" (2:12).

But by his grace, God brought the Gentiles near to himself "in Christ Jesus" (v. 13). That is, God brought previously godless and hopeless Gentiles to himself by uniting them to Christ and his atonement. Union with Christ is a key soteriological principle in Paul. It is also an ecclesiological principle, for those united to Christ are also united to all others united to him. For this reason Paul describes Gentile believers in Ephesus as "coheirs [with believing Jews], members of the same body [of Christ, the church], and partners [with Jewish Christians] in the promise in Christ Jesus through the gospel" (3:6).[13]

This whole passage is autobiographical, because Jesus called Saul, the persecutor of himself and his church, to become Paul, the apostle to the Gentiles (Acts 9:5–6, 15):

---

[12] In fact, of fives uses of "Gentiles" in Ephesians, three occur in Eph 3:1, 6, 8, one in 2:11, and one in 4:17.

[13] For more on union with Christ and the unity of the church, see Kristen Ferguson and Christopher W. Morgan, "Baptists, the Unity of the Church, and the Christian Tradition," in *Baptists and the Christian Tradition*, ed. Matthew Y. Emerson, Christopher W. Morgan, and R. Lucas Stamps (Nashville: B&H Academic, 2020), 5–25.

I was made a servant of this gospel by the gift of God's grace that
was given to me by the working of his power. This grace was given
to me—the least of all the saints—to proclaim to the Gentiles the
incalculable riches of Christ, and to shed light for all about the
administration of the mystery hidden for ages in God who created
all things. (Eph 3:7–9)

This autobiographical text takes us back to the beginning, when the
risen Christ appeared to Saul of Tarsus, "to one born at the wrong time" (1
Cor 15:8). Saul knew that God had appeared in a light from heaven that
knocked him to the ground (Acts 9:3–4). The questions and answer that
followed revolutionized Paul's life and laid the foundation for his ministry.
Jesus asked, "Saul, Saul, why are you persecuting me?" (v. 4). To which he
replied, "Who are you, Lord?" Jesus answered, "I am Jesus, the one you are
persecuting" (vv. 4–5). After this encounter Paul would never be the same.
Has anyone ever been more zealous for the wrong cause? God turned the
greatest persecutor of the church into its greatest proponent. On the road to
Damascus Paul learned that to persecute the church was to persecute Jesus,
its Lord and Savior. Thus, before he understood union with Christ, he experienced it at Christ's hands and was taught it from Christ's mouth. In time,
union would come to dominate Paul's thinking, something for which we are
very grateful.

Summary

Union with Christ stretches back to the OT notion of representation. All
human beings are represented by Adam, and then Israel is represented by
Abraham, Moses, and David. We have also seen that "Son of Man" and
"Servant of the Lord" refer to Israel in the OT, but even in the OT there
were indications of an individual Son of Man and Servant of the Lord. The
NT clarifies that Jesus is the true son of Abraham, the greater Moses, and
the Messiah promised to Israel—the new and final David. He is also the
Son of Man and the Servant of the Lord. Those who desire to belong to
Israel must be united to Jesus Christ, for he is the true vine, and those in him
are the branches. The notion of union with Christ is also communicated
in Paul's "in Christ" theology, and we see that virtually every soteriological

blessing is ours in Christ. Salvation is ours because we are in Christ and no longer in Adam.

Systematic Formulations

The Definition of Union with Christ

Union with Christ is the Holy Spirit's work of joining people to Christ and all his saving benefits. God the Father plans salvation, for he chooses people for salvation before creation. God the Son accomplishes salvation, for he redeems the people of God through his death and resurrection. God the Holy Spirit applies the salvation planned by the Father and accomplished by the Son. The most comprehensive category of the application of salvation is union with Christ.

Our Need for Union with Christ

Our need for union with Christ is separation from him. Before God rescued us, we were "separated from Christ . . . having no hope and without God in the world" (Eph 2:12 ESV). God sent his Son as Reconciler, and because the Spirit united us to him, "in Christ Jesus" we "who were far away have been brought near by the blood of Christ" (v. 13). As a result, we believers "have access in one Spirit to the Father," and we "are no longer foreigners and strangers, but fellow citizens with the saints, and members of God's household" (vv. 18–19).

The Trinity and Union with Christ

Being united to Christ we are united to the Trinity. To understand this superb truth, we must summarize trinitarian doctrine.

The Trinitarian Persons Are in Each Other

Both Testaments testify to monotheism—the reality that there is only one living and true God (Deut 6:4; 1 Tim 2:5). The Old Testament hints at this fact, and the New Testament reveals that this one God exists eternally in three persons: Father, Son, and Holy Spirit. The persons are inseparable, for

God is one. But we must distinguish the persons and not confuse them (Matt 3:16–17). For example, only the Son became incarnate and died on the cross. We distinguish the Father, Son, and Holy Spirit but do not separate them.

Because God is one, the three persons of the Godhead indwell one another. Theologians call this *perichoresis*, circumincession, or co-inherence. The Gospel of John sets this forth most clearly. The Father indwells the Son (John 14:10); the Father is in the Son (17:23). The Son is in the Father (14:20). And the Father and Son are in one another (10:38; 14:10–11, 20; 17:21).

The Holy Spirit Joins Us to the Father, Son, and Holy Spirit

As a result of the Spirit's uniting us to the Trinity, God indwells us. Paul customarily says that the Holy Spirit indwells us. However, six times he ascribes indwelling to the Son (Rom 8:10; 2 Cor 13:5; Gal 2:20; Eph 3:17; Col 1:27; 3:11), and twice to the Father (2 Cor 6:16; Eph 2:22). This means that God the Father, Son, and Holy Spirit indwell believers. Jesus promised to ask the Father to send the Holy Spirit to be with believers forever (John 14:16). Jesus taught his disciples concerning the Spirit, "You do know him, because he remains with you and will be in you" (v. 17). Jesus said that the Father (17:21) and the Son are in believers (14:20; 17:23, 26) and will come to make their home with them (14:23).

Furthermore, Jesus encouraged his disciples, telling them that when the Spirit came they would know that "I am in my Father, you are in me, and I am in you" (John 14:20). He and believers remain in one another (6:56; 15:4–5). In his famous priestly prayer Jesus prays that future believers would be in the Father and the Son as the Father and Son are in one another! (17:20–21). Although it is little known, Paul teaches that believers are in the Father and the Son: the Thessalonians are "in God the Father and the Lord Jesus Christ" (1 Thess 1:1; 2 Thess 1:1).

Such teaching is overwhelming. How can we comprehend that the Trinity indwells us in a way similar to how the three persons indwell each other? First, we must guard the distinction between the Creator God and us his creatures. God's indwelling us does not mean that we become divine. God is always our Lord and Savior, and we are always his redeemed creatures. Second, the Father, Son, and Spirit have eternally indwelled one another, and their indwelling of us begins at our conversion. Third, the mutual indwelling of the Trinity belongs to their divine nature, but God's indwelling us is by his grace through faith in Christ.

A Description of Union with Christ

Our union with Christ is definitive, personal, and enduring.

Union with Christ Is Definitive

Union defines our existence as the people of God. Peter pictures God as using believers as "living stones" to build a temple to God through Christ, the "living stone" (1 Pet 2:4, 5) After this "beautiful picture of union with Christ,"[14] Peter adds, "Once you were not a people, but now you are God's people; you had not received mercy, but now you have received mercy" (v. 10). Union with Christ defines us—we are God's people who have tasted his mercy through union with his Son. We, like the Corinthians, have received God's grace "in Christ Jesus" (1 Cor 1:4).

Union with Christ Is Personal

Christ loved us outside of us; he died for us when we could not rescue ourselves. In union with Christ, however, God works inside of us. Union with Christ brings God's grace up close and personal to us. For that reason, Paul uses the intimate picture of marital relations to depict union:

> Don't you know that your bodies are a part of Christ's body? So should I take a part of Christ's body and make it part of a prostitute? Absolutely not! Don't you know that anyone joined to a prostitute is one body with her? . . . But anyone joined to the Lord is one spirit with him. (1 Cor 6:15–17)

Paul draws a parallel between the union of husbands' and wives' bodies in marital relations and out spiritual union between Christ and us.

Ajith Fernando of Sri Lanka underlines this personal aspect of our union:

---

[14] We credit Robert A. Peterson with insights from his *Salvation Applied by the Spirit: Union with Christ* (Wheaton: Crossway, 2014), 240.

The doctrine of fellowship in Christ's sufferings is a natural extension of the doctrine of our union with Christ. Christ is a suffering Savior, and if we are to be truly one with him, we too must suffer. There is a depth of union with Christ that comes to us only through suffering. But not only do we share in his sufferings; he also shares in our sufferings. The exalted Christ, sharing in the glory of God, is not deaf to our cries of pain as we suffer; he himself suffers with us when we suffer. Paul came to understand this on the road to Damascus when he heard Jesus ask, "Saul, Saul, why are you persecuting me?" (Acts 9:4). He had been hitting the church, but Christ had been feeling the pain.[15]

Our union with Christ is personal indeed!

Union with Christ Is Enduring

Union with Christ is not temporary but permanent. Paul writes, "In him you also were sealed with the promised Holy Spirit when you heard the word of truth, the gospel of your salvation, and when you believed" (Eph 1:13). This text presents the Trinity as active in sealing believers. The divine passive shows that God the Father is the sealer who takes the initiative in sealing God's people. God's seal is the Holy Spirit, promised by Old Testament prophets. The sealing takes place "in him," that is, in union with Christ. As the next verse suggests, the main meaning of this sealing is the permanence of salvation: "The Holy Spirit is the down payment of our inheritance, until the redemption of the possession, to the praise of his glory" (v. 14).

This is underscored by Paul's use of sealing later in Ephesians: "And don't grieve God's Holy Spirit. You were sealed by him for the day of redemption" (Eph 4:30). The chief theological significance of the Father's sealing believers' union with Christ with the seal of the Spirit is thus God's preservation of his saints. Our union with Christ is so permanent that even death cannot break its bond, as John reveals. God eulogizes those who die in union with Christ, "Blessed are the dead who die in the Lord from now on" (Rev 14:13).

---

[15] Ajith Fernando, "Heaven for Persecuted Saints," Christopher W. Morgan and Robert A. Peterson, eds., *Heaven*, Theology in Community 6 (Wheaton: Crossway, 2014), 232.

In sum: Union with Christ is definitive; it defines who we are, God's blessed people linked savingly to his Son forever. Union with Christ is personal: we are spiritually married to Christ, our bridegroom, and love him dearly. Union with Christ is enduring: we are linked to the Son of God our Savior with the unbreakable seal of the Holy Spirit.

Jesus's Story and Union with Christ

The apostle Paul ministers union with Christ to us by placing us as participants in Jesus's story. By the grace of God we die with Christ, are raised with him, ascend and sit down in heaven with him, and even in a sense return with him:

> We died with Christ. (Rom 6:3–8; 2 Cor 4:10; Gal 2:20; Phil 3:10; Col 2:20)
> We were raised with Christ. (Rom 6:4–8; 2 Cor 4:10–14; Eph 2:6; Col 3:1)
> We ascended with Christ and sat down in heaven with him. (Eph 2:6)
> We will even "come again," so to speak, with him. (Rom 8:19; Col 3:4)

Christ's death uniquely makes atonement for sins. When the Holy Spirit joins us to Christ, he unites us to his death, so that we died spiritually with Christ. Similarly, the Spirit unites us to the living Christ and his resurrection. Though Jesus's saving work ranges from his incarnation to his second coming, the heart and soul of his salvation are his death and resurrection.

Christ's atoning death and resurrection accomplish salvation past, present and future. Christ saves us with regard to the past, for "He was delivered up for our trespasses and raised for our justification" (Rom 4:25). Christ's death pays the penalty for our sins, and his resurrection brings acquittal and new life to us who were condemned and spiritually dead.

Christ saves us with regard to the present, for "we were buried with him by baptism into death, in order that, just as Christ was raised from the dead by the glory of the Father, so we too may walk in newness of life" (Rom 6:4). Christ's death broke sin's tyranny over our lives; his resurrection enables us to live new lives.

Christ's death and resurrection save us with regard to the future, for "if, while we were enemies, we were reconciled to God through the death of his Son, then how much more, having been reconciled, will we be saved by his life" (Rom 5:10).

Christ's ascension and session save us too, for God, "because of his great love that he had for us, made us alive with Christ. . . . He also raised us up with him and seated us with him in the heavens in Christ Jesus, so that in the coming ages he might display the immeasurable riches of his grace through his kindness to us in Christ Jesus" (Eph 2:4–7). God puts his love, grace, and kindness on display when he unites us to Christ, seated at God's right hand.

Twice Scripture says that we share in Christ's return. First, "The eager expectation of the creation awaits eagerly the revelation of the sons of God" (Rom 8:19, Morgan's translation). The word "revelation" is the same word Scripture sometimes uses for the second coming of Christ (1 Cor 1:7; 2 Thess 1:7; 1 Pet 1:13; Rev 1:1). There is a sense in which believers have a revelation, a return. Paul means that our true identity is so wrapped up in Christ that it will be fully revealed only when he (and we!) come again.

Second, Paul again says believers will return when Christ does: "When Christ, who is your life, appears, then you also will appear with him in glory" (Col 3:4). Both Jesus and Christians will "appear" at his second coming. Believers are so united to Christ and his saving events that at his return the sin that obscures our identity in Christ will be removed so that we "will shine like the sun in their Father's kingdom" (Matt 13:43).

The Aspects of Salvation and Union with Christ

Gaffin's words are apt: "The central soteriological reality is union with the exalted Christ by Spirit-created faith. That is the nub, the essence, of the way or order of salvation for Paul."[16] For this reason each individual aspect of the application of salvation is "in Christ." Regeneration, justification, adoption, sanctification, preservation, and glorification are blessings we receive not apart from Christ but in union with him. Regeneration is "in Christ," for "God, who is rich in mercy, because of his great love that he had for us, made

---

[16] Richard B. Gaffin, *By Faith, Not by Sight: Paul and the Order of Salvation* (Milton Keynes, UK: Paternoster, 2006), 43.

us alive *with Christ* even though we were dead in trespasses. You are saved by grace!" (Eph 2:4–5).

Likewise, we are justified in union with Christ, for God "made the one who did not know sin to be sin for us, so that *in him* we might become the righteousness of God" (2 Cor 5:21). Paul values gaining Christ above all, and this means to "be found in him," that is, in union with him, and that entails "not having a righteousness of my own from the law, but one that is through faith in Christ—the righteousness from God based on faith" (Phil 3:9).

It is the same for adoption, as Paul teaches: "Through faith you are all sons of God in Christ Jesus. For those of you who were baptized into Christ have been clothed with Christ" (Gal 3:26–27). "Being clothed with Christ" speaks of union with Christ—as clothing covers the body so Christ "covers" believers. Union is the embracive concept of which adoption is a part— "through faith you are all sons of God *in Christ.*"

The Spirit's work of sanctification is not separate from Christ but in union with him: "We are his workmanship, created *in Christ Jesus* for good works, which God prepared ahead of time for us to do" (Eph 2:10). Indeed, our union with Christ in his death and resurrection is the basis for successful Christian lives (Rom 6:1–14).

God's preservation of his saints is done in union with his Son: "There is now no condemnation for those *in Christ Jesus*" (Rom 8:1). On the last day God will save and not condemn all human beings "in Christ Jesus," in union with him. In fact, because believers are "more than conquerors through" Christ, "who loved us" (v. 37), Paul is confident that nothing at all "will be able to separate us from the love of God that is in Christ Jesus our Lord" (v. 39).

Our glorification is also in union with Christ. As we saw when discussing our participation in Jesus's story, we will have a "second coming": "When Christ, who is your life, appears, then you also will appear with him in glory" (Col 3:4). Our full identity will be disclosed only when Jesus comes back, and this is because we will appear "with him," in union with him, "in glory." Our final salvation will thus involve great glory, for by God's grace we will obtain "the glory of our Lord Jesus Christ" (2 Thess 2:14), even "an absolutely incomparable eternal weight of glory" (2 Cor 4:17).

2

Election

The doctrine of election is perhaps the most debated doctrine of the Christian faith. Believers have divided over where the emphasis belongs regarding God's sovereignty and human freedom. Sometimes, because of these divisions, Christians have been reluctant to study election. This is a mistake, for Scripture has much to say about it. Though all will not agree with our conclusions, we will press on in an attempt to understand the Bible's mysterious teaching that God "chose us in [Christ], before the foundation of the world, to be holy and blameless in love before him" (Eph 1:4).

Scripture uses many different words for God's electing or choosing or predestining. The most common Hebrew word is "choose" (*bāḥar*), but we also find "know" (*yāḏaʿ*) and "call" (*qārāʾ*). Many Greek words are used: "choose" (*eklegomai*), "predestine" (*proorizō*), "choose" or "select" (*haireomai* and *exaireomai*), and "foreknow" (*proginōskō*). Important nouns are "election" (*eklogē*) and "will" (*boulē*), as well as the adjective "elect" (*eklektos*). The purpose in this chapter is not to distinguish carefully between these various terms but to focus on what Scripture teaches about election when it uses these terms.

Exegetical Foundations

God's Choice of Abraham and Israel

God's choice of his people is an expression of his grace and mercy, as we see in his election of Abraham and Israel. The context for election is crucial, because Adam's sin had led to death, as we see in the roll call of death in Genesis 5. The pernicious and radical evil present in human beings accounted for the flood (Gen 6:5); after the flood, despite God's gracious covenant with Noah, the evil in human hearts had not been eradicated (8:21). The story of the tower of Babel illustrated that human beings had continued to live to "make a name" for themselves (11:4). At this point in the story, we wonder how God would fulfill the promise that the offspring of the woman would crush the head of the serpent and his offspring (3:15). One thing is clear: the evil in human beings is so deep and profound that salvation will come only from the Lord. This is where election enters the picture: since salvation is of the Lord (Jonah 2:9), it must come ultimately from God's choice rather than from human initiative. God's plan was to bless the world through one man, Abraham. The Lord made a covenant with Abraham and promised him offspring, land, and universal blessing.[1] The promise of salvation pledged to Adam and Eve (Gen 3:15) would be realized through Abraham.

Abraham, however, was the recipient of the promise not because of his own goodness or virtue. God in his grace chose him (lit. "I have known him," $y^e\underline{d}a\,{}'tiw$) so that the covenant promises given to Abraham would be realized in his children (Gen 18:19). Before Abraham was chosen, he was, as Paul says in Rom 4:5, "ungodly." His ungodliness is verified by Josh 24:2: "Thus says the LORD, the God of Israel, 'Long ago, your fathers lived beyond the Euphrates, Terah, the father of Abraham and of Nahor; and they served other gods'" (ESV). Before God called him, Abraham was not a worshiper of the one true God but an idolater. The Lord chose Abraham because of his gracious love, despite Abraham's sin, and Abraham and his offspring would become the channel through which the world would be blessed.

Abraham was the father, the progenitor, of the Jewish people. The promises made to Abraham were made also to his descendants, to Isaac and Jacob and Jacob's sons. Just as the Lord made a covenant with Abraham, he also made a covenant with Israel (see Exod 24:3–8). They were his "kingdom of priests" and his "holy nation" (Exod 19:6). Just as the Lord chose Abraham, so too he chose Israel. We see the connection in Isa 41:8–9: "You, Israel, my servant, Jacob, whom I have chosen, descendant of Abraham, my friend—I

---

[1] For simplicity, we won't distinguish between the names Abram and Abraham but will identify him as Abraham throughout.

brought you from the ends of the earth and called you from its farthest corners. I said to you: You are my servant; I have chosen you; I haven't rejected you." Isaiah was not addressing the historical Jacob but his descendants—the nation of Israel. The Lord didn't reject Israel but chose the nation and freed them from Egypt. The OT often reiterates Israel's special position as God's people: "Yet the Lord had his heart set on your fathers and loved them. He chose their descendants after them—he chose you out of all the peoples, as it is today" (Deut 10:15; cf. 14:2; Pss 105:6, 43; 106:5; Acts 13:17); "For the Lord has chosen Jacob for himself, Israel as his treasured possession" (Ps 135:4). Israel can be described simply as "chosen" (1 Chr 16:13; Isa 43:20; 44:1–2; 45:4; 49:7; cf. 65:9, 15, 22).

The question arises: Why did God choose the Jews? A rabbinic tradition argued that the Lord offered all the nations of the world the Torah and the nations rejected it, whereas Israel chose to live under its authority.[2] But the OT's answer is dramatically different. Two texts in particular stand out. First, we read in Deut 4:37: "Because he loved your fathers, he chose their descendants after them and brought you out of Egypt by his presence and great power." God chose Israel because he loved the fathers, Abraham, Isaac, and Jacob. We have seen, however, that the Lord didn't choose Abraham because Abraham was seeking after him. And, as we shall see, Paul emphatically denies that Jacob was chosen for his virtue (Rom 9:10–13), which is not surprising when we read the story of Jacob's life! The second text, Deut 7:6–8, reaffirms what we see in Deut 4:37 and helps us grasp the rationale for Israel's election:

> "You are a holy people belonging to the Lord your God. The Lord your God has chosen you to be his own possession out of all the peoples on the face of the earth. The Lord had his heart set on you and chose you, not because you were more numerous than all peoples, for you were the fewest of all peoples. But because the Lord loved you and kept the oath he swore to your fathers, he brought you out with a strong hand and redeemed you from the place of slavery, from the power of Pharaoh king of Egypt."

---

[2] *Mekhilta de Rabbi Ishmael,* tractate *Baḥôdeš* 5.63–80 on Exod 20:2; *Sipre* 343 on Deut 33:2.

Israel was distinct among all the nations on earth, for the Lord chose
them alone. He didn't choose them because of their strength or their massive
population. The ultimate reason for the Lord's choice and election of Israel is
his love. The Lord loved Israel because he loved her! We may desire another
answer, but this text takes us into the deepest mysteries of God himself. The
Lord chose Israel because he desired to do so, because it was his will to do so,
because he had chosen to love her. Since all are sons and daughters of Adam
and since none has a claim on God's mercy, God's love is free and sovereign.
His love and election represent his merciful and free choice of Israel. The
joy of being chosen by God and enjoying the sunshine of his presence is
expressed in Ps 65:4: "How happy is the one you choose and bring near to
live in your courts! We will be satisfied with the goodness of your house, the
holiness of your temple."

God's Choice of Priests and Prophets

We have seen that the Lord chose the fathers (Abraham, Isaac, and Jacob),
and he also chose Israel to be his people. In addition, the Lord chose some for
certain ministries and tasks, such as priests, prophets, and kings. For instance,
the Lord chose Aaron to serve him as high priest (Ps 105:26). In the dispute
with Korah, Dathan, and Abiram, the Lord clarified that he chose Aaron as
priest (Num 17:1–11). Korah and his followers rebelled against the order the
Lord had chosen, and the Lord revealed those whom he had truly chosen
(Num 16:5, 7). The Lord also chose Levi and his sons for service (Deut
18:5; 21:5). David remarks, "No one but the Levites may carry the ark of
God, because the LORD has chosen them to carry the ark of the LORD and
to minister before him forever" (1 Chr 15:2). Being chosen for ministry is a
great privilege, but it must not be abused. Hophni and Phinehas abused their
privileges (1 Sam 2:34), and the Lord judged and destroyed them for their
blatant and unrepentant evil.

The Lord also chose prophets as messengers of the covenant. The
prophets reminded Israel of covenant stipulations, of the judgment coming because of Israel's defection, and of God's great promises to save his
people despite their sin. When Amaziah threatened him for intervening in
the political affairs of the northern kingdom of Israel, Amos told of his calling as a prophet: "I was not a prophet or the son of a prophet; rather, I was

a herdsman, and I took care of sycamore figs. But the Lᴏʀᴅ took me from following the flock and said to me, 'Go, prophesy to my people Israel'" (Amos 7:14–15). Amos didn't choose his vocation, but the Lord called him from his work to proclaim the word of the Lord. Usually, we aren't told specifically that the Lord "chose" a prophet. The prophets' calling is relayed by the coming of "the word of the Lᴏʀᴅ" to them (Hos 1:1; Jonah 1:1; Mic 1:1; Zeph 1:1; Hag 1:1; Zech 1:1) or by a vision (Obad 1:1) or oracle (Nah 1:1; Hab 1:1; Mal 1:1) coming to a prophet. The Lord also summoned Ezekiel to prophesy to rebellious and recalcitrant Israel (Ezekiel 2–3).

Isaiah's calling is relayed in Isaiah 6, and in 49:1 we also read about the Lord's choosing him before he was born: "The Lᴏʀᴅ called me before I was born. He named me while I was in my mother's womb." One didn't volunteer or train to be a prophet, for prophets were called by the Lord even before their time on earth. We see this also in the life of Jeremiah. He was a young and reluctant prophet, but the Lord assured him, "I chose you before I formed you in the womb; I set you apart before you were born. I appointed you a prophet to the nations" (Jer 1:5). The word for "chose" is actually "knew" ($y^e\underline{d}a\,'t\bar{\imath}$), but it clearly refers to what the Lord ordained for Jeremiah, as the parallel verbs "set apart" and "appointed" confirm. The three verbs are roughly synonymous, showing that the Lord called and chose Jeremiah before he was conceived.

God's Choice of Kings

The Lord also chose kings in Israel. The people were to follow the Lord's prescriptions and not their own inclinations in choosing a king: "You are to appoint over you the king the Lᴏʀᴅ your God chooses. Appoint a king from your brothers. You are not to set a foreigner over you, or one who is not of your people" (Deut 17:15). The Lord chose Saul as king (1 Sam 10:24) but later rejected him for his disobedience (15:23). The Lord's sovereignty and wisdom are evident in the choice of David as the next king, since Samuel was certain that Eliab was the one the Lord had chosen (16:6). Samuel was astonished because the Lord didn't choose any of Jesse's sons who stood before him but instead chose the youngest son of Jesse, David, who was not even invited to the meal (v. 13). The Lord's criteria for choosing differs from those of human beings, as he tells Samuel, "Do not look at his appearance or his stature because I have rejected him. Humans do not see what the LORD sees, for humans see what is visible, but the LORD sees the heart" (v. 7). The Lord's choice of David is reiterated often in the narrative (2 Sam 6:21; 1 Kgs 8:16; 11:34; 1 Chr 28:4; 2 Chr 6:6).

The Lord in choosing David rejected others. The Lord "rejected the tent of Joseph and did not choose the tribe of Ephraim. He chose instead the tribe of Judah, Mount Zion, which he loved. . . . He chose David his servant and took him from the sheep pens" (Ps 78:67–68, 70). The choosing of David is linked with the covenant made with him: "The LORD said, 'I have made a covenant with my chosen one; I have sworn an oath to David my servant'" (89:3; cf. v. 19). The covenant with David was everlasting and would never be withdrawn, and it was the means by which the promises made to Abraham would be realized. The coming worldwide blessing would be realized through a Davidic son (cf. 2 Samuel 7; 1 Chronicles 17; Psalms 2, 72, 89, 132). Solomon was also chosen as king, and the Lord ordained that he would build the temple (1 Chr 28:6, 10).[3]

God's Choice of Jerusalem and the Temple

There is a remarkable emphasis in Scripture on the Lord's choosing Jerusalem (1 Kgs 8:44, 48; 11:13, 32, 36; 14:21; 2 Kgs 21:7; 23:27; 2 Chr 6:6, 38; Zech 1:17; 3:2). It is designated "the city the LORD had chosen from all the tribes of Israel to put his name" (2 Chr 12:13; cf. 33:7; Zech 1:17; 3:2). The psalmist declares, "The LORD has chosen Zion; he has desired it for his home" (Ps 132:13). The choice of Jerusalem cannot ultimately be separated from its being the place where God's name is specially present, since his temple was in the city (2 Chr 7:12, 16; cf. Neh 1:9). Israel must sacrifice only at the place where the Lord puts his name, and Jerusalem, though not chosen at first, ends up being that place (Deut 12:5, 11, 14, 18, 21, 26; 14:23, 24, 25; 15:20; 16:2, 6, 7, 11, 15, 16; 17:10; 18:6; 26:2; 31:11; Josh 9:27). The Lord's choice of Jerusalem and his dwelling in the temple point to a greater reality: Ultimately, the entire world will be God's temple as he dwells in the new Jerusalem, the new creation (Rev 21:1–22:5).

---

[3] Note also the choosing of Zerubbabel (Hag 2:23).

Jesus's Choice of the Apostles

When we think of those chosen for a special task, the apostles of Jesus Christ come to mind. The choosing of the Twelve was one of the most important decisions in Jesus's life, and he spent the entire night in prayer before choosing them (Luke 6:12–13; cf. Acts 1:2). As was true for prophets, one didn't volunteer to serve as an apostle. Jesus asked, "Didn't I choose you, the Twelve?" (John 6:70). In the Gospel of John, Jesus reminds the apostles that he has chosen them for their ministry (13:18), and we realize that being chosen as an apostle is not the same as being chosen for salvation. Judas, after all, was chosen, and yet Jesus characterizes him as a "devil" (6:70). When it comes to selecting the twelfth apostle after Jesus's resurrection and before Pentecost, the disciples ensure that they don't exercise their selfish will but instead select the one the Lord has chosen (Acts 1:24). Paul's calling as an apostle on the Damascus Road stands out (cf. Acts 9, 22, 26). As the Lord told Ananias about Paul, "This man is my chosen instrument to take my name to Gentiles, kings, and Israelites" (9:15; cf. 26:17). The apostles along with prophets functioned as the foundation of the church (Eph 2:20), and thus their role as authoritative teachers of the gospel of Jesus Christ can scarcely be exaggerated.

Jesus as the Chosen One

The most important choice in history is God's election of Jesus of Nazareth as the Christ. At Jesus's transfiguration God spoke to the disciples with a voice from the cloud of his presence, "This is my Son, the Chosen One; listen to him!" (Luke 9:35; cf. Acts 3:20). We saw from Isaiah that the Lord chose Israel to be his servant, but the servant par excellence, the true Israel, is Jesus Christ. He was the true servant and the true Israel because he always and without fail obeyed the Lord. Matthew, quoting Isaiah, affirms that Jesus is the chosen servant of the Lord: "Here is my servant whom I have chosen, my beloved in whom I delight; I will put my Spirit on him, and he will proclaim justice to the nations" (Matt 12:18, citing Isa 42:1). The people and religious leaders believed that Jesus could not be the Christ and chosen one if he suffered on the cross (Luke 23:35), but God's plan was hidden from many. Jesus was rejected by the people, but he was God's chosen one, the cornerstone of the new temple (Matt 21:42, citing Ps 118:22). Peter says that Jesus is "a living stone—rejected by people but chosen and honored by God" (1 Pet 2:4; cf. v. 6). Identifying Jesus as the anointed one, the Christ, the Messiah, confirms that he is the chosen one. He is the fulfillment of the promise to David that a man would always sit on his throne (Acts 2:29–36), and he fulfills the promise to Abraham, for all nations are blessed through him (cf. Gal 3:8–9, 16).

God's Choice of People for Salvation

We have seen that God chose prophets, priests, and kings, as well as Jerusalem as the place where he specially dwelt with his people. Along the same lines, he chose Jesus to be the Messiah. However, God does not only choose people for special tasks or ministries, but he also chooses them for salvation. The salvation of those in the church of Jesus Christ can be traced back to election, God's choice of his people. We will trace God's election of people for salvation through the New Testament corpora.

The Gospel of Matthew

We find election in Matthew. At the end of the parable of the wedding banquet Jesus concludes, "Many are invited, but few are chosen" (Matt 22:14). Many are summoned or invited to believe, but only those who are elect respond to the summons with faith. A crucial text about election in Matthew lacks the word "election," but the concept is clearly present. We cite this passage in full:

> At that time Jesus said, "I praise you, Father, Lord of heaven and earth, because you have hidden these things from the wise and intelligent and revealed them to infants. Yes, Father, because this was your good pleasure. All things have been entrusted to me by my Father. No one knows the Son except the Father, and no one knows the Father except the Son and anyone to whom the Son desires to reveal him." (Matt 11:25–27)

Jesus has just finished denouncing the cities in which he has performed many miracles and yet the people have not believed (Matt 11:20–24). Then, in a text similar to 1 Cor 1:18–31, he praises the Father that truth is "hidden" from those who deem themselves to be intelligent but "revealed" to those who are "infants" (those who humble themselves like little children; Matt 11:25). We are curious to discover why revelation has been given to infants when nothing is said about their receptiveness or goodness. The revelation is attributed instead to the Father's "good pleasure" (*eudokia*) and will (v. 26). Jesus follows with a remarkable statement on the reciprocal and exclusive knowledge between the Father and the Son (v. 27). What catches our attention is that knowing the Father is given to "anyone to whom the Son wishes to reveal him." "Infants" know the Father, then, because of the good pleasure of both the Father and the Son. When the Son chooses to reveal the Father savingly to a person, that person will receive the revelation and be saved.

Matthew also teaches the irrevocability of election. Jesus predicted a day in which "false messiahs and false prophets will arise and perform great signs and wonders to lead astray, if possible, even the elect" (Matt 24:24; cf. Mark 13:20). Interpreters understand these words in various ways, and there is not universal agreement about the time period to which these words point. But regardless of when this prophecy is fulfilled, no one who puts his or her faith in false messiahs will be saved! If someone believes in a false messiah, that person does not believe Jesus is the Messiah—and one must put one's trust in Jesus to be saved. The signs and wonders spoken of here will be so amazing that even the elect could be led astray, and yet Jesus says it is not possible for that to happen. The reason the elect cannot be shifted from the faith is not because they are wise or godly. The word "elect" is stressed and placed last in word order to accent God's grace, confirming that election cannot and will not be reversed (cf. Matt 24:22; Mark 13:22).

The Gospel of John

John paints three pictures of God's election of people for salvation. First, the Father gives people to the Son (John 6:37, 39; 17:2, 6, 9–10, 24). In his Bread of Life discourse Jesus equates "coming to him" with "believing in him" (6:35). Next, he contrasts the unbelief of some with the faith of those whom the Father gives to him (vv. 36–37). Jesus reassures, "Everyone the Father gives me will come to me, and the one who comes to me I will never cast out" (v. 37). The Father's giving people to Jesus portrays election. All the Father gives to Jesus will believe in him. Here we learn that election precedes faith.

Later, in his great prayer, Jesus asks the Father to glorify the Son since the Father "gave him authority over all flesh, so that he may give eternal life to everyone you have given him" (John 17:2). Eternal life is a gift granted not to all people but to those whom the Father has given to the Son. Jesus revealed the Father's name to the people the Father had given him (v. 6). Jesus prays for them, not for the world (v. 9). He asks the Father to bring to those he gave Jesus to heaven to see his glory (v. 24).

Second, God's people have an identity prior to their faith in Christ. Jesus contrasts the sheep with those who are not his sheep (we'll call them goats):

> "You don't believe because you are not of my sheep. My sheep hear my voice, I know them, and they follow me. I give them eternal life, and they will never perish. No one will snatch them out of my hand. My Father, who has given them to me, is greater than all. No one is able to snatch them out of the Father's hand. I and the Father are one." (John 10:26–30)

Jesus could have said, "You are not my sheep because you don't believe," and of course this is true. Instead, he said, "You don't believe because you are not of my sheep" (10:26), contrasting the goats with his sheep to whom he gives eternal life and whom he keeps saved forever. The sheep and the goats are identifiable so to speak before they believe or reject Jesus. Their faith or unbelief reveals God's sovereign will. Those who belong to Jesus's flock are those who believe. This is another way of saying that divine election precedes human belief.

Third, Jesus is the author of election. John alone presents Jesus as the author of election, whereas everywhere else the Father plays that role. Although John presents Jesus as choosing his disciples for service (6:70), his choosing of them in John 15 goes deeper. Jesus uses the illustration of the vine and the branches to motivate the disciples to remain in him and bear much fruit. They are responsible to bear fruit, but Jesus stands behind their efforts, for he chose and appointed the disciples to bear fruit. He declared:

> "You did not choose me, but I chose you. I appointed you to go and produce fruit and that your fruit should remain. . . . If the world hates you, understand that it hated me before it hated you. If you were of the world, the world would love you as its own. However,

because you are not of the world, but I have chosen you out of it, the world hates you." (John 15:16, 18–19)

Though Jesus's choice in 6:70 was a choice of the Twelve for discipleship, his choice in 15:16, 19 is a choice of the eleven disciples out of the world so that they now belong to Jesus instead of the world. This is Jesus's choice of them for salvation, as D. A. Carson explains: "The disciples cannot even legitimately boast that they are believers on the ground that they, unlike others, wisely made the right choice. On the contrary, Jesus chose them. Merit theology is thus totally savaged."[4]

Acts 13:48

Paul and Barnabas have an up-and-down experience in Pisidian Antioch on the first missionary journey. Their hearers in turn receive their message (Acts 13:42–44, 47–49) and persecute them (vv. 45–46, 50–51). Nevertheless, when the Gentiles hear Paul and Barnabas quote Isa 49:6—"I will also make you a light for the nations, to be my salvation to the ends of the earth"—they turn to the Lord. How are we to account for the Gentiles' conversion? Luke explains: "When the Gentiles heard this, they rejoiced and honored the word of the Lord, and all who had been appointed to eternal life believed" (Acts 13:48). Luke presents a divine classification or appointment to eternal life. And that appointment to eternal life precedes faith on the part of the believers.[5]

Acts 18:9–10

On his second missionary journey Paul has a discouraging start in Corinth. He has preached to the Jews that Jesus is the Christ, but they oppose him, and in protest he says that he is going to the Gentiles (Acts 18:5–6). Paul does so, and God gives him a fruitful ministry (vv. 7–8). One night the Lord speaks to Paul in a vision to strengthen him. He instructs him to keep preaching and promises to be with him and to protect him: "Don't be afraid, but keep

---

[4] D. A. Carson, *Divine Sovereignty and Human Responsibility: Biblical Perspectives in Tension* (Grand Rapids: Baker, 1994), 191.

[5] In contrast to William Klein, *The New Chosen People* (Eugene, OR: Wipf and Stock, 2015), 121; cf. 109–10.

on speaking and don't be silent. For I am with you, and no one will lay a hand on you to hurt you, because I have many people in this city" (vv. 9–10). In obedience Paul stays in Corinth a year and a half, ministering God's Word (v. 11). F. F. Bruce notes, "The Lord had many people in Corinth whom He had marked out for His own."[6] An Arminian appeal to divine foreknowledge is read into this passage, not out of it.[7] The text does not speak about God's foreseeing faith. Rather, God tells Paul that many Corinthians belonged to God before they trusted Christ to strengthen Paul's preaching in difficult circumstances. Although it is sometimes said that emphasizing God's sovereignty in salvation impedes evangelism, the opposite is true—it encourages Paul to continue preaching.

Paul's Epistles: 2 Thessalonians 2:13

Paul is Scripture's principal teacher of election. Second Thessalonians 2:13 introduces us to his thought: "We ought to thank God always for you, brothers and sisters loved by the Lord, because from the beginning God has chosen you for salvation through sanctification by the Spirit and through belief in the truth." Textually it is uncertain whether God chose "from the beginning" (CSB) or as "the firstfruits" (ESV), but the meaning of the verse does not change significantly on either reading. Salvation is anchored in God's gracious choice of his people. God works out his sovereign plan through the use of means, here definitive sanctification and faith in the gospel. This text also demonstrates that believers ought to give thanks to God for his love and election of their fellow believers.

Paul's Epistles: Ephesians 1:4–5, 11

Our reading of 2 Thess 2:13 is confirmed by Eph 1:4–5: God "chose us in him, before the foundation of the world, to be holy and blameless in love before him. He predestined us to be adopted as sons through Jesus Christ for himself, according to the good pleasure of his will." God's choice of his

---

[6] F. F. Bruce, *The Book of Acts*, NICNT (Grand Rapids: Eerdmans, 1988), 372.

[7] I. Howard Marshall, *Kept by the Power of God: A Study of Perseverance and Falling Away* (1969; repr., Eugene, OR: Wipf and Stock, 2008), 85. Cf. Grant Osborne, "Exegetical Notes on Calvinist Texts," in *Grace Unlimited*, ed. Clark H. Pinnock (Minneapolis: Bethany Fellowship, 1975), 175.

people was not made in history as he observed the choices and actions of human beings. He chose believers before the world dawned on the basis of his own will and grace (cf. Eph 1:11). Verse 4 teaches that believers are chosen both unto salvation as a whole and unto holiness in particular. This holiness will be complete only when Jesus returns (1 Thess 5:23–24).

The reference to predestination in Eph 1:5 points in the same direction. English translations aren't as precise here (but cf. ASV, NET), since the word "predestined" (*proorisas*) modifies the main verb "chose" in verse 5. Predestination is not a separate topic in Ephesians 1 but clarifies election: believers are predestined for adoption. Adoption is a picture of salvation and means that believers are the children of God, members of his family. Being chosen for holiness and being predestined to adoption, then, are two different ways of looking at the same reality. One shakes the kaleidoscope and sees one perspective and then shakes the kaleidoscope again and sees another perspective. In both cases, however, it is the same kaleidoscope. God's grace is comprehensive: "We were predestined according to the plan of the one who works out everything in agreement with the purpose of his will" (Eph 1:11; cf. 1:10). It is important to observe in Eph 1:6 that election is "to the praise of [God's] glorious grace." Election raises our hearts to praise when we realize that the Father has been so kind and gracious to deliver us from the death we deserved and pursued.

Ephesians 1:11 powerfully combines God's sovereignty and election: "In him we have also received an inheritance, because we were predestined according to the plan of the one who works out everything in agreement with the purpose of his will." Believers are God's children and heirs ultimately because he chose us. All this depends on God's freely working according to his plan and will. The next verse points us toward election's goal: so that believers "might bring praise to his glory" (v. 12).

Ephesians 1 also teaches that believers are the object of God's election. While Christ is the elect one in passages previously treated, here believers are the object of God's election. They are chosen "in Christ," which means that they are chosen either through Christ or in union with Christ. In either case ultimacy does not lie in human choice. Paul speaks similarly in 1 Cor 1:30: "It is from [God] that you are in Christ Jesus, who became wisdom from God for us—our righteousness, sanctification, and redemption." It is because of God's work, not ours, that we are in Christ.

Paul's Epistles: 1 Corinthians 1:30

What Paul says in 1 Cor 1:30 fits with the near context. He notes that not many intellectuals, not many who have influence, not many from the upper classes are among the saved. Instead, "God has chosen what is foolish in the world to shame the wise, and God has chosen what is weak in the world to shame the strong. God has chosen what is insignificant and despised in the world—what is viewed as nothing—to bring to nothing what is viewed as something" (1 Cor 1:27–28). God's typical pattern is to choose those who are foolish, those without power and influence, those who are nothings in this world. Those who are proud of their wisdom and strength will experience eschatological shame on the last day; those who think they are something will be shown to have nothing. God has wisely planned history so that his wisdom, rather than that of human beings, will be praised on the final day (v. 21). The Lord has chosen the foolish, the weak, and the lowly so that no one could boast in his presence (v. 29). Since salvation is due to God's choice, believers should boast in him. We thus see one of the vital truths about election. The purpose of the doctrine was not so that we would have something to argue about theologically! God's choice of us, God's election, indicates that all the praise, all the glory, all the honor go to God alone for our salvation.

Paul's Epistles: 1 Thessalonians 1:4–5

The election of God's people is emphasized also in 1 Thess 1:4: "We know, brothers and sisters loved by God, that he has chosen you." Paul has just given thanks to God for the faith, hope, and love of the Thessalonians, but in verse 4 he reaches deeper and explains the origin of faith, hope, and love in their lives. Yes, the Thessalonians have believed, hoped, and loved, yet all these qualities derive from God's grace in their lives. We also see here that election is not a cold and impersonal reality. Just as we saw in the OT, God's love is stressed. In addition, the next verse tells us how we can know that God has chosen people for salvation: "because our gospel did not come to you in word only, but also in power, in the Holy Spirit, and with full assurance" (v. 5). God's choice of people for salvation is seen in history when they believe the gospel. We are not to try to figure out whom God has chosen. Instead, we know his choice by people's response to the message of salvation.

Paul's Epistles: Romans 11:5–6

To put it another way, election showcases God's grace since it is based on grace, not works. Paul makes this very point in Rom 11:5–6: "There is also at the present time a remnant chosen by grace. Now if by grace, then it is not by works; otherwise grace ceases to be grace." The subject here is the election of a remnant from Israel (vv. 1–4). Elijah was in despair in his day because he believed that he was the only elect person left in the land and that his demise was imminent. The Lord corrected Elijah's misapprehension. God revealed, "I have left seven thousand for myself who have not bowed down to Baal" (v. 4). The text does not say that seven thousand remained faithful. Rather, the preservation of the remnant was the Lord's work; he had *left* seven thousand among Israel in the land who were faithful. God's promises to Israel will not fail, because they depend upon his grace! Romans 11:5–6, quoted above, unpacks the nature of such grace. By definition grace excludes works as a basis, for, if one's works, if one's deeds enter in the equation, then human merit becomes part of the basis for salvation. Salvation is all of grace, and what we see here is that election underlines that it is a work of grace all the way down.[8]

Paul's Epistles: Romans 9

Paul's words about Jacob and Esau help us clarify further the relationship between election and works. The promise was given to Jacob rather than Esau (Gen 25:23). The promise is reiterated in Mal 1:2, where the brothers' names are applied to the two nations that came from Jacob and Esau: Israel and Edom, respectively. Malachi's statement is cited in Rom 9:13, where it is applied to individual believers and unbelievers: "I have loved Jacob, but I have hated Esau." The words are shocking, but we need to remember that both Jacob and Esau were sinners and undeserving of God's grace. Love is associated elsewhere with election (cf. Deut 7:6–7; Isa 41:8; 44:2 LXX; Rom 8:28; 11:28; Col 3:12; 1 Thess 1:4). God's love for Jacob and hatred of Esau, then, is another way of saying that he chose Jacob instead of Esau, that he set his love on Jacob rather than Esau (cf. Rom 11:7). The question

---

[8] John M. G. Barclay, *Paul and the Gift* (Grand Rapids: Eerdmans, 2015) provides a fresh perspective on God's grace in second temple Judaism that critiques both new and old perspectives on Paul.

before us is why the Lord selected Jacob instead of Esau. Was it because
he looked ahead and saw that Esau would be wicked and Jacob would live
righteously? Such a scenario obviously does not fit the narrative about Jacob
and Esau in Genesis 25–36. Nor does it accord with what Paul writes about
the same events. He emphasizes, just as we saw in Rom 11:5–6, that God's
choice of Jacob was not based on his works (9:12). Jacob's reception of the
promise is attributed to "God's purpose according to election" (v. 11). In fact,
the actions or decisions of Jacob and Esau were not factors in God's choice,
since God chose Jacob before he and Esau were born and "had done anything good or bad" (v. 11).[9]

God's election is before time (Eph 1:4; 2 Tim 1:9) and is not based
on the foreseen merit or decisions of human beings. Paul is explicit. God's
promise, as Rom 9:16 says, does not "depend on human will or effort." God's
election of any depends upon his merciful will (vv. 15, 17–18). That is, the
basis for God's choosing lies in his mercy and will, his grace and purpose, his
love and sovereignty. We did not deserve mercy, for the salvation of any is a
stunning and amazing gift. And it is based on God's mercy and will.

Paul affirms God's prerogative to show mercy to whomever he wants: "I
will show mercy to whom I will show mercy, and I will have compassion on
whom I will have compassion" (v. 15, quoting Exod 33:19). Paul goes further,
this time affirming God's prerogative to show mercy and to harden whomever he wants: "So then, he has mercy on whom he wants to have mercy and
he hardens whom he wants to harden" (Rom 9:18). Paul's following question
and answer show that we have understood him correctly: "You will say to me,
therefore, 'Why then does he still find fault? For who resists his will?' On

---

[9] For a different reading, one that fits into Arminian parameters, see Brian
Abasciano, *Paul's Use of the Old Testament in Romans 9.1–9: An Intertextual and
Theological Exegesis*, LNTS (New York: T & T Clark, 2005); Abasciano, *Paul's Use of
the Old Testament in Romans 9.10–18: An Intertextual and Theological Exegesis*, LNTS
(New York: Bloomsbury T & T Clark, 2011), 317; Abasciano, *Paul's Use of the Old
Testament in Romans 9.19–33: An Intertextual and Theological Exegesis*, LNTS (New
York: Bloomsbury T & T Clark, 2013); Abasciano, "Corporate Election in Romans
9: A Reply to Thomas Schreiner," *JETS* 49 (2006): 351–71. For my response, see
Thomas R. Schreiner, "Corporate and Individual Election in Romans 9: A Response
to Brian Abasciano," *JETS* 49 (2006): 373–86.

the contrary, who are you, a human being, to talk back to God?" (vv. 20–21). Creatures have no right to question their Creator's divine prerogatives.

Some argue that election and predestination in Romans 9 are about historical destiny, about the political fortunes of nations. Paul contrasts, according to this view, the destiny of Isaac and Ishmael, of Jacob (i.e., Israel) and Esau (i.e., Edom). He also brings in Pharaoh, which shows that the history of nations and peoples are in view. Paul indeed does think of the historical destiny of Israel here, but the historical destiny of Israel cannot be separated from salvation.

Romans 9–11 is a unit. The chapters deal with the same issue and the same question, and that is the *salvific destiny* of Israel. Paul thinks of the historical destiny of Israel here, but the historical destiny of Israel cannot be separated from salvation. We see this from the outset of chapter 9, where Paul's intense grief and his willingness to be separated from Christ forever is traced to the fact that many in Israel were unsaved (Rom 9:1–3). Israel's political misfortunes are insufficient to explain Paul's grief and willingness to experience eschatological destruction! When he says that God's word will not fail, that God is faithful, he has in mind God's promise to save his people (v. 9:6).

It is evident that Paul refers to salvation, for the issue is of those who belong to the children of Abraham (Rom 9:7), and Paul has made it clear in both Romans (4:9–12) and Galatians (Gal 3:6–9) that the children of Abraham are saved. Paul also refers to those who are the "children of God" (Rom 9:8 ESV), which in Paul always refers to believers (v. 8:16–17, 21; Phil 2:15). Furthermore, Paul contrasts "calling" with "works" in Rom 9:12, and both of these words are consistently and regularly used in salvific contexts. (For the term "works," see Rom 3:20, 28; 4:2, 4, 5, 6; 9:32; 11:6; Gal 2:16; 3:2, 5, 10; Eph 2:9.) It is significant that two of these instances occur in Romans 9–11 (9:32; 11:6), for Paul addresses the destiny of Israel in these chapters. The salvific character of "calling" is also clear (Rom 8:28, 30; 9:24–26; 11:29; 1 Cor 1:9, 24; Gal 1:6; Eph 4:1). The term "election" in Rom 9:11 also has salvific import. In the same way the word "destruction" in v. 9:22 denotes eschatological judgment in Paul (e.g., Phil 1:28; 3:19; 2 Thess 2:3; 1 Tim 6:9), and the term "wrath" refers to his final judgment as well (Rom 2:5, 8; 3:5; 5:9; Eph 5:6; Col 3:6; 1 Thess 1:10; 5:9). So too, "glory" often refers in Paul's writings to the eschatological reward awaiting believers (Rom 2:7, 10; 5:2; 8:18, 21; 1 Cor 2:8; 2 Cor 4:17; 1 Thess 2:12). The word "mercy" (Rom 9:15–16, 18, 23) often has a salvific import as well (Rom 11:31–32; 15:9; 1 Tim 1:13, 16; 2 Tim 1:16, 18). The evidence that Paul refers to salvation is overwhelming, and we shouldn't be surprised, for Paul hasn't left the subject of his grief stated in Rom 9:1–3!

When we come to Romans 10, the same subject is on his mind. Paul prays for Israel's salvation (10:1), but Israel has come up short because it has relied on works instead of putting its faith in Jesus Christ (Rom 9:30–10:8). All interpreters recognize that Israel's plight in chapter 10 is that they are not saved, and we must see that Paul hasn't gotten off the subject in chapter 10. He considers the same question he addressed in chapter 9 from a different angle. Indeed, all three chapters consider the question of Israel's salvation, and they climax with the remarkable statement, "All Israel will be saved" (Rom 11:26). Yes, Paul is concerned about the historical destiny of Israel, but its historical destiny here is inextricably tied up with its *salvific destiny*.

Paul urges his understudy Timothy to be bold in his service for Christ (2 Tim 1:8). Believers' confidence in salvation and service lies not in themselves but in God, for "he has saved us and called us with a holy calling, not according to our works, but according to his own purpose and grace, which was given to us in Christ Jesus before time began" (v. 9). Paul rejects any notion of salvation by works and instead succinctly summarizes the ground of election—God's "purpose and grace." As in Eph 1:4, so here election is pretemporal, for God's grace was granted to us "in Christ before time began." That means God chose us before we existed or had done anything; he set his love on us in eternity past according to his own mysterious purpose and love. Once more Paul combines eternal election with union with Christ (as in Eph 1:4). No sooner had God chosen a people for himself than he devised a plan to apply salvation to them: he would send his Son to die, rise, and send the Spirit to unite the elect to Christ in salvation.

The General Epistles: James 2:5

This teaching is not limited to Paul. James says, "Listen, my dear brothers and sisters: Didn't God choose the poor in this world to be rich in faith and heirs of the kingdom that he has promised to those who love him?" (Jas 2:5). James clearly teaches here that faith is a gift of God (cf. Eph 2:8; Phil 1:29). By "poor" here James denotes believers, since he designates them as "rich in faith and heirs of the kingdom."[10] Their faith, however, is a consequence of being chosen by God.

The General Epistles: 1 Peter 2:9

A striking text is 1 Pet 2:9: "You are a chosen race, a royal priesthood, a holy nation, a people for his possession, so that you may proclaim the praises of the one who called you out of darkness into his marvelous light." The privileges of Israel (Exod 19:6; Isa 43:20) belong to the church of Jesus Christ. In fact, what Peter writes here is amazing, since he writes to majority Gentile churches (cf. 1 Pet 1:18; 4:3–4). The church of Jesus Christ is the true Israel, though this doesn't mean there aren't future promises for ethnic Israel as well (cf. Rom 11:26). We focus here on the truth that the church of Jesus Christ, like Israel of old, was chosen. The election of the church is quite interesting here, since Peter emphasizes that Jesus was God's elect in the same context (1 Pet 2:4, 6). In addition, Peter stresses that believers are chosen immediately after saying that some were appointed or destined to stumble (v. 8). Like Paul, Peter emphasizes that his addressees have received mercy as God's chosen people (2:10) and that their transfer from darkness to light should propel them to praise God (v. 9).

Revelation 17:14

John foresees battle between the Lamb and "ten kings" who support "the beast" and fight against God's kingdom (Rev 17:12–13). The outcome of this fight is not in doubt: "These will make war against the Lamb, but the Lamb will conquer them because he is Lord of lords and King of kings. Those with him are called, chosen, and faithful" (v. 14). God's foes wage war against Christ and his own, but the invincible Christ will conquer them. Christ's followers, who share in his victory, are "called, chosen and faithful." Scripture links God's election of his people before creation and his effectively calling them in time to himself in salvation: they are "called" and "chosen." God draws to himself through the gospel "everyone whose name was . . . written from the foundation of the world in the book of life

---

[10] For more on the identity of the poor in James, see Christopher W. Morgan, *A Theology of James: Wisdom for the Community*, EBT (Philipsburg, NJ: P&R, 2010), 17–18, 77–94, 164–67.

of the Lamb who was slaughtered" (13:8; cf. 17:8). God's people are also "faithful" because they refuse to worship the "beast" and instead remain devoted to God.

Revelation: The Book of Life

An image from Revelation related to election is the "book of life" (3:5; 17:8; 20:12, 15) or the "book of life of the Lamb" (13:8; 21:27). This image appears first in the letter to the church in Sardis, where Jesus promises the conqueror, "I will never erase his name from the book of life but will acknowledge his name before my Father" (3:5). God keeps those who overcome, Jesus will own them in his Father's presence, and they will enjoy eternal life.

The "beast," God's great enemy, will exert great influence over much of humanity. Indeed, "Those who live on the earth whose names have not been written in the book of life from the foundation of the world will be astonished when they see the beast that was, and is not, and is to come" (17:8). Those omitted from the book of life are lost, for God shields from spiritual danger only those whose names are written there. As in Eph 1:4 and 2 Tim 1:9, so here God's choice of his people is "from" or "before" creation. God chose people for salvation even before creation.

Because the names of those God has chosen appear in the book of life, it serves as the register of the city of God. It records the names of God's people. The kings of the earth will bring into that city, the New Jerusalem, "the glory and the honor of the nations," and "Nothing unclean will ever enter it, nor anyone who does what is detestable or false, but only those written in the Lamb's book of life" (Rev 21:26–27).

When John calls it the "Lamb's book of life" (21:27) and the "book of life of the Lamb who was slaughtered" (13:8), he shows that the book belongs to Jesus because he offered himself as the ultimate sacrifice for the sins of his people. At the Last Judgment the unsaved will be "judged according to their works" and condemned for their sins (20:12). Human responsibility is accented at the Last Judgment. However, divine sovereignty is not absent, for John declares, "And anyone whose name was not found written in the book of life was thrown into the lake of fire" (20:15).

Arminians understand Jesus's words "I will never erase his name from the book of life" (Rev 3:5) to imply that Christians' unfaithfulness may lead to their names being blotted out of that book.[11] But this misses the point of Rev 3:5 in the context of the letters to the seven churches. Each letter promises final salvation to overcomers. The promises are generally expressed in positive terms (2:7, 17, 26–28; 3:5, 12, 21), but three times in negative terms (2:11; 3:5, 12). Both the positive and negative terms have the same purpose—to assure the conquerors of eternal life with God. So, when Jesus promises, "The one who conquers will never be harmed by the second death" (2:11), he means that conquerors will certainly experience eternal life. Likewise, when he says, "I will never erase his name from the book of life" (3:5), he means that overcomers will certainly be found in the book of life. He does not mention names being blotted out of the book of life; rather he uses *litotes* to underline his promise. Litotes is a figure of speech in which the denial of a negative makes a strong positive statement. Therefore, never blotting out names from the book means ensuring that those persons will be included in it. It is an error, therefore, to appeal to Rev 3:5 to make the strong consolation offered by the book of life passages contingent on human faithfulness. In fact, the main purpose of the book of life in Revelation is to assure those listed in that book of God's spiritual protection (3:5; 13:8; 17:8; 20:15; 21:27). Those written in the book of life from creation (17:8) will be spared the lake of fire (20:15) and will enter the New Jerusalem (21:27).[12]

Historical Reconnaissance

Augustine and Pelagius

The historical roots of predestinarian debates go back to the North African bishop Augustine (354–430) and the British moralist Pelagius (354–418). Augustine's worldly background, teaching of rhetoric, and immersion in Manicheism and Neoplatonism are well known from his autobiographical *Confessions*. Ambrose, bishop of Milan, directed Augustine to Paul's letters, through which he became convicted of his great guilt before a holy God,

---

[11] Grant R. Osborne, *Revelation*, BECNT (Grand Rapids: Baker, 2002), 180–81.
[12] G. K. Beale, *The Book of Revelation. A Commentary on the Greek Text*, NIGTC (Grand Rapids: Eerdmans, 1999), 281–82.

especially by Rom 13:13–14: "Let us walk with decency, as in the daytime: not in carousing and drunkenness; not in sexual impurity and promiscuity; not in quarreling and jealousy. But put on the Lord Jesus Christ and make no provision for the flesh to gratify its desires."

Augustine returned to North Africa as a believer and in time became bishop of Hippo. His writings brought him popularity, and through them the concept of monergism in salvation gained acceptance as far as Rome. Here the British monk Pelagius encountered the concept in 405.

Pelagius was known for his interest in monasticism and Christian moralism. Arriving in Rome, the capital of Christendom, in 405 to teach, he was shocked at the city's dreadful moral condition. After hearing Christians repeating Augustine's prayer, "Grant what you command, and command what you will,"[13] Pelagius concluded that Augustine's theological views fostered sin, and he opposed Augustine's teaching out of concern for Christian ethics.

Like the apostle Paul, Augustine's doctrines of sin and grace grew in part out of his conversion experience. His great sense of sinfulness and of God's redeeming mercy led him to formulate a monergistic doctrine of grace, in which salvation was all of God's doing and none of humans'. Augustine conveyed this understanding of God's saving grace in his *Confessions* and later more systematically in his anti-Pelagian writings.[14] He taught that free will is simply the ability for humans to do what they will. We are free to act according to our natures, which since the fall are corrupted and in bondage to sin.[15] This view of free will has been under attack ever since Augustine's time.

Corresponding to these views of the fall, free will, and sin, Augustine held that salvation is a gift of God's efficacious grace. Grace does not enable sinners to cooperate with God; it effects God's sovereign and gracious will.

---

[13] Augustine, *Confessions*, trans. Henry Chadwick (Oxford: Oxford University Press, 1991), 202.

[14] These are, in chronological order: *On the Spirit and the Letter* (412); *On Nature and Grace* (415); *On the Grace of Christ and Original Sin* (418); *On Grace and Free Will* (427); and *On the Predestination of the Saints* (429).

[15] Augustine, *The Enchiridion*, 30–32, in vol. 3, first series, *Nicene and Post-Nicene Fathers*, 247–48.

An Augustinian view thus teaches that God's *prevenient grace* is not universal but particular and effective.[16] But why do some receive God's grace and others don't? Augustine was forthright: "The reason why one person is assisted by grace and another is not helped must be referred to the secret judgments of God."[17]

Augustine held to absolute divine election. Before creation God chose some to eternal life and others to eternal punishment. The elect receive what they do not deserve—God's grace and salvation. The non-elect receive what they do deserve—the judgment of a holy and just God.

Predestination and grace are divine matters, not human, and we dare not pry into God's secret counsels.

Foundational to Pelagius's theology is the idea that humans' responsibility before God assumes their ability as well. If God did not grant us the ability to respond as he demands, he would be unjust. Since God commands us to believe the gospel, we must, then, have the ability to believe it. This in turn led Pelagius to deny Augustine's view of original sin, the idea that all Adam's descendants inherited guilt and corruption from his primal sin. Instead, Pelagius held that Adam's sin affects us only by setting a poor example for us. To Pelagius, all humans are free to choose good or evil, and nothing inclines them to the evil. Pelagius rejected Augustine's view that grace is God's powerful love that saves and keeps us. Rather, according to Pelagius, grace includes free will, God's commandments, and Jesus's example.

As we would expect, Pelagius's doctrine of election clashed with Augustine's. Pelagius emphasized God's foreknowledge of human faith or unbelief as the key to election:

> To predestine is the same as to foreknow. Therefore, those [God] foresaw would be conformed [to the image of Christ] in life, he intended to be conformed in glory. . . . So too, then, he has now chosen those whom he foreknew would believe from among the

---

[16] Augustine, *On Predestination* 10.19, in vol. 5 first series, *Nicene and Post-Nicene Fathers*, 507.

[17] Augustine, *On Grace and Free Will* 23.45, in vol. 5 first series, *Nicene and Post-Nicene Fathers*, 464.

Gentiles, and has rejected those whom he foreknew would be unbelieving out of Israel.[18]

Allison clarifies Pelagius's theology by citing his interpretation of Rom
9:15 (where Paul quotes Exod 33:19): "I will show mercy to whom I will
show mercy, and I will have compassion on whom I will have compassion."
Pelagius wrote, "I will have mercy on him whom I have foreknown will be
able to deserve compassion."[19]

Augustine's and Pelagius's theologies were on a collision course. Both
attracted supporters, and their disputes lasted twenty years. Finally, however,
the church decided for Augustine and against Pelagius, as the ecumenical
Council of Ephesus condemned his views in 431.

Martin Luther

Martin Luther (1483–1546) was an Augustinian monk who became a professor of Bible and then a Protestant Reformer. He protected the free grace
of God in justification by underscoring God's election of sinners, who suffered under the bondage of the will. Desiderius Erasmus (1466–1536), the
renowned Dutch humanist, generally welcomed Luther's critique of Roman
abuses but broke ranks with him in 1524 when Erasmus wrote *On the
Freedom of the Will.* Luther applauded him for pointing to the key issue—the
debate between monergism and synergism. What do failed humans contribute to God's grace in salvation?

Erasmus's position on free will reflected that of the sixth-century
Semi-Pelagians, who held to a weakened free will as a result of Adam's fall:
"Although free choice is damaged by sin, it is nevertheless not extinguished
by it. And although it has become so lame in the process that before we
receive grace we are more readily inclined toward evil than good, yet it is not
altogether cut out."[20] Although Erasmus appealed to humanity's need for

---

[18] Pelagius, *Pelagius's Commentary on St. Paul's Epistle to the Romans*, 8:29; 9:10;
9:15, trans. Theodore de Bruyn (Oxford: Clarendon, 1993), 112, 116–17, quoted in
Gregg R. Allison, *Historical Theology* (Grand Rapids: Zondervan, 2011), 456.

[19] Allison, *Historical Theology*, 456.

[20] E. Gordon Rupp and Philip S. Watson, eds., *Luther and Erasmus: Free Will
and Salvation* (Philadelphia: Westminster, 1969), 51.

God's cooperating grace, which made repentance possible, Luther labeled Erasmus's views Pelagian and criticized him for lacking the courage to take a stand for the truth of the gospel.

Luther responded by penning *On the Bondage of the Will*, a direct attack on Erasmus's theology. Luther agreed with Erasmus that absolute free will exists, but Luther insisted that only God possesses it. He accepted Augustine's doctrine of original sin and with it the corollary that the human will is bound in sin and unable to extricate itself. Luther was concerned with exegesis and particular theological conclusions but was much more concerned with the place of election and free will systematically. Luther juxtaposed the theology of glory (synergism) with the theology of the cross (monergism). The former exalts human accomplishment in salvation and human pride. The latter focuses on Christ on the cross, gives God the glory, and squashes human pride. Christ's cross, the basis of justification and saving faith, highlights man's utter inability to aspire to grace. Election is important in that it shows God's great grace and humans' great helplessness.

However, Luther's strong Augustinian doctrine of election was diluted by Philipp Melanchthon, his disciple and heir to the Lutheran Reformation. He turned from Luther's monergistic view of election to a gracious synergism. In *Loci Communes* (Theological Commonplaces), Melanchthon taught that there are three causes of salvation: Scripture, the Holy Spirit, and free will. Why does one person believe and another does not? He answered, "The reason is in us."[21]

John Calvin

Although John Calvin (1509–1564) respected Melanchthon for his scholarship, he took issue with his synergism and preferred Luther's monergism. Calvin, the Reformer of Geneva, devoted himself to biblical exegesis to build a Christocentric theology. He emphasized God's sovereignty and developed a strong doctrine of election. Calvin stated his views on predestination in his famous *Institutes of the Christian Religion*: "In conformity, therefore, to the clear doctrine of Scripture, we assert that by an eternal and immutable

---

[21] Philip Melanchthon, 1555 *Loci Communes* (variata).

counsel God has once for all determined both whom he would admit to salvation and whom he would condemn to destruction."[22]

Opponents attacked Calvin's views on election and free will, and he responded with *Concerning Free Will* (1543) and *Concerning the Eternal Predestination of God* (1552). Calvin acknowledged his debt to Augustine's theology: "If I wanted to weave a whole volume from Augustine, I could readily show my readers that I need no other language than his."[23]

After Calvin's death, leadership of the Geneva Academy fell to his successor, Theodore Beza (1519–1605). Beza accepted Calvin's theology but pursued a different theological method. He was a leader in Protestant scholasticism that followed the time of Luther and Calvin, a movement that emphasized philosophical theology more than the magisterial Reformers. Beza's theological system was more complete and stronger than Calvin's. Jacob Arminius, a young Dutch ministerial candidate, was taught this strong Calvinism at the Geneva Academy at the end of the sixteenth century.

Arminius and the Synod of Dordt

Jacob Arminius (1550–1609) was a theological student in Geneva under Theodore Beza. After graduation he returned to Amsterdam and accepted a call to pastoral ministry in the Dutch church. Later he taught theology at the University of Leiden, where he found success in his teaching. He also encountered criticism from a colleague, Franciscus Gomarus (1563–1642), a strong Calvinist who took exception to Arminius's soteriology. They disputed for a time, and then Gomarus formally accused Arminius of aberration from the doctrinal standards of the Dutch church (the Belgic Confession and the Heidelberg Catechism). In response, Arminius wrote a systematic defense of his views, the *Declaration of Sentiments* (1608).

Arminius followed his former teacher Beza's approach to systematic theology but forged a different path concerning the plan of salvation. Against Augustine, Luther, and Calvin, he taught that God planned to save all those

---

[22] John Calvin, *Institutes of the Christian Religion* 3.21.7, ed. John T. McNeill, trans. Ford Lewis Battles (Philadelphia: Westminster, 1960), 931.

[23] Calvin, *Institutes* 3.22.8, 942.

whom he foresaw (foreknew) would believe in Christ. This means that election to salvation is contingent upon God's foreseeing people's faith.

Arminius agreed with Augustine and Calvin regarding sinners' inability to do anything to save themselves, including believe. However, he attempted to ameliorate spiritual inability by positing that God gives prevenient (preceding) grace to everyone: "The grace sufficient for salvation is conferred on the elect and on the non-elect, that, if they will, they may believe or not believe."[24] Augustine and Calvin had taught that prevenient grace was particular and efficacious, but for Arminius it was universal and not efficacious. Following Calvin and Beza, Arminius affirmed God's foreknowledge. But he diverged from their view when he said that foreknowledge was not causal: "A thing does not come to pass because it is foreknown . . . but it is foreknown because it is yet to be."[25] The determining factor in salvation resides not in God but in human beings—it is not God's sovereign grace but humans' free will. Although man's will is naturally corrupt and cannot choose the good, God's universal prevenient grace enables all to exercise saving faith in Christ, if only they will. According to Arminius, God's part in salvation is to foresee what sinners freely choose, and then to elect (or reject) based on this foreknowledge.

Arminianism grew among the Dutch Reformed clergy, and an influential minority had developed by a few years after Arminius's death. The Arminians drew up a systematic defense of their views, called the Remonstrance or Protest, and the protestors themselves came to be called the Remonstrants. The Remonstrance consisted of five points of debated doctrine:

1. Conditional election
2. Universal atonement
3. Total depravity/prevenient grace
4. Resistible grace
5. Conditional perseverance

A brief summary of the five Arminian points is in order. Conditional election means God chooses for salvation conditioned or contingent upon

---

[24] Jacob Arminius, *Apology against Thirty-one Theological Articles 28* in *The Works of James Arminius*, trans. James Nichols and William Nichols. 3 vols. (Grand Rapids: Baker, 1999), 2:53

[25] Jacob Arminius, *Private Disputations* 28.14, trans. James Nichols (Grand Rapids: Baker, 1986), 2:368.

his foreknowledge of persons' faith. Universal atonement means that Jesus died to make the salvation of everyone possible. Total depravity means that, because of Adam's fall and human sin, people cannot save themselves. But, as stated previously, universal prevenient grace nullifies the effects of Adam's sin on the human will so that sinners have gracious ability to believe and be saved. Resistible grace means that sinners can and do reject the grace of God and perish. Conditional perseverance indicates that the Arminians were uncertain if believers could fall away from grace and be lost again.

Though it is not common knowledge, these "five points of Arminianism" were promulgated before the five points of Calvinism. These five articles of the Remonstrance moved the Calvinist majority to respond by calling a church synod at Dordrecht in 1618. The Synod of Dort was a general assembly of the Dutch church. Because the synod was a court of the church, it was a deliberative and judicial body, convened to evaluate and judge the Remonstrants' views. After the synod deliberated it published the five points of the Synod of Dort, a point-by-point response to the five points of the Remonstrance. The five canons were:

1. Total depravity
2. Unconditional election
3. Limited atonement
4. Irresistible grace
5. Perseverance of the saints

A summary of these five points is also in order. The Calvinists agreed with the Arminians that sinners cannot rescue themselves, but the Calvinists rejected the Arminian concept of universal prevenient grace. There is no gracious ability but rather inability, which is often called total depravity. Unconditional election means that the ground of election resides in God himself, not in anything in humans. Limited or definite or particular atonement means that, although universal benefits flow from the cross, Jesus died to save the elect, not each and every person. Irresistible grace denies not that sinners "successfully" resist God's saving grace until death, but that none of the chosen do so. Perseverance of the saints means both that God preserves his saved people until the end and that they persevere in the faith; they do not merely profess faith in Christ but continue to believe.

Today we recognize these five canons as the five points of Calvinism. Despite this name, it is important to note that the five points did not come from John Calvin in the sixteenth century but from the seventeenth-century Synod of Dort. They do not represent a complete presentation of Calvinism, which holds to many truths besides the five points. The five canons of Dort represent the rebuttal of the Dutch Calvinists to the Arminians' Remonstrance. By promulgating them, the Dutch Reformed church officially reaffirmed its acceptance of Augustine and Calvin's view of predestination and judged Arminius's interpretation of the Reformed confessions to be out of bounds. The canons of the Synod of Dort were added to the Belgic Confession and Heidelberg Catechism to constitute the "three forms of unity," the doctrinal standards of Reformed churches in Holland and around the world.

Spurgeon and the "Hyperists"

Charles Haddon Spurgeon (1834–1892) grew up in a rural Congregationalist church that basically espoused Calvinism. Showing extraordinary preaching ability, at twenty he was ordained as a Particular Baptist and later called to preach at New Park Street Church in London. No sooner had he arrived than he was drawn into controversy with "Hyperism," an extreme form of Calvinism. Here are its main points:

1. God loves the elect, not the non-elect.
2. There is no universal gospel call, only an efficacious call to the elect.
3. Unbelief is not a sin because the non-elect cannot possibly believe.
4. Any views that do not accept this Calvinism are not Christian.

This Calvinistic system holds to divine agency that totally overwhelms any human agency. That is why Spurgeon called it Hyperism and its advocates Hyperists. Since his time, it has come to be known as Hyper-Calvinism. James Wells, a Hyperist leader, wrote blistering condemnations of Spurgeon in Particular Baptist magazines. Spurgeon disappointed many believers when he failed to respond to these attacks except in sermons.

First, Spurgeon said, besides God's sovereign love for the elect, God has a general love for all humans. Second, despite Hyperist claims to the contrary, the gospel call is universal. Spurgeon said that the Hyperists "are too orthodox to obey the Master's will; they desire to understand first who are appointed to come to the supper, and then they will invite them."[26] Third, Christ invites whosoever will to come to him, and this means that those who reject him bring condemnation on themselves. Spurgeon's teaching was not original but instead a restatement of the historic views on predestination taught by Augustine and Calvin.

Partly because of Spurgeon's Christian testimony and excellence as a preacher of the Word, traditional Calvinism eventually met with wider approval than Hyperism among the Particular Baptists in England. In fact, the Hyperists became an entrenched minority. But by the end of the nineteenth century, Calvinism had been overtaken by Arminianism among English evangelicals. This did not matter much, however, because neither party was any longer concerned about the other, as both were preoccupied with a new, third party that was outstripping them both—theological liberalism, which had little concern for any orthodox doctrines, including election.

Systematic Formulations

God chooses some for service, including prophets, priests, and kings. However, election is not just for service but is also the means by which God's saving plan will be realized. God chose Abraham, Isaac, and Jacob for salvation, and he chose Israel to be his people. In the same way, he chose the church of Jesus Christ to be the children of God. God's election is not based on works or foreseen faith but is due entirely to God's free and loving choice. God's election of sinners confirms that salvation is by grace alone, giving all the glory to God alone. It is time to pull themes together and move toward a systematic theology of election.[27]

Election's Author: God

Scripture is clear: "Our God is a God of salvation" (Ps 68:20), and "Salvation belongs to the LORD" (3:8). We are not surprised, then, when consistently

---

[26] Charles Haddon Spurgeon, *Metropolitan Tabernacle Pulpit*, 63 vols. (Pasadena, TX: Pilgrim Publications, 1969–1980), 11:495.

[27] We received help from Peterson, *Election and Free Will*, 37–124.

in Scripture God is the author of election. God chose Abraham out of all humanity: "You, the Lord, are the God who chose Abram and brought him out of Ur of the Chaldeans, and changed his name to Abraham" (Neh 9:7). From Abraham, God brought the nation of Israel, which he chose as his own out of all the nations on the earth. God told Israel to pursue holiness, "For you are a holy people belonging to the Lord your God. The Lord has chosen you to be his own possession out of all the peoples on the face of the earth" (Deut 14:2).

Most important for our purposes is God's choosing people for salvation. This theme occurs from the beginning to the end of the New Testament:

"Many are invited, but few are chosen." (Matt 22:14)

"Those with [the Lamb] are called, chosen, and faithful." (Rev 17:14)

Every New Testament passage that addresses election either ascribes election to God or implies that fact by using the divine passive. Election is the work of God alone.

In every such passage but one God the Father is the author of election. The exception is in John's Gospel. The New Testament in general ascribes to the Son works that in the Old Testament God performs. This is true of creation (John 1:3; Col 1:16), providence (Col 1:17; Heb 1:3), judgment (John 5:22–23; 2 Thess 1:7–8), and salvation (John 5:28–29; Heb 1:3). John extends this tendency, for he alone teaches that Jesus adopts believers (1:12) and raises himself from the dead (2:19–21; 10:17–18).

John alone also presents Jesus as the elector. After emphasizing disciples' responsibility to bear fruit by remaining in him, the true vine, Jesus explains that the disciples' choice of him is not ultimate. Behind it lies Jesus's choice of them for salvation: "You did not choose me, but I chose you. . . . However, because you are not of the world, but I have chosen you out of it, the world hates you" (John 15:16, 19). Jesus's election of the Eleven results in their salvation because it entails their belonging to him, not the world.

We note that election is for both salvation and service, as Jesus taught: "You did not choose me, but I chose you. I appointed you to go and produce fruit and that your fruit should remain" (v. 16).

The truth that God is election's author is reinforced by a consideration of its timing.

Election's Timing: Before Creation

Four New Testament texts place election "before" or "from" creation. Paul does so twice:

> God chose us in [Christ], before the foundation of the world, to be holy and blameless in love before him. (Eph 1:4)

> [God] has saved us and called us with a holy calling, not according to our works, but according to his own purpose and grace, which was given to us in Christ Jesus before time began. (2 Tim 1:9)

Paul affirms God is the elector and that he chose his people "before the foundation of the world" for sanctification. Placing election before creation removes human faith or works from the equation. The apostle's similar use of election "before" in Rom 9:11 sheds light on Eph 1:4:

> Though her sons had not been born yet or done anything good or bad, so that God's purpose according to election might stand—not from works but from the one who calls—[Rebekah] was told, "The older will serve the younger." As it is written: "I have loved Jacob, but I have hated Esau." (Rom 9:11–13)

Paul speaks of God's choice of Jacob over Esau before their birth, that is, before they "had done anything good or bad." God's choice before their birth precluded anything they might do, including believe. God's choice before their birth guaranteed that his "purpose according to election might stand." Similarly, God's election before creation means the basis of election is entirely within God and not us. In a word, it shows that salvation "does not depend on human will or effort but on God who shows mercy" (Rom 9:16).

Second Timothy 1:9 also speaks of election before creation. God saved us "not according to our works, but according to his own purpose and grace, which was given to us in Christ Jesus before time began." God gave saving grace to his own prior to time, that is, in eternity past. Once more, a pretemporal election precedes our faith.

Twice Revelation speaks of people following "the beast" if their names are not in the book of life "from the foundation of the world":

> All those who live on the earth will worship it, everyone whose name was not written from the foundation of the world in the book of life of the Lamb who was slaughtered. (Rev 13:8)

> "The beast that you saw was, and is not, and is about to come up from the abyss and go to destruction. Those who live on the earth whose names have not been written in the book of life from the foundation of the world will be astonished when they see the beast that was, and is not, and is to come." (17:8)

To have one's name in the book of life means to be enrolled in the city of God, whereas to have one's name omitted means not to be enrolled. By implication the positive, like the negative, is "from the foundation of the world," that is, from creation.

The facts that God alone elects and does so before creation mean that election and subsequent salvation are all of him, not based on foreseen human faith or deeds. And this is exactly what we find when we inquire as to the basis of election.

Election's Basis: God's Love and Will

Scripture consistently locates the basis of election in God, not us. Specifically, it presents God's will and love as the grounds of election. The Old Testament tells why God chose Israel out of all the nations on earth. Israel alone belongs to God for this reason:

> "The LORD your God has chosen you to be his own possession out of all the peoples on the face of the earth. The LORD had his heart set on you and chose you, not because you were more numerous than all peoples, for you were the fewest of all peoples. But because the LORD loved you and kept the oath he swore to your ancestors. . . ." (Deut 7:6–8)

God's will and love lay behind his choice of Israel. God certainly did not choose Israel because he foresaw that Israel would exercise faith and obedience, for he repeatedly characterizes the Israelites as a "stiff-necked people" (Exod 32:9; 33:3, 5; 34:9; Deut 9:6, 13; 10:16; 31:27; Neh 9:16–17). Stephen speaks of his contemporaries as well as their forebears, "You stiff-necked people with uncircumcised hearts and ears! You are always resisting the Holy Spirit. As your ancestors did, you do also" (Acts 7:51).

Paul is Scripture's most prolific teacher of the election of Christians, and he situates its basis in God's love and will. Three examples will suffice. First, in Ephesians 1 we learn that God "chose us. . . . In love he predestined us for adoption to himself as sons through Jesus Christ, according to the purpose of his will, to the praise of his glorious grace" (Eph 1:4–6 ESV). A few verses later he writes, "In [Christ] we have also received an inheritance, because we were predestined according to the plan of the one who works out everything in agreement with the purpose of his will" (v. 11). Paul's teaching is unambiguous: God chooses based on his "love" (v. 4) and "the purpose of his will" (v. 11).

Second, in Romans 9 Paul teaches the same truths with greater emphasis. God's choice of people for salvation is according to his "purpose according to election" (v. 11), love (v. 13), "mercy" (vv. 15, 18, 23), and "compassion" (v. 15). He sums up the basis of election both negatively and positively: "So then, it does not depend on human will or effort but on God who shows mercy" (v. 16). The ground of election is God's sovereign grace, as the next text succinctly summarizes.

Third, Paul's most pithy summary of the basis of election appears in 2 Tim 1:9. Paul exhorts Timothy to boldness in the gospel, even to the point of suffering (v. 8). He reminds Timothy of God's power and declares, "He has saved us and called us with a holy calling, not according to our works, but according to his own purpose and grace, which was given to us in Christ Jesus before time began" (v. 9). As always in Paul, salvation is not by human effort but by God's "purpose and grace," his will and love. As we have seen, this is one of two places where Paul locates God's electing grace "before time began." That grace is efficacious, for, although planned in eternity, God manifested it in time "through the appearing of our Savior Christ Jesus, who has abolished death and has brought life and immortality to light through the gospel" (v. 10).

God's election of his people for salvation is based on his sovereignty and grace, his purpose and mercy, his will and love. He chooses both individuals and the church, as the next section shows.

Election's Scope: Individuals and the Church

God chooses individuals for salvation, individuals that corporately constitute his church. Scripture plainly teaches God's individual and corporate election of his people. We begin with corporate election because it is not contested.

God's corporate election of his people is taught in every New Testament corpus:

> *Gospels*: Mark 13:20, 22, 26–27; 22:14; John 6:37; 10:26–27; 17:2, 24;
> *Acts*: 18:9–10;
> *Paul's Epistles*: Eph 1:4; cf. Rom 8:29–30, 33; cf. 9:23; Col 3:12; 1
> Thess 1:4–5; 2 Thess 2:13; 2 Tim 1:9; 2:10; Titus 1:1;
> *General Epistles*: Jas 2:5; 1 Pet 1:1–2; cf. 2:9; 2 Pet 1:10; 1 Pet 5:13;
> 2 John 1, 13;
> *Revelation*: 17:14: "book of life" texts: 13:8; 17:8.

We have not previously discussed three texts:

> She who is in Babylon, chosen together with you, sends you greetings, as does Mark, my son. (1 Pet 5:13)

> The elder: To the elect lady and her children, whom I love in the truth—and not only I, but also all who know the truth. . . . The children of your elect sister send you greetings. (2 John vv. 1, 13)

The woman "in Babylon, chosen," "the elect lady" (2 John 1), and her "elect sister" (v. 13) are references to churches and thus to corporate election.

Scripture teaches corporate election, and it also teaches individual election in the Gospels, Acts, and Paul's letters. Jesus tells of the Son's choosing to reveal the Father to some people: "All things have been handed over to me by my Father, and no one knows the Son except the Father, and no one knows the Father except the Son and anyone to whom the Son chooses to reveal him" (Matt 11:27 ESV). The Father and Son have unique reciprocal knowledge of one another. The Father has granted authority to the incarnate Son to make the Father known as the Son chooses.

After healing a man who had been lame for thirty-eight years, Jesus says that he always does the Father's will and at the same time performs works that only God can do (John 5:19–29). The purpose of the latter?

"That all may honor the Son, just as they honor the Father" (v. 23). One work performed by Father and Son is giving life: "Just as the Father raises the dead and gives them life, so the Son also gives life to whom he wants" (v. 21). "Whom" is plural and consists of the individuals chosen and quickened by Jesus.

Acts stresses the significance of repentance and faith and underlines God's sovereignty. It speaks of election only twice, once of corporate election (Acts 18:9–10) and once of individual election (13:48). After being rejected by the Jews in Perga of Pamphylia, Paul turns to the Gentiles, citing Isa 49:6: "'I have made you a light for the Gentiles, that you may bring salvation to the ends of the earth.' When the Gentiles heard this, they rejoiced and honored the word of the Lord, and all who had been appointed to eternal life believed" (Acts 13:47–48). God's appointment to life results in saving faith.

Paul teaches both corporate and individual election.[28] In Romans 9 he cites Moses's teaching of the divine prerogative from Exod 33:19: God "tells Moses, I will show mercy to whom I will show mercy, and I will have compassion on whom I will have compassion" (Rom 9:15). The words "to whom" and "on whom" are singular. So are Paul's words applying Moses's words to Paul's ministry: "So then, he has mercy *on whom* he wants to have mercy and he hardens *whom* he wants to harden" (v. 18). "On whom" and "whom" are singular, pointing to God's choice of individuals as recipients of God's saving mercy and to his rejection of other individuals.

A neglected election text appears among Paul's greetings at the end of Romans: "Greet Rufus, chosen in the Lord" (Rom 16:13). After considering the possibility that Paul was referring to a man named Rufus as an "outstanding" or "choice" believer, Douglas Moo interprets this as a reference to God's choice of Rufus for salvation: "Probably Paul simply means that he was a Christian, 'chosen' as all Christians are."[29] We agree.

---

[28] For interaction with such views, see Thomas R. Schreiner, "Does Romans 9 Teach Individual Election unto Salvation?" in *Still Sovereign: Contemporary Perspectives on Election, Foreknowledge, and Grace*, ed. T. R. Schreiner and B. A. Ware (Grand Rapids: Baker, 2000), 89–106.

[29] Douglas Moo, *The Epistle to the Romans*, NICNT (Grand Rapids: Eerdmans, 1996), 926.

Election's Goals: Our Salvation and God's Glory

God chose people in eternity past with a view to eternity future—the new heavens and new earth. God set goals pertaining to election for the church and for himself. For the church, the goal is final salvation communicated in many ways, including holiness (Eph 1:4), adoption (v. 5), conformity to Christ (Rom 8:29), an inheritance (Eph 1:11), and glory (Rom 8:30; 2 Thess 2:14). Paul combines election and final salvation in 2 Timothy: "This is why I endure all things for the elect: so that they also may obtain salvation, which is in Christ Jesus, with eternal glory" (2 Tim 2:10).

Concerning God himself, the goal of election is his own glory. God chose Jews and Gentiles for salvation with the goal that they "might bring praise to his glory" (v. 12). Arnold is correct: "God's ultimate purpose in selecting and predestining a people for himself is that it would lead to his own glory."[30] Believers feel compelled to join the apostle when he sings, "To [God] be glory in the church and in Christ Jesus throughout all generations, forever and ever. Amen" (Eph 3:21).

Election: Historical and Eternal

John Frame helps distinguish between historical and eternal election.[31] God's choosing Israel is an *historical election*—although God chose the nation in history, his choice did not necessarily result in the salvation of every Israelite. Those who opposed him and continually broke covenant were not saved. In a similar way, God chooses via historical election the visible New Testament church as a corporate people, but not every individual in the church experiences salvation. By contrast, *eternal election* always results in salvation, for God chooses individuals for salvation before creation as revealed in the New Testament. Both historical election and eternal election are types of election because both involve God's choice. But Frame clarifies differences between them: "All of the eternally elect are historically elect, but not vice versa."[32]

---

[30] Clinton E. Arnold, *Ephesians*, Zondervan Exegetical Commentary on the New Testament (Grand Rapids: Zondervan, 2011), 84.

[31] John Frame, *The Doctrine of God* (Phillipsburg, NJ: P&R, 2002), 317–30.

[32] Frame, 329.

Historical election puts one in the community of faith but does not guarantee that one has been eternally elected for salvation. Elect individuals ultimately believe and obey God.

Election and Foreknowledge

In the Arminian tradition, election is subordinated to foreknowledge. After all, Paul says, "Those he foreknew [*proginōskō*] he also predestined to be conformed to the image of his Son, so that he would be the firstborn among many brothers and sisters" (Rom 8:29). Arminians hold that predestination depends upon foreknowledge (*prognōsis*), which they understand as God's foreseeing beforehand who would believe. When human beings foreknow something, they simply foresee what will happen (2 Pet 3:17). Biblically, God's foreknowledge, although it includes prescience, the idea that God sees beforehand what will occur, also includes the notion of foreordination. Such a conclusion is not merely philosophical but is textually grounded.

God's knowledge of persons, when it is knowledge that leads to salvation, has a covenantal and personal dimension.[33] This is evident in how the word "know" (*yāda '*) is used in the OT. God "chose," literally "knew" (*yᵉda 'ti*), Abraham (Gen 18:19). The translation rightly represents the significance of the word "know," for the text does not merely say that the Lord had mental cognition of Abraham but also signifies that the Lord set his love upon him. Another example stems from Amos 3:2, where the Lord addresses Israel, "I have known only you out of all the clans of the earth; therefore, I will punish you for all your iniquities." Here again the word *yᵉda 'ti* occurs for "known," and some translations for good reasons translate the word as "chosen" (NIV, NET, NASB1995). Obviously, God cognitively knows all the nations of the earth, and thus in Amos 3:2 the word "know" has a personal and covenantal dimension. The Lord has known Israel in that he has chosen it as his special possession among all nations. We noted earlier that Jeremiah was "known" as prophet (Jer 1:5) in the same way. We see a similar usage in Ps 1:6, where "the LORD watches over [lit. "knows,"

---

[33] See the study of S. M. Baugh, "The Meaning of Foreknowledge," in *Still Sovereign: Contemporary Perspectives on Election, Foreknowledge, and Grace*, ed. T. R. Schreiner and B. A. Ware (Grand Rapids: Baker, 2000), 183–200.

*yôdea*ʾ] the way of the righteous." Certainly, the Lord "knows" cognitively the way of the wicked as well, for the next line says, "The way of the wicked leads to ruin." God's knowing the path of the righteous means that he cares for and protects his people.

Paul also uses the word "know" of God's setting his love, for his own good pleasure, on his people. Paul reproves the Galatians, "Now, since you know God, or rather have become known by God, how can you turn back again to the weak and worthless elements? Do you want to be enslaved to them all over again?" (Gal 4:9). The Galatians' knowing God signifies their conversion, but then Paul considers a deeper reality, the ultimate reason they know God, and he traces it to God's knowledge of them. He set his covenant affection upon them. Believers know God only because God knew them first.

A similar text occurs in an introductory paragraph addressing the issue of food offered to idols (1 Cor 8:1–3). The "knowers" were those proud of their knowledge of idols and foods but not caring for the weak (vv. 1–13). They were proud of their knowledge but were using it as a club on the heads of weaker Christians. Paul reminds and reproves them, "But if anyone loves God, he is known by him" (v. 3). The fundamental issue is not how much "the knowers" know but whether they are known by God. Those who love God, that is, believers (cf. Rom 8:28; 1 Cor 2:9), are previously known by God. The perfect tense of "known" (*egnōstai*) indicates that human love is a result of God's knowing. Love springs up in human hearts in those who have been known by God, in those who been the objects of his covenant love.

Another example of the word "knowing" signifying God's covenant affection surfaces in 2 Tim 2:19: "Nevertheless, God's solid foundation stands firm, bearing this inscription: The Lord knows those who are his, and let everyone who calls on the name of the Lord turn away from wickedness." Paul considers the influence of false teachers who were undermining the faith of those who confessed faith in Jesus Christ (vv. 15–18). As a result of the machinations of such teachers, the faith of some was ruined (v. 18). Does that mean some who were truly believers are now lost? Certainly not. Paul alludes in 2 Tim 2:19 to Num 16:5 and the story of Korah, Dathan, and Abiram, who rebelled against the leadership of Moses and Aaron. The point of the story is that the Lord knows those who are truly his. Korah and his friends by their apostasy showed that they didn't truly belong to the Lord, and the same is true of those who defected from the faith according to 2 Tim 2:18. Those whom the Lord knows, however—those upon whom God has set his covenant affection—will never depart from him.

In the NT, then, God's foreknowledge is not mere cognition but refers to his covenant affection and relationship with his people. We see this clearly in Rom 11:2, where we read, "God has not rejected his people whom he foreknew." Paul asks here whether "God rejected his people" Israel, and the answer is absolutely not, and the preservation of a remnant demonstrates that there is a future for Israel. In the midst of this discussion the meaning of "foreknew" is evident from the context and its use in the sentence. In context it clearly refers to Israel's election (Rom 11:5) and preservation (v. 4). The meaning is also clear in the sentence because the word "foreknew" stands in contrast to "rejected." We could put it this way: Israel was not rejected but selected. "Foreknew" here means that God set his covenant affection and love upon Israel.

We see another example of foreknowledge in Rom 8:29: "Those he foreknew he also predestined to be conformed to the image of his Son." We have seen from the OT and from Rom 11:2 that there are good reasons to think that "foreknow" means "foreordain" and designates God's covenant affection that he bestows on his people. These ideas fit well in 8:29, for Paul's meaning would then be: those he sovereignly foreloved he also predestined. Such an understanding of foreknowledge is also supported by 1 Pet 1:20, where we read that Christ "was foreknown before the foundation of the world, but was revealed in these last times for you." Certainly, God foreknew when Christ would come, but he didn't merely foreknow his arrival. He also foreordained and determined when Christ would come. Similarly, the death of Christ was not an accidental event. Jesus "was delivered up according to God's determined plan and foreknowledge" (Acts 2:23). The word "determined" (*hōrismenē*) assists us in defining "foreknowledge" (*prognōsei*), showing that foreknowledge includes the notion of foreordination. The interpretation proposed here is supported also by Acts 4:27–28, which teaches clearly that Jesus's death was predestined: "In this city both Herod and Pontius Pilate, with the Gentiles and the people of Israel, assembled together against your holy servant Jesus, whom you anointed, to do whatever your hand and your will had predestined to take place." Limiting foreknowledge to foresight falls short of the actual usage of the word.

We have seen in both Acts 2:23 and 1 Pet 1:20 that foreknowledge includes the idea of foreordination. The same applies in 1 Pet 1:1–2: "To those chosen, living as exiles dispersed abroad in Pontus, Galatia, Cappadocia, Asia, and Bithynia, chosen according to the foreknowledge of God the Father . . ." The elect are chosen "according to foreknowledge." Just as God foreordained the coming of Christ (1 Pet 1:20), he also elected believers based on his choice to set his covenant affection upon them (1:2). Thus, foreknowledge combines God's foreordination and commitment to love.

Election and Union with Christ

Paul often uses the words "in Christ" to speak of union with Christ. Twice he ties union with Christ to pretemporal election. Paul teaches that God chose people in Christ before the foundation of the world (v. 4). He says that God gave us grace "in Christ Jesus," "before time began" (2 Tim 1:9). The difference between Paul's normal use of "in Christ" and these two texts is temporal. Every other time Paul uses the phrase "in Christ" to speak of union he tells of God's uniting people to Christ *in history*. In Eph 1:4 and 2 Tim 1:9 Paul speaks of union with Christ *in eternity*.

Paul thus teaches that God united the elect to Christ before creation. What does this mean? It does not refer to actual union with Christ, for before creation we did not exist. Rather, Paul includes union with Christ in God's plan. God not only chose to save people but also planned the means to save them; he planned to unite them spiritually to his Son. This helps us understand 2 Tim 1:9 better: God "has saved us . . . according to his own purpose and grace, which was given to us in Christ Jesus before time began." Union with Christ was not a divine afterthought. It was a part of God's plan of salvation from the beginning.

Election and Calling

Three times Paul connects election and calling. God effectively brings people to salvation through the gospel. First,

> We know that all things work together for the good of those who love God, who are called according to his purpose. For those he foreknew he also predestined. . . . And those he predestined, he also called; and those he called, he also justified; and those he justified, he also glorified. (Rom 8:28–30)

Paul explains that lovers of God are those "called according to his purpose" (Rom 8:28). He then connects God's choice of people to his calling them to Christ: "Those he predestined, he also called" (v. 30). Without fail, he will glorify them (v. 30).

Second,

> What if God, wanting to display his wrath and to make his power known, endured with much patience objects of wrath prepared for destruction? And what if he did this to make known the riches of his glory on objects of mercy that he prepared beforehand for glory—on us, the ones he also called, not only from the Jews but also from the Gentiles? (Rom 9:22–24)

Although Romans begins by holding both Jews and Gentiles responsible, accountable, and culpable before a holy God (1:18–3:20), here it treats more ultimate matters. God is sovereign over every human being's destiny. There are "objects of wrath prepared for destruction" (9:22) and "objects of mercy that he prepared beforehand for glory" (v. 23). God's choices are not mere hypotheticals, because Paul identifies first-century believing Jews and Gentiles as among the objects of God's mercy, namely, "us, the ones he also called, not only from the Jews but also from the Gentiles" (v. 24).

Third, Paul declares, "God . . . has saved us and called us with a holy calling, not according to our works, but according to his own purpose and grace, which was given to us in Christ Jesus before time began" (2 Tim 1:8–9). We do not save ourselves, but God saves us. One aspect of his salvation is calling, God's drawing us to himself through the gospel: "He called us with a holy calling" (v. 9). Paul contrasts "our works" with God's "own purpose and grace," which he gave us before creation (v. 9). God gives grace "before time began," and he summons people to himself in time and space when they believe the good news.[34]

Election and Faith

Scripture clearly teaches that the means of salvation is faith in Christ. This is evident in Acts, where Paul and Silas tell the Philippian jailer, "Believe in the

---

[34] Revelation 17:14 fits under this heading too when it speaks of God's people as "called" and "chosen."

Lord Jesus, and you will be saved—you and your household" (Acts 16:31). Paul speaks plainly: "The righteousness of God is through faith in Jesus Christ to all who believe, since there is no distinction" (Rom 3:22).

In several passages we learn that election is the cause of faith and that faith is the result of election. In John 6:35, after Jesus defines "coming to him" as "believing in him" (6:35), he says, "Everyone the Father gives me will come to me, and the one who comes to me I will never cast out" (v. 37). The Father's giving people to Jesus is one of John's pictures of election. All the Father gives to Jesus will believe in him. John here teaches that election precedes faith.

Second, in Acts 13:48, after Paul and Barnabas turn from the Jews to the Gentiles in Antioch of Pisidia, many Gentiles believe the gospel. Luke combines election and faith: "When the Gentiles heard this, they rejoiced and honored the word of the Lord, and all who had been appointed to eternal life believed" (Acts 13:47–48). The text puts a divine appointment to eternal life prior to the faith of the Gentiles. David Peterson concurs, "Luke draws attention to the way in which God uses the gospel to call out his elect and to save them. . . . Those who seek the Lord from among the nations are those whom he has already claimed as his own. Yet this happens as God enables some to believe through the proclamation of the gospel."[35] God ordained persons to salvation and then drew them to Christ in the preaching of the gospel. Once again election is the cause of faith, not its result.

Third, Paul leads us to the same conclusion. He is grateful to God for his loving election resulting in the salvation of the Thessalonians: "We ought to thank God always for you, brothers and sisters loved by the Lord, because from the beginning God has chosen you for salvation through sanctification by the Spirit and through belief in the truth" (2 Thess 2:13). In his love and will, God eternally elects his people for salvation. He then manifests the results of that election in history by means of initial sanctification and faith. Faith is thus the result of election. In Romans 9 Paul says that God chose Jacob and rejected Esau before they were born for this reason: "so that God's purpose according to election might stand" (Rom 9:11). A few verses later

---

[35] David G. Peterson, *The Acts of the Apostles*, PNTC (Grand Rapids: Eerdmans, 2009), 399–400.

the apostle rules out all human effort in salvation, including faith, when he concludes, "So then, [salvation] does not depend on human will or effort but on God who shows mercy" (Rom 9:16). John, Luke, and Paul agree: God's eternal election results in faith.

Election and the Gospel

Election is a biblical doctrine, but it is not the only one. And if we are to understand it rightly, we must see it in relationship to and in proportion with other truths of the Christian faith. It might be helpful to take a step back and ask, Why are we saved? The Bible answers this in many ways (beginning with the more ultimate reasons):

- Because God deserves to be praised.
- Because God loves us.
- Because God planned to save us.
- Because Jesus died for us.
- Because we heard the gospel.
- Because the Holy Spirit convicted us of sin and drew us to faith.
- Because we trusted Christ.

Our salvation is tied to God's glory, God's love, God's plan, Christ's death, the Spirit's work, the gospel message, and our faith in Christ. Our faith does not save us; God saves us through Christ. But our faith receives what God has done for us in Christ. We are never the source, ground, or cause of our salvation; God is. He is the Savior; we are the saved. He is the Redeemer; we are the redeemed. But salvation is by grace through faith, so we trust, we believe, we have faith, we repent (Eph 2:8–9). We are not the cause, but we are active as we receive salvation through faith.

Further, it is important to remember that Paul teaches that salvation comes through hearing "the word of truth, the gospel of your salvation" (Eph 1:13). Anyone speaking of election without speaking of missions fails to do justice to the Bible.

In Gen 12:1–3 God chooses Abraham. Barnabe Assohoto of Benin and Samuel Ngewa of Kenya helpfully point out how God gives Abraham promises in the form of five "I wills":

- I will make you into a great nation.
- I will bless you.
- I will make your name great.
- I will bless those who bless you.
- I will curse whoever curses you.[36]

And God commissions Abraham: "You will be a blessing . . . and all the peoples on earth will be blessed through you." Abraham is chosen for the sake of mission.

In Exod 19:5–6 God expresses his choice of Israel. They are his covenant people—his treasured possession, his kingdom of priests, his holy nation. The particularity is striking: out of all the nations, you are mine, God says. Even more striking is that God's particularity is for the sake of universality: out of all the nations, you are mine; *and* the whole earth is mine, so you will be for me a kingdom of priests and a holy nation. God is on a mission to save, and he plans to reach the nations through his chosen people. They will witness to him and his ways through their distinctiveness as his holy nation. And they will witness to him through their proclamation as a kingdom of priests, "bringing the knowledge of God to the nations, and bringing the nations to the means of atonement with God."[37]

Paul writes similarly in Romans 9–10. Note how he begins and ends this incredibly complex treatment on salvation history, Israel, the church, divine election, and human responsibility. He begins this theological discourse by stating his intense and unceasing burden for the salvation of his people, the Jews. Paul so longs for their salvation that he would almost be willing to go to hell in order for them to be saved, if that were actually possible (9:1–5). Then, after a heavy and detailed treatise, Paul stresses his deep desire and prayer for the conversion of the Jews. He then reminds that "everyone who calls on the name of the Lord will be saved" (10:13). But how will others call on Jesus without believing in Jesus? How will they believe without hearing

---

[36] Barnabe Assohoto and Samuel Ngewa, "Genesis," *Africa Bible Commentary*, ed. Tokunboh Adeyemo (Grand Rapids: Zondervan, 2006), 29.

[37] Christopher J. H. Wright, *The Mission of God: Unlocking the Bible's Grand Narrative* (Downers Grove: IVP Academic, 2006), 331. Wright also helped us overall on Genesis 12 and Exodus 19.

the gospel? And how will they hear without someone telling them? Paul then reiterates the necessity of the gospel: faith comes through hearing, and hearing through the Word of God, the gospel (vv. 14–17).[38]

How do we respond to such marvelous yet inscrutable truths?[39] Two voices from the past offer much help. First, we humbly worship, as nineteenth-century Baptist pastor Charles H. Spurgeon reminded:

I cannot expect to understand the mysteries of God, neither do I wish to do so. If I understood God, He could not be the true God. A doctrine which I cannot fully grasp is a truth of God which is intended to grasp me. When I cannot climb, I kneel. Where I cannot build an observatory, I set up an altar. . . . How idle it is to dream of our ever running parallel in understanding with the infinite God! His knowledge is too wonderful for us. It is so high—we cannot attain to it.[40]

Second, we share the gospel, as Baptist missionary William Carey stressed:

As our blessed Lord has required us to pray that his kingdom may come, and his will be done on earth as it is in heaven, it becomes us not only to express our desires of that event by words, but to use every lawful method to spread the knowledge of his name. . . . Expect great things; attempt great things. . . . Do not the goodness of the cause, the duties incumbent on us as the creatures of God, and Christians, and the perishing state of our fellow men, loudly call upon us to venture all and use every warrantable exertion for their benefit?[41]

---

[38] See J. I. Packer, *Evangelism and the Sovereignty of God* (Downers Grove: InterVarsity, 1973).

[39] For more on how the doctrine of election functions in the Christian life, see chapter 13, "Salvation and the Christian Life."

[40] Charles H. Spurgeon, "The Hairs on Your Head Numbered," in *Metropolitan Tabernacle Pulpit*, vol. 34, 1888 (Pasadena, TX: Pilgrim Publications, 1974), 54.

[41] William Carey, "An Enquiry into the Obligations of Christians to Use Means for the Conversion of the Heathens," in Timothy George, *Faithful Witness: The Life and Mission of William Carey* (Worcester, PA: Christian History Institute, 1998), E.3, E.49.

3

Calling

The words for "calling" in Hebrew (*qārā'*) and Greek (*kaleō*) are both verbal forms. The word "call" is often used for identification, such as when Naomi says, "Don't call me Naomi. Call me Mara" (Ruth 1:20; cf. Judg 6:32; 1 Sam 9:9; Jer 19:6; 23:6; Lam 2:15; Hos 2:1; Matt 5:9; Luke 1:32). In other contexts, the word signifies an invitation, such as in Matt 9:13: "Go and learn what this means: I desire mercy and not sacrifice. For I didn't come to call the righteous, but sinners" (cf. also 22:9; Luke 14:12–13). "Call" may signify the calls (sounds) made by owls or herons (Zeph 2:14), or one may hear a human voice calling out something (Deut 31:14; 1 Sam 3:10; Jer 31:6; 38:12; Dan 8:16). Also, human beings call on God in prayer and for help when in need (2 Sam 22:4; Jer 29:12; Hab 1:2; Zeph 3:9). These uses of "call" in Scripture are quite ordinary and are what we would expect the word to mean even from its English meaning, but here we will concentrate on the distinctive and theological usage of the word.

God calls unbelievers to saving faith in Christ, and this calling is a neglected aspect of the application of salvation. That is unfortunate, because calling combines God's lordship and human responsibility in salvation. God calls; we do not call ourselves to Christ. But some respond to Christ as he is offered in the gospel, while some don't. Accounting for these facts has produced different understandings of calling.

Exegetical Foundations

Calling in Isaiah

An Invitation

The living and true God issues a wonderful invitation to sinners through Isaiah: "Turn to me and be saved, all the ends of the earth. For I am God, and there is no other" (Isa 45:22). John Oswalt situates this invitation in its OT context: "In many OT texts the unrepentant and unbelieving world has destruction meted out on it. But the point here is that salvation is not the sole preserve of the Israelites whose God the Lord is."[1] Israel's God offers a universal invitation to come to him for salvation in repentance and faith.

An Effective Call

In several texts in Isaiah "calling" is used in a distinctive way. In these instances, the calling is performative in the sense that God effects what he calls. His call has an inherent power that creates a new reality. We see this in the summoning of Cyrus, God's agent by whom Babylon would be defeated: "Who has stirred up someone from the east? In righteousness he calls him to serve. The LORD hands nations over to him, and he subdues kings. He makes them like dust with his sword, like wind-driven stubble with his bow" (Isa 41:2). The calling of Cyrus here isn't an invitation, and in Hebrew parallelism it is matched with the verb "stirred," which centers on God's action. God summoned Cyrus to serve him by creating in him the desire to overthrow Babylon.

A subsequent reference to Cyrus, which also contains a call, is one of the most powerful texts on divine sovereignty in the Scriptures: "Remember what happened long ago, for I am God, and there is no other; I am God, and no one is like me. I declare the end from the beginning, and from long ago what is not yet done, saying: my plan will take place, and I will do all my will. I call a bird of prey from the east, a man for my purpose from a far country. Yes, I have spoken; so I will also bring it about. I have planned it; I will also do it" (Isa 46:9–11). God's incomparability, his superiority to other so-called

---

[1] John N. Oswalt, *The Book of Isaiah: Chapters 40–66*, NICOT (Grand Rapids: Eerdmans, 1998), 223.

gods, is evident from his ability to foretell what will happen from all eternity. Nor does he merely foresee what will occur. Instead, the events of history represent his plan and will, which here focus on the calling of "a bird of prey from the east." The bird of prey is Cyrus, as the Lord had planned and would fulfill his plan for Cyrus to overturn the kingdom of Babylon. This call is not a mere invitation but is performative in the sense that God's call is effective.

Isaiah also emphasizes the call of Israel. In Isa 41:8 Israel is identified as the servant of the Lord, and in v. 9 we see the Lord's calling of Israel: "I brought you from the ends of the earth and called you from its farthest corners. I said to you: You are my servant; I have chosen you; I haven't rejected you." Here "calling" emphasizes the Lord's gracious work. The verbs "I brought" and "I have chosen" highlight what the Lord has done for Israel, and thus calling here isn't a mere invitation. God's calling is closely related to his choosing, representing a summons that creates a response. The same use of "call" occurs in 48:12: "Listen to me, Jacob, and Israel, the one called by me: I am he; I am the first, I am also the last."

We step out of Isaiah a moment to note a striking use of "call" in Hos 11:1: "When Israel was a child, I loved him, and out of Egypt I called my son." Matthew picks up this word and applies it to Jesus Christ (Matt 2:15), while Hosea is certainly thinking of Israel's exodus from Egypt, her liberation from Egyptian slavery. The calling out of Egypt is matched here with God's love, showing that the Lord had set his covenant affection upon Israel. The Lord's call out of Egypt was certainly effective in that it created a new reality so that Israel was freed from slavery.

A similar use of the word appears in the life of Abraham: "Look to Abraham your father, and to Sarah who gave birth to you. When I called him, he was only one; I blessed him and made him many" (Isa 51:2). "Called" could mean "invited" here, but the emphasis on the Lord's work suggests the effectiveness of the calling. The Lord assures and comforts his people, pledging to complete the work he started by making the land like the garden of Eden (vv. 1–3). Since the text highlights God's new creation work, the call of Abraham most likely refers to God's grace in summoning Abraham. The Lord's tender love for Israel shines in 54:6: "The LORD has called you, like a wife deserted and wounded in spirit, a wife of one's youth when she is rejected, says your God." Israel is "deserted" and "wounded" by virtue of her exile, being severed from the land promised to her. The Lord promises in Isaiah 54 that he will have mercy on his people and restore them to their land. "Calling" here stands in contrast to "rejected." Israel isn't rejected by the Lord but called to him. We can compare the image here to that of a king calling an unfaithful queen and lovingly restoring and comforting her.

Two other texts on the servant of the Lord also feature God's calling. We don't have space to comment on Isaiah's figure of the servant of the Lord. We have already seen that the servant is Israel, but in the course of reading Isaiah it becomes clear that the servant is Israel and yet sometimes distinct from Israel. He must be distinct from Israel because he will bring Israel back to the Lord (Isa 49:5–6), and in contrast to Israel he is obedient to the Lord (v. 50:5) and even suffers for the sake of Israel, accomplishing atonement (52:13–53:12). The servant of the Lord, then, is the true Israel, Jesus Christ. This distinctive use of "servant" is found in Isaiah 42 (v. 1). We read further about the servant in 42:6, "I am the LORD. I have called you for a righteous purpose, and I will hold you by your hand. I will watch over you, and I will appoint you to be a covenant for the people and a light to the nations." Possibly "called" has the meaning "invite" here, indicating that the servant needs to respond to God's righteous purpose and be a light for the nations. Such an understanding would not contradict other passages that feature God's sovereignty in calling. On the other hand, the effectiveness of God's call is probably in view, given the context. It is the Lord who strengthened, chose, and gave his Spirit to the servant (42:1), and verse 5 stresses the Lord's sovereignty as Creator of all. Furthermore, verse 6 speaks not of the servant's obedience but of God's work in his life. God will "hold" him by the hand, and God has appointed him as a "covenant for the people and a light to the nations." We have good reasons, then, to think that the calling represents God's gracious work in the life of the servant.

Another servant text is Isa 49:1–7. The servant worries that his work has been futile, but the Lord assures him that Israel will be restored to the Lord through him and also promises him that nations will be joined to the Lord through him (vv. 5–7). The servant here is ultimately Jesus Christ, but there are good reasons to think that the calling of Isaiah as a prophet is depicted here as well. Isaiah's servant theology is complex, and what Isaiah means by the servant can't be limited to one referent, though ultimately and finally the servant is Jesus himself. In any case, the calling in Isa 49:1 is effective: "Coasts and islands, listen to me; distant peoples, pay attention. The LORD called me before I was born. He named me while I was in my mother's womb" (v. 1). Since the Lord called and named Isaiah before he was born, the call here represents a summons that is heeded.

Calling in the New Testament

Acts 2:39: God's Effective Call

As we turn to the NT, a fascinating reference to calling appears in Peter's sermon on the day of Pentecost.[2] He admonishes those hearing to repent and be baptized to be forgiven of their sins and to receive the Spirit (Acts 2:38). Peter then says, "For the promise is for you and for your children, and for all who are far off, as many as the Lord our God will call" (v. 39). Peter could be saying that the Lord *invites* both children and those who are far off to receive the promise of the Spirit and the forgiveness of sins. If we understand calling as an invitation to respond to the Lord, it makes good sense of the command to repent and be baptized in verse 38.

Still, there are reasons to think that the calling here is effective instead of being a mere invitation. "Promise" focuses on what God does instead of what human beings do. For instance, the law and promise are contrasted in Gal 3:18, for the law depends on human performance while the promise looks to God's grace. Similarly, Rom 4:14 says that if the inheritance is given based on keeping the law, "faith is made empty and the promise is nullified" (Rom 4:14). The promise was given to Abraham through faith instead of via the law (v. 13). If this understanding of promise is correct, then calling highlights what God does. "Promise" in Acts 2:39 probably alludes to Jer 31:31–34 and Ezek 36:26–27, which are both new covenant promises. We read in these texts that the Lord will inscribe his law on the hearts of his people, that he will give us his Spirit so that we obey his decrees, and that he will forgive our sins. The probable allusion to the new covenant suggests that calling here refers to God's overcoming of human resistance to his overtures by his grace. A final reason to think the call is effective is the probable allusion to Isa 57:19, where we find the word "far," the same term (*makran*) used in Acts 2:39. Paul cites this verse in Eph 2:17 as well. Even though Isaiah doesn't use the term "new

---

[2] For a study on calling in the NT, see J. Eckert, "*Kaleō*," *EDNT*, 2:240–43.

covenant," we clearly have a new covenant text in terms of material content, for the Lord promises to revive his people (Isa 57:15), to refrain from accusing them (v. 16), and to heal and comfort them (vv. 18–19). I suggest that Acts has this promise in mind, and, if this is the case, then the calling is effective. Peter anticipates that God will call both Jews and Gentiles to himself.

Acts 17:30: God's Universal Call

God's call is sometimes effective; at other times it is universal and not always effective. The latter is the case when Paul declares to the Athenians, "Having overlooked the times of ignorance, God now commands all people everywhere to repent, because he has set a day when he is going to judge the world in righteousness by the man he has appointed" (Acts 17:30–31). God warns sinners of the need to repent, even commanding them to do so. In fact, God in grace issues a universal gospel call, for he loves the world that hates him, giving his Son to save sinners (John 3:16–18). Jesus gave such a call when he invited the lost, "Come to me, all of you who are weary and burdened, and I will give you rest" (Matt 11:28).

Jesus's poignant lament over Jerusalem reflects his heart toward sinners: "Jerusalem, Jerusalem, who kills the prophets and stones those who are sent to her. How often I wanted to gather your children together, as a hen gathers her chicks under her wings, but you were not willing!" (Matt 23:37). God works in hearts to make the universal gospel call effective, as in Lydia's case; when she heard the gospel message, "The Lord opened her heart to give heed to what was said by Paul" (Acts 16:14).

Calling in Paul. Before we begin looking at the word *call* in Paul, we should consider Matt 22:14. Jesus concludes a parable by saying, "Many are called, but few are chosen" (ESV). Obviously "called" here means invited, as translated by the CSB. We recognize, then, that the meaning of "called" must be discerned in context. Matthew uses the verb "called" to mean "invite" on other occasions as well (9:13; 22:3, 4, 8, 9). We are not arguing that "called" invariably means an effective call. Instead, the point is that "called" often has this meaning in context, especially in Paul's writings.[3]

---

[3] In 1 Cor 10:27 the word clearly means "invite," but here Paul considers an unbeliever inviting a believer to dinner. He is not speaking about God's calling.

"Call" is used to refer to Paul's commission as an apostle. For instance, we read in Rom 1:1 (cf. 1 Cor 1:1) that he was "called as an apostle and set apart for the gospel of God." Paul was "set apart" before he was born, but he was called to be an apostle in history, on the Damascus Road—as we read in Acts 9; 22; 26. The effectiveness of Paul's call to apostleship is communicated unmistakably in Gal 1:15–16: "When God, who from my mother's womb set me apart and called me by his grace, was pleased to reveal his Son in me, so that I could preach him among the Gentiles, I did not immediately consult with anyone." Paul reflects on his calling as an apostle, his Damascus Road experience. The text is quite similar to Rom 1:1. Paul was set apart before his birth and called by God's grace. The calling overwhelmed him, changed him, and transformed him so that Paul became a messenger, an apostle of Jesus Christ.

The effectiveness of God's call, the power of God's summons, is evident in Rom 4:17: "As it is written: I have made you the father of many nations. He is our father in God's sight—in the presence of the God in whom he believed, the one who gives life to the dead and calls things into existence that do not exist." The parallelism between granting life to the dead and calling into existence what doesn't exist is striking. In the latter instance the reference is to God's creative power, the power by which he called into existence by his word the sun, moon, stars, and everything else in the created order (Gen 1:1–31). God's word has inherent power so that whatever he speaks comes into existence. In Romans 4 Paul thinks of God's creating life in the body of Abraham and the womb of Sarah. They were, so to speak, dead (v. 19). God's word, God's calling, created life and produced a child where there was no possibility of one being born.

Thus far we have seen God's call summoning Paul to ministry and granting life where life was absent. Paul also teaches that God calls people to salvation. This is very clearly in view in 1 Cor 1:23–28. Paul *preaches* (*kēryssō*) to all, both Jews and Greeks, but Jews stumble over the notion that the Messiah was crucified, while Gentiles think the idea ridiculous that God saved the world through a crucified man (v. 23). But the *called* among "both Jews and Greeks" recognize that "Christ is the power of God and the wisdom of God" (v. 24). The "called" aren't merely those invited to be saved; the notion of all being invited is found in the word "preached." Paul proclaimed the gospel to all without distinction, but only the effectively called responded by seeing

Christ as God's power and wisdom. God's call here, then, is clearly effective in that it brings people to faith. We could misunderstand what is being said here, because the calling occurs in history, in contrast to foreknowledge, election, and predestination. Those who are chosen for salvation, who are elected before the world began (2 Thess 2:13), are called to that salvation through the gospel (v. 14). Since the calling comes via the gospel, it takes place in history as people hear the gospel. All to whom the good news is proclaimed *hear* the gospel, but only some are *called* through the gospel.

It is important to underscore God's desire that all hear the message of salvation. As we have seen, this is the *gospel call*. Anthony Hoekema regards 2 Cor 5:20 as the "clearest New Testament passage on this point": "Therefore, we are ambassadors for Christ, since God is making his appeal through us. We plead on Christ's behalf, Be reconciled to God."[4] Only God can save the lost, but he has ordained to do so through the preaching of the gospel: "To this he called you through our gospel so that you may obtain the glory of our Lord Jesus Christ" (2 Thess 2:14). In fact, without the gospel call no one could be saved! "How, then, can they call on him they have not believed in? And how can they believe without hearing about him? And how can they hear without a preacher?" (Rom 10:14).

Paul often speaks of God's effective call. The subsequent context confirms this interpretation of calling in 1 Cor 1:23–28. Paul moves from the power of the gospel he preaches (1 Cor 1:18–25) to the conversion of the Corinthians (vv. 26–31). He describes their conversion as their "calling" (v. 26), noting that it isn't the intelligent, the powerful, or the upper class that are called but the foolish, the weak, and the lower class (vv. 27–28). What is instructive for us in terms of calling is that Paul describes the calling in terms of God's *choosing* the believers for salvation. Indeed, he uses "chosen" three times in 1:27–28 to describe further the word "called."

We do not claim that "called" and "chosen" have the same meaning; only that they are closely related. The close relationship here shows that God's call is effective, that it creates life in those he calls. The use of "calling" in 2 Tim 1:9 is quite close to that in 1 Corinthians: God has "saved us and called us with a holy calling, not according to our works, but according to his own purpose and grace, which was given to us in Christ Jesus before time began."

---

[4] Anthony A. Hoekema, *Saved by Grace* (Grand Rapids: Eerdmans, 1989), 76.

Salvation and calling are historical events, taking place when people put their faith in Jesus Christ, and yet the call is ordained by God's grace before the beginning of time and accords with God's eternal purpose and intention. Believers aren't called on account of the works they have done. God calls by virtue of his grace, and this provides further evidence that God's call is performative, accomplishing his will.

We have already seen the emphasis on election in Romans 9, and we have also observed the close relationship, though not identification, between election and God's call in 1 Cor 1:24–28. We are not surprised, therefore, that "called" surfaces in Rom 9:12. We also see the term "purpose" (*prothesis*, v. 11) that was also present in 2 Tim 1:9, and a reference in the same verse to God's election. God's call here is opposed to works as a basis for salvation. Often in Paul faith and works stand in contrast when it comes to salvation, but here and in 2 Tim 1:9 calling and works are contrasted. Certainly, Paul doesn't contradict what he said about salvation being by faith instead of works, but here he considers the matter from a comprehensive perspective, asking what accounts for the faith of human beings. The power of God's grace provides the answer. Human beings aren't saved based on what they do; salvation is God's work and is accomplished by his calling people to faith.

As Paul considers the inclusion of the Gentiles in the people of God, he attributes their participation in salvation to God's calling. Both Jews and Gentiles are saved because they have been called by God (Rom 9:24–25). Ultimately, "All Israel will be saved" (11:26), which means that God's promises to ethnic Israel will be fulfilled, since God always keeps his promises (9:6). Or, as Paul puts it in 11:29, "God's gracious gifts and calling are irrevocable." It is again instructive that in the previous verse Paul refers to Israel's election (v. 28), indicating that Israel continues to be God's beloved people because of his electing grace. God will not revoke his calling of Israel to be his people. What is true of Israel is true of all believers in Jesus Christ: they belong to God by virtue of his calling of them, and hence Paul simply designates believers on occasions as "the called" (e.g., Rom 1:1, 6–7; 1 Cor 1:1).

We have not yet examined one of the most significant texts on calling in the NT. We read in a verse that is rightly celebrated, "We know that all things work together for the good of those who love God, who are called according to his purpose" (Rom 8:28). We see again the close relationship between "calling" and God's purpose; this is the third verse from Paul in which calling and purpose (*prothesis*) are linked (9:11–12; 2 Tim 1:9). Paul begins by saying that everything works for the good of those who love God, but he pauses and corrects a possible misapprehension. The saints' love for God is not the ultimate reality; behind their love lies God's purpose and calling. Our love flows from God's grace in our lives where he effectively summons us to faith.

Nor is Paul finished with calling in this context, for in Rom 8:30 he goes on to say, "And those he predestined, he also called; and those he called, he also justified; and those he justified, he also glorified." The objects of every one of these verbs is personal, and there is a chain here—what William Perkins called the golden chain—that actually reaches back to verse 29: God foreknew, predestined, called, justified, and glorified his people. Here we want to attend to the verb "called," noting that those who are called are also justified. If all those who are called are also justified, the calling can't merely be an invitation. The reason for this is not difficult to see. If to call means to invite, then Paul teaches that all those who are invited to be saved—all those who are exhorted to be saved—are justified. But this is clearly wrong, since many of those who are invited to put their faith in Christ don't believe, and Paul makes clear that no one is justified apart from faith (5:1). It is evident, then, that "called" here refers to a performative call, a call that creates faith. If those who are called are justified, then the calling is effective.

We are interested here in concepts, not merely words; therefore one of the most fascinating verses on calling in Paul, even though "call" isn't used, is 2 Cor 4:6: "God who said, 'Let light shine out of darkness,' has shone in our hearts to give the light of the knowledge of God's glory in the face of Jesus Christ." Paul alludes to the first day of creation, when God's word created light where there was darkness (Gen 1:3). So too, when God speaks to an unbelieving heart, he shines a supernatural light into the heart so that that person sees the beauty and wonder of Jesus Christ and is converted. Another way of describing God's call is to say that Christ's loveliness dawns upon the mind and heart of people so that they are drawn to Christ.

Another text in the same arena as those that speak of God's call is Phil 1:29: "It has been granted to you on Christ's behalf not only to believe in him, but also to suffer for him." "Granted" is the verbal form of the word "grace" (*charizomai*) and indicates that faith is a gift, that God bestows faith. We have already seen this idea clearly (see esp. Rom 8:30) in the word "calling." Because of his great mercy and by virtue of his own infinite wisdom and kind will, God bestows faith as a gift upon some. Ephesians 2:8 confirms the fact that faith is God's gift because in that text Paul contrasts faith and works: "You are saved by grace through faith, and this is not from yourselves; it is God's gift." Some object that "this" (*touto*) is neuter and "faith" (*pistis*) is feminine, and thus faith can't be the gift in view since the pronoun is another gender. This objection on first glance seems to be persuasive, but it actually fails to convince. "Saved" (*sesōsmenoi*) is a masculine plural participle, and so the neuter "this" doesn't agree with the gender or number of the participle. "Grace" (*chariti*) is also feminine, so "this" doesn't match this word either. What is the antecedent of "this"? It doesn't clearly refer to any of the words of the verse. There is actually a good explanation, however, for its inclusion. When Paul wants to include the whole of what he said previously, he uses a neuter pronoun (cf. Rom 13:11; 1 Cor 6:6; Phil 1:29). "This," then, comprehends the whole verse. Everything Paul refers to is a gift of God, including faith as a quality that God grants to those who are his own.

Since the call is effective in bringing believers to faith, we are not surprised to learn that God's calling can't be revoked, that those who are called will be preserved until the end. God promises to "strengthen [believers] to the end" so that they will be "blameless" on the day of Christ (1 Cor 1:8). The reason believers have such assurance is because "God is faithful; you were called by him into fellowship with his Son, Jesus Christ our Lord" (v. 9). The God who called believers into saving fellowship with Christ will faithfully preserve them until the final day.

A similar emphasis appears in 1 Thess 5:23–24. Paul prays that the Thessalonians would be sanctified entirely so that they would be "blameless at the coming of our Lord Jesus Christ" (v. 23). Do the prayer and the necessity of sanctification and blamelessness on the last day suggest that future salvation is uncertain? Paul gives the answer in the next verse: "He who calls you is faithful; he will do it" (v. 24). The prayer for sanctification and blamelessness will certainly be answered, since God is faithful. The one who calls believers to salvation will complete the work he has begun. This same theme is evident when Paul speaks twice in Ephesians of the hope to which believers are called (Eph 1:18; 4:4). The hope isn't an uncertain confidence but represents what will certainly be realized in the life of believers. Philippians 3:14 should be understood along the same lines: "I pursue as my goal the prize promised by God's heavenly call in Christ Jesus." In the context Paul emphasizes that he must run the race to the end to receive the prize of eternal life (vv. 12–16). At the same time God's call guarantees that he will finish the race. There is tension here between divine sovereignty and human responsibility, but there is no contradiction.

Paul also uses "calling" to designate the life to which believers are summoned, to the kind of life believers are supposed to live. We are called to freedom (Gal 5:13), to live in a way that befits our calling (Eph 4:1; 1 Thess 2:12; 2 Thess 1:11), to "the peace of Christ" (Col 3:15), to holiness and sexual purity (1 Thess 4:7). Paul reproves the Galatians for turning away from the one who called them (Gal 1:6) and warns that their fascination with the false teaching doesn't "come from the one who calls you" (5:8). Timothy must "take hold of eternal life to which you were called" (1 Tim 6:12). None of these exhortations renders the calling or final preservation uncertain, but they all signify that one must live out one's calling. God's grace doesn't negate commands or warnings but undergirds and grounds them. The relationship between promise and warning is a longer discussion that will be pursued in the chapter on preservation and perseverance.

Finally, Paul also uses "calling" in terms of the circumstances of life when one is called to faith. This emphasis can be seen in 1 Cor 7:17–24. Paul refers to being "called while uncircumcised" (v. 18), of remaining "in the situation in which" one "was called" (v. 20), of being "called while a slave" (v. 21; cf. v. 22), and again of remaining "in the situation in which [one] was called" (v. 24). Paul here uses the term "calling" as he does elsewhere, to refer to the call to salvation. What he considers here is the station of life a person had *when* he or she was saved. He envisions the *circumstances* in which one was called—whether one was circumcised or a slave, for instance. Paul uses "call" to refer to the salvation to which believers were summoned by God's wonderful grace.

Calling in Peter, Jude, and Revelation

Peter, like Paul, mentions both God's effective call and his gospel call. The latter is featured in Peter's words answering scoffers mocking Jesus's delay in returning: "The Lord does not delay his promise, as some understand delay, but is patient with you, not wanting any to perish but all to come to repentance" (2 Pet 3:9). This is not a statement of God's decretive will in choosing to save people before creation. It is an expression of God's heart, his desire that people turn from their sins and be saved.

Peter also teaches God's effective call. It is striking that 1–2 Peter have the same themes as Paul with regard to calling, even though they don't have as many references to calling, which is understandable since these two books only contain eight chapters. In 1 Pet 2:9 Peter affirms, "You are a chosen race, a royal priesthood, a holy nation, a people for his possession, so that you may proclaim the praises of the one who called you out of darkness into his marvelous light." God's call has an inherent power and effectiveness since it transfers people from the realm of darkness to the realm of light (cf. 1:15; see also 3:9). We see again the close relationship between being "chosen" and God's call, which is a common Pauline theme. The reference to light and darkness bears some similarity to 2 Cor 4:6, where God's light shines on people in Jesus Christ and brings them to faith. First Peter 5:10 declares similar themes: "The God of all grace, who called you to his eternal glory in Christ, will himself restore, establish, strengthen, and support you after you have suffered a little while." The performative nature of the call stands out here as well. The call comes from the God of grace, and his grace is transformative and life-changing. We also see that the call is to eschatological glory and is accompanied by the promise that God will complete the work he began in believers.

At their conversion believers are called to suffer as Christ did (1 Pet 2:21), and they are called to bless instead of curse, like Jesus Christ (3:9). We again see a similarity to Paul, who says believers must live up to their calling. The call to end-time glory and the call to salvation are not grounds for moral laxity. Believers confirm and validate their calling by their godly lives: "Brothers and sisters, make every effort to confirm your calling and election, because if you do these things you will never stumble" (2 Pet 1:10). If the godly qualities found in vv. 5–7 are not present in someone's life, then there is reason to question whether he or she is truly called by God.

Jude mentions calling in only one verse, referring to "those who are the called, loved by God the Father and kept for Jesus Christ" (Jude 1). Calling is closely associated with God's love, and Jude emphasizes the grace of God before he enjoins the readers to resist false teachers and persevere to the end (vv. 3–23). The call to endurance isn't minimized in the least but is undergirded by the mercy of God that called them to faith in Christ.

The book of Revelation rarely mentions calling but includes both the gospel call and the effective call. We find the gospel call without the words "call" or "calling" at the end of the book: "Both the Spirit and the bride say, 'Come!' Let anyone who hears, say, 'Come!' Let the one who is thirsty come. Let the one who desires take the water of life freely" (Rev 22:17). John wrote this book so that believers would persist in the faith, for they faced a great battle from Rome and ungodly forces. The only place that uses the word "calling" is Rev 17:14, which speaks of the enemies of God's people: "These will make war against the Lamb, but the Lamb will conquer them because he is Lord of lords and King of kings. Those with him are called, chosen, and faithful" (v. 14). Believers are described as faithful, but John recognizes that those who persevere in their faith are also elect and called. What accounts for perseverance is God's amazing grace, a grace that chose believers before the world was created and effectively called them to faith through the gospel.

Calling in the Gospel of John

John does not use the words "call" or "calling," but his teaching overlaps that of Paul. The fourth Gospel contains both the gospel call and the effectual call. The gospel call is famously communicated thus: "For God loved the world in this way: He gave his one and only Son, so that everyone who believes in him will not perish but have eternal life. For God did not send his Son into the world to condemn the world, but to save the world through him" (John 3:16–17). At the Feast of Tabernacles Jesus proclaims, "If anyone is thirsty, let him come to me and drink" (John 7:37). Here the Savior invites all to believe in him for salvation.

The Gospel of John doesn't use the language of calling to designate the summons to faith, but the concept of God's drawing people to himself effectually is clearly present.[5] This appears in the discourse where Jesus identifies himself as the "bread of life" (John 6:48). The Johannine description of calling surfaces in v. 37, where Jesus says, "Everyone the Father gives me will come to me, and the one who comes to me I will never cast out." "Come" refers here to a coming to Jesus for salvation, and such an interpretation is

---

[5] See Bruce A. Ware, "Effectual Calling and Grace," in *Still Sovereign: Contemporary Perspectives on Election, Foreknowledge, and Grace*, ed. T. R. Schreiner and B. A. Ware (Grand Rapids: Baker, 2000), 203–27.

confirmed by v. 35: "No one who comes to me will ever be hungry, and no one who believes in me will ever be thirsty again." In verse 35 "comes" and "believes" are parallel ways of describing the same reality. Therefore, we can paraphrase verse 37 as follows: "Everyone the Father gives to the Son will believe in the Son, and those who believe will never fall away." The notion of an effective call is clearly present, since all those and only those the Father gives to the Son will believe in him. Those who will believe in Jesus will come to him for salvation if and only if they are given by the Father to the Son. The corollary is also true: those who are not given will not come. Jesus says this very thing to the religious leaders complaining about his claim to be the bread of life: "No one can come to me unless the Father who sent me draws him, and I will raise him up on the last day" (v. 44). Verse 44 makes explicit what was implicit in verse 37: all those given by the Father to the Son *will come*, and those who are not drawn *will not come*.

John 6:45 reaffirms this understanding. Jesus cites Isa 54:13: "It is written in the Prophets: 'And they will all be taught by God.' Everyone who has listened to and learned from the Father comes to me." Isaiah 54 follows the great chapter about the servant's atoning work in Isaiah 53, pledging the restoration and rebuilding of Jerusalem and Judah. The Lord doesn't merely promise to restore the nation externally; in Isa 54:13 we learn that the people will be taught by the Lord, and in context the teaching will be received. Isaiah doesn't contemplate a situation in which the children are taught but refuse to listen. His point is that their hearts are softened so that *they will be taught*. This is Isaiah's way of speaking of the new covenant, of the law being imprinted on the heart (cf. Jer 31:31–34).[6]

As the story continues in John 6, many disciples turn away from Jesus because he teaches that he is the bread of life and that people must eat his flesh and drink his blood to enjoy eternal life (vv. 50–63). Jesus remarks that he knows from the outset who will not believe (v. 64), but he doesn't account for unbelief on the basis of God's foresight alone, as if God simply foresaw

---

[6] A parenthetical word should be said about 1 Thess 4:9: "About brotherly love: You don't need me to write you because you yourselves are taught by God to love one another." "Taught by God" (*theodidaktoi*) probably alludes to Isa 54:13 as well, which confirms further that the teaching there is effective, for God imprints on the heart of believers the desire to love one another.

what people would do. Instead, he explains in v. 65, "No one can come to me unless it is granted to him by the Father." If the Father grants or gives someone to the Son, that person will come to him. If the Father doesn't give someone to the Son, that person will not believe and cannot come.

Jesus reaffirms in his prayer in John 17 that he grants life to those who are given to him by the Father. For instance, Jesus tells the Father in verse 2 that the Son grants "eternal life to everyone you have given him." We see again that eternal life in the age to come is restricted to those given by the Father to the Son. According to 10:28 Jesus gives to his sheep eternal life, and the foundation for Jesus's granting life is the Father's giving these sheep to the Son (v. 29). The specificity and exclusivity of divine revelation is evident in 17:6, where Jesus prays, "I have revealed your name to the people you gave me from the world. They were yours, you gave them to me, and they have kept your word." The Son did not reveal the Father to all but only to those given to him by the Father, and thus he prays specifically for them (John 17:9). Indeed, he doesn't pray for the world but only for the disciples, "because" the disciples "are yours" (v. 9). Jesus asks that those who are given will be preserved and protected so that they aren't lost but will enjoy final salvation (vv. 11–19).

Summary

"Calling" is often used to identify someone's name or to signify an invitation given to someone. However, the term can refer specifically to God's call, both the gospel call that invites people to faith in Jesus and the effective call by which God works through the gospel call to bring people to salvation. Salvation is the work of God in both his free, universal offer of the gospel and his effective call.

Systematic Formulations

God's calling people to salvation is a noteworthy and neglected theme of soteriology. As we have shown, this call has two aspects. The gospel call is universal; the church is to preach the gospel indiscriminately to all people. Scripture teaches and experience shows that not all who hear the gospel believe in Christ. God holds responsible for their unbelief those who refuse to believe (John 3:18, 36; 8:24; 2 Thess 1:8; 1 John 5:10). Paul Jaesuk Jo observes how John "forcefully" shows the consequence of unbelief in John 3:36: it is not only that unbelievers will not see life, but that the wrath of God abides on them.[7] Scripture affirms genuine human responsibility and at the same time teaches absolute divine sovereignty. Thus, along with the gospel call there is an effective call by which God draws some to salvation in Christ. God issues his effective call through the gospel call.

Traditionally, these two aspects of calling were called the "external call" and the "internal call," respectively. All hear the message of salvation outside of them (external call). But only some are saved—these receive God's internal, effective call to salvation. These designations were somewhat confusing because they could be understood to mean that some people receive only the external call and some only the internal call. In truth, however, the internal call works through the external call. Thus better names would be "external call" and "external/internal call." Even better, however, are the names we have used: "gospel call" and "effective call." The first speaks of calling as gospel invitation; the second speaks of calling as performative summons.

Calling as Gospel Invitation

To place these teachings in a larger biblical perspective, we continue systematizing by noting that God does not take pleasure in the judgment of lost persons, as the prophet Ezekiel declares:

> "Do I take any pleasure in the death of the wicked?" This is the declaration of the Lord GOD. "Instead, don't I take pleasure when he turns from his ways and lives?" (Ezek 18:23)

> "This is the declaration of the Lord GOD—I take no pleasure in the death of the wicked, but rather that the wicked person should turn from his way and live." (33:11)

Therefore, Isaiah declares, "Turn to me and be saved, all the ends of the earth. For I am God, and there is no other" (Isa 45:22). The Old Testament

---

[7] Paul Jaesuk Jo, *Introduction to the Literary Art of the Gospel of John* (Eugene, OR: Wipf & Stock, 2022), 76–77.

thus declares God's desire to save sinners. Jonah's reluctant mission to Nineveh likewise shows God's heart, as the prophet confesses to him, "That's why I fled toward Tarshish in the first place. I knew that you are a gracious and compassionate God, slow to anger, abounding in faithful love, and one who relents from sending disaster" (Jonah 4:2). Peter in the New Testament delivers the same message: "The Lord . . . is patient with you, not wanting any to perish but all to come to repentance" (2 Pet 3:9).

Jesus and his apostles proclaim the gospel call in the New Testament. It is the sincere desire on the part of God and preachers that sinners repent, believe, and be saved. This involves sharing the gospel and its invitation and promises. As its name implies, this call includes the gospel: we are lost and cannot save ourselves, the Son of God died and was raised to redeem sinners, and it is through faith in him that we are saved. The gospel includes an invitation, asking people to trust Christ alone for salvation. The gospel includes promises: eternal life and the forgiveness of sins to everyone who believes. Many biblical texts feature the gospel:

"This is the will of my Father: that everyone who sees the Son and believes in him will have eternal life, and I will raise him up on the last day." (John 6:40)

"Believe in the Lord Jesus, and you will be saved—you and your household." (Acts 16:31)

A person is not justified by the works of the law but by faith in Jesus Christ, even we ourselves have believed in Christ Jesus. This was so that we might be justified by faith in Christ and not by the works of the law, because by the works of the law no human being will be justified. (Gal 2:16)

Christ has appeared as a high priest of the good things that have come. . . . [And] he entered the most holy place once for all time . . . by his own blood, having obtained eternal redemption. (Heb 9:11–12)

God intends the gospel call to be universal and to go to all without discrimination. God loves a sinful world and gave his Son to rescue it (John 3:16–17). Jesus poured out his heart over Jerusalem's stubborn rejection of God's prophets and himself (Matt 23:37). He opens his arms and heart wide, inviting the weary and burdened to come to him for the rest of salvation (11:28). He commands his followers to make disciples of "all nations" (28:19).

The apostles declare the same message: "God now commands all people everywhere to repent" (Acts 17:30). God not only commands sinners to repent but also pleads with them to do so. He does this through his apostles, including Paul: "God is making his appeal through us. We plead on Christ's behalf, 'Be reconciled to God'" (2 Cor 5:20). Although not all who hear the gospel call believe and are saved, the gospel call is necessary for salvation. Paul offers the most extensive and explicit teaching on this:

> This is the message of faith that we proclaim: If you confess with your mouth, "Jesus is Lord," and believe in your heart that God raised him from the dead, you will be saved. One believes with the heart, resulting in righteousness, and one confesses with the mouth, resulting in salvation. For the Scripture says, "Everyone who believes on him will not be put to shame," since there is no distinction between Jew and Greek, because the same Lord of all richly blesses all who call on him. For "everyone who calls on the name of the Lord will be saved." How, then, can they call on him they have not believed in? And how can they believe without hearing about him? And how can they hear without a preacher? And how can they preach unless they are sent? As it is written: "How beautiful are the feet of those who bring good news." But not all obeyed the gospel. For Isaiah says, "Lord, who has believed our message?" So faith comes from what is heard, and what is heard comes through the message about Christ. (Rom 10:8–17)

The only way to salvation is through hearing the message about the crucified and risen Christ (v. 17) and confessing his lordship (v. 9). Paul similarly stresses, "I am not ashamed of the gospel, because it is the power of God for salvation to everyone who believes, first to the Jew, and also to the Greek" (Rom 1:16). This is the free offer of the gospel call to whoever will come.

Calling as Performative Summons

As we have seen, calling is used another way in Scripture: as a performative summons. In the effective call God works internally and mysteriously by his

Spirit in the lives of many who hear the gospel call to draw them to saving faith in his Son. The calls are interrelated. The gospel is powerful (Rom 1:16), like a seed that takes root (Matt 13:1–23; Jas 1:18; 1 Pet 1:22–25). The Spirit powerfully uses the gospel to enable faith. In the Cape Town Confession of Faith global leaders reminded:

> We love the Holy Spirit within the unity of the Trinity, along with God the Father and God the Son. He is the missionary Spirit sent by the missionary Father and the missionary Son, breathing life and power into God's missionary Church. We love and pray for the presence of the Holy Spirit because without the witness of the Spirit to Christ, our own witness is futile. Without the convicting work of the Spirit, our preaching is in vain. Without the gifts, guidance and power of the Spirit, our mission is mere human effort. And without the fruit of the Spirit, our unattractive lives cannot reflect the beauty of the gospel.[8]

Both calls are at work in Acts 13:48–49. After Paul and Barnabas turn from the Jews to the Gentiles, Luke reports, "When the Gentiles heard this, they rejoiced and honored the word of the Lord, and all who had been appointed to eternal life believed" (Acts 13:48). Inextricably woven together are the apostles' free offer of the gospel, God's plan to save, and genuine faith on the hearers' part.

If we enlarge our perspective on the divine side, we see that Scripture connects our being chosen "in eternity" and our being "called in time," as Matthew Ebenezer from India puts it.[9]

> Those he predestined, he also called; and those he called, he also justified; and those he justified, he also glorified. (Rom 8:30)

> What if he did this to make known the riches of his glory on objects of mercy that he prepared beforehand for glory—on us, the ones

---

[8] The Cape Town Confession of Faith, pt. 1, no. 5, Lausanne Movement, accessed June 24, 2019, https://www.lausanne.org/content/ctc/ctcommitment.

[9] Matthew Ebenezer, "The Great Truths of the Bible," in *ESV Global Study Bible* (Wheaton: Crossway, 2012), 1881.

he also called, not only from the Jews but also from the Gentiles? (9:23–24)

We ought to thank God always for you, brothers and sisters loved by the Lord, because from the beginning God has chosen you for salvation through sanctification by the Spirit and through belief in the truth. He called you to this through our gospel, so that you might obtain the glory of our Lord Jesus Christ. (2 Thess 2:13–14; see also 2 Tim 1:9)

When God effectively calls people through the gospel call, he brings about both short-term and long-term results. In the short term, God intends the effective call to produce a life that is praiseworthy: "I, the prisoner in the Lord, urge you to walk worthy of the calling you have received" (Eph 4:1). Specifically, God wants his calling to produce freedom, harmony, holiness, and suffering in the lives of his people:

You were called to be free, brothers and sisters; only don't use this freedom as an opportunity for the flesh, but serve one another through love. (Gal 5:13)

Let the peace of Christ, to which you were also called in one body, rule your hearts. (Col 3:15)

God has not called us to impurity but to live in holiness. (1 Thess 4:7; cf. 2 Tim 1:9)

You were called to this, because Christ also suffered for you, leaving you an example, that you should follow in his steps. (1 Pet 2:21)

Along with short-term effects, God also intends for his calling to have glorious long-term effects in believers' lives:

I pray that the eyes of your heart may be enlightened so that you may know what is the hope of his calling. (Eph 1:18; cf. 4:4)

He called you to this through our gospel, so that you might obtain the glory of our Lord Jesus Christ. (2 Thess 2:14)

He is the mediator of a new covenant, so that those who are called might receive the promise of the eternal inheritance. (Heb 9:15)

You were called for this, so that you may inherit a blessing. (1 Pet 3:9)

The God of all grace, who called you to his eternal glory in Christ, will himself restore, establish, strengthen, and support you after you have suffered a little while. (1 Pet 5:10)

4

Regeneration

One of the most familiar phrases referring to salvation in contemporary evangelicalism is that of being "born again." Many refer to Jesus's words: "Truly, truly, I say to you, unless one is born again, he cannot see the kingdom of God" (John 3:3). Theologians call this "regeneration," for it stresses God's gracious work of giving new life in Christ to those who were spiritually dead. Scripture refers to regeneration in many other ways: God's making us alive with Christ, being born of God, the new creation, God's bringing us forth, God's giving us new life, spiritual resurrection, the new birth, and God's moving us from death to life. Does this mean that we believe and as a result are born again? Or does God make the first move? This chapter explores these questions and more.

Exegetical Foundations

Here we focus on texts that refer to regeneration or being born again.

Regeneration in the OT

The OT communicates the concept of regeneration using the image of circumcision of the heart, signifying a radical change within. The necessity of heart circumcision is plainly taught:

> "Circumcise your hearts and don't be stiff-necked any longer." (Deut 10:16)

"Circumcise yourselves to the LORD; remove the foreskin of your hearts, men of Judah and residents of Jerusalem. Otherwise, my wrath will break out like fire and burn with no one to extinguish it because of your evil deeds." (Jer 4:4)

In these verses Yahweh commands the Israelites to circumcise their hearts, to take a compliant attitude toward him, the opposite of being stubborn. The nation as a whole is lacking such heart circumcision.[1] Along with these commands are texts that declare circumcision of the heart to be God's work. Moses prophesied, "The LORD your God will circumcise your heart and the hearts of your descendants, and you will love him with all your heart and all your soul so that you will live" (Deut 30:6). Craigie interprets this passage in light of the new covenant; in it heart circumcision "is seen . . . to be an act of God and thus indicates the new covenant, when God would in his grace deal with man's basic spiritual problem. . . . The new covenant, involving the direct operation of God in man's heart, would still involve . . . an obedience springing out of love for God in his continuing mercy and grace."[2]

The OT's promise of a circumcised heart comes to a climax in Jeremiah's prediction of a new covenant, which includes the writing of the law upon the heart (31:31–34). The problem with the old covenant was that Israel was disobedient, that they repeatedly violated the covenant stipulations (v. 32), showing that they weren't regenerated. New life would be theirs when the Lord wrote the law upon their hearts, which is a vivid picture of what it means to be born again (v. 33). The inscribing of the law on the heart means that new covenant members know the Lord, that they are regenerate (v. 34).

Jeremiah describes the new covenant again in a text that is not as well known:

"I will give them integrity of heart and action so that they will fear me always, for their good and for the good of their descendants after them. I will make a permanent covenant with them: I will never

---

[1] Certainly, there were exceptions, but we are talking about the general state of the nation.

[2] P. C. Craigie, *The Book of Deuteronomy*, NICOT (Grand Rapids: Eerdmans, 1976), 364.

turn away from doing good to them, and I will put fear of me in their hearts so they will never again turn away from me. I will take delight in them to do what is good for them, and with all my heart and mind I will faithfully plant them in this land." (32:39–41)

The granting of "integrity of heart" is another way of describing regeneration, since those who are given such a heart fear the Lord. Paul distinguishes mere physical circumcision from true spiritual circumcision: "A person is not a Jew who is one outwardly, and true circumcision is not something visible in the flesh. On the contrary, a person is a Jew who is one inwardly, and circumcision is of the heart—by the Spirit, not the letter" (Rom 2:28–29). The Holy Spirit performs spiritual circumcision, the equivalent of regeneration.

Regeneration in John's Writings

When we come to the NT, the first text to consider is that which recounts the conversation between Jesus and Nicodemus (John 3). Nicodemus came at night, which signifies, among other things, that he lived in spiritual darkness. Nicodemus probably believed that he was wise and insightful since he commended Jesus for his signs. But Jesus abruptly changed the subject, confronting Nicodemus's spiritual poverty: "Truly I tell you, unless someone is born again, he cannot see the kingdom of God" (v. 3). Nicodemus was baffled and perplexed, misunderstanding Jesus by taking him literally; he thought the idea that one could be born again was nonsensical. The word rendered "again" (*anōthen*) could also be translated "from above." John often uses words with double meanings when both meanings are intended, and such is probably the case here. Jesus speaks of being born from above *and* of being born again.

Jesus responded to Nicodemus's misunderstanding, "Truly I tell you, unless someone is born of water and the Spirit, he cannot enter the kingdom of God" (John 3:5). The necessity of being born again could hardly be clearer; those who aren't regenerated will not enter the kingdom. Much discussion has centered on the phrase "of water and the Spirit" (*ex hydatos kai pneumatos*). Both nouns are modified by the same preposition, which suggests that water and Spirit should be understood together. The notion, then, that "water" refers to the breaking of water in physical birth is quite unlikely, since water and

Spirit are conjoined here, not opposed. Others think Christian baptism is intended, but Nicodemus could not have grasped a reference to a practice that did not yet exist. Others see a reference to John's baptism, but it is unlikely that John would have signaled adherence to a practice irrelevant to his post-resurrection readers. Linda Belleville has given us the most likely solution, which is that John draws on Ezek 36:25–27: "I will also sprinkle clean water on you, and you will be clean. I will cleanse you from all your impurities and all your idols. I will give you a new heart and put a new spirit within you; I will remove your heart of stone and give you a heart of flesh. I will place my Spirit within you and cause you to follow my statutes and carefully observe my ordinances."[3] "Water" refers to the cleansing water noted in Ezekiel and "Spirit" to the regenerating work of the Spirit in the heart of human beings.

What we find in Ezekiel is that the ability to keep God's statutes and ordinances is the result and consequence of the granting of the Spirit. We can say, then, that the giving of the Spirit isn't predicated on anything humans do. The obedience of human beings is the consequence and result of the Spirit's work. Jesus reminded Nicodemus of the truth Ezekiel taught: all people (even religious Pharisees!) need to be regenerated and born again by the Spirit to enter the kingdom.

Jesus also emphasized the Spirit's freedom in his regenerating work: "The wind blows where it pleases, and you hear its sound, but you don't know where it comes from or where it is going. So, it is with everyone born of the Spirit" (John 3:8). We can't calculate or predict who will be born again, since the granting of such life is the prerogative of God's will. We have good grounds from John 3:9–10 as well for seeing an allusion to Ezek 36:26–27 in this text. Jesus reproved Nicodemus for failing to understand what he was talking about as a "teacher of Israel." Presumably Nicodemus should have known about these matters since they are plainly taught in Ezek 36:26–27.

John uses the image of being born for new life in the prologue of his gospel as well. He remarks that those who believe, who receive Christ, are by right God's children (John 1:12), but he goes on to explain in verse 13 that they "were born, not of natural descent, or of the will of the flesh, or of the will of man, but of God" (v. 13). What is the relationship between believing

---

[3] Linda Belleville, "'Born of Water and Spirit': John 3:5," *Trinity Journal* 1, no. 2 (1980): 125–41.

and receiving in verse 12 and being born again in verse 13? These two verses alone don't resolve the question; believing and being born are parallel concepts in the verse, and John doesn't give clear signals here about their logical or temporal relationship. We have to go elsewhere to resolve the question, and I would suggest John's first letter does precisely that.

John's first letter was written to address a situation in which many had left the church and had probably formed a rival congregation. John wants to assure those who had stayed that they truly belonged to God by pointing to evidence of their new life, which includes obedience, love, and belief that the historical Jesus is the Christ. In several statements John speaks of those who are born of God, and these statements are quite instructive as to the relationship between faith and regeneration. The first appears in 1 John 2:29: "Everyone who does what is right has been born of him." The words "has been born" (*gegennētai*) are in the perfect tense, while the participial construction that speaks of doing what is right (*ho poiōn tēn dikaiosynēn*) is present tense. From the grammar itself we have good reasons to believe that being born again *precedes* doing what is right. If the grammatical argument doesn't convince, it is almost certain that this is John's point anyway. Surely John maintains here that, first, one is born of God, and the evidence and proof that one is born of God is that one practices righteousness. It is unthinkable that John would be saying that believers, first, do what is right and as a consequence are born of God.

The same reading applies to the next text: "Everyone who has been born of God does not sin, because his seed remains in him; he is not able to sin, because he has been born of God" (1 John 3:9). Once again, being born of God is in the perfect tense (*gegennēmenos*), while not practicing sin is in the present tense. It is clear that one is born of God *first* and that the *result* of such new life is freedom from the tyranny of sin. The same observation applies to loving one another: "Dear friends, let us love one another, because love is from God, and everyone who loves has been born of God and knows God" (4:7). Once again being born of God is in the perfect tense, while loving is present tense. John is not teaching that loving one another leads to our being born of God. Instead, believers are born of God, and their new life produces love in them.

This established pattern helps us interpret what John means in 5:1, where he writes, "Everyone who believes that Jesus is the Christ has been born of God, and everyone who loves the Father also loves the one born of him." Believing is a participle in the present tense, whereas "has been born of God" (*gegennētai*) is in the perfect tense. There is good reason to think John maintains the pattern here, and thus we have solid exegetical grounds for concluding that our belief in Jesus as the Christ is a *consequence* of being born of God. Our continued faith is certainly the result of our new birth: those who are believing in Christ show evidence of being born of God. It is plausible that John intends us also to see that our initial faith follows being born of God. If this is the case, then *logically* regeneration precedes faith, even though *temporally* faith and regeneration occur at the same instant.

We should interpret 1 John 5:4–5 the same way, although the logical connection there isn't as clear. John affirms that "Everyone who has been born of God conquers the world. This is the victory that has conquered the world: our faith." The words "has been born" (*gegennēmenon*) are once again in the perfect tense, while "conquers" (*nika*) is present tense. Believers triumph and overcome (cf. v. 18) because they are born of God, and to conquer is to exercise faith. John clarifies the nature of this conquering and overcoming faith in verse 5: "Who is the one who conquers the world but the one who believes that Jesus is the Son of God?" It isn't just any faith that triumphs, but faith that the historical person Jesus of Nazareth is the Son of God.

Regeneration in Paul's Letters

Although Paul doesn't use "born again" terminology in Eph 2:1–5, the concept is clearly present. Paul begins by sketching the state of human beings before conversion: they are "dead in . . . trespasses and sins" (v. 1; cf. 2:5). Human beings aren't merely weakened or enfeebled by sin, as if it dimmed our potential capacities. They are excluded from God's life entirely (4:18), and, as those who are spiritually dead, they have no capacity to respond to God (cf. Rom 8:7–8). We could say that they are enslaved to evil psychologically, spiritually, and socially (Eph 2:1–3). They are in bondage psychologically in that their desires stem from the flesh, which is unregenerate. When they follow their desires, they sin because they have no inclination or aspiration to trust in God (Rom 14:23) or glorify him (4:20–21; 1 Cor 10:31). Spiritually they are under the control of Satan—"the ruler of the power of the air" (Eph 2:2), and they don't even have an inkling of their subjection to him (cf. 2 Cor 4:4; 1 John 5:19). Socially they are enslaved to the fashions and dictates of the culture that envelopes them. The cultural air they breathe is contrary to God and his will and ways. The dire state of humanity is capsulized in the admission, "We were by nature children under wrath" (Eph 2:3).

Ephesians 2:1–3 certifies that new life can't come from human beings; many have noted that the words, "But God," in v. 4 are among the most glorious words in Scripture. Paul doesn't stop with these words, of course, but contemplates the richness of God's mercy and his astonishing love for believers. Such mercy and love generate action. As Paul says in verse 5, God "made us alive with Christ even though we were dead in trespasses. You are saved by grace!" Those who were spiritually dead were made alive, and the granting of such life describes regeneration. Those who are regenerated are dead, with no capacity to produce life. No wonder Paul says that salvation is by grace. Grace does more than make salvation possible, for God by his grace grants us new life. Grace raises us from the dead! Grace, then, is a transforming power; it changes us. We could say that we are regenerated by grace.

In Titus 3:5 we find the actual word "regeneration," and the line of thought is remarkably similar to that of Eph 2:1–5. The evil of human beings is painted in depressing colors: "We too were once foolish, disobedient, deceived, enslaved by various passions and pleasures, living in malice and envy, hateful, detesting one another" (Titus 3:3). Perhaps the most striking word is "enslaved," which shows the dire state of human beings in Adam. We think here of the title of Martin Luther's famous work *The Bondage of the Will*. Once again, however, human depravity is not the last word, for human beings are the recipients of God's saving kindness and mercy (v. 4). Salvation is not by virtue of human works—how could it be, given the litany of evil depicted in verse 3? The salvation of believers is ascribed to God's "mercy through the washing of regeneration and renewal by the Holy Spirit" (v. 5). The phrase "washing of regeneration" has precipitated much discussion. Some have argued that "washing" doesn't refer to baptism, but this is quite unlikely. Since baptism, as is evident in Acts (2:38, 41; 8:12, 13, 16, 36, 38; 9:18; 10:47, 48; 11:16; 16:15, 33; 18:8; 19:5), almost always immediately follows conversion in the NT, a reference to washing (cf. Acts 22:16) would naturally bring to mind baptism. Others claim that baptism here signifies baptismal regeneration, but such a reading doesn't account for the necessity of faith for new life. Baptism is regularly applied to those who repent and believe (Acts 2:38; 3:19; 4:4; 8:12, 13; 16:31, 34; 18:8; 19:4).

Paul isn't seeking to distinguish temporally between baptism and regeneration here, since they both take place at conversion, and thus his purpose isn't to construct the logical relationship between baptism and regeneration, although theologically regeneration precedes baptism. Baptism symbolizes the new life granted to believers. "Regeneration" (*palingenesias*) and "renewal" (*anakainōseōs*) are synonyms here, designating the new life of believers. The term used here for "regeneration" occurs in only one other place in the NT (Matt 19:28), where it designates the coming new creation. Here in Titus regeneration and renewal are attributed to the Holy Spirit—the genitive "Holy Spirit" (*pneumatos hagiou*) is almost certainly a genitive of source. The new life believers enjoy is from the Holy Spirit, as we have already seen in Jesus's conversation with Nicodemus in John 3. The miraculous work of regeneration is evident, since, before being born again, believers were enslaved to sin. If we consider what human beings do in the natural sphere in order to be born, the answer, of course, is nothing! So too, regeneration is the work of God and God alone.

The notion of regeneration is found in texts that don't mention the new birth or regeneration or being born again but do emphasize that life comes from the Holy Spirit. Paul remarks in 2 Cor 3:6, "The letter kills, but the Spirit gives life." The law doesn't transform human beings; it actually provokes sin instead (cf. Rom 5:20; 7:7–11; 1 Cor 15:56). New life, eternal life, comes from the Holy Spirit. As Jesus says in John 6:63, "The Spirit is the one who gives life. The flesh doesn't help at all. The words that I have spoken to you are spirit and are life." Romans 8:2 contains a similar theme: "The law of the Spirit of life in Christ Jesus has set you free from the law of sin and death" (v. 2). "Law" here probably means something like "principle" or "rule" and doesn't refer to the Mosaic law, since Paul has just emphasized in Romans 7 that the Mosaic law doesn't furnish life. New life comes from outside human beings and is the work of the Spirit.

Regeneration in James's Epistle

The image of new birth or regeneration is found also in James and 1 Peter. James reminds wavering believers of God's goodness in the midst of their trials (Jas 1:12). Temptation to sin comes not from God but from our own desires and inclinations (vv. 12–14). God gives believers "every good and perfect gift," including the beauty of the natural world he has made (v. 17). Indeed, God never changes in his character, so he is unalterably and permanently good; his goodness won't suddenly vanish tomorrow! The Lord shows his goodness supremely by granting believers new life in Christ. James puts it this way: "By his own choice, he gave us birth by the word of truth so that we would be a kind of firstfruits of his creatures" (v. 18). "Word of truth" here refers to the gospel, and thus, as was the case with effectual calling, regeneration comes through the gospel. The new birth here, since James refers to the gospel, certainly refers to regeneration, which finds its origin not in the will of human beings but in the will of God, in his marvelous grace.

Regeneration in Peter's First Epistle

Peter in his first epistle also introduces the notion of regeneration, in two texts. The first reference comes in the first major section of the letter, where Peter blesses God for the great salvation enjoyed by believers: "Blessed be the God and Father of our Lord Jesus Christ. Because of his great mercy he has given us new birth into a living hope through the resurrection of Jesus Christ from the dead" (1 Pet 1:3). Peter reminds suffering believers that they have every reason to bless and praise God since he has, because of his amazing mercy, caused them to be born again. God deserves all the praise, because regeneration is entirely his work and stems from his mercy, and thus afflicted believers have hope no matter what comes their way. The next reference to regeneration is found a few verses later, in a paragraph in which Peter summons his readers to love one another (v. 22). But the call to love doesn't appeal to the inherent capacity of human beings. Rather, Peter's readers have resources to love "because you have been born again not of perishable seed but of imperishable—through the living and enduring word of God" (v. 23). Their regeneration, as we saw in Jas 1:18, comes from God's living Word, from what is identified in 1 Pet 1:25 as the gospel.

Regeneration as New Creation

God's regenerating work is communicated also by the language of new creation, which picks up from Isa 65:17; 66:22, where the Lord promises to create "new heavens and a new earth." The conclusion of the letter to the

Galatians sums up the fundamental issues addressed in the letter, and it is significant that we find here a reference to the new creation: "Both circumcision and uncircumcision mean nothing; what matters instead is a new creation" (Gal 6:15). Circumcision was mandated forever (Gen 17:9–14), but the command was required only during the era of the old creation. Now that the new creation has dawned in Jesus Christ, the practice of circumcision is passé since regulations like this are part and parcel of the old creation. The new creation has an anthropological dimension: now the world is crucified for Christians, and Christians are crucified to the world (Gal 6:14). This is another way of saying that believers have died with Christ, been crucified with Christ, and have come to life with him (2:19–20). The resurrection in Jewish thought signals that the old age is over and the new age has commenced (cf. Ezek 37:12–14). We are not surprised, then, that in the first verse of Galatians Paul announces the resurrection of Christ (1:1) and then a few verses later proclaims Christ's death, which frees believers from the "present evil age" (v. 4). Believers belong to the new creation by virtue of God's transforming work in Jesus Christ.

A noteworthy text on the new creation is found at 2 Cor 5:17: "If anyone is in Christ, he is a new creation; the old has passed away, and see, the new has come!" Just as we saw in Galatians, believers are a new creation; they have new life (are regenerated) because they have died and been raised with Christ (vv. 14–15). The new creation comes only where there is death and resurrection. The new creation signifies that believers have been raised with Christ. A similar theme appears in Colossians: believers have "died with Christ" (Col 2:20) and "been raised with him" (3:1). Therefore, believers have now died, and their "life is hidden with Christ in God" (v. 3). The new creation means that the old self is crucified with Christ (Rom 6:6) and that the life of the new creation has begun (v. 4). Since believers have died with Christ, they have put off the old self, i.e., who they were in Adam, and have put on the new self, i.e., who they are in Jesus Christ (Col 3:9–10). The "new self," as Paul says in Eph 4:24, is "created according to God's likeness in righteousness and purity of the truth." The new self, the self that died and is raised with Christ, is a new creation, is born again. The new life of believers, the "good works" they do (2:10), is attributed to the new creation work of God in Jesus Christ.

Summary

We find in the OT the language and promise of regeneration in the circumcision of the heart, in the promised gift of the Spirit in Ezek 36:25–27, and in the new covenant promise of the transformation of the heart (Jer 31:31–34). Both John's Gospel and his first epistle use the language of birth or regeneration to describe the new life of believers. The regenerating work of God is the work of his sovereign will. Regeneration in Paul is a work of the Holy Spirit (Titus 3:5) and is described by him and elsewhere as resurrection or the new creation work of God. We see in both 1 Peter and James that God regenerates believers through his Word, through the preaching of the gospel of Jesus Christ.

Systematic Formulations

Regeneration Described

Scripture uses many images of God's bringing grace to bear on sinners' lives, including regeneration. Regeneration is God's gracious act of giving new life to those who were spiritually dead. God "made us alive with Christ even though we were dead in trespasses. You are saved by grace!" (Eph 2:5). John taught that regeneration is supernatural by contrasting it with natural birth: "To all who did receive him, he gave them the right to be children of God, to those who believe in his name, who were born, not of natural descent, or of the will of the flesh, or of the will of man, but of God" (John 1:12–13). Jesus taught that regeneration is instantaneous: "Truly I tell you, anyone who hears my word and believes him who sent me has eternal life and will not come under judgment but has passed from death to life" (5:24).

Paul compares regeneration to circumcision of the heart: "A person is a Jew who is one inwardly, and circumcision is of the heart—by the Spirit, not the letter" (Rom 2:29). God warned rebellious Israel, "Circumcise your hearts and don't be stiff-necked any longer" (Deut 10:16). Mercifully, God told Israel that he would circumcise their hearts so that they would "love him with all [their] heart and all [their] soul" (30:6). God promised to renew his people inwardly, replacing hardened hearts with receptive ones. In the new covenant his Spirit indwells his people and prompts their obedience (Ezek 36:26–27).

Regeneration and Our Need

Before being born again we were spiritually dead. In great kindness and love God "saved us—not by works of righteousness that we had done, but according to his mercy—through the washing of regeneration and renewal by the Holy Spirit. He poured out his Spirit on us abundantly through Jesus Christ our Savior" (Titus 3:5–6). Spiritual death heads up the list of our need for salvation: "You were dead in your trespasses and sins in which you previously walked . . . according to the ruler of the power of the air. . . . We too all previously lived among them in our fleshly desires, . . . and we were by nature children under wrath" (Eph 2:1–4). Before regeneration we were dead spiritually, lacked God's life, and could not make ourselves alive.

Regeneration and the Trinity

Each person of the Holy Trinity plays a role in regeneration. God the Father wills that we be born anew: "Blessed be the God and Father of our Lord Jesus Christ. Because of his great mercy he has given us new birth into a living hope" (1 Pet 1:3). God the Son's resurrection unleashes the power of the new birth: the Father causes our regeneration "through the resurrection of Jesus Christ from the dead" (v. 3).

The Holy Spirit plays the most prominent role in regeneration. In the context of John 3, Jesus makes a play on words, for the same Greek word can mean "breath," "wind," "spirit," or "Spirit": "The wind blows where it pleases, and you hear its sound, but you don't know where it comes from or where it is going. So it is with everyone born of the Spirit" (John 3:8). As the blowing wind is beyond our control, so it is with the Holy Spirit's bringing people from spiritual death to spiritual life. Those regenerated are "born of the Spirit" (v. 8). Indeed, Packer underlines the necessity of the Spirit's role in the new birth:

> Without the Holy Spirit there would be *no faith* and *no new birth*—
> in short, *no Christians*. The light of the gospel shines; but "the
> god of this world hath blinded the minds of them which believe
> not" (2 Cor 4:4), and the blind do not respond to the stimulus of
> light. . . . And because the Spirit does bear witness in this way, men

come to faith when the gospel is preached. But without the Spirit there would not be a Christian in the world.[4]

Regeneration and Jesus's Work

Jesus's death and resurrection are the basis of regeneration. Paul contrasts Adam and Christ, the second Adam: "As through one trespass there is condemnation for everyone, so also through one righteous act there is justification leading to life for everyone" (Rom 5.18). Even as Adam's primal sin plunged the human race into condemnation, so Christ's "one righteous act," his death on the cross, brings justification and eternal life to all believers. Jesus's death brings life.

Christ's death must not be severed from his resurrection, which also is the basis of regeneration, as we saw in 1 Pet 1:3—the power that gives us new life comes "through the resurrection of Jesus Christ from the dead." After affirming that "Christ has been raised from the dead" (1 Cor 15:20), Paul again contrasts the two Adams: "For since death came through a man, the resurrection of the dead also comes through a man. For just as in Adam all die, so also in Christ all will be made alive" (vv. 21–22). The risen Christ makes spiritually dead people alive now, and his resurrection will be the cause of theirs at the end of the age.

Regeneration and the Word of God

Twice we have seen that the Holy Spirit is God's agent in regeneration (Titus 3:5–6; John 3:8). We now add that the Spirit uses the Word to give new life. "The gospel . . . is the power of God for salvation to everyone who believes," and this includes salvation when viewed as regeneration. Peter teaches that God uses the living Word to create new life: "You have been born again—not of perishable seed but of imperishable—through the living and enduring word of God" (1 Pet 1:23). James, underscoring God's sovereignty in regeneration, teaches that God uses the "word of truth" to make us

---

[4] Quoted from Robert A. Peterson and Michael D. Williams, *Why I Am Not an Arminian* (Downers Grove: InterVarsity, 2004), 172, citing J. I. Packer, *Knowing God*, 20th anniversary edition (Downers Grove: InterVarsity, 1993), 62–63.

alive: "By his own choice, he gave us birth by the word of truth so that we would be a kind of firstfruits of his creatures" (Jas 1:18). Therefore, it is not difficult to understand the relationship between regeneration and preaching. Mysteriously and sovereignly the Spirit uses the preaching of the Word to give life to men and women who are dead in their trespasses and sins.

Jesus, speaking to Nicodemus, correlates regeneration and the kingdom of God: "Truly I tell you, unless someone is born again, he cannot see the kingdom of God" (John 3:3). Regeneration is God's door into the kingdom, God's reign begun by the Messiah. When in God's grace we enter the kingdom, we experience it, become its citizens, and long for its full manifestation at Christ's return.

Regeneration and Baptism

Several Christian traditions have erroneously taught infant or believers' baptismal regeneration, the view that God automatically conveys spiritual life through the waters of baptism. Appeal is made to several Scriptures, one of which contains Jesus's words, "Truly I tell you, unless someone is born of water and the Spirit, he cannot enter the kingdom of God" (John 3:5). Views of "water and the Spirit" were explored in the exegetical section (see pages 113–14), so here we simply summarize conclusions. John 3:5 does not refer to baptism. Jesus expected Nicodemus to have knowledge of the new birth; Jesus could not expect him to know about a not-yet-existent practice (Christian baptism). Jesus in John 3 probably refers to Ezek 36:25–27, so that being "born of water" refers to eschatological cleansing and being born of "the Spirit" refers to the Spirit's regenerating work in human hearts. Appeal is made also to Titus 3:5 and salvation "through the washing of regeneration and renewal by the Holy Spirit." We agree that this refers to baptism, but not baptismal regeneration, because, as noted above, in the NT conversion precedes baptism, and those who repent and believe are baptized.

Regeneration and Faith

Believers agree that regeneration and faith are simultaneous. However, they debate as to which has causal priority. Is faith the cause of regeneration (the Arminian view), or is regeneration the cause of faith (the Calvinist view)? Or are they simply distinct pictures of salvation that are complementary and do not necessarily fit into a certain order of salvation? As mentioned previously (pages 115–16), it is possible that 1 John answers these questions. We saw a pattern established in 1 John 2:29; 3:9; and 4:7:

> If you know that he is righteous, you know this as well: Everyone who does what is right has been born of him. (1 John 2:29)

> Everyone who has been born of God does not sin, because his seed remains in him; he is not able to sin, because he has been born of God. (3:9)

> Dear friends, let us love one another, because love is from God, and everyone who loves has been born of God and knows God. (4:7)

The new birth results in holiness (1 John 2:29; 3:9) and in loving one another (4:7). First John 5:1 affirms, "Everyone who believes that Jesus is the Christ has been born of God." Following the pattern of the three previous texts, we see that being born of God results in faith. John refers to our ongoing faith (as an evidence of our being born of God) and plausibly includes our initial faith.[5] Regeneration and faith/conversion are not to be distinguished chronologically, as they occur at the same time. But what should be distinguished is that regeneration is a picture of salvation that stresses God's work in giving us life, whereas conversion is a picture of salvation that stresses our response of faith toward God.

Regeneration and the Christian Life

Regeneration produces much fruit in believers' lives. Paul tells how the new creation spawned by Christ's death and resurrection issues forth in "good works" (Eph 2:10). "The Spirit gives life" (2 Cor 3:6) and transforms believers into Christ's "image from glory to glory" (v. 18). Peter praises God the

---

[5] Initial faith is most likely included because (if we look at the parallels established earlier) there is no basis for saying that our initial love or our first acts of righteousness or our first experiences of victory over sin *precede* regeneration. All of these fruits are the result of God's regenerating work in our life. So both our initial faith *and* ongoing faith are the consequence of regeneration, just as both our initial and ongoing righteousness, love, and obedience are the fruit of being born again.

Father, who regenerated us to a "living hope" of an "inheritance that is imperishable, undefiled, and unfading, kept in heaven for" believers (1 Pet 1:3–4). Because we "have been born again—not of perishable seed but of imperishable—through the living and enduring word of God," we "show sincere brotherly love for each other, from a pure heart" and "love one another constantly" (1:22–23).

First John continually applies its teaching on regeneration to the Christian life. John teaches that the new life affects what people believe, how they live, and how they love. Regeneration affects faith, for John enjoins, "Dear friends, do not believe every spirit, but test the spirits to see if they are from God, because many false prophets have gone out into the world. This is how you know the Spirit of God: Every spirit that confesses that Jesus Christ has come in the flesh is from God, but every spirit that does not confess Jesus is not from God" (1 John 4:1–3). John assures his readers that those who have been born again do believe in Jesus (5:1).

Regeneration affects lifestyle, for "God is light, and there is absolutely no darkness in him. If we say, 'We have fellowship with him,' and yet we walk in darkness, we are lying and are not practicing the truth. If we walk in the light as he himself is in the light, we have fellowship with one another, and the blood of Jesus his Son cleanses us from all sin" (1 John 1:5–7). "Walking in the light" means putting God's truth to work and living a holy life. A godly life does not mean sinless perfection but involves regular confession of sin (vv. 8–10).

Regeneration shapes whom and how we love, for the new life shows up in love for God and for fellow believers. Samuel Ngewa of Kenya puts it well: "Belief and practice are inseparable. The sincerity of one's belief about Jesus is demonstrated by one's love for God's other children (5:2)."[6] This is because love is an essential characteristic of God: "God is love" (4:8; cf. also v. 16). John Stott states it simply: "God's love, which originates in himself (7–8) and was manifested in his Son (9–10), is made complete in his people (12)."[7] More specifically, John is stressing that God is love. He seeks

---

[6] Samuel Ngewa, "1 John," *Africa Bible Commentary*, ed. Tokunboh Adeyemo (Grand Rapids: Zondervan, 2006), 1535.

[7] John R. W. Stott, *The Letters of John*, TNTC (1964; repr., Grand Rapids: Eerdmans, 1990), 167.

the good of others and eternally gives of himself for their good. His love is intrinsic, eternal, and interrelated to all his divine attributes. It is expressed within the Trinity as the Father loves the Son, the Son loves the Father, each loves the Spirit, etc.

This intrinsic love flows out to others as well, even us. Indeed, the indwelling Spirit communicates God's love to us, particularly displayed in Christ's coming and saving work. The Spirit gives us new birth and communicates God's love through us back to God. We love God because he loved us first. The fact that we love God shows we are born of God, and our love for others does the same (4:7–8). Robert Yarbrough notes that God's love "gives rise to love in those whom God grants spiritual rebirth."[8] Jonathan Edwards explains, "When the Spirit, by His ordinary influences, bestows saving grace, He therein imparts Himself to the soul in His own holy nature. . . . By His producing this effect, the Spirit becomes an indwelling vital principle in the soul, and the subject becomes spiritual." Such divine grace reaches to the "very bottom of the heart. It consists in a new nature, and therefore it is lasting and enduring."[9] In other words, the Spirit communicates God's love *to us*; the Spirit communicates God's love *through us back to God*; and the Spirit communicates God's love *through us toward others*. The Spirit also communicates God's love *to others*; he communicates God's love *through others back to God*; and he communicates God's love *through others toward us*. We are a part of God's people, the church, the community characterized by love. As such, we not only give love—we receive it too. The love we give and the love we receive all flow ultimately from God's own love. Just as God genuinely seeks the good of others and gives himself for their good, as his people we too genuinely seek the good of others and give ourselves for their good.[10]

---

[8] Robert W. Yarbrough, *1–3 John*, BECNT (Grand Rapids: Baker Academic, 2008), 235.

[9] Jonathan Edwards, *Charity and Its Fruits* (repr., Orlando: Soli Deo Gloria, 2005), 32–33, 257.

[10] For more on how regeneration leads to our love for God and others, see Christopher W. Morgan, "How Does the Trinity's Love Shape Our Love for One Another?" *The Love of God*, Theology in Community, ed. Christopher W. Morgan (Wheaton: Crossway, 2016), 130–42.

5

Conversion

We have been examining in the last few chapters salvation, election, calling, and regeneration, which all describe aspects of the Lord's great work of saving us. We now consider conversion, another beautiful picture of the Lord's work of salvation. The picture of conversion focuses on our *response* to the grace of God and the gospel call. A response is necessary for salvation, and thus the call to be converted is proclaimed with urgency. When the gospel is proclaimed in the book of Acts, the apostles do not declare to their hearers, "You are chosen! You are regenerated!" Instead, they call their hearers to a response, to repentance and faith. In this chapter we will zero in on repentance and faith as the two elements of conversion. The primary Hebrew word for conversion or turning is *šûb*. Greek words for repentance include the verb "repent" (*metanoeō*), the noun "repentance" (*metanoia*), and the verb "turn" (*epistrephō*). The most common Hebrew verb for believing is *ʾāman*, while in Greek we find the noun "faith" (*pistis*) and the verb "believe" (*pisteuō*).

Exegetical Foundations

Repentance

The call to repentance, even for Gentiles, is not uttered for the first time in the NT. Many times in the OT the Lord calls on Israel or sometimes the nations to turn to God, though there isn't space to remark upon all of those instances here (e.g., Jer 25:5; Lam 3:40; Joel 2:12). A striking case is found in Isa 45:22: "Turn to me and be saved, all the ends of the earth. For I am

God, and there is no other." Here all people everywhere are summoned to turn to the one and only God (see also Jonah 3:8–9). The whole of Ezekiel 18 stresses that only those who repent will have life, and the Lord says he doesn't take pleasure in the death of the wicked, and so he summons them to "repent and live!" (Ezek 18:32). Perhaps the most beautiful text on repentance in the OT is found in Hos 6:1–3:

> Come, let us return to the LORD. For he has torn us, and he will heal us; he has wounded us, and he will bind up our wounds. He will revive us after two days, and on the third day he will raise us up so we can live in his presence. Let us strive to know the LORD. His appearance is as sure as the dawn. He will come to us like the rain, like the spring showers that water the land.

Perhaps Paul derived the teaching that "God's kindness is intended to lead you to repentance" (Rom 2:4) from texts like Ezek 18:32 and Hos 6:1–3. The call for repentance should be interpreted not as an onerous requirement but as a kind and gracious invitation to be forgiven.

Conversion and repentance are not identical, but, although different, they portray the same thing: when God converts sinners, they *turn to him* in faith, and they *turn from sin* in repentance. The word "repent" has unfortunately become a religious word in the sense that it isn't often used in our culture today, but in the biblical world the term was a common way of designating those who had forsaken and turned away from evil. One of the best descriptions of conversion is found in 1 Thess 1:9, as Paul reminds the Thessalonians of his visit with them and their response to his preaching: "They themselves report what kind of reception we had from you: how you turned to God from idols to serve the living and true God." The Thessalonians "turned [*epistrepsate*] to God," and such turning means they also turned away from idols, which are fantasies—the false gods to which many in the Greco-Roman world gave their allegiance. Those who are converted, then, *turn away* from idolatry, from serving the gods that played such a prominent role in their social world. Repentance is fundamentally relational; it means that we turn back to God, and the result of that repentance is good works.[1] Good works are inseparable

---

[1] For the relational nature of repentance, see the unpublished master's thesis shared with me by Adrian Birks, "Returning to God: The Relational Nature

from repentance, but they should be distinguished from it. The relational nature of repentance should be emphasized, since when we repent we turn back to the Lord, and thus we turn away from sin. Conversion, however, isn't only turning away from false gods. At the same time the Thessalonians *turned to* the true God and dedicated themselves "to serve" (*douleuein*), to give their total allegiance to the one true and living God. Perhaps the words of Joshua were in Paul's mind here, words that Joshua proclaimed to his generation: "Get rid of the foreign gods that are among you and turn your hearts to the LORD, the God of Israel" (Josh 24:23).

A fascinating call to conversion is found in Acts 14, where Paul and Barnabas are evangelizing in Lystra. The people to whom they are speaking are pagans, as is evident when a lame man is healed and the people are ready to worship Paul and Barnabas. Paul and Barnabas vigorously protest, exclaiming, "People! Why are you doing these things? We are people also, just like you, and we are proclaiming good news to you, that you turn from these worthless things to the living God, who made the heaven, the earth, the sea, and everything in them" (v. 15). The pagans at Lystra need to change—they need to *turn away* (*epistrephein*) from the futility of idol worship and *turn to* the true God, the living God, the creator God.

The call to repent was no Pauline innovation. John the Baptist emphasized in his ministry the need to repent, saying, "Repent, because the kingdom of heaven has come near!" (Matt 3:2). And in Matthew the first public words of Jesus reiterate the same call to repentance uttered by John the Baptist (cf. 4:17). Jesus sends out his disciples to proclaim to the people that they must repent (Mark 6:12), and he rebukes Galilean cities because they refused to repent (Matt 11:21; Luke 10:13). Jesus warns his contemporaries, "Unless you turn and become like children, you will never enter the kingdom of heaven" (Matt 18:3). Clearly repentance isn't optional, for those who don't repent will be condemned and perish on the last day (12:41; Luke 11:32; 13:3, 5; 16:10). Since repentance is vital for new life, heaven and angels rejoice over those who repent (15:7, 10).

Teaching on repentance isn't limited to texts that contain the word but is found also in accounts in the Gospels that capture the essence of repentance.

of Repentance in Luke-Acts," MTh in Biblical Studies, Spurgeon's College, London, 2005.

Space is lacking to consider all the accounts, and so we will limit ourselves to representative examples. For instance, people haven't truly repented simply because they say, "Lord, Lord." Only those who do what the Father commands will enter the kingdom (Matt 7:21), showing that repentance can't be separated from a changed life. People may prophesy, exorcise demons, and perform miracles in Jesus's name, but if they don't live a life that befits repentance, they will be excluded from Jesus's presence forever (vv. 22–23). Jesus portrays the truth in a colorful way in another text: if the tree is good, the fruit will be good (12:33–34). Those who repent must show that they are good trees by their fruit. The parable of the sower communicates the same truth (13:3–9, 18–23, par.). Hearing the Word of God isn't enough to deliver one from judgment, nor is an initial response without perseverance sufficient. Some fall away because of persecution or because they are dazzled by the things of this world or distracted by the stresses of life. Still, those who truly repent yield good fruit; repentance can't be separated from living in a new way.

Although Jesus doesn't use the word "repentance" in Matthew 16, he describes it as denying oneself, taking up one's cross, and following him (Matt 16:24). We see again the relational character of repentance, that when we repent, we turn to Christ. Jesus insists that the rich young ruler surrender all if he wants to enjoy eternal life, if he desires to enter the kingdom (19:16–24 par.). The parable of the two sons beautifully illustrates repentance (22:28–32). The first son initially refuses to work in the vineyard but later changes his mind and works in the vineyard in accord with his father's will. The second son promises to work in the vineyard but never lifts a finger to help. The first son represents the tax collectors and prostitutes who repent and do the Father's will, while the son who claims to be obedient but does nothing represents the religious leaders. The religious leaders remind us of what Nehemiah prays to the Lord concerning his contemporaries' forefathers: "When they were in their kingdom, with your abundant goodness that you gave them, and in the spacious and fertile land you set before them, they would not serve you or turn from their wicked ways" (Neh 9:35).

John the Baptist warned the crowds that they needed to "produce fruit consistent with repentance" (Luke 3:8). Genuine repentance doesn't consist merely of saying one is sorry and isn't limited to words hanging in the air. Changes in life verify and substantiate repentance, and thus the Baptist gives practical examples of what repentance looks like in everyday life (vv. 3:10–14). We can also say that Luke describes the nature of repentance in texts about discipleship. Jesus emphasizes that one must be willing to surrender all, even family and possessions, to follow him (9:57–62; 14:25–33). Zacchaeus doesn't merely claim that he has been saved as a disciple of Jesus, though he certainly is (19:9–10). He proves his salvation as he pledges to give half of what he owns to the poor and to repay those he has cheated (v. 8).

The theme of repentance continues in Acts. On the day of Pentecost, Peter preaches that Jesus as the crucified and risen one is Lord. He concludes the sermon by urging, "Repent and be baptized, each of you, in the name of Jesus Christ for the forgiveness of your sins, and you will receive the gift of the Holy Spirit" (Acts 2:38). The Spirit and forgiveness (cf. 2 Chr 7:14) will be granted only to those who repent. We see the same emphasis in Peter's next speech, in Acts 3: "Repent and turn back, so that your sins may be wiped out" (v. 19). When Paul is in Athens he concludes his speech by declaring, "Having overlooked the times of ignorance, God now commands all people everywhere to repent" (17:30). We find an explanation about the nature of repentance in Paul's speech before Agrippa and Festus, where Paul clarifies the purpose of his ministry: "to open their eyes so that they may turn from darkness to light and from the power of Satan to God, that they may receive forgiveness of sins and a share among those who are sanctified by faith in me" (26:18; cf. 15:19). In Acts 3:26 repentance is described as "turning . . . from your evil ways." Similarly, Paul preaches to both Jews and Gentiles that "they should repent and turn to God, and do works worthy of repentance" (26:20). The works that follow repentance demonstrate its authenticity and reality. Repentance is vital and necessary, for we read in Acts 11:18 that God granted to Gentiles "repentance resulting in life," and thus life in the age to come is impossible without repentance.

Many other passages also underscore the importance of repentance. We see God's patience and kindness (cf. Rom 2:4) in giving people time to repent (Rev 2:21). We are reminded of 2 Pet 3:9, where Peter remarks that God is "patient with you, not wanting any to perish but all to come to repentance." John emphasizes that those who refuse to repent will be judged (Rev 2:16, 22; 3:3). God brings judgments in history to induce people to repent, but often those resisting the Lord become even more stubborn and continue to resist him and refuse to give him glory (9:20–21; 16:9–11). Indeed, they become enraged at God and blaspheme his name. Those who turn back to the Lord are restored to a relationship with him (Jas 5:19–20). Indeed, conversion can be described as "[returning] to the Shepherd and Overseer of your souls" (1 Pet 2:25), showing us again that repentance means a restored relationship with God. Or, as Paul puts it in 2 Tim 2:25, repentance leads "to the knowledge of the truth," and the truth here is the gospel. It follows that, without repentance, people don't experience gospel blessings. We must distinguish between true and false repentance, as Paul does in 2 Cor 7:10: "Godly grief produces a repentance that leads to salvation without regret, but worldly grief produces death." Worldly grief is present when people feel bad about their actions but exhibit no genuine change in their lives.

Faith

Those who are converted repent, but they also put their trust in God. It is important to observe from the outset that the centrality of faith isn't limited to the NT. In a key verse in the OT we see that "Abram believed the LORD, and he credited it to him as righteousness" (Gen 15:6). Paul picks up on this verse, emphasizing that Abraham was justified by faith instead of by works (Rom 4:1–6; Gal 3:6–9). One of the striking features of the OT is the emphasis on obedience, as demonstrated by Abel, Noah, Abraham, Moses, and David. We might even think that obedience is more fundamental than faith, but a canonical reading yields a different conclusion, for Hebrews 11 informs us that faith is the root of obedience. A few examples should suffice. Many interpreters of Genesis 4 have asked why Abel's gifts were pleasing to God but Cain's weren't. The author of Hebrews answers the question: "By faith Abel offered to God a better sacrifice than Cain did. By faith he was approved as a righteous man, because God approved his gifts, and even though he is dead, he still speaks through his faith" (Heb 11:4). The author of Hebrews pauses in the middle of his parade of OT examples to explain how crucial faith is: "Without faith it is impossible to please God, since the one who draws near to him must believe that he exists and that he rewards those who seek him" (v. 6).

We should also consider Abraham, for Genesis 12 centers on Abraham's leaving his homeland to go to the land of Canaan (v. 1). The author of Hebrews, however, gives us, in an inspired commentary, a deeper look at what animated Abraham: "By faith Abraham, when he was called, obeyed, and set out for a place that he was going to receive as an inheritance. He went out, even though he did not know where he was going" (Heb 11:8). The emphasis on Abraham's faith matches Gen 15:6 and verifies that Abraham's obedience flowed from his faith even in Genesis 12. When the author of Hebrews summarizes the lives of Abraham, Isaac, and Jacob, he says, "These all died in faith" (Heb 11:13), which shows that faith characterized the nature of their relationship to the Lord. There is no need to rehearse all of the examples recorded in Hebrews 11. The author summarizes his teaching in verse 39: "All these were approved through their faith." What we find in Hebrews 11 is enormously important for understanding the message of the Scriptures, for we might read about OT characters and think faith didn't play a vital role in their lives. Hebrews clarifies that their obedience—and, yes, their approval before God—was due to their faith. The notion that those who are converted repent *and believe* is confirmed in the OT.

Another OT text that plays a central role in the NT is Hab 2:4, where the prophet says, "The righteous one will live by his faith." Paul picks up on this text twice (Rom 1:17; Gal 3:11), and Hebrews cites it as well (Heb 10:38) right before the great faith chapter just considered, showing this to be a decisive text for understanding how people were considered right before God.

The importance of belief and trust is evident in a number of places in the OT. The wilderness generation didn't enter the land "because they did not believe God or rely on his salvation" (Ps 78:22; cf. 78:32). The same theme appears in Ps 106:24: "They despised the pleasant land and did not believe his promise." Hebrews picks up on the unbelief and disobedience of the wilderness generation, warning its readers about "an evil, unbelieving heart that turns away from the living God" (Heb 3:12), concluding that this generation was "unable to enter because of unbelief" (v. 19).

Another crucial text is Isaiah 28, where the Lord pronounces judgment on Israel and yet in the midst of the judgment says, "Look, I have laid a stone in Zion, a tested stone, a precious cornerstone, a sure foundation; the one who believes will be unshakable" (v. 16). Those who believe will be spared judgment; the NT appeals to this text on several occasions, emphasizing the importance of belief for salvation (Rom 9:33; 10:11; 1 Pet 2:6). Jonah describes what is probably the conversion of the Ninevites, and he calls attention to their faith: "Then the people of Nineveh believed God. They proclaimed a fast and dressed in sackcloth—from the greatest of them to the least" (Jonah 3:5).

The statement "your faith has saved you" shows the necessity of faith (in Luke 7:50; 8:48; 17:19; 18:42). We also see that the centurion's servant is healed because of the centurion's faith (Matt 8:10, 13; cf. 15:28), and Jesus in the same context speaks of Gentiles who are included because of their faith, whereas "The sons of the kingdom will be thrown into the outer darkness where there will be weeping and gnashing of teeth" (8:12). Clearly the centurion's faith signified that he was converted. Along the same lines, Jesus often reproves his disciples for their "little faith" (6:30; 8:26; 14:31; 16:8; 17:20), showing that faith is vital for one's relationship with God.

The Gospel of John underlines the importance of faith. Although John does not use the noun "faith" (*pistis*), he uses the verb "believe" (*pisteuō*) almost 100 times. The verb signifies both the activity of faith and its vitality. The Gospel's purpose statement teaches that faith is essential for obtaining eternal life: "These are written so that you may believe that Jesus is the Messiah, the Son of God, and that by believing you may have life in his name" (John 20:31). Eternal life isn't given for just any sort of believing but for believing that Jesus is the Christ and God's Son. Martha's confessional statement, in the account in which Jesus raises Lazarus from the dead, shows that she understands who Jesus is. "Yes, Lord," she tells him, "I believe you are the Messiah, the Son of God, who comes into the world" (11:27). Other confessional statements play a key role in John's Gospel, reminding us of its central theme. When many disciples abandon Jesus, Peter exclaims, "We have come to believe and know that you are the Holy One of God" (6:69). Jesus is encouraged the day before his death when the disciples confess that they believe that Jesus has come from God, that he was sent by the Father (16:30; 17:8). The blind man also confesses his belief by acknowledging that Jesus is the Son of Man and by worshipping him (9:35–38).

John returns repeatedly to the necessity of believing in Jesus in order to obtain life, and he centers on the same theme, expressing it in a variety of ways. We see this in John's portrayal of the ministry of John the Baptist, who came not to exalt himself but to testify about Jesus so his hearers would believe in Jesus (John 1:7). God's love for the world is demonstrated in the sending of his Son so that those who believe will escape condemnation and enjoy eternal life (3:15–18; cf. also 1:12). What God desires fundamentally isn't that human beings work *for God*, showing by their work their passion and desire for him. Instead, they are called to believe in Jesus Christ as the sent one (6:29). The one who believes in Jesus already enjoys the life of the age to come and has left behind the shadowlands of death (5:24; cf. 6:47). Jesus will quench the thirst of those who believe on him, and those who believe will be raised from the dead on the final day (6:35, 40). Since Jesus is "the resurrection and the life," those who believe in him "will live" even if they die (11:25). Indeed, those who believe in Jesus "will never die" (v. 26). On the other hand, those who don't believe in Jesus will die because of their sin (8:24), and God's wrath is on them even now (3:36).

Acts demonstrates the importance of repentance, and at the same time Luke highlights that faith is necessary for conversion. When the Philippian jailer asks what he must do to be saved, Paul and Silas reply, "Believe in the Lord Jesus, and you will be saved—you and your household" (Acts 16:31). Five thousand are added to the church because they believe the message that is proclaimed (4:4). Similarly, the Samaritans are converted when they believe (8:12; cf. 9:42). Peter declares the same truth to Cornelius and his friends, emphasizing that God invites all people everywhere to believe: "All the prophets testify about him that through his name everyone who believes in him receives forgiveness of sins" (10:43). Luke regularly records stories of those who are converted, and he attributes their conversion to their believing in the gospel that is proclaimed (e.g., Acts 11:21; 13:12, 48; 14:1; 17:12, 34; 18:8; 28:24), and he clarifies that it is believing and not keeping the law of Moses that leads to justification (13:39), and thus all people are saved through faith (15:9).

Paul also teaches that those who are converted, those who are saved, and those who are righteous believe (Rom 1:16; 2 Tim 3:15). This salvation is open to all from every ethnic group (Rom 3:22, 30; 4:9–12; 10:11). It isn't the one who works but the one who believes who stands in the right before God (4:5). Salvation doesn't come from the works of the law or from any other works but belongs to those who put their trust in Jesus (3:20, 28; 4:13–16; 9:30–32; 10:3–8; Gal 2:16; 3:2, 5, 10–12; Eph 2:8; Phil 3:9; 2 Tim 1:9; Titus 3:5). Those who believe confess Jesus as the risen Lord (Rom 4:24; 10:9), and believers receive eternal life (1 Tim 1:16).

The discussion here is brief on the necessity of faith, and we will return to many of these texts. The necessity of faith, as noted above, is emphasized in Hebrews 11, and the author draws on Hab 2:3–4 to underscore how faith is necessary for eschatological preservation (Heb 10:38–39). Only those who believe enter God's rest (4:3). What James means by justification by works will be discussed later, but we can't miss the fact that he indicates that faith is necessary as well (Jas 2:14–26). James insists on the necessity of works, but in doing so he does not exclude or minimize the indispensable role that faith plays in salvation.

John in his first letter picks up where his Gospel leaves off, emphasizing that those who believe in the Son of God have assurance of eternal life (1 John 5:13). Those who believe that "Jesus is the Christ" are "born of God" (v. 1; cf. 3:23), and those who believe in Jesus as God's Son have an inner testimony, an inner conviction that they are God's children (5:10).

The Relationship between Faith and Repentance

Faith and repentance are two sides of the same coin—faith isn't genuine if repentance isn't included. If someone claims to believe in the Lord but doesn't give himself to the Lord and turn from sin, then his lifestyle contradicts his profession of faith. We see the indissoluble relationship between faith and repentance often in the NT. For instance, when Jesus begins to proclaim his message, he announces, "The time is fulfilled, and the kingdom of God has come near. Repent and believe the good news!" (Mark 1:15). Repentance *and* belief are brought together here as two aspects of the same reality, and there is no suggestion that one could experience one dimension (say, belief) while the other reality (repentance) is left out.

Luke also puts belief and repentance together, and we saw earlier that this makes sense given the relational character of repentance since those who repent turn from sin and to the Lord. Luke speaks of the conversion of many in Syrian Antioch in the early days of the church, remarking, "The Lord's hand was with them, and a large number who believed turned to the Lord" (Acts 11:21). We see a genetic and organic relationship between believing and repenting, in that those who "believed" also "turned"—and this is precisely what we would expect, for what does it mean truly to believe something if that belief doesn't affect one's life and the decisions one makes? Similarly, when Paul describes his ministry in Ephesus, he reports, "I testified to both Jews and Greeks about repentance toward God and faith in our Lord Jesus" (20:21). Repentance and faith belong together, just like love between a man and a woman is proven by a commitment to God's vision for marriage. The comparison is apt, for affirmations of love mean little if the one who professes love refuses to commit in marriage. The same theme reverberates in Acts 26:18, where Paul proclaims his gospel to King Agrippa, the procurator Festus, and other honored guests. Paul's commission as an apostle is "to open their eyes so that they may turn from darkness to light and from the power of Satan to God, that they may receive forgiveness of sins and a share among those who are sanctified by faith in me." Those whose eyes are opened, those who truly see the glory of Christ, move away from the darkness in which they lived and from the authority of Satan. Their faith manifests itself in turning to God.

Faith alone saves, but the faith that saves is bound up with repentance, for repentance is faith in action, faith with clothes on. John explains that those who are God's children, those who love God, keep his commands (1 John 5:2–3), but he goes on immediately to say that it is faith that conquers and overcomes (v. 4). The faith that "conquers the world . . . believes that Jesus is the Son of God" (v. 5). Faith has a propulsive power, an inherent energy that leads to a transformed life. Twice in his letters, at the beginning and end of Romans, Paul tells of "the obedience of faith" (Rom 1:5; 16:26). This phrase communicates the truth that genuine faith produces a life of obedience and discipleship. This concept overlaps Paul's phrase "work produced by faith" in 1 Thess 1:3, that once again features the organic relationship between faith and works. We immediately think here of James's insistence that faith must lead to works (Jas 2:14–26); the import of what James says will be examined in due course.

Once we understand the organic relationship between faith and obedience, faith and repentance, we are not surprised to read of conversion as described by Luke in Acts 6:7. Luke reflects on the many who had become disciples and then reports that "A large group of priests became obedient to the faith." Their conversion is described in terms of obedience! Similarly, Paul speaks of the necessity of *obeying* the gospel (Rom 10:16), and his entire ministry is designed to bring about "the obedience of the Gentiles" (15:18)—and by "obedience" he means conversion. Peter also describes conversion in terms of obedience (1 Pet 1:2), describing it as "obedience to the truth" (v. 22).

Summary

Faith and repentance are necessary for salvation. Faith and repentance are inseparable but distinguishable. They are two sides of one coin when it comes to conversion, for true faith always leads to repentance. People do not truly believe unless turning from sin occurs. Faith is turning to God, and repentance is turning to God and away from sin.

Systematic Formulations

Conversion Is Shorthand for Repentance and Faith

Paul, Silvanus, and Timothy are proud of the Thessalonian believers, for their testimony has become well known to people throughout their region:

> In every place . . . your faith in God has gone out. Therefore, we don't need to say anything, for they themselves report what kind of reception we had from you: how you turned to God from idols to serve the living and true God and to wait for his Son from heaven, whom he raised from the dead—Jesus, who rescues us from the coming wrath. (1 Thess 1:8–10)

Conversion involves turning *from* as well as turning *to*, as the Thessalonians exemplify, for they have turned away from idols to serve God. Conversion has two parts: repentance (turning from sin) and faith (turning to Christ in faith). It is wise not to regard these as two steps in salvation, because doing so appears to make salvation a human work, involving steps we perform. These are not two steps but two sides of one coin, because turning is one act. Turning from (repentance) automatically involves turning toward (faith). "Conversion" is shorthand for repentance and faith.

Repentance and faith are related but not identical. When John the Baptist and Jesus call people to repentance, they do not mention faith, although it may be implied:

> In those days John the Baptist came, preaching in the wilderness of Judea and saying, "Repent, because the kingdom of heaven has come near!" (Matt 3:1–2)

From then on Jesus began to preach, "Repent, because the kingdom of heaven has come near." (Matt 4:17)

Repentance and faith are not identical, but they are inseparable.

There is not only one style of conversion in Scripture, for we read of God's dramatic conversion of Saul of Tarsus and God's quiet conversion of Timothy.[2] The ascended Christ met Saul in power as he was traveling to Damascus to persecute believers in that city. When Christ knocked Saul to the ground, Saul knew it was God, for he asked, "Who are you, Lord?" (Acts 9:5). The answer Saul received is as shocking as any in Scripture: "I am Jesus, the one you are persecuting" (v. 5).

Timothy's conversion makes a sharp contrast. Though he had an unsaved father, "from infancy" Timothy had learned "the sacred Scriptures, which are able to give you wisdom for salvation through faith in Christ Jesus" (2 Tim 3:15). Paul tells us whom God used to lead Timothy to Christ: "I recall your sincere faith that first lived in your grandmother Lois and in your mother Eunice and now, I am convinced, is in you also" (v. 1:5). The important thing is not whether one's conversion is dramatic or quiet but that it is genuine, as it was for Paul and Timothy. Further, Scripture records the conversions of both individuals and families. Paul's and Timothy's were individual conversions. Whole families also turned to Christ (Acts 16:14–15, 31–34).

Repentance and Faith, Combined or Alone

It is not customary, but several times Scripture combines repentance and faith as conditions of salvation:

> Paul said, "John baptized with a baptism of repentance, telling the people that they should believe in the one who would come after him, that is, in Jesus." (Acts 19:4)

> I testified to both Jews and Greeks about repentance toward God and faith in our Lord Jesus. (Acts 20:21)

---

[2] Sam Chan, *Evangelism in a Skeptical World* (Grand Rapids: Zondervan, 2018), 26–38.

Let us leave the elementary teaching about Christ and go on to maturity, not laying again a foundation of repentance from dead works, faith in God, teaching about ritual washings, laying on of hands, the resurrection of the dead, and eternal judgment. (Heb 6:1–2)

More frequently the Bible mentions only repentance:

[Jesus said,] "I have not come to call the righteous, but sinners to repentance." (Luke 5:32; we quoted Matt 4:17 earlier)

[Jesus] also said to them, "This is what is written: The Messiah would suffer and rise from the dead the third day, and repentance for forgiveness of sins would be proclaimed in his name to all the nations, beginning at Jerusalem." (Luke 24:46–47)

I now rejoice, not because you were grieved, but because your grief led to repentance. For you were grieved as God willed. . . . For godly grief produces a repentance that leads to salvation without regret, but worldly grief produces death. (2 Cor 7:9–10)

The Lord does not delay his promise, as some understand delay, but is patient with you, not wanting any to perish but all to come to repentance. (2 Pet 3:9)

Most frequently Scripture lists faith as the sole condition of salvation:

"God loved the world in this way: He gave his one and only Son, so that everyone who believes in him will not perish but have eternal life." (John 3:16)

I am not ashamed of the gospel, because it is the power of God for salvation to everyone who believes, first to the Jew, and also to the Greek. For in it the righteousness of God is revealed from faith to faith, just as it is written: The righteous will live by faith. (Rom 1:16–17)

We know that a person is not justified by the works of the law but by faith in Jesus Christ even we ourselves have believed in Christ Jesus. This was so that we might be justified by faith in Christ and not by the works of the law, because by the works of the law no human being will be justified. (Gal 2:16)

You are saved by grace through faith, and this is not from yourselves; it is God's gift. (Eph 2:8)

Scripture, then, at times names both repentance and faith as conditions of salvation, but more often it mentions repentance or faith, especially the latter, as the sole condition. Repentance and faith are distinguishable but inseparable in God's plan. They are not two separate conditions but two sides of one coin. So, when Scripture names only repentance or faith as the correct response to the gospel, it implies the other one. John Murray hits the nail on the head:

The question has been discussed: which is prior, faith or repentance? It is an unnecessary question and the insistence that one is prior to the other is futile. There is no priority. The faith that is unto salvation is a penitent faith and the repentance that is unto life is a believing repentance.[3]

Repentance

A further distinction is necessary when discussing both faith and repentance. Both are ways of speaking of initial salvation. Both also are ways of describing ongoing salvation. Repentance often speaks of people's turning from sin toward Christ in salvation. Graciously God enables sinners to repent and be saved:

When they heard this they became silent. And they glorified God, saying, "So then, God has given repentance resulting in life even to the Gentiles." (Acts 11:18)

The Lord's servant must not quarrel, but must be gentle to everyone, able to teach, and patient, instructing his opponents with gentleness. Perhaps God will grant them repentance leading them to the knowledge of the truth. (2 Tim 2:24–25)

---

[3] John Murray, *Redemption Accomplished and Applied* (Grand Rapids: Eerdmans, 1955), 113.

Another name for this is evangelical repentance. In these verses repentance is God's gift. Earlier we cited verses that show repentance to be humans' responsibility:

> Jesus [said], "Repent, because the kingdom of heaven has come near." (Matt 4:17)

> Godly grief produces a repentance that leads to salvation without regret, but worldly grief produces death. (2 Cor 7:10)

Repentance is initial and saving (evangelical); it is also ongoing and sanctifying. Daily repentance is a normal part of the Christian life and a fruit of initial repentance. Christian repentance is repeatedly turning from sins to God out of gratitude to Jesus and a desire to further God's glory. Repentance is a way of life, as Christians walk in the Spirit and battle sin each day. Sometimes believers stumble but then repent to walk rightly. This process is lifelong. It involves saying yes to God and righteousness and no to sinful thoughts, speech, and actions again and again.

To the church at Laodicea Jesus has words of rebuke and encouragement: "As many as I love, I rebuke and discipline. So be zealous and repent. See! I stand at the door and knock. If anyone hears my voice and opens the door, I will come in to him and eat with him, and he with me" (Rev 3:19–20).

The concept of Christian repentance occurs often in Scripture without the words "repent" or "repentance," as in Eph 4:20–24:

> That is not how you came to know Christ, assuming you heard about him and were taught by him, as the truth is in Jesus, to take off your former way of life, the old self that is corrupted by deceitful desires, to be renewed in the spirit of your minds, and to put on the new self, the one created according to God's likeness in righteousness and purity of the truth. (See also Rom 6:15–23; Col 3:5–10; Heb 3:12–15; 1 Pet 2:1–3; 1 John 1:8–10).

Faith

Faith is believing in Christ, trusting him as Savior, and owning him as Lord. The Bible teaches that faith is necessary for salvation. Indeed, according to Heb 11:6, "Without faith it is impossible to please God, since the one who draws near to him must believe that he exists and that he rewards those who seek him." Salvation comes only by faith in Christ, as every part of the New Testament bears witness: John 14:6; Acts 4:12; Rom 10:9–10; Jas 2:1; Rev 14:12.

The Scriptures depict faith in a variety of ways:

> There are many Old Testament descriptions of faith, including believing the Lord (Gen 15:6), taking refuge in him (Ps 5:11), trusting him (9:10), relying on him (21:7), waiting for him (27:14), putting hope in him (42:5, 11), and more. It is the same for the New Testament, as the Gospel of John alone speaks of faith predominantly as believing (1:7), believing in Jesus's name (v. 12), believing in him (3:16), and believing his word (4:50), but also as receiving Christ (1:12), accepting his testimony (3:33), coming to him (6:35), and remaining in him (15:4–7).[4]

A traditional post-Reformational Reformed analysis of faith is helpful. Faith includes *notitia*, *assensus*, and *fiducia*. *Notitia* means "knowledge": in order to believe, a certain amount of knowledge is necessary. One must hear the gospel message, including one's need of salvation, the facts of Jesus's death and resurrection, and the need for saving faith. *Assensus* means "assent": one must agree with the facts of the gospel to be saved. Knowing the facts is insufficient. One must accept them as God's truth. *Fiducia* means "trust": even agreeing with the facts of the gospel is insufficient. One must personally trust Christ as Lord and Savior to be saved. We should keep in mind that these are not three *steps to* saving faith but three *aspects of* saving faith.

We underscore the need to extol Christ in his saving work as the object of saving faith. The only basis for salvation is Jesus crucified in the place of sinners. Stott is emphatic: "Substitution is not 'a theory of the atonement.' Nor is it even an additional image to take its place as an option alongside the others. It is rather the essence of each image and the heart of the atonement itself."[5] This is important, because faith is only as good as its object. Great faith in unworthy objects is not only misplaced but tragic. Think of

---

[4] Christopher W. Morgan, *Christian Theology: The Biblical Story and Our Faith* (Nashville: B&H, 2020), 354.

[5] John Stott, *The Cross of Christ* (Downers Grove: InterVarsity 1986), 202–3.

the Jonestown massacre of 1978, when hundreds of people committed mass suicide at the direction of cult leader Jim Jones in Guyana. Those people had great faith in Jones, sadly, and their misplaced faith cost them their lives. By contrast, Luther correctly said that a little faith in Jesus saves because of who Jesus is and what he has done. Paul is our trustworthy guide: "Faith comes from what is heard, and what is heard comes through the message about Christ" (Rom 10:17).

Previously, we distinguished initial evangelical repentance from ongoing repentance in Christians' lives. Similarly, we distinguish initial saving faith from ongoing faith. When we cited passages presenting faith as the sole condition of salvation (John 3:16; Rom 1:16–17; Gal 2:16; Eph 2:8), we stressed the importance of initial saving faith. Now we affirm that faith is a key part of the ongoing lives of Christians as well. Faith is initial and saving, and it is lifelong, for we aren't merely saved by faith once for all, but we also live by faith every day of our lives:

> We are always confident and know that while we are at home in the body we are away from the Lord. For we walk by faith, not by sight. (2 Cor 5:6–7)

> I have been crucified with Christ, and I no longer live, but Christ lives in me. The life I now live in the body, I live by faith in the Son of God, who loved me and gave himself for me. (Gal 2:20)

> We ought to thank God always for you, brothers and sisters, and rightly so, since your faith is flourishing and the love each one of you has for one another is increasing. (2 Thess 1:3)

Like repentance, faith is both the gift of God and the responsibility of human beings. Faith is God's gift:

> When the Gentiles heard this, they rejoiced and honored the word of the Lord, and all who had been appointed to eternal life believed. (Acts 13:48)

> "I am the bread of life," Jesus told them. "No one who comes to me will ever be hungry, and no one who believes in me will ever be thirsty again. . . . No one can come to me unless the Father

who sent me draws him, and I will raise him up on the last day." (John 6:35, 44)

Faith is God's gift, but it is also human beings' responsibility. Many New Testament texts bear this out:

He said to them, "Why are you afraid, you of little faith?" Then he got up and rebuked the winds and the sea, and there was a great calm. (Matt 8:26)

"I told you that you will die in your sins. For if you do not believe that I am he, you will die in your sins." (John 8:24)

"Believe on the Lord Jesus, and you will be saved—you and your household." (Acts 16:31)

Since [the Israelites] are ignorant of the righteousness of God and attempted to establish their own righteousness, they have not submitted to God's righteousness. For Christ is the end of the law for righteousness to everyone who believes. (Rom 10:2–4)

What should we say to these wonderful truths? Believers respond with gratitude to God for his good gifts of saving faith and evangelical repentance. We thank him for converting us, for turning us from sin to Christ as he is offered in the gospel. We look to him for enabling grace to strengthen us to live a life of repentance and faith. We also look to share the good news with others so that they can know Jesus and the new way of life he offers. Global church leaders captured it well, penning this in the Lausanne Covenant:

We, members of the Church of Jesus Christ, from more than 150 nations . . . praise God for his great salvation. . . . We believe the gospel is God's good news for the whole world, and we are determined by his grace to obey Christ's commission to proclaim it to all mankind and to make disciples of every nation. . . . We affirm that there is only one Saviour and only one gospel. . . . We recognize that everyone has some knowledge of God through his general revelation in nature. But we deny that this can save, for people suppress the truth by their unrighteousness. We also reject as derogatory to

Christ and the gospel every kind of syncretism and dialogue which
implies that Christ speaks equally through all religions and ideolo-
gies. . . . Rather [to proclaim Jesus as the 'Saviour of the world'] is to
proclaim God's love for a world of sinners and to invite everyone to
respond to him as Saviour and Lord in the wholehearted personal
commitment of repentance and faith.[6]

---

[6] https://www.lausanne.org/content/covenant/lausanne-covenant.

Justification

Justification is one of the most important topics in soteriology, for it deals with how people find acceptance with God. Protestant and Roman Catholic theologies agree on a number of important doctrines, including the Trinity, the sinfulness of humanity, the person of Christ, and his second coming. They also have serious areas of disagreement, and perhaps the most important is over the doctrine of justification. Divergent views of justification played a central role in the split between Roman Catholicism and Protestantism in the Reformation. In this chapter we will pay special attention to what "justification" means, for it is the term most sharply disputed among all the words studied in this book.[1]

Exegetical Foundations

Righteousness in the Old Testament

Conformity to a Norm

The key words in Hebrews are "righteous" (*ṣaḏiyq*), "just, righteous" (*ṣaddiq*), "righteousness" (*ṣeḏeq*), "righteousness" (*ṣᵉḏāqâ*), and "be righteous" (*ṣāḏeq*). In Greek we find the word "righteous" (*dikaios*), "righteousness" (*dikaiosynē*), and "to declare righteous" (*dikaioō*). Other words could be considered, such

---

[1] For a very helpful study of justification that takes into account recent work in NT studies, see Stephen Westerholm, *Justification Reconsidered: Rethinking a Pauline Theme* (Grand Rapids: Eerdmans, 2013).

as "justice" (*mišpāṭ*) and "judging" (*šāpaṭ*), and they will be introduced when relevant. Many contend that in the OT righteousness depicts covenant faithfulness and not conformity to a norm.[2] Despite the popularity of this view, it is almost certainly mistaken.[3] That righteousness has to do with conformity to a norm is clear in Lev 19:36: "You shall have just balances, just weights, a just ephah, and a just hin: I am the LORD your God, who brought you out of the land of Egypt" (ESV). The word "just" here translates the Hebrew word for what is right, and we clearly see here the idea of a righteous norm, since the weights and measures must meet a certain standard (cf. Deut 25:15; Ezek 45:10). The notion of conforming to a righteous standard is evident in Lev 19:15 as well: "Do not act unjustly when deciding a case. Do not be partial to the poor or give preference to the rich; judge your neighbor fairly" (cf. Eccl 3:16; 5:8).

Jeremiah wondered about the Lord's justice, since the wicked prosper (Jer 12:1; cf. also Job 34:5, 12, 17), which suggested to Jeremiah (who was mistaken, of course!) that the Lord wasn't judging according to a righteous norm. Cases are to be decided by what is right, by an objective norm, and not by the whims of judges (see also Deut 1:16). We see this conception of a standard also in Isaiah, where the Lord says, "I will make justice the measuring line and righteousness the mason's level" (Isa 28:17). As Deut 16:20 says, "Pursue justice and justice alone."

Another argument for a normative meaning of righteousness is the frequent collocation of the words "justice" and "righteousness" (e.g., 2 Sam 8:15; 1 Kgs 10:9; 1 Chr 18:14; 2 Chr 9:8; Pss 33:5; 72:2; 103:6; Isa 5:7; 9:7; Amos 5:7). For instance, we read in 2 Sam 8:15, "David reigned over all Israel, administering justice and righteousness for all his people." David's rule as

---

[2] See, e.g., N. T. Wright, *Justification: God's Plan & Paul's Vision* (Downers Grove: InterVarsity, 2009), 64–71.

[3] Rightly, Mark A. Seifrid, "Righteousness Language in the Hebrew Scriptures and Early Judaism," in *Justification and Variegated Nomism*, vol. 1: *The Complexities of Second Temple Judaism*, ed. D. A. Carson, P. T. O'Brien, and M. A. Seifrid, WUNT (Tübingen: Mohr Siebeck, 2001), 415–42; M. A. Seifrid, *Christ, Our Righteousness: Paul's Theology of Justification*, NSBT 9 (Downers Grove: InterVarsity, 2000), 38–45. See now especially Charles Lee Irons, *The Righteousness of God: A Lexical Examination of the Covenant-Faithfulness Interpretation*, WUNT 2/386 (Tübingen: Mohr Siebeck, 2015).

king was fair and just; he rendered to people what they deserved. In Ezekiel 18 the person who is just and righteous doesn't commit idolatry, doesn't commit sexual sin, doesn't rob or exploit the poor but cares for them (vv. 5–9). He keeps God's standards and laws; he conforms to the norm!

We see other indications that "justice" (*mišpāṭ*) points to a norm. God is "just" and doesn't "kill the righteous and the wicked" by "treating the righteous and wicked alike" (Gen 18:25). He judges according to a norm, though the norm isn't above and outside of God himself. The Lord himself is the standard of righteousness (Job 8:3), for righteousness describes who he is, his very character and being (Deut 32:4; Pss 7:17; 36:6; 48:10; 97:6; Isa 51:8), and thus all his judgments are righteous (Pss 9:8; 35:24, 28; 50:6; 96:13; 98:9). "The righteous LORD is in her; he does no wrong. He applies his justice morning by morning" (Zeph 3:5). Justice accords with a norm, as we read in Lev 19:15: "Do not act unjustly when deciding a case. Do not be partial to the poor or give preference to the rich; judge your neighbor fairly." We also find justice in verse 35, where a standard of justice is obviously present: "Do not be unfair in measurements of length, weight, or volume." The notion of a righteous standard using the word "justice" is clear in Num 15:16: "The same law and the same ordinance will apply to both you and the alien who resides with you." There can't be a different standard, a different law, a different norm; the same law must apply to all (cf. Deut 16:18–19; 2 Sam 15:4). Jeremiah 22:3 clearly shows the normative nature of justice: "This is what the LORD says: Administer justice and righteousness. Rescue the victim of robbery from his oppressor. Don't exploit or brutalize the resident alien, the fatherless, or the widow. Don't shed innocent blood in this place." Those who act justly conform to a norm: they don't let the robber get away with what he does, they ensure weaker members of society aren't taken advantage of, and they don't wink their eyes at murder.

Kings and judges in particular are to be characterized by justice and righteousness in their executive capacity as rulers and administrators (2 Sam 8:15; 1 Kgs 10:9; Isa 9:7; 11:4; 16:5; 32:1; Jer 22:13; Pss 45:4; 72:2; Prov 31:9). Human beings are righteous if they do what God commands. "Righteousness will be ours if we are careful to follow every one of these commands before the LORD our God, as he has commanded us" (Deut 6:25). Human beings by nature stand guilty before the Lord because of their unrighteousness, because they fail to do what God has ordained and stipulated (9:4–6; Isa 5:7). On the other hand, David, who was certainly a sinner (cf. 2 Sam 11), also spoke of the Lord's rewarding him for his righteousness (22:21, 25; 1 Kgs 3:6). For example, David didn't take Saul's life when he had an opportunity but lived in fear of the Lord, keeping his commandments.[4]

Those who define righteousness as covenant faithfulness instead of conformity to a norm appeal to Gen 38:26 (cf. also Jer 3:11; Ezek 16:52; Hab 1:13),[5] where Judah confesses that he wronged Tamar by not giving her his son. Judah says that Tamar "is more in the right than I, since I did not give her to my son Shelah." How can righteousness consist of conformity to a norm, say those who dispute such a notion, if Judah says Tamar was righteous since she had sex with her father-in-law? The argument supporting covenant faithfulness here isn't convincing. Judah doesn't say that Tamar was completely righteous but that she was more righteous than he was, and she could be *more righteous* only if she was closer to the norm than he was.

"Righteousness" and "righteous" are often used to describe a person's relationship to God. Noah was spared the judgment of the flood because he was "righteous" (Gen 6:9; 7:1). In a famous text we read, "Abram believed the LORD, and it was credited to him as righteousness" (15:6). Phinehas's decisive action in killing the Hebrew man and Midianite woman having sex near the tabernacle "was credited to him as righteousness" (Ps 106:31). David lived before the Lord "in faithfulness and righteousness" (1 Kgs 3:6). Job clung to his "righteousness" (Job 27:6). The Psalms also often speak of the righteous (e.g., 11:3, 5; 14:5; 18:20, 24; 31:18; 32:11; 33:1; 34:15, etc.), as does Proverbs (2:20; 3:33; 4:18; 9:9; 10:3, 6, 7, 11, 16, 20, etc.). Other texts could be noted; it is sufficient to point out that some people are designated righteous because of their godly behavior (Isa 3:10; 26:7; 29:21; 57:1; Ezek 13:22; 18:9, 20, 22; Amos 2:6; 5:12; Hab 1:4; Mal 3:18).

God's Judging Righteousness

Some scholars argue that righteousness in the OT refers only to God's saving righteousness (and covenant faithfulness) instead of his judging

---

[4] The murder of Uriah and adultery with Bathsheba stand out as shameful exceptions.

[5] In these texts the righteousness of the one who is more righteous was nothing to boast about.

righteousness. This understanding of righteousness is linked with their rejection of the notion that righteousness has to do with conformity to a norm. We will see shortly that righteousness in the OT often designates God's saving righteousness, but the claim that the term never refers to God's judging righteousness doesn't withstand scrutiny, for there in a number of texts "righteousness" language is linked with God's judging righteousness. For instance, Pharaoh acknowledges that Yahweh is righteous and that he and his people are sinners and guilty and thus deserving of punishment (Exod 9:27). Or, when Rehoboam is punished by Shishak, it is clear that the difficulties the nation experiences are due to its sin, and the leaders confess that Yahweh is "righteous" in punishing them (2 Chr 12:6). Similarly, Ezra, after Israel has returned from exile, affirms that Yahweh was "righteous" in punishing the nation for its guilt (Ezra 9:15). We see the same sentiment in Nehemiah's prayer: "You are righteous concerning all that has happened to us, because you have acted faithfully, while we have acted wickedly" (Neh 9:33). God's judging righteousness is clearly on display in Ps 7:11: "God is a righteous judge and a God who shows his wrath every day" (cf. 14:5).

Psalm 50 emphasizes God's judgment of the wicked and affirms that "The heavens proclaim his righteousness, for God is the Judge" (Ps 50:6; cf. 58:11). Similarly, God's righteousness is displayed in his judgment of David's sin (51:4), and in vindicating the oppressed he judges the wicked (103:6). Or, as 129:4 says, "The Lord is righteous; he has cut the ropes of the wicked." Isaiah focuses on the judgment of Israel and says, "The Lord of Armies is exalted by his justice, and the holy God demonstrates his holiness through his righteousness" (Isa 5:16). The Lord who "judges righteously" will pour out vengeance on the wicked (Jer 11:20). As Daniel laments Israel's sin and exile he prays, "The Lord kept the disaster in mind and brought it on us, for the Lord our God is righteous in all he has done. But we have not obeyed him" (Dan 9:14). The author of Lamentations cries out over the destruction of Judah and Jerusalem and the exile of the people. Still, he confesses, "The Lord is just, for I have rebelled against his command. Listen, all you people; look at my pain. My young women and young men have gone into captivity" (Lam 1:18). The punishment that has come upon the people is what they deserve. The notion that God's justice is retributive is clear in a number of texts, and we have seen that God's righteousness expresses itself in judgment.

God's Saving Righteousness

What might be surprising to some readers is the other end of the spectrum, for God's righteousness isn't limited to his judging righteousness. God's righteousness is expressed also in salvation, in what we could call his saving righteousness. For instance, the plural "righteous acts" (*ṣidqôt*) at key junctures points to God's saving intervention of his people. After Barak and Deborah win a great victory against Sisera they voice praise to the Lord, recounting "the righteous acts of the Lord" (Judg 5:11), which recall the victory and deliverance Israel experienced in the battle against Sisera. Similarly, in 1 Sam 12:7, as Samuel reaffirms the Lord's covenant with Israel, he reminds the people of "all the righteous acts" the Lord "has done for you and your ancestors." Samuel is referring not to the Lord's judgments but to his saving acts for the sake of Israel. Micah sounds the same theme: "My people, remember what King Balak of Moab proposed, what Balaam son of Beor answered him, and what happened from the Acacia Grove to Gilgal so that you may acknowledge the Lord's righteous acts" (Mic 6:5). Balak wanted Balaam to come and curse Israel, and Micah reminds Israel that the Lord didn't curse Israel but blessed her with his "righteous acts," i.e., his saving work on her behalf. As the psalmist says, "The Lord executes acts of righteousness and justice for all the oppressed" (Ps 103:6), which means that he delivers and saves them in their oppressed situation.

In many texts "righteousness" is used in the singular and refers to God's saving activity. "Lord, I seek refuge in you; let me never be disgraced. Save me by your righteousness" (Ps 31:1). David asks for God to *save* him in his righteousness. Or, in Ps 35:24, "Vindicate me, Lord my God, in keeping with your righteousness." A striking example of God's saving righteousness is found in Ps 51, where David confesses his sins of murdering Uriah and committing adultery with Bathsheba: "Save me from the guilt of bloodshed, God—God of my salvation—and my tongue will sing of your righteousness" (v. 14). David will sing not of God's judging righteousness for David's sin, but of his saving righteousness that brings David forgiveness. David's prayer in 143:1–2, alluded to in Rom 3:20, runs along the same lines: "Lord, hear my prayer. In your faithfulness listen to my plea, and in your righteousness answer me. Do not bring your servant into judgment, for no one alive is righteous in your sight." David pleads for God not to judge him, since as a sinner he deserves judgment; David knew that he was unrighteous before the Lord. At the same time, he asks God to spare him in his *righteousness*! We might think God's righteousness would not deliver David but judge him, and yet it is clear that David refers here to God's saving righteousness. David appeals to the Lord again near the end of the psalm: "For your name's sake, Lord, let me live. In your righteousness deliver me from trouble" (Ps 143:11). David asks the Lord to rescue him and save his life for the sake of God's name, because of God's saving righteousness.

Often "righteousness" is present in constructions involving Hebrew parallelism, with the parallels confirming that salvation is in view. For instance, "I did not hide your righteousness in my heart; I spoke about your faithfulness and salvation" (Ps 40:10). "Faithfulness," "salvation," and "righteousness" describe God's saving work from different perspectives. We can consider also Ps 71:15, where "righteousness" and "salvation" are in parallel: "My mouth will tell about your righteousness and your salvation all day long." The parallel between salvation and righteousness is evident also in Ps 98:2: "The Lord has made his salvation known and revealed his righteousness to the nations" (NIV).

Isaiah, one of the books the NT cites most often, in several places appeals to the Lord's saving righteousness. The Lord proclaims, "Let the earth open up so that salvation will sprout and righteousness will spring up with it" (Isa 45:8). The Lord's saving righteousness is evident in 51:5–8:

> My righteousness is near, my salvation appears, and my arms will bring justice to the nations. The coasts and islands will put their hope in me, and they will look to my strength. Look up to the heavens, and look at the earth beneath; for the heavens will vanish like smoke, the earth will wear out like a garment, and its inhabitants will die like gnats. But my salvation will last forever, and my righteousness will never be shattered. Listen to me, you who know righteousness, the people in whose heart is my instruction: do not fear disgrace by men, and do not be shattered by their taunts. For moths will devour them like a garment, and worms will eat them like wool. But my righteousness will last forever, and my salvation for all generations.

We see three times in these verses that the Lord's righteousness stands in parallelism to his salvation, and for Israel this salvation will express itself in the new exodus, its return from Babylon. Another remarkable example appears in 59:16–17: "He saw that there was no man—he was amazed that there was no one interceding; so his own arm brought salvation, and his own righteousness supported him. He put on righteousness as body armor, and a helmet of salvation on his head; he put on garments of vengeance for cloth-ing, and he wrapped himself in zeal as in a cloak." Human beings were not the agent of salvation; they didn't actualize saving righteousness, and thus the Lord promises that he will both save and judge, saving his people and judg-ing their enemies. A day of salvation is coming for Jerusalem, and this day is described as the day of her righteousness: "I will not keep silent because of Zion, and I will not keep still because of Jerusalem, until her righteousness shines like a bright light and her salvation, like a flaming torch" (62:1).

The question that arises is how God can be said to be righteous in saving Israel, in saving and delivering those who are sinners. This question isn't fully resolved until we come to the NT, to the cross of Jesus Christ. Some scholars answer this question by appealing to the covenant, arguing that God saves according to his covenant promises. Actually, this answer reflects part of the truth. We have to be very careful here, however. God's righteousness should not be *defined as his covenant faithfulness*, but his saving righteousness *fulfills his covenant promises*. To put it another way, the *rightness* of God's salvation is still preserved in the Lord's deliverance of his people, but we must consider the message of the entire canon of Scripture before we can understand fully how the righteous God who judges sinners can also be right in saving them.

Righteousness as Forensic

It should be also noted that righteousness in the OT is often forensic, espe-cially when the verbal form is used (*ṣādeq*). Moses considers a court case in Deut 25:1: "If there is a dispute between men and they come into court and the judges decide between them, acquitting the innocent and condemning the guilty" (ESV). "Acquitting" (*weḥiṣdîqû*) means "declare righteous," not "make righteous." Judges in condemning the guilty don't *make* the wicked guilty; they assess whether the facts of the case indicate that the accused is guilty. The same is true of the righteous; a just judge determines whether the person under trial is innocent and makes a pronouncement accordingly.

Indeed, Prov 17:15 confirms the interpretation proposed here: "Acquitting the guilty and condemning the just both are detestable to the LORD." A judge who declares innocent a person who is in fact guilty of the crime flouts justice heinously. The judges in Isaiah's day are condemned since they "acquit the guilty for a bribe and deprive the innocent of justice" (Isa 5:23). In a legal context, where laws are prescribed for the nation of Israel, the Lord declares, "I will not acquit the wicked" (Exod 23:7 ESV), which means the Lord will not declare righteous the one who is wicked. We see the same theme in 1 Kgs 8:32, where Solomon is praying to the Lord at the dedication to the temple. He asks the Lord to "act and judge your servants, condemning the guilty by bringing his conduct on his own head, and vindicating the righteous by rewarding him according to his righteousness" (ESV). The text could scarcely be clearer so that this verse teaches that the Lord doesn't *make* anyone righteous; he *declares* people righteous if they are in fact so. Both Prov 17:15 and Exod 23:7 raise questions about Rom 4:5, where the Lord is said to justify the ungodly, but we will delay that discussion until we come to the NT. Here we see clear evidence that the verbal form of "righteous" signifies a declaration rather than a transformation. The judge doesn't make people righteous; he declares them righteous.

The question of righteousness plays a significant role in Job, and the issue isn't whether Job will be *made* righteous but whether there are grounds for him to be *declared* righteous. Job and his friends disagree, of course, but they are asking the same question (cf. 4:17; 9:2). Job insists that he is righteous (13:18) and complains that, even so, he can't stand before God (9:15, 20; 10:15). Elihu disputes Job's contention that the Lord has deprived him of justice (33:12; 34:5). On this score the Lord agrees with Elihu, reproving Job for his effrontery in challenging the Lord's justice: "Would you really challenge my justice? Would you declare me guilty to justify yourself?" (40:8). The matter is complex, of course, since Job is righteous but goes astray when he casts aspersions on God's justice. The legal character of righteousness pervades the book of Job, since Job's standing before God is the basis of the dispute.

Isaiah imagines a courtroom in which all the peoples of the world are gathered to assess the case. They are to "present their witnesses to vindicate themselves" (Isa 43:9). "Vindicate" (*wᵉyiṣdāqû*) here means that they should go to court with the Lord to attempt to show that they are in the right. Their so-called righteousness would demonstrate to all that they deserve to win the judicial proceeding. Yahweh invites Israel in a similar way to proceed to court to prove its alleged innocence, but it is clear that they will lose the court case: "Remind me. Let's argue the case together. Recount the facts, so that you may be vindicated" (v. 26). When Judah appears before his brother Joseph, though he doesn't know it is Joseph, he asks, "How can we justify ourselves?" (Gen 44:16), and these words appear in a context where it is clear that Judah and his brothers are guilty. They can't make themselves righteous if they are not! All they can do is admit their guilt. When judges are instructed to "Provide justice for the needy and the fatherless; uphold the rights of the oppressed and the destitute" (Ps 82:3), this doesn't mean that judges make the needy and fatherless righteous! No, they uphold and enforce the right they already had. They recognize that they are being mistreated unlawfully.

Isaiah promises that "All the descendants of Israel will be justified and boast in the LORD" (Isa 45:25), which fits with 53:11, where we are told, "By his knowledge my righteous servant will justify many." The servant of the Lord will vindicate his people and declare them to be in the right. Furthermore, the servant himself is confident of his vindication, and the legal character of the dispute is quite evident: "The one who vindicates me is near; who will contend with me? Let us confront each other. Who has a case against me? Let him come near me!" (50:8). To sum up, the forensic character of righteousness in the OT is evident in many texts.

Righteousness in the NT

When we come to the NT understanding of righteousness, we see that it is informed by use of the term in the OT, which we have investigated above, and thus the OT informs, as we would expect, the usage of the term in the NT.

Conformity to a Norm

Often "right" and "righteousness" denote those who live righteously, those who do what is right, those who live according to God's standards. Joseph, the husband of Mary, was a "righteous man" (Matt 1:19), living in a way that pleases God. On the last day the "righteous will shine like the sun in their Father's kingdom" (13:43) and inherit eternal life (25:34, 46). It is apparent in the parable of the sheep and the goats (25:31–46) that some are righteous because of their behavior: they cared for the sick, prisoners, and the hurting. On that same day angels will "separate evil people from the righteous" (13:49).

In Luke both Zechariah and Elizabeth are considered to be "righteous" because they have kept God's commands (Luke 1:6). Similarly, Simeon is described as "righteous and devout" (2:25) for his godly behavior. Jesus envisions the day of "the resurrection of the righteous" (14:14; cf. Acts 24:15), though it is possible that someone may claim to be "righteous" when he actually is not (Luke 18:9; 20:20). The centurion recognizes that Jesus was "righteous" (23:47), and Joseph of Arimathea is described as a "good and righteous man" (23:50). Paul speaks to the procurator Felix about the righteousness God demands (Acts 24:25).

Paul also uses "righteousness" of the ethical and godly lives believers are to live. They are to give every part of themselves to God "as weapons for righteousness" (Rom 6:13, 19). Obedience leads to "righteousness" (v. 16; cf. v. 18), and before believers were saved they "were free with regard to righteousness" (v. 20). Along the same lines, there is no "partnership . . . between lawlessness and righteousness" (2 Cor 6:14). Those who give generously to the poor are attested as righteous (9:9), and the false teachers claim to be "servants of righteousness" (11:15), but their profession is contradicted by their lives. Those who "put on the new self" will live in "righteousness" (Eph 4:24). Timothy is enjoined to "pursue righteousness" (1 Tim 6:11; 2 Tim 2:22), and elders and all believers are to live "righteous" lives (Titus 1:8; 2:12). We need to pay attention to context when Paul uses "righteousness," for it means different things in different contexts, and there are plenty of instances in which it simply means righteous behavior.

An ethical use of "righteousness" is found also in the General Epistles and Revelation. The Son rules over the entire universe for a number of reasons, including because he "loved righteousness" (Heb 1:9). Those who dine only on milk spiritually are "inexperienced with the message about righteousness" (5:13), while those who are disciplined by the Lord enjoy the "peaceful fruit of righteousness" (12:11). James in a similar way refers to the "fruit of righteousness" (Jas 3:18), and he also warns that "human anger does not accomplish God's righteousness" (1:20). Christ has died for believers so that they would "live for righteousness" (1 Pet 2:24), and they are called to "suffer for righteousness" (3:14), even though they too were not "righteous" before their conversion (v. 18). Noah is characterized as a "preacher of righteousness" (2 Pet 2:5), there is a "way of righteousness" (v. 21), and the future world will be characterized by "righteousness" (3:13). John reminds us that the one "who does what is right is righteous" (1 John 3:10) and that Abel was "righteous" in contrast to Cain (v. 12). The "righteous" live godly and holy lives (Rev 22:11). The examples noted here show without a doubt that the words for righteousness and righteous often denote *righteous behavior* in the NT. The reference to righteous behavior makes it clear that behavior that is righteous conforms to a norm, to a standard—and that standard is ultimately God himself.

God's Judging Righteousness

We noted in the discussion of the righteous word-group that some argued that God's righteousness is restricted to salvation and doesn't include the idea of judgment. When we considered the word in the OT it became evident that such a conception is too narrow. The same conclusion should be drawn from the NT: God's righteousness isn't limited to salvation but also includes his judging righteousness, his condemnation of the wicked. We see the rightness of God's judgment in Acts 17:31, where Paul tells the Athenians that God will "judge the world in righteousness." Similarly, the multitude are full of praise because God's "judgments are true and righteous" (Rev 19:2), and Jesus at his second coming "in righteousness . . . judges and makes war" (v. 11).

Although some contend that righteousness in Paul is only saving and that retributive judgment is absent from his theology, the textual warrant for such claims is unpersuasive. Paul warns those who are resisting repentance that they "are storing up wrath" for themselves "in the day of wrath, when God's righteous judgment [*dikaiokrisias*] is revealed" (Rom 2:5). The Greek word here combines the ideas of righteousness and judgment, and thus it is evident that God's righteous judgment includes the idea of judging. We see the same thing in Rom 3:4–5. In verse 4 Paul cites Ps 51:4, where David contemplates God's response to his adultery with Bathsheba and murder of Uriah and affirms that God is "justified" in his words and triumphs when he judges. The context here is one of judgment, showing that God vindicates his character, his own righteousness, when he judges sinners. So too, in verse 5 human "unrighteousness highlights God's righteousness" in judging sinners.

I will argue below that "righteousness" in 3:25–26 also refers to God's judging righteousness, and in this case the judgment is experienced by Jesus Christ, who dies in the place of sinners.

In some cases we find the concept of judging righteousness, and the notion is more evident in Greek than in English. For example, the word translated "vengeance" often has the same *dik-* root as those used for rightness and righteousness. God's end-time wrath is described as the manifestation of his "vengeance" (*ekdikēsis*), which means that his judgment expresses his righteousness. Perhaps the most important text for retributive justice is 2 Thess 1:5–9. In verse 5 we find a reference to God's "righteous judgment" (*dikaias kriseōs*), and verse 6 elaborates by saying that God's judgment is "just" (*dikaion*). In other words, it is righteous for God to "repay with affliction those who afflict you." The timing of the repayment is unpacked in verse 7 and is clearly eschatological, since it "will take place at the revelation of the Lord Jesus from heaven with his powerful angels." The judgment is retributive, since God will inflict "vengeance" (*ekdikēsin*) on unbelievers (v. 8), and the punishment is permanent: "They will pay the penalty [*dikēn*] of eternal destruction from the Lord's presence and from his glorious strength" (v. 9). What is striking is that eternal punishment, permanent exclusion from the Lord's presence, is described as just and righteous. God punishes according to a righteous standard, according to a norm: his own character. Paul isn't the least embarrassed by the truth that God punishes the wicked forever. Quite the contrary: God's judgment of the wicked demonstrates his righteousness and justice.

God's Saving Righteousness in the Teaching of Jesus

Is the Pauline teaching on justification by faith present in the teaching of Jesus? If we rely simply on word studies, we find that the notion isn't common in the Gospels, but scholars today recognize that a word-study approach is inadequate. If we look at the concept of God's merciful saving grace, it is clearly present and prominent in Jesus's teaching. In fact, the word "justification" isn't entirely absent, for it appears in the parable of the Pharisee and the tax collector (Luke 18:9–14). Luke informs us about the target for the parable before we read it—a remarkable hermeneutical clue. Jesus "told this parable to some who trusted in themselves that they were righteous and looked down on everyone else" (v. 9). Apparently, human beings are tempted to trust in their own righteousness, and Jesus espied this tendency among his contemporaries. The temptation to self-righteousness isn't merely a Jewish problem; it is a human problem, as anyone who knows human beings and his or her own heart knows! The parable is addressed, then, to the self-righteous, to those who despise others because they consider themselves morally superior. The Pharisee, even though he thanked God for his righteousness, actually gave the credit to himself, emphasizing that he wasn't like the tax collector since he wasn't greedy, a sexual sinner, or unrighteous (v. 11). We should not be fooled by the Pharisee's thanking God in the parable, for he wasn't truly thankful to God—the conclusion of the parable tells us that he *exalted himself* (v. 14). One isn't genuinely thankful for God's grace if one is filled with pride and narcissism. Indeed, the Pharisee was impressed with his piety, evidenced in fasting and tithing (v. 12). Meanwhile, the tax collector put his hope entirely on the mercy of God (v. 13), imploring God to forgive him of his transgressions. Jesus declared that the tax collector was "justified" rather than the Pharisee. The tax collector was declared to be in the right before God, not based on what he did but by appealing to God's mercy. We have a striking example here of the justification of the ungodly!

Jesus's table fellowship with tax collectors and sinners also shows that there is forgiveness for those who repent of their sins (Matt 9:10–11 par.). Jesus is the doctor for the spiritually sick (v. 12 par.), and he "didn't come to call the righteous, but sinners" (v. 13 par.). Fellowship with Jesus is offered to all, and those who have sinned grievously may join him in such fellowship if they receive Jesus's love and repent of their sins. We think also of the woman who came to Jesus's table when he was eating with Simon the Pharisee (Luke 7:36–50). We studied this account earlier, but here we notice what it teaches us about justification, since forgiveness of sins is another way of speaking of justification. Jesus declares, "Her many sins have been forgiven" (v. 47). Her relationship with God is based not on her obedience but on putting her trust in the God who by his mercy absolves her of all her sins. We hear the same gospel of justification in the words Jesus speaks to the man on the stretcher: "Son, your sins are forgiven" (Mark 2:5 par.). The unforgettable parable of the two lost sons in Luke 15:11–32 should be interpreted along the same lines. Both sons were lost; both sons had strayed, for the older son was full of self-righteousness like the Pharisees. Still, the younger son discovered when he returned home to his father that his past sins weren't held against him, that the father (who represents God) had forgiven him completely and utterly. God as Father longs for sinners to return to him, and he forgives them entirely despite their many sins.

Forgiveness in Acts

Luke in Acts doesn't speak often of justification, but he does refer several times to forgiveness of sins, which is in the same orbit as justification (cf. Acts 2:38; 5:31; 8:22; 26:18). Peter declares that forgiveness is available to those who believe in Jesus (10:43), and he emphasizes at the Jerusalem Council, where the apostles, elders, and the church gather to consider whether circumcision and the law are required for salvation (15:1, 5), that salvation comes not through obedience to the law but "through the grace of our Lord Jesus" (v. 11). The clearest statement about justification in Acts is found in 13:38–39, where Paul addresses the church in Pisidian Antioch as he preaches the gospel to them for the first time. We realize that Luke gives us an abbreviated account of the speech, and thus Paul must have elaborated for some time on what he says here: "Let it be known to you, brothers and sisters, that through this man forgiveness of sins is being proclaimed to you. Everyone who believes is justified through him from everything that you could not be justified from through the law of Moses." Forgiveness comes through Jesus Christ; justification doesn't come through the law of Moses, since human beings can't keep the law (cf. 15:10). Instead, justification belongs to those who put their trust in Jesus Christ.

God's Righteousness in Paul

The forensic and declarative character of righteousness is often evident in Paul. A clear example is Rom 2:13: "The hearers of the law are not righteous before God, but the doers of the law will be justified." The verse fits with what we have seen in the OT. Those who do what the law says will be declared to be righteous by God, the divine judge. God's forensic judgment is featured also in 3:4, though here the reference is to God's judgment of sinners, which points to God's being "justified in his words and triumph[ing] when he judges." God is vindicated and declared to be in the right when he pronounces his verdict against human beings. The status of human beings before God is evident also in verse 10: "There is no one righteous, not even one." Along the same lines Paul declares, "No one will be justified in his sight by the works of the law, because the knowledge of sin comes through the law" (v. 20). The thought is quite similar to 2:13, but here the matter is considered from the opposite perspective. Since all people sin, since no one keeps what the law commands, no one can stand in the right before God; all are declared to be sinners. We will examine later what Paul means in saying that people are justified by works, since he also asserts that that no one is justified by works of law. Here we focus on the forensic meaning of the term.

The judicial and forensic character of righteousness is seen also in 1 Cor 4:4, where Paul considers his stance before the Lord at the final judgment: "I am not conscious of anything against myself, but I am not justified by this. It is the Lord who judges me." Paul believed there was no public stain on his ministry, but whether he would be declared to be in the right was the Lord's prerogative, not his, and the Lord, as the divine judge, would bring to light Paul's life on the final day.

We see the same forensic theme in Rom 8:33–34: "Who can bring an accusation against God's elect? God is the one who justifies. Who is the one who condemns? Christ Jesus is the one who died, but even more, has been raised; he also is at the right hand of God and intercedes for us." The legal and forensic character of this text is obvious. Paul considers a situation in which one is either condemned or justified, is found either guilty or innocent. The verdict for all those in Christ is "not guilty" by virtue of Christ's death, resurrection, and intercession. The forensic character of justification is taught also in 5:9: "How much more then, since we have now been declared righteous by his blood, will we be saved through him from wrath." The CSB translates the verb "justify" as "declared righteous" here, and for good reason. Christ's blood atones for sin (Lev 17:11), and thus those who are justified will be spared from God's wrath on the last day.

Paul often says that righteousness doesn't come from works of law (cf. Rom 3:28; Gal 2:16; 3:2, 5, 10), and in such cases it is clear that justification is forensic. The new perspective on Paul[6] claims that he has in mind the

---

[6] For further discussion, see Scot McKnight and B. J. Oropeza, *Perspectives on Paul: Five Views* (Grand Rapids: Baker Academic, 2020); D. A. Carson, Peter O'Brien, and Mark A. Seifrid, eds., *Justification and Variegated Nomism: Volume 1: The Complexities of Second-Temple Judaism* (Grand Rapids: Baker, 2001); *Justification and*

boundary markers that segregate Jews from Gentiles, such as circumcision, food laws, and Sabbath. Certainly these matters are part of what Paul has in mind, but the fundamental criticism here isn't sociological but theological.[7] Paul's primary concern isn't that the Jews exclude Gentiles but that they are sinners. When Paul mentions specific Jewish sins, he brings up stealing, adultery, and robbing temples (Rom 2:21–22), not ethnic separation or segregation from Gentiles. So too, in his summary of the plight of human beings in 3:10–18, the godlessness and unrighteousness of human beings is featured, along with sins of the tongue and sins of action (including murder). Nothing is said about boundary markers. It isn't the case that boundary markers are of no concern (cf. Gal 2:11–14), but they are not the fundamental critique leveled by Paul.

Paul explains in Gal 3:10 that one must do *everything* written in the law in order to stand in the right before God. Those who fail to keep the entire law are cursed—and all are cursed, since no one keeps what the law demands (cf. Eccl 7:20; Prov 20:9; 1 Kgs 8:46). Only those who keep the law will live (Rom 10:5; Gal 3:12), but the problem is that everyone violates the law, and thus law obedience can't be the basis of justification. As Paul says of himself in Phil 3:9, he does not enjoy a "righteousness of my own from the law." Sometimes people object against the interpretation put forward here and contend that perfect obedience isn't required since forgiveness could be obtained under the law through the sacrificial system. Such an observation fails to see that such sacrifices no longer atone for sins now that Christ has

---

Variegated Nomism: Volume 2: The Paradoxes of Paul (Grand Rapids: Baker, 2004); N. T. Wright, *Justification: God's Plan and Paul's Vision* (Downers Grove: IVP Academic, 2016); John Piper, *The Future of Justification: A Response to N. T. Wright* (Wheaton: Crossway, 2007); James D. G. Dunn, *The New Perspective on Paul* (Grand Rapids: Eerdmans, 2005); Guy Prentiss Waters, *Justification and the New Perspectives on Paul: A Review and a Response* (Phillipsburg, NJ: P&R, 2004); E. P. Sanders, *Paul and Palestinian Judaism: A Comparison in Patterns of Religion* (London: SCM, 1977); Seyoon Kim, *Paul and the New Perspective: Second Thoughts on the Origin of Paul's Gospel* (Grand Rapids: Eerdmans, 2002); Thomas R. Schreiner, *Paul: Apostle of God's Glory in Christ*, 2nd ed. (Downers Grove: IVP, 2020); Stephen Westerholm, *Perspectives Old and New on Paul: The "Lutheran" Paul and His Critics* (Grand Rapids: Eerdmans, 2003).

[7] For a good survey of the new perspective and the old perspective, see Westerholm, *Perspectives Old and New on Paul.*

come. If forgiveness could be obtained through the law and animal sacrifices, then Christ died for nothing (Gal 2:21)!

We should also note that Paul doesn't merely say that human beings aren't justified by works of law, but he also excludes *works* in general. For instance, he explains that Abraham wasn't justified by works, for, if Abraham did the requisite works, he could boast and would deserve a reward (Rom 4:2, 4). The reason Abraham wasn't declared to be in the right by works was his ungodliness (v. 5). It isn't the case that Abraham did good works and God condemned him anyway! If he had done what God required, he would not have been condemned but rewarded. Abraham stood guilty before God because of his unrighteousness, because of his sin.

We should also point out the significance of Paul's shifting from *works of law* to *works* in the life of Abraham. Obviously, Abraham could not be condemned with reference to works of law, since Abraham did not live under the law. The works of the law didn't commence until the days of Moses, until the covenant with Israel was enacted. We also see the role that works play with reference to justification in the life of David. When Paul thinks of the forgiveness of David (Rom 4:6–8), the subject is works in general, not works of law, and nothing is said about the exclusion of Gentiles. Paul uses the term "works," not "works of law." It seems that Paul here has in mind David's *moral infractions*, specifically his adultery (with Bathsheba) and murder (of her husband Uriah). So too, when Paul excludes righteousness by works in 9:30–10:4, he uses the term "works," not "works of law," and he doesn't breathe a word about boundary markers like circumcision, Sabbath, or food laws.

We have been considering the forensic nature of justification, but we have taken a bit of an excursion and explained why justification (a declaration of righteousness) doesn't come by the works of the law or by works. God declares all persons everywhere to be unrighteous since they don't do what he commands.

The forensic character of justification is evident also when Paul says that justification is by faith and not by works of law (Rom 5:1; Gal 2:16; 3:2, 5, 6, 8, 11, 24). One of Paul's most well-known statements is that we are "justified by faith apart from the works of the law" (Rom 3:28). Luther concluded from this verse that justification was by faith alone, and a number of

Roman Catholic commentators agree.[8] Justification is by faith whether one is circumcised or uncircumcised, a Jew or a Gentile (v. 30; cf. 4:9–12). When Paul uses the noun "righteousness," he also insists that righteousness is by faith (3:21–22; 4:13). Paul sharply disputes the notion that righteousness can be obtained by works, contending that it comes by faith alone (9:30–10:13). Righteousness can't be obtained through works or keeping the law, since human beings are sinners. Faith, however, receives Christ as crucified and risen. Indeed, God "justifies the ungodly" (4:5 ESV), which means that he declares the ungodly to be in the right. How God as the divine judge can make such a declaration will be answered in due course, but here we must see that in justifying the ungodly God is making a declaration as judge of all. He gives a legal pronouncement; he announces that sinners aren't guilty, by virtue of their faith.

Eschatological Righteousness in Paul

It is also important to recognize that righteousness in Paul is eschatological—and this is scarcely surprising, since Paul's theology as a whole is thoroughly eschatological, in that God's end-time promises are fulfilled in an inaugurated way with the coming of Jesus Christ. The eschatological character of justification is clear in Rom 2:13 (CSB): "The doers of the law will be justified," and this declaration will be announced on the last day. The same end-time perspective is communicated in 8:33–34, where Paul says because Christ is crucified, risen, seated at God's right hand, and intercedes for believers, he will justify them at the Last Judgment. In 1 Cor 4:4–5 as well Paul recognizes that his justification will come on the last day, when God assesses him and brings to light what is hidden. Paul also speaks of the "hope of righteousness" (Gal 5:5), and hope points to the future. Paul doesn't simply mean here that we hope for hope!

---

[8] E.g., see J. A. Fitzmyer, *Romans: A New Translation with Introduction and Commentary*, AB 33 (New York: Doubleday, 1993), 360–62; Karl Kertelge, *Rechtfertigung bei Paulus: Studien zur Struktur und zum Bedeutungsgehalt des paulinischen Rechtfertigungsbegriffs*, 2nd ed., NTAbh 3 (Münster in Westfalen: Aschendorff 1967), 225; Ulrich Wilckens, *Der Brief an die Römer*, teilband 1: *Röm 1–5*, EKK 6/1 (Zürich: Benziger/Neukirchen-Vluyn: Neukirchener Verlag, 1978), 247, 254. This doesn't mean, of course, that they agree with a Reformed understanding of justification by faith alone.

Instead, believers hope for righteousness, for a declaration from God himself that they are righteous before him. When Paul speaks of being "found" in Christ, the term "found" is legal, and Paul's eye is cast to the last day, to the day of judgment (Phil 3:9). Paul is confident that the Lord will find in his favor because he does not have "a righteousness of my own from the law, but one that is through faith in Christ—the righteousness from God based on faith."

Saying that justification is eschatological doesn't mean that justification is exclusively a *future* reality, for it is clearly a past reality as well. Abraham was justified and right before God when he believed (Rom 4:2–3; Gal 3:6). Paul affirms as well that believers are justified by faith even now (Rom 5:1). If there are any doubts about whether justification is past, such doubts are removed by Rom 5:9: "We have now been declared righteous by his blood." "Now" demonstrates that justification is an accomplished reality. We also see that justification is an accomplished work in 8:30: "Those he called, he also justified; and those he justified, he also glorified." We can say the same about 1 Cor 6:11: "You were washed, you were sanctified, you were justified in the name of the Lord Jesus Christ and by the Spirit of our God." The Corinthians should live new lives since they are already justified in Christ (cf. Titus 3:7). The "justification" of Jesus is also past, for he "was vindicated by the Spirit" (1 Tim 3:16 NIV).

In many texts the temporal character of justification isn't easy to assess (Rom 3:20, 24, 26, 38; 4:5; Gal 3:8, 11, 24; 5:4), but the matter isn't of great consequence if we accept that justification is eschatological through and through. We just saw in 1 Tim 3:16 that Jesus himself was justified or acquitted at his resurrection, for his resurrection demonstrated that he wasn't a messianic pretender. He was vindicated as the Messiah of Israel and of the world. At the same time, the resurrection signified that the last days have come, for in the OT the resurrection indicates that the new creation is a reality (Isa 26:19; Ezek 37:13–14; Dan 12:1–3).

Believers in Jesus Christ are "not guilty" by virtue of Jesus's death and resurrection (Rom 4:25). Since they are "in Christ" (Eph 1:3–14) and united to him by faith, they are no longer in Adam (Rom 5:12–19; 1 Cor 15:21–22). Hence Jesus's vindication at his resurrection is their vindication; his status is their status. Every text that speaks of past justification is also an eschatological text, for justification belongs to believers inasmuch as they are united to Jesus Christ as the crucified and risen Lord. The future is revealed and announced in the present.

Believing God's Word, Christians look forward to Christ's return when God will *publicly* and universally declare our justification. At present, believers know their justification by faith, not sight, and therefore they may doubt their right standing before God. Nevertheless, Christ's finished atonement means that the final verdict of justification is already a reality for believers, while they await its public announcement to the whole world. It is the same for Jesus's kingship. Scripture teaches that he already rules and reigns, but this is hidden from the world, and unsaved persons therefore doubt or even reject that the risen Christ is Lord. But the day is coming when God will reveal to all that Jesus is the risen Lord and Christ, and then he will announce to all that those who have put their trust in Jesus are acquitted of all their sins.

Forensic Righteousness—Not Transformative

Earlier we saw that "righteousness" may be used of our ethical righteousness as believers, but here we are asking whether the gift of righteousness God grants to believers is transformative or forensic. We have already seen that the verb "justify" (*dikaioō*) is forensic, but some have argued that the noun "righteousness" (*dikaiosynē*), and even the verb on some occasions, has a transformative sense. We should recognize that such a transformative view of righteousness in the history of interpretation is classically Roman Catholic, not Protestant.[9] Still, we must investigate Scripture anew and consider why some prominent scholars think God's righteousness is transformative.[10] The following arguments are particularly relevant. First, "the righteousness of God" (Rom 1:17) is said to be transformative because it is parallel with "the power of God" (v. 16) and "the wrath of God" (v. 18). The argument is that since God's power and wrath are effective and dynamic, so too is his righteousness. Second, God's righteousness is "revealed" (*apokalyptetai*, v. 17) and "manifested"

---

[9] We should note, however, that today some Roman Catholics understand God's righteousness forensically, while some Protestants conceive of God's righteousness as transformative.

[10] E.g., Ernst Käsemann, "'The Righteousness of God' in Paul," in *New Testament Questions of Today*, trans. W. J. Montague (Philadelphia: Fortress, 1969), 168–82.

(*pephanerōtai*, 3:21), suggesting that God's power is unleashed apocalyptically. Third, we read in Rom 5:19, "Just as through one man's disobedience the many were made sinners, so also through the one man's obedience the many will be made righteous." This verse is interpreted to teach that human beings are *made righteous*, not just counted righteous. Fourth, Rom 6:7 says, "Anyone who has died has been set free from sin" (NIV). The verb translated "set free" is *dedikaiōtai*, from the verb "justify" (*dikaioō*), and the translation "set free" signifies that sinners are transformed by God's grace. Fifth, God's righteousness is transformative because justification includes both the death and the resurrection of Christ (4:25), and the inclusion of the resurrection indicates that those who are justified are changed—they are given life. Sixth, the parallel in 2 Cor 3:8–9 supports a transformative view. Verse 8 speaks of the "ministry of the Spirit" and verse 9 of the "ministry of righteousness." Those who enjoy the ministry of righteousness also enjoy the ministry of the Spirit, and the Spirit changes and renews and transforms believers. Seventh, it is argued that the Lord's verdicts in the OT are effective: "He executes justice for the fatherless and the widow, and loves the foreigner, giving him food and clothing" (Deut 10:18; cf. Ps 68:5). God's judgments aren't empty verdicts; they change the situation. The same reality is envisioned in Ps 72:4, which is fulfilled in Jesus as Messiah: "May he vindicate the afflicted among the people, help the poor, and crush the oppressor." God's verdicts create a new reality; they are not a legal fiction but transform the world.

The arguments for a transformative view are impressive, but they do not finally convince. First, we have already shown in both the OT and the NT that the verbal forms of the words for righteousness are almost invariably forensic. The only real question for the discussion of the verb in our discussion is Rom 6:7. We should begin by saying that verse 7 may stand as an exception to the rule. Words don't always have the same meaning, as anyone who knows his or her own language understands. One exception doesn't cancel out the ordinary meaning of a word. Nevertheless, it is possible that even in verse 7 the verb has a forensic meaning, so that the forensic is the basis of the transformative. In any case, an unusual case shouldn't determine what the word typically means. One mouthful doesn't make a dinner.

Second, the argument from parallels isn't convincing. We must avoid saying that, simply because God's righteousness is parallel to his power, wrath (1:16–18) and the ministry of the Spirit (2 Cor 3:8–9), the word has a transformative meaning. The distinct meaning of each word must be respected and acknowledged. We must be careful of collapsing words so that they are no longer distinguished from one another. Righteousness and reconciliation (Rom 5:9–10) and righteousness and sanctification (1 Cor 6:11) are closely related. They all describe our salvation, but it doesn't follow lexically or logically that they all mean the same thing. If this procedure were followed in Hebrew parallelism, all the words in parallel would mean the same thing, but it is clear that words that are parallel to one another still have distinct meanings.

Third, God's righteousness is "revealed" (Rom 1:17) and "manifested" (3:21 ESV) in the gospel, and it is correct to say that God's attribute of righteousness is manifested. Such a conception, however, doesn't necessarily lead to the idea that God's righteousness transforms. God reveals and manifests his attribute of righteousness in salvation history, and thus human beings see both God's saving and judging righteousness in the gospel. Such a state of affairs doesn't lead to the conclusion that righteousness isn't a gift. God gives us the gift of his own righteousness!

Fourth, the meaning of Rom 5:19 is contested, and space is lacking to enter into a technical discussion here, but there are good reasons for thinking that *kathistēmi* has the meaning "appoint" here (cf. Matt 24:45, 47; 25:21; Luke 12:14; Acts 6:3; Titus 1:5; Heb 7:28); which would mean that the forensic is the *basis* of the transformative. Such a reading fits with the entirety of Rom 5:12–19, for human beings are sinners because Adam's sin is imputed to them.

Fifth, God's verdicts are indeed effective. There is a danger of confusing terms so that, as mentioned earlier, words aren't distinguished from each other. For example, if a psalm speaks of righteousness, deliverance, victory, etc., we shouldn't make the mistake of thinking that righteousness means victory or deliverance. In that case the meaning of words collapses into each other. Just because deliverance and righteousness are found together, we shouldn't draw the conclusion that righteousness consists in deliverance.

We affirm that God's forensic verdict is efficacious. Jesus's resurrection confirms that God vindicated him. God's words are never empty; they do create a new reality, but the new reality doesn't lead us to the conclusion that "justification" *means* to be "made righteous" or "transformed." For the sake of clarity, a parenthetical comment needs to be added. Of course believers are transformed! The question we are pursuing here isn't whether believers are transformed but *whether the word "righteousness" has such a meaning*. So, what does it mean to say that God's verdict is effective? It means that sinners who trust in Jesus Christ for salvation are truly righteous before God. Still, their righteousness lies not in themselves but in Jesus Christ crucified and risen. Our justification is the result of the Spirit's uniting us to Christ, who is our righteousness. Our righteousness is not a legal fiction but a legal reality. We are truly righteous in Christ—all that Christ is belongs to us. As Luther said, we are married to Christ, or, as Calvin says so clearly, Christ's righteousness is imputed to us.

Sixth, the close association between the verb "justify" (*dikaioō*) and the noun "righteousness" (*dikaiosynē*) indicates that both terms should be interpreted similarly in soteriological contexts. We have seen that "justify" is almost invariably forensic and declarative; since the verb and the noun are placed together in the same contexts, we have good reasons for thinking that the noun is forensic as well. A couple of examples should suffice. For instance, Rom 3:20 says no one is "justified" by works of law, and then 3:21–22 speaks of righteousness by faith, and then 3:24 returns to the verb "justified." It is most natural to read both the noun and the verb here as forensic—both denote the saving righteousness of God, which is given as a gift to us. We find the same phenomenon in Galatians. Paul affirms justification by faith in Gal 2:16–17 and then says that if "righteousness comes through the law, then Christ died for nothing" (v. 21). The verb and noun are two different ways of describing the same reality: the gift of righteousness. Similarly, Abraham's faith is counted as "righteousness" (3:6), and then verse 8 affirms that God justifies the Gentiles by faith. The noun and the verb both designate the gift of righteousness, a forensic righteousness, a declarative righteousness granted to believers (cf. also 3:21, 24). Finally, 5:4 rules out being "justified by the law," and then verse 5 refers to the "hope of righteousness," which is by faith. The verb and noun once again refer to the same reality.

Seventh, we see that God's righteousness refers to his gift of righteousness if we compare what Paul says about God's righteousness in Romans 10 and in Philippians 3. The two texts are rightly set next to each other because they examine the same themes. In Philippians 3 we see the matter from the standpoint of Paul's life under the law, while in Romans 10 the same issues are explored in terms of the experience of Israel under the law. Israel's experience was Paul's experience, and Paul's experience mirrors Israel's experience. Israel attempted to "establish their own righteousness" by observing the law (Rom 10:3), and Paul tried to establish his own righteousness based on his law obedience (Phil 3:6, 9). In both texts Paul contrasts righteousness by law and righteousness by faith (Rom 10:4–8; Phil 3:9). It is very unlikely, since both texts refer to God's righteousness, the role of the law, and the necessity of faith, that God's righteousness in Philippians has a different meaning from what we find in Romans. In Philippians Paul emphasizes that "righteousness" is a gift "from God" (*dikaiosynēn tēn ek theou*), and in Romans we find "righteousness of God" (*dikaiosynē tou theou*). The parallels and contextual similarities between Philippians 3 and Romans 10 indicate that "righteousness of God" in Romans 10 shouldn't be interpreted differently from "righteousness from God" in Phil 3:9. If in Philippians righteousness is "from God," which means it is a gift from his hand, then the same meaning of righteousness should be assigned to the term in Romans 10. And, if righteousness is God's gift in Rom 10:3, which it almost certainly is, then God's righteousness in 1:17 and 3:21–22 is surely the gift of his righteousness as well, for it is quite unlikely that the word would be used in a different way, since in 1:17 and 3:21–22 Paul considers the same matter he addresses in chapter 10.

Eighth, other texts clearly indicate that God's righteousness is a gift. We have no doubt about Rom 5:17, since Paul speaks of the "gift of righteousness." We shall see shortly that 2 Cor 5:21 also refers to the gift of God's righteousness to sinners.

Imputation of Righteousness

Paul also teaches the imputation of righteousness. This doctrine is disputed by Roman Catholics, and some Protestants reject it as well. The noted Puritan Richard Baxter rejected the doctrine, contending over it with John Owen, among others.[11] Contemporaries who reject imputation include Robert Gundry and N. T. Wright.[12]

---

[11] See my discussion in Thomas R. Schreiner, *Faith Alone: The Doctrine of Justification. What the Reformers Taught . . . and Why It Still Matters* (Grand Rapids: Zondervan, 2015), 68–77.

[12] For a discussion of Wright, see Schreiner, *Faith Alone*, 253–61.

Imputation is supported by a number of texts. Romans 5:12–19 offers a contrast between Adam and Christ, who are to be understood as covenant heads, as federal heads of all humanity. Just as Adam's sin was imputed to all human beings, Christ's righteousness is imputed to all those who receive him by faith (v. 17). When Paul says that Jesus's one act of righteousness leads to righteousness (v. 18), he probably focuses on his act of obedience at the cross.

However, his "becoming obedient to the point of death—even to death on a cross" (Phil 2:8) would not have saved us apart from his obedient life. His single act of obedience shouldn't be separated from the obedience that marked his whole life, since he could hardly suffer for the sake of sinners if he had sinned previously. What does this have to do with imputation? When the Spirit unites us savingly to Christ, God credits to us Jesus's entire obedience, his whole righteous life. When we are united to Christ, we receive the whole Christ, all of who he is, and that means his righteousness is given to us as believers.

Another text teaching imputation is Rom 4:1–8, where Paul teaches that the faith that justifies is apart from works and that faith justifies the ungodly. The word "reckoned" or "counted" or "credited" (*logizomai*) is used eleven times in Romans 4 (vv. 3, 4, 5, 6, 8, 9, 10, 11, 22, 23, 24). It is imperative to see that faith's being counted as righteousness in Romans 4 is subsequent to Paul's exposition of the death of Christ (3:21–26). Those who reject imputation claim that *faith is our righteousness.* Such a reading, however, misses the flow of thought of Romans, in which 3:21–26 function as the decisive text in explaining the saving event at the cross. Once we see that it is the cross of Christ that saves, we realize that what justifies believers is not ultimately their faith but the object of their faith. Faith can't constitute our righteousness because it isn't our faith that saves us but God who saves. Our salvation is of the Lord; our salvation is accomplished by Jesus Christ. Faith is the instrument whereby we receive Christ as our righteousness, just as an electric cord becomes the vehicle for electricity to flow to an object. The power doesn't come from the electric cord but from the source the cord connects to. Such a reading fits with Paul's claim that our righteousness comes from God as a gift (10:3; Phil 3:9). Faith can't be our righteousness as well, since our faith is imperfect and inadequate and stained with sin.

Another passage pointing to imputation is 2 Cor 5:21: "He made the one who did not know sin to be sin for us, so that in him we might become the righteousness of God." We have here what is typically called the great exchange, and such a teaching isn't a novelty in church history but is clearly and emphatically taught in the Epistle of Diognetus (9:1–5). Christ who never sinned became sin for believers. In other words, he was counted as a sinner by God even though he had never sinned or fallen short of the glory of God. This is another way of saying that our sin was put on Christ, that he died in our place as a substitute and took the penalty we deserved. The doctrine is rightly described as penal substitution. But Paul doesn't only say that Christ bore our sin and took our place. He also says that by virtue of our union with Christ we receive God's righteousness. We receive God's righteousness, however, because we are united with Jesus Christ, and all that he is becomes ours, including his righteousness.

We have seen that 2 Cor 5:21 introduces us to the great exchange, but we should note two other crucial texts that teach penal substitution, and we should consider the implications for understanding God's righteousness. We saw in Gal 3:10 that perfect obedience is necessary to be justified by works of the law, since one must do *everything* the law commands in order to escape God's curse. But no human being (except Jesus Christ) does all that God commands, and thus a curse lies upon every human being. Paul explains, however, in verse 13 that the curse is removed for those who trust in Christ since he became "a curse for us." We see again the great exchange: the curse human beings deserved was taken by Christ, and he bore the penalty we deserved. We see again why imputation fits with the whole story of the Scriptures. It isn't our faith that saves us but Jesus Christ crucified and risen.

We also find the same truth in some of the most important verses in Scripture, i.e., Rom 3:21–26. Paul has finished explaining that no one stands in the right before God since all, both Gentiles and Jews, fail to do what God commands (1:18–3:20). As Paul says in 3:23, "All have sinned and fall short of the glory of God." God has fulfilled his covenant promises, however, in Jesus Christ, and now God's saving righteousness is given to all who put their faith in Jesus Christ (vv. 21–22).

Still, a significant problem arises. We have seen in the OT that judges who declare that the wicked are righteous are evil judges (Deut 25:1; Isa 5:23). In fact, those who acquit the guilty are themselves guilty of an abomination (Prov 17:15). Here is where everything we have studied so far on righteousness comes into play. We have seen that righteousness conforms

to a norm, to a standard, and this standard is ultimately God's very character. We have also seen that God's righteousness is both saving and judging.
Because of God's holiness, he judges those who have sinned against him.
The vital question, then, asks how God can declare the ungodly, those who
are sinners, to be righteous, since such an action contradicts his righteous
character. We have already seen that Gal 3:10–13 and 2 Cor 5:21 answer this
question, as do other texts in the NT. Still, the answer given in Rom 3:25–26
is particularly important. Here we see that God has set forth his Son as a
"propitiation" (ESV; Gk. *hilastērion*), as the mercy seat. This word has to do
with the satisfaction and appeasement of God's wrath. At the same time the
word also has the idea of "expiation," the wiping away or erasing of sin.[13]
What is vital to see is that Christ satisfied the Father's wrath "to demonstrate" God's "righteousness" (3:25). The demonstration of God's righteousness is so important that it is repeated in the next verse (v. 26) so that the
readers don't skate over this vital point.

The question we must ask here is what is meant by God's righteousness. We might think this refers to God's saving righteousness, since "righteousness" clearly refers to God's salvation, to God's saving righteousness,
in 3:21–22. But we have also encountered in the argument of 1:18–3:20
the judging righteousness, the holiness, of God. God's "wrath is revealed
from heaven against all godlessness and unrighteousness of people who by
their unrighteousness suppress the truth" (1:18). In fact, Paul engages in a
sustained argument about human sin, and such sin warrants God's judging righteousness, as Paul explicitly says (2:5; 3:5). Christ's propitiatory and
expiatory death demonstrated his righteousness, his holiness, his conformity
to a norm (which is his own character), for God doesn't simply declare that
the guilty are innocent—an abomination, according to Prov 17:15. Instead,
he satisfies his justice in the death of Christ.

A crucial piece of the argument is found in the words "because in
his restraint God passed over the sins previously committed" (Rom 3:25).
What role does this statement play in the argument—why were these words
included? They are tucked into the argument on God's righteousness. The
passing over of sins, which clearly means the failure to punish sin, called into

---

[13] For a fuller discussion, see Thomas R. Schreiner, *Romans*, 2nd ed., BECNT
(Grand Rapids: Eerdmans, 2018).

question God's righteousness, and this certainly means that it called into question God's justice. How could God, because of his awesome and fearsome holiness, leave sin unpunished? How could he tolerate sin? The answer is that his holiness and justice and wrath would be satisfied in the cross of Jesus Christ. Thus, in the cross God is both "just" and the "justifier" of the one who has faith in Jesus (v. 26). In the cross, the mercy of God and the wrath of God are reconciled. God's holiness and his love are both expressed and revealed. We see that his saving righteousness does not compromise his judging righteousness. Nor should we make the mistake of thinking that an angry Father sent a loving Son to quench his anger. The reality is deeper and thicker and more complex, for the Father in love sent his Son, who because of his great love was willing to go. At the same time, the righteous wrath of God was satisfied through the death of his Son when he died as the penal substitute for sinners. We see here the deeper logic of imputation, for we see why faith can't be our righteousness—our righteousness comes only from Jesus Christ as the crucified and risen Lord.

The final verse we will consider is 1 Cor 1:30, where Christ is "our righteousness, sanctification, and redemption." The verse isn't a clear argument for imputation (cf. also Phil 3:9). Some say that, if imputation is claimed, then Jesus would be our imputed wisdom, our imputed sanctification, and our imputed redemption. This objection doesn't necessarily stand, for the words used have different meanings, and imputation could be suggested by the very word "righteousness," which has a distinct meaning from "sanctification" and "redemption."

One final objection to imputation will be considered. N. T. Wright says imputation isn't credible since judges don't give their righteousness to defendants, and such a thing is unheard of in legal cases.[14] Wright's objection fails because he imposes his understanding of the legal background on the text instead of letting the biblical text shape how the legal background is employed. Wright is correct, of course, in saying that judges don't give their righteousness to defendants, but he fails to see that the divine courtroom in this respect differs dramatically from human courtrooms. In no other courtroom are the ungodly justified (Rom 4:5). Such an action would be

---

[14] N. T. Wright, *What Saint Paul Really Said: Was Saul of Tarsus the Real Founder of Christianity?* (Downers Grove: InterVarsity, 1997), 98.

unthinkable and detestable and a great evil in ordinary courtrooms (Prov 17:15). We must interpret Paul's use of legal imagery by what he teaches, and here we find that the Father sent his Son to bear the wrath that human beings deserved. That doesn't happen and shouldn't happen in human courtrooms! No human being, after all, can take the punishment deserved by another. Ultimately, all analogies fail when we speak of the sacrifice of Christ on the cross. What Paul emphasizes is that God's judging and saving righteousness meet at the cross. To sum up, there are good grounds for believing in imputation. Faith itself isn't our righteousness, but our righteousness is in the crucified and risen Christ.

Can James and Paul Be Reconciled?

Paul teaches, as we have seen, that justification is by faith, while James teaches that justification is by works. As James says, "What good is it, my brothers and sisters, if someone claims to have faith but has no deeds? Can such faith save them?" (2:14). A "claiming" faith, a "saying" faith, an "assenting" faith without any accompanying works isn't a saving faith. Faith without works, according to James, is "dead" (vv. 17, 26) and "useless" (v. 20). Even devils have faith, and yet they are not saved. "You believe that there is one God. Good! Even the demons believe that and shudder" (v. 19). Genuine faith is transforming: "You see that his faith and his actions were working together, and his faith was made complete by what he did" (v. 22). Faith and works belong together. James argues, then, that Abraham was "justified by works" in the offering of Isaac (v. 21), and he goes on to say that Rahab was "justified by works" in receiving the Israelite spies and sending them away so that they were not put to death (v. 25). James affirms, then, that "A person is justified by works and not by faith alone" (v. 24).

Scholars interpret James in various ways. Some who don't see a coherent and consistent scriptural teaching maintain that there is a contradiction between Paul and James, with Paul teaching justification by faith and James justification by works.[15] Such scholars posit not an apparent contradiction

---

[15] Martin Hengel, "Der Jakobusbrief als antipaulinische Polemik," in *Tradition and Interpretation in the New Testament: Essays in Honor of E. Earle Ellis for His 60th Birthday*, ed. G. F. Hawthorne with O. Betz (Grand Rapids: Eerdmans, 1987), 248–65.

but a real contradiction, for Paul cites Gen 15:6 to teach that justification is by faith (Rom 4:3; Gal 3:6), and James quotes the same verse to support justification by works (Jas 2:23). Many scholars of this persuasion maintain that James actually wrote to counteract Paul's view, and thus the difference between James and Paul was fundamental and far-reaching.

It isn't our purpose here to respond in detail to the claim that Paul and James contradict one another. We think it is legitimate to say, among other things, that such a view should be rejected because Scripture is inspired, authoritative, and wholly true. When all of Scripture is rightly understood, there can't be contradictions, since God is a God of truth. Nor are we dealing with a minor matter here! If one writer teaches we are justified by faith and another that we are justified by works, then we have no sure word from God as to how we are right before him. On one of the most important matters in life we wouldn't have clarity. It should quickly be added that there are valid ways of resolving the apparent contradiction between Paul and James. It is not as if we throw up our hands and say that we trust the Scriptures even when the texts make no sense to us. There are good and credible resolutions to the dilemma posed by James and Paul, and we turn to that matter next.

Reformed Protestants trumpet the fact that we are justified by faith alone. Roman Catholics with some delight point out that the Scriptures never explicitly use the language that we are justified by faith alone. In fact, on the only occasion in which Scripture addresses the matter, it denies that we are justified by faith alone. As we saw earlier, James asserts that "a person is justified by works and not by faith alone" (Jas 2:24). So how do Roman Catholics (with the caveat that not all Roman Catholics hold the same view today) understand the relationship between Paul and James on justification? They propose a solution in which James and Paul harmonize. James teaches that we are justified by our works, which means that we are justified by our moral deeds, our good works. Paul, they claim, propounds the same understanding. When Paul says that we aren't justified by works of law, his point is that we aren't justified by the ceremonial law. He agrees with James, however, in asserting that we are justified by our works, by keeping the moral law. The Roman Catholic solution is logically satisfying, and it resolves the apparent contradiction. Paul and James mean the same thing by justification, and the difference between them is resolved by their understanding of the term "works." Paul has in mind the ceremonial law when he says justification isn't by works, while James refers to the moral law when he says that justification is by works.

The problem with the Roman Catholic interpretation isn't logical but exegetical. It doesn't explain convincingly the use of "works" in Paul. Saying that "works of law" refers to the ceremonial law isn't persuasive. We discussed earlier in the discussion of the new perspective on Paul the notion that "works of law" refers to boundary markers such as circumcision and food laws. We saw that limiting "works of law" to boundary markers or the ceremonial law isn't convincing. "Works of law" refers to the entire law and can't be limited to ceremonies. Galatians 3:10 helps us see that "works of law" includes *everything* written in the law. Furthermore, Paul doesn't merely say that justification isn't by works of law. In other texts he affirms that justification isn't by works in general (cf. Rom 4:1–8; 9:30–32; cf. Eph 2:8–9; 2 Tim 1:9; Titus 3:5). The Roman Catholic solution fails to grapple with what Paul actually affirms, for he also teaches clearly that justification isn't by works, which signifies *everything* a person does, and thus "works" can't be restricted to the ceremonial law. The apparent contradiction with James, then, is rather stark, for James says justification is by works while Paul says that it isn't. Claiming that "works" in Paul refers to the ceremonial law doesn't persuade, since "works" is a general term that refers to everything a person does. We can say, then, that the Roman Catholic attempt to resolve James and Paul is noble but unsuccessful.

One common Protestant solution with a venerable history stresses that Paul and James mean different things by justification.[16] In this reading James stresses justification *before human beings* and Paul justification *before God*. James means by justification "proved to be righteous," but Paul means "declared righteous." The problem with this solution is that it is quite improbable that James thinks of righteousness in the sight of human beings in his discussion of justification. Instead, the righteousness that avails, according to James, is clearly before God. We have no hint in the context that justification is before human beings instead of God, and we wonder why James would even be concerned about whether a person is justified in the eyes of other people, since he is concerned about one's relationship to God.

---

[16] E.g., R. C. Sproul, *Faith Alone: The Evangelical Doctrine of Justification* (Grand Rapids: Baker, 1995), 166.

In any case, there is no doubt, when James cites Gen 15:6 (Jas 2:23), that it is *God* who counts Abraham as righteous by virtue of his works. Saying that James thinks of justification before people is a desperate expedient that should be abandoned. It is more plausible to say that justification here means "proved to be righteous" instead of "declared righteous." A couple of texts in the NT may support this meaning of "justify" (Matt 11:19; Luke 7:29), but the meaning of the term even in these texts is disputed. The common meaning of "justify" is "declared righteous," and it seems unlikely that the word should be assigned different meanings in James and in Paul. James also uses "save" (Jas 2:14) to refer clearly to eschatological salvation, as does Paul. The burden of proof is on those who seek to assign a different meaning to the term "justify" in James.

We suggest, then, the following solution to the apparent contradiction between Paul and James. "Justify" in James means "declare righteous," and "works" refers to all that a person does. What James inveighs against is defective faith, empty faith, barren faith, inactive faith, dead faith. For James, such faith is no faith at all, which is to say it isn't saving faith, and we shall point out shortly that Paul agrees. James, then, isn't denying *sola fide*; what he denies is that mere intellectual belief saves. The faith that saves, as we noted earlier in our study, embraces the whole person, so that those who believe also repent. That James has in mind defective faith is clear from 2:19, where he indicts demons who believe but "shudder" at the prospect of their coming judgment. Demons confess that there is only one true God, but they refuse to submit to his lordship. Nor can we say that the demons confess the one true God but deny Jesus. We see in the Gospels that the demons acknowledged that Jesus was "the Holy One of God" (Mark 1:24; cf. Luke 4:34), and in that sense they "believed" in him and knew more about him at that stage in his ministry than almost anyone. They knew Jesus's identity, and in that sense they believed in him, and yet such "faith" didn't lead to commitment, to submission to Jesus as Lord. Intellectual assent to doctrines doesn't qualify as saving faith, and thus one may say he or she believes Jesus died for one's sins, and yet such a statement really means nothing to a person and doesn't lead to embrace and trust in Jesus. Authentic saving faith is dynamic and active and inevitably yields fruit in believers' lives.

Genuine faith is a living and active thing and will inevitably produce results in one's life. We see this plainly in Jas 2:23, where James considers the life of Abraham: "Faith was active together with his works, and by works, faith was made complete." Genuine faith isn't merely a faith that professes belief; it is more than intellectual assent. Genuine faith is completed, brought to fitting fruition, by works. The concept is quite simple: if you have a life-threatening illness and believe a doctor has the ability to save you from death, then you entrust yourself to the surgeon's knife.

Here it is important to bring in Paul, who also says believers are justified by works (Rom 2:13)! Some scholars understand what Paul says in verse 13 to be hypothetical, but such a reading in light of 2:6–10, 26–29 is quite unlikely. Paul gives no hint that he writes hypothetically. Those who are wicked will be judged and condemned for their works (cf. 2 Cor 11:16; 2 Tim 4:14; Titus 1:16), since they practice the "works of the flesh" (Gal 5:19), "fruitless works of darkness" (Eph 5:11). On the other hand, God has prepared believers "for good works" (2:10), which are to be present in the lives of believers (1 Tim 2:10; 5:10, 25; 6:18; Titus 2:7, 14; 3:8, 14). Such works are necessary for salvation, for Paul emphasizes that those who practice the works of the flesh "will not inherit the kingdom of God" (Gal 5:21; cf. 1 Cor 6:9–11). James, then, doesn't differ from Paul in demanding that people practice good works in order to obtain end-time salvation.

It is also evident in Rom 2:26–29 that the obedience of Gentiles demonstrates their salvation, for Paul ties it to the work of the Holy Spirit in their lives (vv. 28–29). So too, in 1 Thess 1:3 and 2 Thess 1:11 the work that believers do is traced to their faith. Their work is an expression of their faith, a result of their faith. The importance of these observations can hardly be overstated, for we must consider how Paul himself can say that justification and salvation are apart from works and then later teach that works are necessary for entering the kingdom. We see that the works are fruit of faith, a consequence of new life in the Spirit. It follows, then, that, although works are necessary for justification, they are not a necessary basis but a necessary fruit and evidence. They are the result of the Spirit's work, not the autonomous contribution of human beings. Works can't be the basis for justification, since God demands perfection, but good works signify that new life has dawned.

James should be interpreted along the same lines. Good works are necessary for justification and salvation (cf. Jas 2:14), but they are the necessary fruit and evidence of justification, not its necessary basis. This reading is confirmed by 3:2, which immediately follows James's exposition on justification by works. James remarks that "We all stumble in many ways." "Stumble" here refers to sin, as the use of the same verb in 2:10 confirms: "Whoever keeps the entire law, and yet stumbles at one point, is guilty of breaking it all." We notice in 3:2 that all without exception stumble and sin, and James even includes himself. He also remarks that we all sin "in many ways." He does not teach that we sin in merely a few ways. No—we all sin in more ways than we can count. We must put what James says about the continuing presence of sin in 3:2 with what he teaches about justification by works in 2:14–26. Justification by works doesn't mean we avoid sin. In fact, those who are justified by works still sin in many ways, which confirms that the works that justify in James aren't the basis (how could they be, when we sin in many ways?) but the evidence of our new life. True faith expresses itself in works, in a changed life, and God declares that those whose lives are changed are righteous—yet their works aren't the basis of their righteousness but the evidence of their new life with God.[17]

Summary

Righteousness in the Scriptures should be defined not merely as covenant faithfulness but as conformity to a norm, conformity to a standard, and the standard is ultimately the character of God himself. Since God is righteous, his righteousness manifests itself when he judges and punishes the wicked for their sin. At the same time, we see God's saving righteousness for those who trust in his salvation. We have also seen that God's righteousness is forensic and not transformative. We are *declared* righteous, not *made* righteous. Remarkably, God's saving and judging righteousness come together at the cross. God in his great love sent his Son to bear his wrath and display his love for the world. The Son because of his great love for the Father and for us willingly bore that wrath so that in the cross both God's holiness (his judging righteousness) and his mercy (his saving

---

[17] See Christopher W. Morgan, *A Theology of James: Wisdom for God's People*, EBT, ed. Robert A. Peterson (Phillipsburg, NJ: P&R, 2010), 127–43.

righteousness) might be displayed. For those who trust in Christ, God's righteousness is imputed to them via union with Christ. Believers are justified by faith alone, and yet, as is often said, such faith is not alone. Good works are necessary for justification, but they function as the necessary evidence or fruit of justification.

Historical Reconnaissance

The Roman Catholic View of Justification

The Council of Trent, 1545–63

The Council of Trent was an ecumenical council of the Roman Catholic Church held in Trent, Italy, in three sessions between 1545 and 1563. The council was the Catholic response to the Reformation's theology and criticism of the church's ecclesiastical abuses. The council elucidated and redefined Rome's doctrine, corrected many ecclesiastical abuses, and strengthened papal authority. It was the beginning of the Counter-Reformation through which many former followers of Rome were reclaimed.

The Council of Trent rejected many Reformation doctrines, including *sola scriptura* (the Bible alone as the ultimate authority for theology and ethics) and *sola fide* (justification by faith alone). In sixteen paragraphs ("chapters") the council's first decree on justification set forth the official Roman Catholic doctrine in opposition to Reformation theology. Here is a summary of that decree, promulgated in January 1547 (the council uses "justice" instead of "righteousness"):

> *Preparation for justification*: Adults must prepare themselves for justification. In the fall, free will was "attenuated and bent down" but not "extinguished" (ch.1). God's prevenient grace allows adults to "convert themselves to their own Justification, by freely assenting to and co-operating with that said grace" (chs. 5, 6).

> *Definition of justification*: Justification is not a declaration of righteousness but an infusion of God's grace (chs. 7, 16). God's grace enables us to be justified from righteousness "inherent in us[;] that same is [the justice] of God, because that it is infused into us of

God, through the merit of Christ. Further, justification does not involve the forgiveness of sin alone "but also the sanctification and renewal of the inward man" (ch. 7).

Faith and justification: We are "justified by faith because faith is the beginning of human salvation, the foundation, and the root of all Justification" (ch. 8).

Good works, merit, and justification: "Life eternal is to be proposed to those working well unto the end, and hoping in God, both as a grace mercifully promised to the sons of God through Jesus Christ, and as a reward which is according to the promise of God himself, to be faithfully rendered to their good works and merits" (ch. 16).

Increase of justification: People, having been justified "through the observance of the commandments of God and of the Church, faith co-operating with good works, increase in that justice which they have received through the grace of Christ, and are still further justified" (ch.10).

Assurance of salvation: This is the "vain confidence of heretics" who claim their "sins are forgiven" or boast of "confidence and certainty of the remission of his sins" (ch. 9). Rather, "He that shall persevere to the end, he shall be saved." Therefore "Let no one herein promise himself anything as certain with an absolute certainty" (ch. 13).

Loss of justification: "God forsakes not those who have been once justified by his grace, unless he be first forsaken by them. Wherefore, no one ought to flatter himself up with faith alone" (ch. 11). "The received grace of Justification is lost, not only by infidelity whereby even faith itself is lost, but also by any other mortal sin whatever, though faith be not lost" (ch. 15).

Recovery of justification: Those justified by grace, if they fall away, "may be again justified . . . through the sacrament of penance." This involves contrition, confession, absolution, and satisfaction, not "for the eternal punishment, which is, together with the guilt, remitted . . . by the sacrament . . . but for the temporal punishment" (ch. 14).

Perseverance and justification: "He that shall persevere to the end, he shall be saved."

There follows a transition from the first decree on justification to "canons": "After this Catholic doctrine on Justification, which whoso receiveth not faithfully and firmly cannot be justified, it hath seemed good to the holy Synod to subjoin these canons, that all may know not only what they ought to hold and follow, but also what to avoid and shun."[18] Then in thirty-three canons (statements) the council condemns all who disagree with Catholic doctrine. Here is a sample:

> CANON IX. If any one saith, that by faith alone the impious is justified; in such wise as to mean, that nothing else is required to co-operate in order to the obtaining the grace of Justification, and that it is not in any way necessary, that he be prepared and disposed by the movement of his own will; let him be anathema.

> CANON XI. If any one saith, that men are justified, either by the sole imputation of the justice of Christ, or by the sole remission of sins, to the exclusion of the grace and the charity which is poured forth in their hearts by the Holy Ghost, and is inherent in them; or even that the grace, whereby we are justified, is only the favour of God; let him be anathema.

> CANON XXXIII: If any one saith, that, by the Catholic doctrine touching Justification, by this holy Synod inset forth in this present decree, the glory of God, or the merits of our Lord Jesus Christ are in any way derogated from, and not rather that the truth of our faith, and the glory in fine [ultimately] of God and of Jesus Christ are rendered (more) illustrious; let him be anathema.[19]

The Catechism of the Catholic Church, 1992

The Roman Catholic Church has not rejected the teachings and anathemas of Trent. *The Catechism of the Catholic Church*, 1992, is not as thorough as Trent, due to its popular genre. This important document was promulgated

---

[18] Council of Trent, session 6, http://www.thecounciloftrent.com/ch6.htm.
[19] Council of Trent, session 6.

by Pope John Paul II and commended by Cardinal Joseph Ratzinger (later Pope Benedict XVI). Protestants find many points of disagreement with it concerning justification. The catechism's doctrine of justification reflects the Council of Trent. A consideration of article 2, "Grace and Justification," bears this out (paragraph numbers are in parentheses).

Some statements contain teachings with which we agree, such as the following, except for its references to baptism and God's making "us inwardly just."

> Justification has been merited for us by the Passion of Christ who offered himself on the cross as a living victim, holy and pleasing to God, and whose blood has become the instrument of atonement for the sins of all men. Justification is conferred in Baptism, the sacrament of faith. It conforms us to the righteousness of God, who makes us inwardly just by the power of his mercy. Its purpose is the glory of God and of Christ, and the gift of eternal life. (Notes cite the Council of Trent and Rom 3:21–26.) (1992)

The catechism defines justification as the Holy Spirit's power to cleanse us from our sins and communicate to us "the righteousness of God through faith in Jesus Christ" and baptism. Three biblical quotations follow, two of which treat progressive sanctification: Rom 6:3–4, 8–11. The next paragraph deals with "dying to sin," "being born to a new life," and union with Christ, none of which belongs to justification proper.

In agreement with Trent, the catechism teaches that "justification establishes cooperation between God's grace and man's freedom." We cannot be saved without the Spirit's enabling our free will, but we say yes or no to God's Word (1993). The catechism goes beyond Trent when it speaks of people's becoming "divinized" and as proof cites Athanasius on deification (1987–88).

The Spirit's "first work of the grace of the Holy Spirit is conversion," defined as when "Moved by grace, man turns toward God and away from sin, thus accepting forgiveness and righteousness from on high." There follows a quotation from Trent: "Justification is not only the remission of sins, but also the sanctification and renewal of the interior man." Once more the catechism includes progressive sanctification in justification: "Justification follows upon God's merciful initiative of offering forgiveness. It reconciles man with God. It frees from the enslavement to sin, and it heals" (1989–90). Again, "The Holy Spirit is the master of the interior life. By giving birth to the inner man justification entails the sanctification of his whole being" (1995).[20]

Further confirmation that Rome's views haven't changed is provided by Rahner and Vorgrimler's *Dictionary of Theology* (1981). This tool defines justification in terms similar to those of the Council of Trent:

> Justification is the event in which God, by a free act of love, brings man . . . into that relationship with him which a holy God demands of man. . . . He does so by giving man a share of his divine nature . . . through the word of faith and the signs of the sacraments. This justice, which is not merely imputed in juridical fashion but makes a man truly just, is at the same time the forgiveness of sins. . . . There can be no reflexive certainty of salvation for any individual. . . . This justice, God-given and received, can also be lost if man rejects divine love by serious sin. . . . Man can both preserve and continually increase [justification].[21]

The Reformation and Justification

The sixteenth-century Protestant Reformation was chiefly a theological movement, although it had repercussions in political, social, economic, and cultural domains as well. The Reformers focused on the rediscovery of the message of salvation. Far from being uniform, the Reformation produced Lutheran, Calvinist, Anglican, and Anabaptist churches, as well as the Roman Catholic Counter-Reformation in reaction to Protestantism. Nevertheless, the several Reformation churches unitedly embraced the gospel.

The Reformation churches agreed on the gospel because they held to *sola scriptura*: the Bible alone is the chief authority for theology and ethics.

---

[20] Catechism of the Catholic Church, pt. 3, sec. 1, chap. 3, art. 2, "Grace and Justification" (1992). https://www.usccb.org/beliefs-and-teachings/what-we-believe /catechism/catechism-of-the-catholic-church (section 3, paragraph 1995), p. 483.

[21] Karl Rahner and Herbert Vorgrimler, *Dictionary of Theology*, 2nd ed. (New York: Crossroad, 1981), 260–61. Cited in Hoekema, *Saved by Grace*, 168–69 (see chap. 3, n. 78).

This was the first of five Reformation *solas*, the others being *sola fide* (salvation is through "faith alone" in Christ, not good works), *sola gratia* (we are saved by God's "grace alone"), *solus Christus* ("Christ alone" is the only Mediator between God and humans), and *soli Deo gloria* (all glory belongs "to God alone").

Practically, *sola scriptura* meant that the Reformers rejected Rome's view that sacred Scripture and sacred tradition were equally authoritative, instead elevating Scripture to the supreme place for doctrine and Christian living. Calvin, to cite one example, acknowledged the authority of reason, tradition, and experience but sought deliberately and consistently to place Scripture over these lesser authorities, judging them.

Applying *sola scriptura* to salvation, Luther came to understand the Bible's central message as one of free justification received by faith alone in Christ, resulting in the forgiveness of sins. The major Reformers accepted Luther's doctrine of justification and strongly opposed the medieval Roman Catholic doctrine of justification. Although Rome's teaching began with God's prevenient grace, such grace enabled sinners' free will to believe in Christ and perform good works that merit eternal life. The Catholic church taught that justification is not forensic, whereby God declares sinners righteous in Christ. Rather it is transformational, beginning a process that may lead to final salvation. Thus Rome conceives of salvation as a synergism between God and humans. By contrast, the Reformers held to a monergistic salvation, with God alone saving sinners from beginning to end.

Further, the Roman church taught that the church alone was the fount of God's saving grace, dispensed through its sacraments of baptism, penance, and Eucharist, among others. Luther objected to this view and committed himself to defending and propagating the good news of God's free grace. Luther and his fellow Reformers held that justification is a judicial picture of God's applying salvation to believers. It is forensic, not transformational. It is a declarative act, not a lifelong process. In justification God once for all declares righteous and forgives every believer in Jesus.

Paul emphatically teaches that justification is received by faith, not by faith and works: "We know that a person is not justified by the works of the law but by faith in Jesus Christ, even we ourselves have believed in Christ Jesus. This was so that we might be justified by faith in Christ and not by the works of the law, because by the works of the law no human being will be justified" (Gal 2:16).

Justification does not purify sinners within and enable them to do good works. When God justifies a sinner, he or she becomes *simul justus et peccator*, to use Luther's famous expression, at the same time righteous and a sinner. God the judge declares believers righteous in Christ, and so they are in God's sight. At the same time, viewed in themselves they are still sinners. Rome's condemnation of Luther's doctrine as promoting license misses the mark. Although justification is not transformational, it is correlative with other aspects of the application of salvation that *are* transformational. God's justifying sinners is inseparable from his regenerating and sanctifying them. In regeneration God gives sinners new life, which is seen in their believing the gospel, loving fellow believers, and living godly lives, as 1 John attests. In progressive sanctification God enables believers to grow in grace, the knowledge of Christ, and practical holiness.

Rome's confusing justification with progressive sanctification is an egregious error, for it results in "good Christians" seeking to gain or keep salvation by living for God. As the Reformers recognized, Paul inseparably linked God's saving grace and faith in Christ for justification: "This is why the promise is by faith, so that it may be according to grace, to guarantee it to all the descendants . . . to the one who is of Abraham's faith" (Rom 4:16). Merit theology is impossible, for it sets aside "the grace of God, for if righteousness comes through the law, then Christ died for nothing" (Gal 2:21). Salvation means turning our attention away from ourselves to Christ alone (Rom 4:22–25).

When God joins us to Christ, he imputes our sins to him and his righteousness to us: God "made the one who did not know sin to be sin for us, so that in him we might become the righteousness of God" (2 Cor 5:21). Christ's "active" or lifelong obedience is counted to us, as is his "passive" or suffering obedience, his death on the cross: "Just as through one man's disobedience the many were made sinners, so also through the one man's obedience the many will be made righteous" (Rom 5:19). God accepts us freely in his grace when we trust Christ alone for salvation.

In sum: though we are saved by grace through faith alone, saving faith never remains alone, for "In Christ Jesus neither circumcision nor uncircumcision accomplishes anything; what matters is faith working through love" (Gal 5:6). Consequently, "We love because he first loved us" in Christ (1 John 4:10). Because Christ loved us and laid down his life for us, we love one another (John 15:12–13). Out of gratitude for grace received in justification, we are "[re]created in Christ Jesus for good works, which God prepared ahead of time for us to do" (Eph 2:10).

Systematic Formulations

Having laid a solid exegetical foundation and explored the history of doctrine, we move to a systematic theology of justification. Biblical pictures of the application of salvation arise from various spheres. Calling comes from the realm of our senses, particularly that of hearing. Regeneration hails from the sphere of death and life. Sanctification is related to ritual uncleanness and holiness. Conversion concerns a change of direction, both turning from (repentance) and turning to (faith).

Both justification and adoption are legal images, though hailing from different sections of the court. Adoption comes from the family court, presenting God as Father, Christ as older Brother and Redeemer, and believers as God's beloved children to whom he gives the benefits and responsibilities of family life.

Justification, like adoption, is a legal image, but it belongs in a different division—the criminal court. It is a part of a larger biblical legal picture that portrays God as lawgiver and Judge of all the earth, to whom every person will give an account. Fallen humans appear before him as guilty sinners who have rebelled against their Maker and broken his law. Christ was "born under the law, to redeem those under the law" (Gal 4:4–5). How did he do this? "Christ redeemed us from the curse of the law by becoming a curse for us, because it is written, 'Cursed is everyone who is hung on a tree'" (3:13).

God the Judge declares righteous all who trust his Son as Lord and Savior. That is, he *justifies* them. In answer to the question "What is justification?" the Westminster Shorter Catechism answers, "Justification is an act of God's free grace, wherein he pardons all our sins, and accepts us as righteous in his sight, only for the righteousness of Christ imputed to us, and received by faith alone."[22]

---

[22] Question and answer 33, language updated.

Justification's Necessity: Condemnation

Adam and Eve did not need to be justified prior to the fall, for they were "created after the likeness of God in true righteousness and holiness" (Eph 4:24 ESV). But after the fall they and all their progeny needed justification. Paul presents this need in two ways. First, we need Christ's righteousness because of Adam's original sin: "One trespass led to condemnation for all men. . . . By the one man's disobedience the many were made sinners" (Rom 5:18–19 ESV). Second, we have all committed actual sins: "All have sinned and fall short of the glory of God" (3:23). In fact, this verse may refer to both Adam's primal transgression (the aorist "we all have sinned") and our actual sins (the present tense "fall short"), as Dunn suggests.[23]

Paul's developing argument in Romans underscores humanity's universal need for justification in Christ. Immediately after announcing the theme of the book, the revelation of God's righteousness in the gospel (1:16–17), Paul begins a long section treating another revelation, that of God's judgment on sin: "God's wrath is revealed from heaven against all godlessness and unrighteousness of people who by their unrighteousness suppress the truth" (v. 18). He finishes this section with a summary that begins, "There is no one righteous, not even one. There is no one who understands; there is no one who seeks God" (3:10–11), and ends, "There is no fear of God before their eyes" (v. 18). The goal of Romans 1:18–3:20? "So that every mouth may be shut and the whole world may become subject to God's judgment. For no one will be justified in his sight by the works of the law, because the knowledge of sin comes through the law" (3:19–20).

Paul's strategy is shrewd. Before we can embrace God's good news of salvation, we must understand the bad news of our sin and what it deserves—the wrath of a holy and just God. Paul presents sin and judgment not as ends in themselves but as preparation for the gospel of God's grace. Each one of us is guilty in God's eyes, unable to rescue oneself, and therefore in need of a Savior.

Justification's Source: God's Grace

Paul juxtaposes Adam's sin and Christ's righteousness: "If by the one man's trespass, death reigned through that one man, how much more will those

---

[23] James D. G. Dunn, *Romans 1–8*, WBC (Dallas: Word, 1988), 168.

who receive the overflow of grace and the gift of righteousness reign in life through the one man, Jesus Christ" (Rom 5:17). Paul contrasts the reign of death begun by Adam's sin with the reign of life brought by Christ. The apostle upsets the balance between the two Adams and their influence on their people by writing not of life reigning through Christ but of *those* who will reign through him. Far greater than the deleterious influence of Adam's sin, Christ's saving work produces an "overflow of grace and the gift of righteousness" that causes his people to reign in eternal life. Moo correctly says that "righteousness" here is "clearly the status of a new relationship with God."[24] It is the status of those justified by the "overflow of God's grace" in Jesus.

It is no surprise, then, that Scripture combines grace and justification:

They are justified freely by his grace through the redemption that is in Christ Jesus. (Rom 3:24)

He poured out his Spirit on us abundantly through Jesus Christ our Savior so that, having been justified by his grace, we may become heirs with the hope of eternal life. (Titus 3:6–7)

Scripture speaks clearly: the ultimate source of the justification of God's people is his matchless grace. Luther explains it beautifully:

Rather than seeking its own good, the love of God flows forth and bestows good. Therefore sinners are attractive because they are loved; they are not loved because they are attractive. . . . Thus Christ says: "For I came not to call the righteous, but sinners" [Matt. 9:13]. This is the love of the cross, born of the cross, which turns in the direction where it does not find good which it may enjoy, but where it may confer good upon the bad and needy person.[25]

Justification's Basis: Christ's Work

The Bible paints a panoramic picture of Christ's saving accomplishment. It begins with the essential precondition for redemption—the incarnation—and

---

[24] Moo, *The Epistle to the Romans*, 339 (see chap. 2, n. 62).
[25] Martin Luther, *Luther's Works, Vol. 31: Career of the Reformer I*, ed. Jaroslav Jan Pelikan, Hilton C. Oswald, and Helmut T. Lehmann, vol. 31 (Philadelphia: Fortress, 1999), 57.

ends with its essential finale—the second coming. In between are Christ's sinless life, death, resurrection, ascension, session, pouring out the Spirit at Pentecost, and intercession. But the core, the heart and soul of Jesus's saving work, is his death and resurrection.

When Paul summarizes the gospel he preaches, he includes both Christ's death and resurrection: "I passed on to you as most important what I also received: that Christ died for our sins according to the Scriptures, that he was buried, that he was raised on the third day according to the Scriptures" (1 Cor 15:3–4). Moreover, the apostle also includes both of Christ's most important deeds when speaking of the ground of justification: Christ "was delivered up for our trespasses and raised for our justification" (Rom 4:25).

People commonly err when they are perplexed by how a God who is love could possibly condemn sinners. They are correct in asserting "God is love" (1 John 4:8, 16). They are incorrect in overlooking that fact that before John says "God is love," he says "God is light and there is absolutely no darkness in him" (1:5). God is both absolutely holy and absolutely loving. To compromise his holiness or his love is to distort the biblical picture of his person. As we saw in the last section, God's grace is the source of our justification. Without his incomparable love we would never be saved. But how can a loving God declare sinners righteous when they are so unrighteous? How in his love can he maintain his moral integrity and justify the ungodly?

The answer lies in the complexity of Christ's cross. Jesus, our substitute, saves because his cross affects our standing before God both negatively and positively. Negatively, Christ's death turns away God's wrath (Rom 3:25–26); positively, his death procures righteousness (5:18–19). These are two ways in which Scripture presents Christ's cross as the basis of justification. We'll treat the former first. Four times Scripture teaches that Christ's death is a propitiation (Rom 3:25–26; Heb 2:17; 1 John 2:2; 4:10).

Christ's Death Is a Propitiation

Romans 3:25–26 is the key because it is most developed. Paul had set forth Roman's thematic statement in 1:17: the revelation of God's righteousness. Then in 1:18–3:20 he expanded on another topic—the revelation of God's wrath against sinners. Now he returns to the epistle's theme: "But now, apart from the law, the righteousness of God has been revealed, attested by the

Law and the Prophets" (3:21). All humans are sinners who lack this saving righteousness and gain it by trusting Christ (vv. 22–23).

God's grace justifies sinners through Christ's vicarious death, which is both a redemption (Rom 3:24) and a propitiation (vv. 25–26). This is Scripture's main text on propitiation:

> Christ Jesus, whom God put forward as a propitiation by his blood, to be received by faith. This was to show God's righteousness, because in his divine forbearance he had passed over former sins. It was to show his righteousness at the present time, so that he might be just and the justifier of the one who has faith in Jesus. (vv. 24–26 ESV)

In light of Scripture's witness to God's holiness, justice, and love, we must ask: How can God save sinners while keeping his moral integrity intact and satisfying his justice? The answer lies in these verses. In his forbearance, his clemency, God did not bring immediate judgment on sins committed before Christ came. Instead, he "passed over former sins" (Rom 3:25 ESV). He forgave OT saints on the basis of final atonement to be made in the future. He forgave them ultimately based on the work of Christ to come and immediately based on the OT saints' response to the gospel message in the OT sacrifices. Although it was "impossible for the blood of bulls and goats to take away sins," they depicted the gospel (Heb 10:4). But God still had to deal with sin; he had to make atonement once and for all with a sacrifice whose efficacy would extend to OT saints (v. 9:15).

God did this when he "put forward [Christ] as a propitiation by his blood" (Rom 3:25 ESV). Luther states it plainly:

> There was no remedy [for guilt and wrath] except for God's only Son to step into our distress and himself become man, to take upon himself the load of awful and eternal wrath and make his own body and blood a sacrifice for sin. And so he did, out of the immeasurably great mercy and love towards us, giving himself up and bearing the sentence of unending wrath and death.[26]

---

[26] Martin Luther, "Epistle Sermon: Twenty-fourth Sunday after Trinity," cited in John Nicholas Lenker, ed., *The Precious and Sacred Writings of Martin Luther* (Minneapolis: Luther Press, 1909), 9:43–45. We owe this quote to Stephen J.

Christ died in our place, dying the death we should have died. God punished his Son with the punishment we sinners deserved. God thus showed "his righteousness at the present time, so that he might be just and the justifier of the one who has faith in Jesus" (v. 26 ESV). God's propitiating his justice in the work of Christ enables God to remain holy and just while justly declaring righteous all who believe in Jesus.

Christ's Death Procures Righteousness

Jesus's cross not only satisfies God's wrath; it also gains the righteousness we need for justification. Paul presents this in his powerful contrast between the first and second Adams:

> As through one trespass there is condemnation for everyone, so also through one righteous act there is justification leading to life for everyone. For just as through one man's disobedience the many were made sinners, so also through the one man's obedience the many will be made righteous. (Rom 5:18–19)

Paul first contrasts Adam's "one trespass" with Christ's "one righteous act" (v. 18). Adam's sin brought condemnation; Christ's act of dying on the cross brought "justification leading to [eternal] life" (v. 18). The apostle then says basically the same thing in different words. Adam's primal sin made many to be sinners in God's sight, and Christ's obedience to death, "even death on a cross" (Phil 2:8), made many to be righteous in God's sight (Rom 5:19).

Paul presents the two Adams as *accomplishing* condemnation and justification for their respective people. Moo correctly interprets Christ's deed in verse 18: "Paul wants to show, not how Christ has made *available* righteousness and life for all, but how Christ has secured the benefits of that righteousness for all who belong to him."[27] Some have interpreted verse 19 in moral categories, but Moo asserts that this is a misinterpretation: "To be 'righteous' does not mean to be morally upright, but to be judged acquitted, cleared of all charges, in the heavenly judgment."[28]

Wellum, *Christ Alone: The Uniqueness of Christ as Savior* (Grand Rapids: Zondervan, 2017), 174.

[27] Moo, *The Epistle to the Romans*, 343.

[28] Moo, 345.

Our performance is never the ground of our justification. Rather, Scripture consistently presents that ground as Christ's saving accomplishment, presented in terms both negative (turning away God's wrath in propitiation) and positive (securing righteousness by his substitutionary death). We are not justified by any faith but by faith in the Christ who atoned for us.

Justification's Means: Faith, Not Works

Paul repeatedly teaches that the instrument that connects us to God's grace in justification is faith. This appears already in his purpose statement, as the italicized words show: "I am not ashamed of the gospel, because it is the power of God for salvation *to everyone who believes*, first to the Jew, and also to the Greek. For in it the righteousness of God is revealed from faith to faith, just as it is written: The righteous will live *by faith*" (Rom 1:16–17).

After dealing with God's judgment on sin from 1:18–3:20, Paul returns to his purpose statement and quickly explains what he is talking about: "The righteousness of God is through faith in Jesus Christ to all who believe" (3:22). Even when explaining propitiation Paul says that it is received "by faith" (v. 25). A verse later he tells of God's justifying "the one who has faith in Jesus" (v. 26). In case we missed it, in the next five verses he underlines the fact that people are justified by faith, not works:

> Where, then, is boasting? It is excluded. By what kind of law? By one of works? No, on the contrary, by a law of faith. For we conclude that a person is justified by faith apart from the works of the law. Or is God the God of Jews only? Is he not the God of Gentiles too? Yes, of Gentiles too, since there is one God who will justify the circumcised by faith and the uncircumcised through faith. Do we then nullify the law through faith? Absolutely not! On the contrary, we uphold the law. (vv. 27–31)

Paul devotes the next chapter of Romans to a discussion of faith and teaches that faith and grace are inseparable—we cannot have one without the other: "This is why the promise is by faith, so that it may be according to grace, to guarantee it to all the descendants—not only to the one who is of the law but also to the one who is of Abraham's faith. He is the father of us all" (Rom 4:16). Paul is even more emphatic later in Romans: "Now if [it is] by grace, then [salvation] is not by works; otherwise grace ceases to be grace" (11:6). As means of salvation, faith and works are antithetical. Grace's natural complement is faith, and faith alone is the means God uses to declare us righteous.

Justification's Imputation: Christ's Righteousness

When God unites believers to Christ, they gain all of his spiritual benefits. Justification, therefore, is never alone, and believing sinners are not merely justified. Simultaneously believers are regenerated, declared righteous, adopted into God's family, set apart as God's saints for a lifetime of growth in holiness, and more. So, although justification itself does not involve moral transformation, no one is justified who is not also transformed by God's grace in regeneration and progressive sanctification. However, to define justification in terms of transformation is to confuse soteriological categories and to harm God's people. It harms them because it encourages them to strive to please God in their lives (a good thing) as a means of being accepted by him (a bad thing). Believers are accepted by God once and for all when they believe in Christ, and he declares them righteous because of Christ's righteousness.

Justification is a forensic term that portrays God as the Judge who declares righteous all believers in his Son. God works moral improvement in the lives of his people as a result of regeneration and by means of sanctification, but not in justification. But if our good works are not the basis of God's declaring us righteous, what is? The answer is the imputation of Christ's righteousness to believers, the topic to which we now turn.

Imputation is the act of crediting something to someone or something. Scripture teaches three imputations: the imputation of original sin, the imputation of our sin to Christ, and the imputation of his righteousness to us. First, God imputes Adam's primal sin to the human race (Rom 5:18–19). Second, God imputes our sin to his crucified Son: "He made the one who did not know sin to be sin for us. . . ." (2 Cor 5:21a). Third, God imputes Christ's righteousness to everyone who believes in him: ". . . so that in him we might become the righteousness of God" (5:21b).

Our concern is with the third imputation. Affirming this imputation is not based on any one passage alone but on the combination of three passages, as Brian Vickers has shown:[29]

> Abraham believed God, and it was credited to him for righteousness. (Rom 4:3)

> Just as through one man's disobedience the many were made sinners, so also through the one man's obedience the many will be made righteous. (5:19)

> He made the one who did not know sin to be sin for us, so that in him we might become the righteousness of God. (2 Cor 5:21)

The first passage looks back at God's appearing to Abram in a vision and declaring, "Do not be afraid, Abram. I am your shield; your reward will be very great" (Gen 15:1). When God promises childless Abram countless offspring, Abraham takes God at his word, and Scripture says, "Abram believed the LORD, and he credited it to him as righteousness" (v. 6). Paul cites this text to prove that Abraham (and everyone else) is justified by faith, not works: "'Abraham believed God, and it was credited to him for righteousness.' Now to the one who works, pay is not credited as a gift, but as something owed. But to the one who does not work, but believes on him who justifies the ungodly, his faith is credited for righteousness" (Rom 4:3–5).

Through the means of faith God imputes (credits) righteousness to Abraham and everyone else who trusts Christ as Lord and Savior.

The second passage, which we have already studied, reveals that, just as Adam's disobedience in the garden of Eden "made many sinners," so Christ's obedience unto death will make "many righteous" (Rom 5:19). In a previous volume we observed,

> To those in Christ, God graciously imputes Christ's righteousness. At precisely this point the contrast between Adam and Christ emerges, and the wonder of grace shines brightly. As sons and

---

[29] Brian Vickers, *Jesus' Blood and Righteousness: Paul's Theology of Imputation* (Wheaton: Crossway, 2006); *Justification by Grace through Faith*, EBT (Phillipsburg, NJ: P&R, 2013).

daughters of Adam we enter the world spiritually dead and sinners. But God, in his grace, has reversed the baleful results of Adam's sin by imputing the righteousness of Christ to us. Such an imputation is an act of grace; it is totally undeserved.[30]

The third passage is justly celebrated: "He made the one who did not know sin to be sin for us, so that in him we might become the righteousness of God" (2 Cor 5:21). Luther labeled this text a happy exchange: "Lord Jesus, you are my righteousness, just as I am your sin. You have taken upon yourself what is mine and have given to me what is yours. You have taken upon yourself what you were not and have given to me what I was not."[31]

God so identified the sinless Christ with our sin that he could say, "He made him . . . to be sin." In Peter's words, "Christ also suffered for sins once for all, the righteous for the unrighteous, that he might bring you to God" (1 Pet 3:18). By virtue of union with Christ we "become the righteousness of God"—God imputes Christ's righteousness to us and accepts us. Harris is clear about the meaning of 2 Cor 5:21:

> Although the term λογίζομαι ["to account, reckon"] is not used in v. 21 (but cf. v. 19), it is not inappropriate to perceive in this verse a double imputation: sin was reckoned to Christ's account (v. 21a), so that righteousness is reckoned to our account (v. 21b). . . . As a result of God's imputing something that was extrinsic to him, namely sin, believers have something imputed to them that was extrinsic to them, namely righteousness.[32]

In another epistle Paul shares the result of this imputation. He regards knowing Christ as his supreme value and is willing to give up everything else. His highest goal is to "gain Christ and be found in him, not having a righteousness of my own from the law, but one that is through faith in Christ—the righteousness from God based on faith" (Phil 3:8–9).

---

[30] Thomas R. Schreiner, *Romans*, BECNT (Grand Rapids: Baker, 1998), 290.

[31] Luther, *Works* 48:12–13; ed. Helmut T. Lehmann (Minneapolis: Fortress, 2002).

[32] Murray J. Harris, *The Second Epistle to the Corinthians*, NIGTC (Grand Rapids: Eerdmans, 2005), 455.

Combining these three texts yields good results. God, the supreme Judge, declares righteous all who trust Jesus's death and resurrection for salvation. God declares us righteous in Christ and accepts us based on his righteousness, not our own. This is what Luther called "alien righteousness." "Now it is certain that Christ or the righteousness of Christ, since it outside of us and foreign to us, cannot be laid hold of by our works."[33] The imputation of Christ's righteousness to believing sinners explains a lot. It explains how Paul says believers "are justified freely by his grace through the redemption that is in Christ Jesus" (Rom 3:24). And it explains how Paul could say of a believer, "To the one who does not work, but believes on him who justifies the ungodly, his faith is credited for righteousness" (4:5). It explains why Luther regarded justification as the article on which the church stands or falls[34] and why Calvin called it the "main hinge" or "principal axis" on which Christianity turns.[35] As with every other biblical teaching, free justification redounds to the glory of God.

---

[33] Martin Luther, "Third Disputation Concerning Justification, 1536," *Luther's Works* (St. Louis: Concordia, 1955–2019), 34:153.

[34] Martin Luther, *What Luther Says: An Anthology*, ed. Ewald M. Plass, 3 vols. (St. Louis: Concordia: 1959), 2:704n5. More precisely Luther said, "If this article stands, the church stands; if this article collapses, the church collapses."

[35] Calvin, *Institutes of the Christian Religion*, 3.11.1 (2:726).

7

Adoption

The meaning of righteousness and of justification has been sharply disputed in scholarship and through church history. The same disputes don't exist when it comes to adoption. In speaking of adoption, we are thinking of texts that refer to human beings' becoming God's sons (or daughters), to their being children of God, or to adoption itself. The word "adoption" never appears in the OT, though the concept exists in that God includes Israel, which is not the Lord's natural son, within his family by virtue of his choosing Israel to be his people. Though the term (Gk. *huiothesia*) isn't found in the Greek OT, Paul uses it in describing Israel's relationship to the Lord in Rom 9:4.

Exegetical Foundations

Israel as God's Son

When Moses returned to Egypt, he commanded Pharaoh to allow Israel freedom to worship the Lord in the wilderness (Exod 4:23). The special place Israel occupied with reference to Yahweh is clear, since he designates Israel as his "son," his "firstborn" (v. 22). The firstborn son enjoyed special status in Israel and in the culture of the day by virtue of primogeniture (cf. Gen 48:14–20). If Pharaoh refused to accede to the Lord's command, then the Lord would slay *his* firstborn (Exod 4:23)—as he in fact does on the night of the first Passover.

Israel's special relationship to the Lord as God's son is sprinkled throughout the rest of the OT, though the theme isn't prominent. Since Israel is
God's son, they are to reflect that sonship in the way they live, supremely in
their loyalty to the Lord. They must not compromise by doing anything that
would indicate subservience to other gods: "You are sons of the LORD your
God; do not cut yourselves or make a bald spot on your head on behalf of the
dead" (Deut 14:1). Cutting oneself and making bald spots probably signified devotion to other gods. Moses predicts in the song he taught Israel that
they would not be faithful children: "His people have acted corruptly toward
him; this is their defect—they are not his children but a devious and crooked
generation. Is this how you repay the LORD, you foolish and senseless people? Isn't he your Father and Creator? Didn't he make you and sustain you?"
(32:5–6; cf. Isa 1:2). The Lord was Israel's kind Father, their creator and
preserver, but they responded as people who were not his children, rejecting
his provision and care.

Since the theme of sonship isn't common in the OT, Jeremiah 3 stands
out, as the language of sonship and fatherhood appears throughout the
chapter. Jeremiah calls Israel to repentance, to turn away from their sin and
idolatry and turn to the Lord. Judah is described as a spiritual harlot for worshipping other gods (vv. 1–3). The Lord reminds his people of their defection by emphasizing that he is their Father: "Haven't you recently called to
me, 'My Father! You were my friend in my youth'" (v. 4). The people aren't
identified as sons here, but the Lord is designated as Father, and he reminds
them of their friendship and devotion in the past, a friendship and intimacy
that have been lost as the people have wandered from their God. The Lord's
kindness is expressed in that he continues to implore Judah and Israel to
return to him. Judah (the southern kingdom) has seen the harlotry and judgment (exile) of Israel (the northern kingdom), and yet she continues to sin
and refuses to repent (vv. 6–13). The Lord implores his people, "Return, you
faithless children—this is the LORD's declaration—for I am your master, and
I will take you, one from a city and two from a family, and I will bring you
to Zion" (v. 14). Even though Judah is guilty of spiritual adultery, the Lord
will forgive, restore, and actually unite the nation again. No one will miss the
ark of the covenant, since the Lord's presence will be present powerfully and
intimately among this people (vv. 15–18).

The Lord's amazing love, despite his people's sin, is evident from Jer 3:19–20: "I thought, 'How I long to make you my sons and give you a desirable land, the most beautiful inheritance of all the nations.' I thought, 'You will call me "My Father" and never turn away from me.' However, as a woman may betray her lover, so you have betrayed me, house of Israel. This is the Lord's declaration" (vv. 19–20). The Lord's desire was to make Israel his sons and to bless them in a beautiful land. The relationship would be one of love and affection. Israel would look to the Lord as its kind Father and never seek protection or help from any other source. Israel, however, has proven to be an unfaithful son and like an unfaithful wife, defecting from the Lord and giving its affection and loyalty to other gods. Still, the Lord, as the Father of Israel, is wondrously patient and forgiving and still stretches out his hands to Israel and implores them, "Return, you faithless children. I will heal your unfaithfulness" (v. 22). God's fatherhood signifies in Jeremiah 3 his tender love of his people.

We also see the Lord's fatherhood of his people and Israel's role as God's son in texts that speak of the future hope of Israel. For instance, Isa 43:1–7 predicts Israel's return from exile to Babylon. The people will come from east and west and from north and south back to the land: "Bring my sons from far away, and my daughters from the ends of the earth, everyone who bears my name and is created for my glory" (vv. 6–7). We have a hint here that the Lord will bestow mercy on his sons and daughters from Israel because they are his covenant people, because they are his children, because they belong to him and he is particularly glorified through them.

Near the end of Isaiah, we find a remarkable prayer by Israel for mercy (Isa 63:7–64:14), beseeching the Lord to renew his work in the nation. Israel reflects on the Lord's goodness, compassion, and faithful love for the people (v. 63:7). The Lord adopted them as his people, his children: "'They are indeed my people, children who will not be disloyal,' and he became their Savior" (v. 8). Israel's role as God's children indicates their special covenant relationship with him, and because of his covenant with them he saved and preserved them (v. 9). Nevertheless, Israel rebelled against the Holy Spirit, and the Lord sent the nation into exile (v. 10). The prophet asks where is the Lord who brought them through the sea, the one who put his Spirit among them, brought them into the land, and glorified his great name (vv. 11–14).

Isaiah then prays for the Lord to look and see the plight of Israel, to remember his zeal, his strength, and his compassion for his people (63:15). And why should the Lord show mercy? Isaiah gives the answer in verse 16: "You are our Father, even though Abraham does not know us and Israel doesn't recognize us. You, LORD, are our Father; your name is Our Redeemer from Ancient Times." Israel is the Lord's dear son, and he is the Father of his people. Even if Abraham and Jacob would not recognize Israel, presumably because of the depth of their sin, as the Father of his people the Lord will not abandon them. The prophet prays, then, that the Lord would come down and fulfill his promises, even though the nation has sinned so blatantly (Isa 64:1–7). The sin of the people is so profound and so defiling that it could lead to despair, but still there is hope in the Lord: "Yet LORD, you are our Father; we are the clay, and you are our potter; we all are the work of your hands. LORD, do not be terribly angry or remember our iniquity forever. Please look—all of us are your people!" (vv. 8–9). Israel has no claim on the Lord, but the Lord is still their Father, and they plead with the Lord to shape them as a potter shapes the clay, to forgive them of their terrible sins, and to remember that they, his dear children, are still his people. They ask the Lord to restore the nation (vv. 10–12).

Jeremiah's reference to sonship sounds out themes similar to those in Isaiah. Jeremiah in chapters 1–29 pounds home the judgment that will come upon Judah for its sin. Chapters 30–33 turn the corner, however, and are often called the book of comfort, for the Lord promises that he will restore the people and make a new covenant with them (Jer 31:31–34). Exile in Babylon will not be the final word; the Lord will bring them back to the land and to Jerusalem and renew and comfort them. The new lease on life is communicated in the promise, "His children will be as in past days" (30:20). Israel's relationship with the Lord will be restored, and the glory of the past days when God smiled upon them will be their portion again. Israel is called upon to burst forth with praise and joy since the Lord will restore his people and bring them back from Babylon (31:7–8): "They will come weeping, but I will bring them back with consolation. I will lead them to wadis filled with water, by a smooth way where they will not stumble, for I am Israel's Father, and Ephraim is my firstborn" (v. 9). Sorrow will not be their permanent possession and ultimate reality, for they will see the Lord's goodness again and will dance and sing for joy (vv. 12–13)!

And why is the Lord so kind? One reason is that he is Israel's father, and Ephraim (which stands for the entire nation here) is his precious and beloved firstborn son. The Lord will never forget or abandon his children. Yes, Israel was filled with grief and sorrow because of its sin, because it went into exile (vv. 15–19). But a new day is promised, a day of restoration and redemption. And Israel's sonship is again given as the explanation: "Isn't Ephraim a precious son to me, a delightful child? Whenever I speak against him, I certainly still think about him. Therefore, my inner being yearns for him; I will truly have compassion on him. This is the LORD's declaration" (v. 20). Despite Israel's sin, Ephraim (the whole nation) is still God's beloved son, and God as Father won't forsake his delightful child. Like a father with a child, the final word isn't judgment but compassion.

We find a similar theme in Hosea. Judgment will come upon Israel for its spiritual adultery, for its forsaking of the Lord. At the same time, Hosea teaches that judgment isn't the final reality. After the prophet rehearses the judgment of Israel, we find a word of promise: "Yet the number of the Israelites will be like the sand of the sea, which cannot be measured or counted. And in the place where they were told: You are not my people, they will be called: Sons of the living God" (Hos 1:10). Despite Israel's harlotry, the promise made to Abraham (Gen 22:17) and Jacob (32:12) that their offspring would be as numerous as the sand hasn't been withdrawn but will certainly be fulfilled. Israel's sonship is still a reality. The same theme appears again in Hosea 11, where the prophet predicts that the northern kingdom will be exiled to Assyria. Still, the Lord will not abandon his people. He won't destroy them totally and permanently as he did Admah and Zeboiim when Sodom and Gomorrah were annihilated; he will bring them back from exile (Hos 11:8–11). The chapter begins with a reminder of Israel's sonship: "When Israel was a child, I loved him, and out of Egypt I called my son" (v. 1). Clearly Hosea refers here to Israel's exodus from Egypt, in which the Lord rescued his people from Egyptian slavery. Why does Hosea refer to Israel's history here? He picks up on Israel's history to remind the people of how the Lord delivered them from exile in the past, and the Lord's past work becomes the basis for confidence in his future deliverance from Assyria. Israel is still the Lord's son!

The Davidic King as God's Son

Israel is God's son, but the Lord also designates the Davidic king as his son. We see this when the Lord makes a covenant with David, a covenant that promises that the Davidic dynasty will never end. The Lord will fulfill his covenant promises made to Abraham through a Davidic king. Furthermore, the Davidic king will be God's son: "I will be his father, and he will be my son. When he does wrong, I will discipline him with a rod of men and blows from mortals" (2 Sam 7:14). Kings will experience God-ordained consequences for their sins, but the Lord's faithful covenant love will never be withdrawn from the Davidic line (vv. 15–16).

The author of Psalm 89 reflects on the same promise. The Davidic king recognizes his dependence upon and relationship to God: "He will call to me, 'You are my Father, my God, the rock of my salvation'" (v. 26). Since the king is God's son and the Lord is his Father, he is assured that the great promises made in the Davidic covenant will be fulfilled. The Lord assures the king, "I will also make him my firstborn, greatest of the kings of the earth" (v. 27). If Israel was the firstborn of the Lord, so too is the king. Indeed, "firstborn" signifies the king's sovereignty and rule, for the king will be the means by which the commission to rule the world, originally given to Adam (Gen 1:26–27), will be realized. The condition present in 2 Sam 7:14 appears again in Ps 89:30–32: "If his sons abandon my instruction and do not live by my ordinances, if they dishonor my statutes and do not keep my commands, then I will call their rebellion to account with the rod, their iniquity with blows" (cf. 132:12). Still, the Lord will not abandon his covenant with his son; it will be fulfilled (89:33–37)!

The promises for the Davidic king, God's son, are relayed in Psalm 2. David considers the opposition of the nations to the Lord in this psalm. The Lord is amused and angered by the opposition, for he has installed his own king—David—in Zion (vv. 4–6). David reflects on the Lord's promise to him in verse 7: "I will declare the LORD's decree. He said to me, 'You are my Son; today I have become your Father.'" The Lord has become David's father by appointing him as king. The promise of universal rule, the inheritance of the nations, will be realized through a Davidic king (vv. 8–9).

How do we put together Israel as God's son and the Davidic king as the son of God? What is the relationship between these two realities? As the leader of the nation, the Davidic king represents Israel before God. He is the son of God par excellence, and so there is a sense in which Israel's sonship is due to its relationship with the Davidic king.

Jesus as God's Son

The purpose of this chapter isn't to establish Jesus as the Son of God, for our subject is restricted to soteriology. Still, we should note that Jesus is often identified as the Son of God. We find the expression more than thirty times in the Gospels, and the word "Son" alone is also quite common. Jesus is identified as the "Son of David" in the first verse of the NT (Matt 1:1), and in Luke his sonship is also linked with his ruling on David's throne (Luke 1:35). The son called out of Egypt is surely Israel in the historical context of Hosea (Hos 11:1), but Matthew sees these words fulfilled in Jesus (Matt 2:15), and even the very use of "Son" with reference to Jesus suggests he is the true Israel. Jesus as the Son is the true Israel, the true Son of David, and the very Son of God. These arguments have been made elsewhere. Here we want to suggest that believers are sons of God, children of God, and adopted through Jesus, the Son of God. Their sonship derives from and is rooted in his sonship. We could say, then, that there is a sense in which the church is the true Israel, the true son of God, without denying that there will be a future eschatological salvation for ethnic Israel (Rom 11:26).

Believers as God's Adopted Children

We should begin by reflecting on the wonder and joy and grace of being God's children, of being members of his family.[1] "See what great love the Father has given us that we should be called God's children—and we are! The reason the world does not know us is that it didn't know him. Dear friends, we are God's children now, and what we will be has not yet been

---

[1] For helpful academic studies on adoption see Trevor J. Burke, *Adoption into God's Family: Exploring a Pauline Metaphor*, NSBT 22 (Downers Grove: InterVarsity, 2006); James M. Scott, *Adoption as Sons of God: An Exegetical Investigation into the Background of Huiothesia in the Pauline Corpus*, WUNT 2/48 (Tübingen: Mohr Siebeck, 1992). For a semi-popular book, see Robert A. Peterson, *Adopted by God* (Phillipsburg, NJ: P&R, 2001).

revealed" (1 John 3:1–2). We can imagine a scenario in which believers were forgiven of their sins but not invited to be members of God's family—a scenario in which God would not be their Father. But this is not the case! Jesus regularly taught his disciples that God was their Father. Only believers know God as the Father who saves them (John 8:19, 41–42), and the father of unbelievers is the devil (v. 44). Indeed, only those who know Jesus truly know the Father (5:22–23; 14:7–11; 15:23). Jesus invited believers to address God as "Father" in the Lord's Prayer (Matt 6:9; Luke 11:2). It was God's intention for Jesus to be "the firstborn among many brothers and sisters" (Rom 8:29). The author of Hebrews affirms that "Jesus is not ashamed to call" us "brothers and sisters" (Heb 2:11; cf. v. 12), and we are "children" of God because God gave us to Jesus as his brothers and sisters (v. 13).

The great blessing of the covenant with David, that he would be God's son (2 Sam 7:14), is democratized and given to all believers, as Paul's allusion to this verse shows: "I will be a Father to you, and you will be sons and daughters to me, says the Lord Almighty" (2 Cor 6:18). God's fatherhood signifies his authority over believers but also his protection and care, for as our Father he knows and provides what we need (Matt 6:8, 26, 32). As Father he grants "good things to those who ask him" (7:11).

It is an inestimable privilege to be the children of God, one reserved for those who "receive" Jesus, for those who "believe in his name" (John 1:12; cf. 12:36). One isn't a child of God simply because one is a child of Abraham. As the Baptist says, "God is able to raise up children for Abraham from these stones" (Matt 3:9; Luke 3:8). Paul makes the same point in Rom 9:7–8: "Neither is it the case that all of Abraham's children are his descendants. On the contrary, 'your offspring will be traced through Isaac.' That is, it is not the children by physical descent who are God's children, but the children of the promise are considered to be the offspring." The children of God are not restricted to Jews but include Gentiles also (John 11:52), and thus the promise given to Abraham that there would be a worldwide family (Gen 12:3) is fulfilled.

Those who are adopted as God's children are inducted into the family by virtue of God's grace, as is evident in Eph 1:5: "He predestined us to be adopted as sons through Jesus Christ for himself, according to the good pleasure of his will." People must believe to become God's children, and such belief is traced to God's grace. For human beings to become God's children they must be set free from their sin, and this freedom was secured through Christ's death; he gave his life "to redeem those under the law, so that we might receive adoption as sons. And because you are sons, God sent the Spirit of his Son into our hearts, crying, "*Abba*, Father!" So you are no longer a slave but a son, and if a son, then God has made you an heir" (Gal 4:5–7). Those who are sons are those who are redeemed, and redemption secures adoption as sons. Those who are God's sons, God's children, know they are God's children because they gladly cry out "*Abba*, Father!" Paul makes the same point in Rom 8:15–16, where he says that those who exclaim that God is their dear Father have the witness in themselves that they are God's children. The Spirit assures believers that they are truly God's children. Paul assures the Gentile Galatians that they, like Isaac, are the children of God, the true heirs of the promise (Gal 4:21–31).

Those who are adopted as God's children show they are the children of God by the way they live. Jesus declares in one of his most famous sayings, "Blessed are the peacemakers, for they will be called sons of God" (Matt 5:9). Those who make peace will be identified as God's sons on the last day, whereas those who cause dissensions don't belong to God. The new life of God's children is clear also in Romans, where Paul remarks, "All those led by God's Spirit are God's sons" (8:14). Those who are truly God's children demonstrate their sonship by their obedience, which is imperfect yet present as demonstrable evidence of new life. We find the same theme in 1 John: "This is how God's children and the devil's children become obvious. Whoever does not do what is right is not of God, especially the one who does not love his brother or sister" (3:10). Certainly, John isn't suggesting perfection, and yet being a child of God isn't an abstraction; it must be seen in the real world in a new way of life. John makes the same point in 5:2: "This is how we know that we love God's children: when we love God and obey his commands." Those who claim to be the children of God manifest their family relationship by their love for God, and love for God manifests itself in obedience— in a new way of life.

We see similar themes in Ephesians: "Be imitators of God, as dearly loved children" (Eph 5:1). The indicative grounds the imperative, and thus the ground for the obedience of believers is that they are "dearly loved children." We imitate God not so that he will love us but because he already does. We are planted securely in the soil of his love and grace in Christ Jesus, and that wonderful love bestowed on us should be evident in the way we live, so that people will recognize that we are children of the One who sent his Son to die for us (v. 2). As Paul puts it in verse 8, "Now you are light in the Lord. Live as children of light."

Believers are instructed to "work out your own salvation with fear and trembling" (Phil 2:12), but it is imperative to see that everything believers do is the result of God's transformation of the human being, so that both desire and doing flow from his grace (v. 13). Believers are to be distinguished from Israel, which fell prey to "grumbling and arguing" (v. 14). Paul alludes in verse 15 to Deut 32:5, where Israel showed that they didn't belong to God, that they were not his children, that they belonged to "a devious and crooked generation." The church of Jesus Christ by its joy reveals that it is "blameless and pure, children of God who are faultless in a crooked and perverted generation, among whom you shine like stars in the world" (Phil 2:15). Those who persevere in the faith (v. 16), who continue to follow the Lord, are the true children of God. John in Revelation teaches the same truth: "The one who conquers will inherit these things, and I will be his God, and he will be my son" (Rev 21:7). Believers are God's sons through the cross of Christ and by virtue of his amazing grace, and God's grace makes a difference in the lives of believers and changes them so that they live like children of the Father.

In the interval between conversion, when believers become God's children and are adopted into his family, and final glorification, believers live out their lives as God's children. The author of Hebrews instructs us, reminding us that God treats us as sons (Heb 12:5–8). Because he loves us as his sons, he disciplines and corrects us, for every loving father disciplines his sons so that they will grow up to be mature adults. Discipline isn't an indication that God doesn't love us as sons but functions as the proof and evidence of his love. On the one hand, believers are *already adopted and God's children* (Rom 8:15; Gal 4:5), but we have seen that there is a *not yet* in terms of our adoption. The pronouncement that we are God's children will be declared and ratified on the last day (cf. Matt 5:9; Phil 2:15; Rev 1:7). Adoption also has an eschatological dimension: "We ourselves who have the Spirit as the firstfruits—we also groan within ourselves, eagerly waiting for adoption, the redemption of our bodies" (Rom 8:23). Believers are now in God's family; they are now God's sons and children, and yet the fullness of adoption will be realized only on the last day, on the day of resurrection, when the bodies of believers are redeemed. Then the full implications of our adoption will be apparent to us and the entire world.

The eschatological character of our sonship reverberates throughout Romans 8. We are now God's children but are also heirs, and yet we won't come into the fullness of our inheritance without suffering (v. 17). There is a sense of anticipation, a sense of longing, a sense of incompleteness that characterizes our present sonship: "The creation eagerly waits with anticipation for God's sons to be revealed" (v. 19). The sonship of believers is tied up with the transformation of the created world: "The creation itself will also be set free from the bondage to decay into the glorious freedom of God's children" (v. 21). As the children of God, we are free now, but we await the day when our freedom is complete and the entire world is changed as well.

Summary

Even though the theme isn't prominent in the OT, the Lord is the Father of Israel and Israel is his son. Since Israel is God's son, his firstborn, God promised to fulfill his saving promises to them, even when they sinned in dramatic ways. The Davidic king also was the son of God, representing the nation before God. When we come to the NT we learn that Jesus is God's true Son and that all those who are children of God, all those who are adopted, are adopted by virtue of the atoning work of Jesus Christ. The wonder and glory of being God's son is celebrated in the NT, and our sonship reveals God's amazing love and care for us. At the same time, believers are to live in a way that befits their adoption so that they reflect to the world the character of their Father. The adoption of believers is an already-but-not-yet reality. Believers are now adopted, but the fullness of their adoption will be consummated on the last day, when believers are granted new bodies at the resurrection.

Systematic Formulations

We build upon the solid exegetical foundation to explore a systematic theology of adoption. This vital yet neglected teaching is perhaps the warmest of the NT, as Packer reminds us:

If you want to judge how well a person understands Christianity, find out how much he makes of the thought of being God's child, and having God as his Father. If this is not the thought that prompts and controls his worship and prayers and his whole outlook on life, it means that he does not understand Christianity very well at all. For everything that Christ taught, everything that makes the New Testament new, and better than the Old, everything that is distinctively Christian as opposed to merely Jewish, is summed up in the knowledge of the Fatherhood of God. "Father" is the Christian name for God.[2]

Adoption's Need: Bondage

As with all aspects of the application of salvation, adoption is best understood against humans' need for it. We need adoption because, due to the fall and our own sins, we are enslaved to sin. Paul says that before adoption we were "in slavery under the elements of the world" (Gal 4:3), but after adoption it is said of each believer, "You are no longer a slave but a son, and if a son, then God has made you an heir" (v. 7). Adoption is thus God's gracious application of the salvation accomplished by Christ in which God frees slaves to sin and welcomes them into his own family as sons and daughters.

John speaks more strongly than Paul: "This is how God's children and the devil's children become obvious. Whoever does not do what is right is not of God, especially the one who does not love his brother or sister" (1 John 3:10). John divides humanity into two easily observable groups: God's children and the devil's. Yarbrough captures John's idea: "Based on his readers' divine parentage, John is confident that God's true children, like those of the devil, ultimately cannot conceal their identity."[3] Specifically, John points to doing right and loving one another as the litmus tests of true spiritual pedigree. God's children reflect their Father, whom John describes as "light" (1:5) and "love" (4:8, 16).

Scripture also describes people's becoming God's children in another way: regeneration. Here the need is spiritual death that separates people

---

[2] J. I. Packer, *Knowing God*, 20th anniversary edition (Downers Grove: InterVarsity, 1993), 201.

[3] Robert W. Yarbrough, *1–3 John*, BECNT (Grand Rapids: Baker, 2008), 196.

from God. His antidote is to make them alive spiritually, causing them to be born again (John 3:3, 7).

Adoption's Source: God's Love

We will see that the means of adoption is faith in Christ—but is faith its ultimate source? The answer is no. The ultimate source of people's becoming God's children is his will and love. Paul sets this forth in Ephesians 1:

> In love [God] predestined us for adoption to himself as sons through Jesus Christ, according to the purpose of his will, to the praise of his glorious grace, with which he has blessed us in the Beloved. (vv. 4–6 ESV)

> In [Christ] we have also received an inheritance, because we were predestined according to the plan of the one who works out everything in agreement with the purpose of his will. (v. 11)

In the first text God's love for people is behind their sonship. All this accords with the "purpose of his will" and redounds "to the praise of his glorious grace." In the second text believers' inheritance, one result of our adoption, follows from his plan to save.

John likewise traces our sonship to God the Father's awesome love for us: "See what great love the Father has given us that we should be called God's children—and we are!" (1 John 3:1). Adoption highlights the Father's love for his children, as Yarbrough asserts: "The love's greatness lies in its effect: it makes people τέκνα θεοῦ (*tekna theou*, children of God). . . . The love's greatness also lies in its purpose. The Father bestows such love 'in order that' (ἵνα, *hina*) John and his readers might enjoy his familial favor."[4]

Adoption's Basis: Christ's Person and Work

On what basis did God adopt slaves to sin as his beloved children? Did he simply pronounce them his own? No, for he had to redeem them from their state of bondage, and for that the death of his Son was necessary. Thus,

---

[4] Yarbrough, *1–3 John*, 175.

the basis for our adoption is the person and work of Christ. First, his person: Unlike believers, who become sons (and daughters) of God by grace through faith, Christ always has been the eternal Son of God by nature. When Scripture ascribes agency in creation to the Son, it implies his eternal sonship. Paul does so: the Father "has rescued us from the domain of darkness and transferred us into the kingdom of the Son he loves. . . . For everything was created by him, in heaven and on earth, the visible and the invisible, whether thrones or dominions or rulers or authorities—all things have been created through him and for him" (Col 1:13, 16). Hebrews does the same: "In these last days, [God] has spoken to us by his Son. God has appointed him heir of all things and made the universe through him" (Heb 1:2). Moreover, Paul teaches that "When the time came to completion, God sent his Son, born of a woman, born under the law" (Gal 4:4). The Second Person of the Trinity did not become the Son at the time of the incarnation, but he who existed eternally as the Son was "sent" by the Father into the world at his incarnation.

Second, Christ's work: The eternal Son of God died to deliver those enslaved to sin. The atonement motif corresponding to adoption is redemption. This involves three elements: a state of bondage, the payment of a ransom price, and the consequent state of freedom of the sons of God. "When the time came to completion, God sent his Son, born of a woman, born under the law, to redeem those under the law, so that we might receive adoption as sons" (Gal 4:4–5). Earlier in the same epistle Paul more explicitly defines the Son's redemption: "Christ redeemed us from the curse of the law by becoming a curse for us, because it is written, 'Cursed is everyone who is hung on a tree'" (3:13). We lawbreakers were under a curse, the penalty the law threatened to the disobedient. In grace Christ paid our penalty by dying as an accursed man in our place. As a result we enjoy the Christian freedom of God's children. Stott does not overstate the importance of this text: "This is probably the plainest statement in the New Testament on substitution. The curse of the broken law rested on us; Christ redeemed us from it by becoming a curse in our place. The curse that lay on us was transferred to him. He assumed it, that we might escape it."[5]

---

[5] John Stott, *The Cross of Christ* (Downers Grove: InterVarsity 1986), 346.

Adoption's Means: Faith

Like justification, adoption is by grace through faith in Christ. Adoption is all of grace, for as slaves of sin and self we could never redeem ourselves. Psalm 49:7–9 is clear: "Truly no man can ransom another, or give to God the price of his life, for the ransom of their life is costly and can never suffice, that he should live on forever and never see the pit" (ESV). That is why Paul finds redemption only in Christ: "In him we have redemption through his blood, the forgiveness of our trespasses" (Eph 1:7). In fact, Paul expresses our final adoption as redemption: "We ourselves who have the Spirit as the firstfruits—we also groan within ourselves, eagerly waiting for adoption, the redemption of our bodies" (Rom 8:23).

Redemption in Christ is appropriated by faith, as Paul testifies: "Through faith you are all sons of God in Christ Jesus" (Gal 3:26). And, although some think John speaks only of regeneration, not adoption (as indeed John 1:13 does), John 1:12 appears to speak of adoption by faith in Christ: "To all who did receive him, he gave them the right to be children of God, to those who believe in his name." Further, the Spirit enables us to believe, resulting in adoption: "You received the Spirit of adoption, by whom we cry out, *'Abba*, Father!'" (Rom 8:15). "Abba" is an Aramaic word children used to address a dear father, but is not baby-talk. I (Tom) formerly wrote, "Some have concluded that the frequency and intimacy of the term indicates that 'Father' is equivalent to *Abba,* which is then rendered 'Daddy.' Surely Jesus's relationship with God was intimate and unique, and his many references to God as 'Father' are distinctive. Still, it goes beyond the evidence, as James Barr has demonstrated, to conclude that 'Father' should be equated with 'Daddy.'"[6] France concurs with

---

[6] Thomas R. Schreiner, "The Centrality of God in New Testament Theology," *SBJT* 16:1 (Spring 2012), p. 9. James Barr, "'Abba' Isn't 'Daddy.'" *Journal of Theological Studies*, 39:28–47. See also the discussion in Geza Vermes, *The Religion of Jesus the Jew* (Minneapolis: Fortress, 1993), 152-83; and David Michael Crump, *Knocking on Heaven's Door: A New Testament Theology of Petitionary Prayer* (Grand Rapids: Baker, 2006), 97–100. The scholarship of Jeremias is essentially vindicated in the judicious study of Aquila H. I. Lee, *From Messiah to Preexistent Son: Jesus' Self-Consciousness and Early Christian Exegesis of Messianic Psalms*, WUNT 2/192 (Tübingen, Mohr Siebeck, 2005), 122–36. Less convincing is the claim of M. M. Thompson that Jesus's relationship with God as Father does not signal a "new intimacy" with God but reflects the same trust Israel had in God. Marianne Meye Thompson, *The Promise of*

Barr but remarks that Jeremias never intended such a conclusion to be drawn since Abba "conveys the respectful intimacy of a son in a patriarchal family."[7]

Justification and adoption are both pictures of salvation taken from the courtroom. Justification is in the criminal division; adoption is in the family court. Both are by God's grace alone through faith alone in Christ alone. Justification is God's declaring believers righteous by imputing Christ's righteousness to them, while adoption is the Father's welcoming believers into his family as his loved children.

Adoption and Union with Christ

Like every other aspect of the application of salvation, adoption occurs in union with Christ. "Through faith you are all sons of God in Christ Jesus" (Gal 3:26). "In Christ Jesus" here speaks of union with Christ. Paul thus teaches that faith is the means by which the believing Galatians are adopted, and this adoption takes place in union with Christ. A majority of scholars and translations take the phrase "in Christ Jesus" independently and not as the object of "faith." Moo agrees and explains, "Taken independently, these two phrases summarize two key elements of Paul's teaching in Galatians and indeed of his theology as a whole: our relationship with God is established by our union with Christ Jesus, and that union is in turn secured by our faith."[8]

Adoption's Blessings: Children

We enjoy at least five wonderful blessings of the Father's adopting us into his family. First, we belong to our heavenly Father and are a part of his family: "God sent his Son . . . to redeem those under the law, so that we might receive adoption as sons" (Gal 4:4–5). God is our Father and we are his sons or daughters. God meets our deep need to belong by placing us as adult

---

the Father: Jesus and God in the New Testament (Louisville: Westminster John Knox, 2000), 30–32. Nor is Thompson persuasive in casting doubts on whether Jesus's use of Abba reflected Jesus's experience and intimacy with God (2000: 30–32). See the evaluation of Thompson's view in Lee, From Messiah to Preexistent Son, 132–35.

[7] R. T. France, The Gospel of Mark, NIGTC (Grand Rapids: Eerdmans, 2002), 584.

[8] Douglas J. Moo, Galatians, BECNT (Grand Rapids: Baker, 2013), 251.

children into his family. We know God and are known by him. All other believers are our brothers and sisters in Christ.

Second, God gives us the Spirit of sonship, who enables us to call God "Father." Paul writes, "You did not receive a spirit of slavery to fall back into fear. Instead, you received the Spirit of adoption, by whom we cry out, '*Abba*, Father!'" (Rom 8:15). The Holy Spirit, "the Spirit of adoption," draws us to saving faith in the Redeemer Jesus so that we enter God's family. The Spirit also plays a second role, for "The Spirit himself testifies together with our spirit that we are God's children" (v. 16). Mysteriously, the Spirit assures us within that God is our Father and we are his own. He replaces our fear with freedom.[9] God's most important means to assure his children is the promises of his Word. But we rejoice that the hope of those promises "will not disappoint us, because God's love has been poured out in our hearts through the Holy Spirit who was given to us" (Rom 5:5).

Third, by God's grace and Spirit we resemble our Father in heaven. We no longer belong to our father the devil and no longer want to carry out his desires (cf. John 8:44). Instead, we belong to God our Father, love him, and want to please him. "All those led by God's Spirit are God's sons" (Rom 8:14). This does not speak of divine guidance, which is a biblical truth. Rather it speaks of believers' following the Spirit's leadership in holiness and love. By God's enabling grace we do so and thereby resemble our heavenly Father.

Fourth, God disciplines us, his children. Our Father loves and corrects us. The writer to the Hebrews shares tough love with Christians enduring persecution for their faith:

> The Lord disciplines the one he loves and punishes every son he receives. Endure suffering as discipline: God is dealing with you as sons. . . . Furthermore, we had human fathers discipline us, and we respected them. Shouldn't we submit even more to the Father of spirits and live? For they disciplined us for a short time based on what seemed good to them, but he does it for our benefit, so that we can share his holiness. (Heb 12:6–7, 9–10)

---

[9] David M. Kasali, "Romans," *Africa Bible Commentary*, ed. Tokunboh Adeyemo (Grand Rapids: Zondervan, 2006), 1363.

Fifth, we have an inheritance. Like other aspects of our salvation, adoption is both already and not yet: "Dear friends, we are God's children now, and what we will be has not yet been revealed. We know that when he appears, we will be like him because we will see him as he is" (1 John 3:2). Paul teaches that adoption is both a present and a future reality: "You are no longer a slave but a son, and if a son, then God has made you an heir" (Gal 4:7). We are now sons and daughters, and we are also heirs of a future inheritance. Because we are God's sons, we are "also heirs—heirs of God and coheirs with Christ—if indeed we suffer with him so that we may also be glorified with him" (Rom 8:17). In fact, we *long* for our final adoption: "We ourselves who have the Spirit as the firstfruits—we also groan within ourselves, eagerly waiting for adoption, the redemption of our bodies" (v. 23).

8

Sanctification

S anctification has long been regarded as the less important stepchild of justification. Thankfully, today evangelicals are giving it more attention than previously. The good news is that evangelicals basically agree on the theological framework for the doctrine of sanctification. It must be examined within an orthodox understanding of the Trinity, anthropology and hamartiology, Christology (including Jesus's death and resurrection), pneumatology, ecclesiology, and eschatology. The bad news is that, although evangelicals share this common framework, they disagree significantly over the details of sanctification. Before we examine those details, we will lay an exegetical foundation, which will help us evaluate the views of sanctification and prepare us to systematize the doctrine.

Exegetical Foundations

Holiness in the OT

God's Holiness

That which is holy is separate and distinct. In the OT we find such words as "holy" (*qādôš*) and "consecrate" (*qādš*), while in the NT we find "holy" (*hagios*), "sanctification" (*hagiasmos*), "holiness" (*hagiōsynē*), and "sanctify" (*hagiazō*).[1] Certainly the concept is wider than the word, and this must be

---

[1] For a fascinating and helpful study of the meaning of *holiness*, see Peter Gentry, "No One Holy Like the Lord," *Midwestern Journal of Theology* 12 (2013): 17–38.

kept in mind as we consider the subject of sanctification. Still, we can explore the central ideas of sanctification by concentrating on the terms for holiness. Holiness is difficult to define, for the Lord himself in his character is holy, and God himself is ultimately incomprehensible and mysterious; "holy" thus points to the incomparability of the Lord. For instance, we read in Exod 15:11, "Lord, who is like you among the gods? Who is like you, glorious in holiness, revered with praises, performing wonders?" Yahweh is incomparable, different from all other gods. In Isa 6:3 the seraphim cry out, "Holy, holy, holy is the Lord of Armies; his glory fills the whole earth" (cf. Rev 4:8). Since Isaiah recognizes his uncleanness in the presence of the Lord's holiness (Isa 6:5), Yahweh's holiness must include his moral purity. As Isaiah stands in the Lord's presence, he recognizes the distance between God and himself, the greatness of God and his own smallness.

The awesome holiness of God, his holy otherness, his burning purity, is reflected in the call of Moses when he sees the burning bush. The Lord tells Moses not to come closer and to remove his sandals, "for the place where you are standing is holy ground" (Exod 3:5). We see a similar encounter in Joshua 5, where Joshua meets a man with a drawn sword, and Joshua challenges him by asking whose side he is on. The man replies that he isn't on any side! He is utterly distinct from both armies, for he has come "as commander of the Lord's army" (Josh 5:14). He is not Joshua's servant but his Lord, and he commands Joshua, "'Remove the sandals from your feet, for the place where you are standing is holy.' And Joshua did that" (v. 15). On both occasions sinful human beings cannot stand in God's presence, for he is the holy one, often described in the OT as "the Holy One of Israel."[2]

The uniqueness and incomparability of Yahweh, the Holy One of Israel, is a recurring theme of the OT. Hannah praises God, saying, "There is no one holy like the Lord. There is no one besides you! And there is no rock like our God" (1 Sam 2:2). Since the Lord is holy, he must be worshiped as the ever holy one: "Ascribe to the Lord the glory of his name; bring an

---

We think, however, the meaning of the word has a wider semantic range than does Gentry.

[2] 2 Kgs 19:22; Pss 71:22; 78:41; 89:18; Isa 1:4; 5:19, 24; 10:20; 12:6; 17:7; 29:19; 30:11, 12, 15; 31:1; 37:23; 41:14, 20; 43:3, 14; 45:11; 47:4; 48:17; 49:7; 54:5; 55:5; 60:9, 14; 50:29; 51:5.

offering and come before him. Worship the LORD in the splendor of his holiness" (1 Chr 16:29). Because the Lord is holy and deserves worship, all people everywhere should "tremble before him" (Ps 96:9). The Lord is the holy king, the one who is exalted above all: "You are holy, enthroned on the praises of Israel" (22:3). Isaiah 57:15 teaches that the Lord's holiness signifies his transcendence, his being separate from us: "The High and Exalted One, who lives forever, whose name is holy, says this: 'I live in a high and holy place, and with the oppressed and lowly of spirit, to revive the spirit of the lowly and revive the heart of the oppressed.'" Despite God's holiness and transcendence, he is also the one who comes to the aid of those who are crushed and oppressed.

The Lord's holiness rightly fills people with dread and fear when they consider being in his presence. For instance, the Lord puts to death seventy people in Beth-shemesh because they look inside the ark. The God of Israel cannot and must not be treated casually, as if he were another utensil for everyday use. After this severe judgment, "The people of Beth-shemesh asked, 'Who is able to stand in the presence of the LORD this holy God? To whom should the ark go from here?'" (1 Sam 6:20). The sinfulness of human beings and the Lord's transcendent holiness make residing in his presence dangerous, and this passage makes it clear that Yahweh's holiness includes his moral purity, so that he judges those who sin. Along the same lines, Joshua warns Israel about the Lord's holiness shortly before his death: "You will not be able to worship the LORD, because he is a holy God. He is a jealous God; he will not forgive your transgressions and sins" (Josh 24:19). The connection is clear between holiness and the sin that affronts God's holiness.

Psalm 99 captures powerfully the Lord's holiness and the judgment that comes because of human sin. We will quote several verses to get a good sense of the psalm:

> Let them praise your great and awe-inspiring name. He is holy. The mighty King loves justice. You have established fairness; you have administered justice and righteousness in Jacob. Exalt the LORD our God; bow in worship at his footstool. He is holy. Moses and Aaron were among his priests; Samuel also was among those calling on his name. They called to the LORD and he answered them. He spoke to them in a pillar of cloud; they kept his decrees and the statutes he

gave them. LORD our God, you answered them. You were a forgiving God to them, but an avenger of their sinful actions. Exalt the LORD our God; bow in worship at his holy mountain, for the LORD our God is holy. (vv. 3–9)

The Lord forgives because he is merciful, but he also avenges sin because he is holy. He is not to be trifled with, and we are to bow in awe and in worship before him. When Nadab and Abihu offer strange fire and are slain by lightning from God, they are punished for taking for granted the Lord's holiness: "This is what the LORD has spoken: 'I will demonstrate my holiness to those who are near me, and I will reveal my glory before all the people'" (Lev 10:3). There is an awe-inspiring gravity about the Lord's holiness, and creatures must never forget that he is the Creator.

Living Holy Lives

The Lord's holiness means that he calls his people to live holy lives so that his holiness is reflected in the world (Deut 7:6; 14:2). The call to holiness is found in several texts in Leviticus. "I am the LORD your God, so you must consecrate yourselves and be holy because I am holy. Do not defile yourselves by any swarming creature that crawls on the ground. For I am the LORD, who brought you up from the land of Egypt to be your God, so you must be holy because I am holy" (Lev 11:44–45). Here Israel is called to be holy, to be a distinct people, by not eating the food the nations eat (vv. 1–43). The call to holiness is reiterated in 19:2: "Speak to the entire Israelite community and tell them: Be holy because I, the LORD your God, am holy." Here holiness is linked with honoring parents, keeping the Sabbath, refraining from idolatry, etc. (vv. 3–4). Holiness is especially interwoven with love (19:18; cf. Exod 19–20).

It is evident, therefore, that holiness includes living in a way that pleases God, living morally in a way that distinguishes Israel from the nations. Holy living reflects God's character in our lives, in their moral quality. We see the same admonition in Lev 20:26: "You are to be holy to me because I, the LORD, am holy, and I have set you apart from the nations to be mine." Israel is to be holy because the Lord himself is holy, because Israel uniquely belongs to him among all the nations of the world, and because he has set Israel apart to be his. In the context of Leviticus 20, most of the commands have to do with avoiding idolatry and sexual sin, though some have to do with ritual matters (v. 25). In any case, the holiness of Israel is reflected in the moral beauty of the people's lives. They are to be different from the nations, distinct from them, and their lives are to reflect the character of the Lord who delivered them from Egypt and entered into covenant with them.

Holy Things

Israel is distinct from the nations and is to be distinguished from them in countless ways. For instance, the tabernacle and temple are divided into the holy place and the most holy place (see 2 Chr 3:8–13). One must not—one cannot—enter the Lord's presence casually. In fact, only the high priest, and only once a year on the Day of Atonement, may enter the most holy place (Lev 16). We also see how Israel is set apart and distinct from the nations with regard to the Sabbath. The Sabbath isn't to be treated like every other day of the week, and thus no work should be done on it (Exod 20:8–11; Jer 17:22–27). Furthermore, Aaron, as high priest, must wear "holy garments" (Exod 30:25) when carrying out his priestly ministry, which signifies that ministry to the Lord is utterly distinct and different from ordinary vocations. In the same way, a special "holy anointing oil" is to be used for worship. "It is holy, and it must be holy to you" (v. 32). Its special character is evident, for "It must not be used for ordinary anointing on a person's body, and you must not make anything like it using its formula" (v. 32). In case Israel failed to see that this oil must be distinguished from everyday oil, the Lord repeats the command (v. 37). This text helps us define holiness, for what is holy isn't ordinary but is special, set apart, consecrated, and devoted to God.

Jerusalem and Zion are designated God's "holy mountain" (Pss 2:6; 3:4; 15:1; 43:3; 48:1; Isa 11:9; 27:13; 56:7; 57:13; 65:11, 25; 66:20; Jer 31:23; Ezek 20:40; Dan 9:16, 20; 11:45; Joel 2:1; 3:17; Obad 16; Zeph 3:11; Zech 8:3), and we also find a number of references to the Lord's "holy temple" (Pss 5:7; 11:4; 79:1; 138:2; Jonah 2:4, 7; Mic 1:2; Hab 2:20). Since priests are holy to the Lord, they must not marry a prostitute or one who is divorced, "for the priest is holy to his God. You are to consider him holy since he presents the food of your God. He will be holy to you because I, the LORD who sets you apart, am holy" (Lev 21:7–8). Priests cannot and must not marry women other Israelites are permitted to marry. Along the same lines, a person who has a physical defect isn't allowed to serve as a priest (v. 23).

Priests are called upon to "distinguish between the holy and the common, and the clean and the unclean" (Lev 10:10; cf. Ezek 44:23). When Israelites fail to live holy lives, when they turn to evil, the Lord judges them, since in doing so they profane the Lord's name. For instance, if someone offers his child to Molech, Yahweh says, "I will turn against that man and cut him off from his people, because he gave his offspring to Molech, defiling my sanctuary and profaning my holy name" (Lev 20:3). Even Moses and Aaron, who were godly men, were not allowed to enter the Promised Land because they "did not trust me to demonstrate my holiness in the sight of the Israelites" (Num 20:12). God's holiness, his matchless character, his holy otherness, must never be taken for granted.

In a crucial text in Ezekiel the prophet explains why Israel went into exile and why God will deliver them from exile:

> "When they came to the nations where they went, they profaned my holy name, because it was said about them, 'These are the people of the LORD, yet they had to leave his land in exile.' Then I had concern for my holy name, which the house of Israel profaned among the nations where they went.
>
> "Therefore, say to the house of Israel, 'This is what the Lord GOD says: It is not for your sake that I will act, house of Israel, but for my holy name, which you profaned among the nations where you went. I will honor the holiness of my great name, which has been profaned among the nations—the name you have profaned among them. The nations will know that I am the LORD—this is the declaration of the Lord GOD—when I demonstrate my holiness through you in their sight.'" (Ezek 36:20–23)

Israel went into exile because they profaned the Lord's holy name, and they will also be delivered and saved in order to "demonstrate" the Lord's holiness. Israel is indicted by Ezekiel and others for provoking and despising "the Holy One of Israel" (Ps 78:41; Isa 1:4; 5:24). The Lord's holiness and his name are closely related, and the Lord judges when his holiness is tarnished—but he also saves to denote his uniqueness. Since the Lord's reputation is aligned with his people's, he also saves to proclaim his holiness.

The Lord Sanctifies

If Israel is to be set apart, if she is to be holy, it will be the Lord's work. In Leviticus a regular refrain reminds that it is the Lord who sets Israel apart; it is the Lord who sanctifies his people, as the following verses teach:

> "Keep my statutes and do them; I am the Lord who sets you apart." (Lev 20:8)

> "I promised you: You will inherit their land, since I will give it to you to possess, a land flowing with milk and honey. I am the Lord your God who set you apart from the peoples." (v. 24)

> "You are to be holy to me because I, the Lord, am holy, and I have set you apart from the nations to be mine." (v. 26)

> "You are to consider him holy since he presents the food of your God. He will be holy to you because I, the Lord who sets you apart, am holy." (21:8)

> "You must not profane my holy name; I must be treated as holy among the Israelites. I am the Lord who sets you apart." (22:32)

Israel was set apart by the Lord's grace, because they belonged to the Lord. Any sanctifying work, the work of setting one apart, is from the Lord. This appears in the life of Jeremiah the prophet: "I chose you before I formed you in the womb; I set you apart before you were born. I appointed you a prophet to the nations" (Jer 1:5). God also promises in the last days to set apart or sanctify Israel: "When my sanctuary is among them forever, the nations will know that I, the Lord, sanctify Israel" (Ezek 37:28). God's promise to Israel will not be revoked since he is faithful to fulfill his covenant promises.

Summary

We have seen that Yahweh is the Holy One of Israel, and his holiness means that he is transcendent and utterly distinct. His holiness includes his moral excellence and purity. Israel was called to be the Lord's holy people, to be distinct from the nations surrounding them. Some of the customs the Lord gave Israel were intended to separate them from the nations and were not moral norms, such as which foods were allowed to be eaten. However, other instructions that God gave to Israel were moral norms. Israel was to reflect Yahweh to the world by living in love, by living in a morally beautiful and excellent way. Since Israel failed to do so, both the northern and the southern kingdoms were sent into exile. Still, the Lord promised to save and deliver them to display the holiness and utter uniqueness of his great name. Finally, Israel's only hope was for the Lord to sanctify them; their holiness would become a reality only in the Lord and by the Lord—and this promise is fulfilled in the NT.

Sanctification in the NT

When we come to sanctification and holiness in the NT, we must remind ourselves again that the concept is wider than the words "holy" and "holiness." The OT conceptions of holiness inform the NT and function as essential background in comprehending what the NT teaches about sanctification.

God Himself

The OT teaching on God's holiness is fundamental and foundational when it comes to understanding God himself. Perhaps the fundamental verse in the NT is Rev 4:8, where we enter the throne room of heaven: "Each of the four living creatures had six wings; they were covered with eyes around and inside. Day and night they never stop, saying, 'Holy, holy, holy, Lord God, the Almighty, who was, who is, and who is to come.'" Isaiah 6, with the seraphim voicing God's holiness, clearly lurks in the background (Isa 6:3). We should note the programmatic role Revelation 4 plays in the entire book. After the letters to the seven churches, John has a vision of God as Creator, and he is revealed as thrice-holy, as the awesome and amazing Lord of the universe. The Lord's judgments and his wrath, poured out on the wicked, also cause people to confess his holiness: "Lord, who will not fear and glorify your name? For you alone are holy. All the nations will come and worship before you because your righteous acts have been revealed" (Rev 15:4). Similarly in the midst of the fierce bowl judgments an angel exclaims, "You are just, the Holy One, who is and who was, because you have passed judgment on these things" (16:5).

Mary's song is filled with OT allusions, and among other things she praises "the Mighty One" who "has done great things for me, and his name is holy" (Luke 1:49). Since God is ever and always the holy one, one of the fundamental prayers of believers, as Jesus taught his disciples, is "Father, your name be honored as holy" (11:2). It is significant that the first element of the Lord's Prayer relates to God's holiness, to praying that his name would be high and lifted up.

Everyday Examples

It is helpful to look for examples of how "holiness" is used when the subject isn't the holiness of God or the sanctification of believers. As in the OT, the word signifies that which is consecrated, devoted, distinct, or different. Peter refers to "the holy mountain" (2 Pet 1:18) where the transfiguration occurred, the mountain set apart because Jesus was transfigured there. So too, the OT tabernacle is divided into the "holy place" and the "most holy place" (Heb 9:2–3). Matthew refers to gold or gifts that are sanctified (Matt 23:17, 19), and such gifts are set apart for the Lord's use. The details about what Paul says in Rom 11:16 are debated, but the point we should notice here is that Israel is still consecrated to God, set apart for God, even though many in Israel have failed to believe: "Now if the firstfruits are holy, so is the whole batch. And if the root is holy, so are the branches." Paul also speaks of Gentile Christians as set apart, as holy. He envisions himself as priest and the Gentiles as an offering and then says that the offering is pleasing and acceptable since the Gentiles have been consecrated and set apart by the Holy Spirit (15:16).

When a believer is married to an unbelieving spouse, some might think that the believer would be defiled by being united to someone who didn't belong to the Lord. We might expect Paul to allege defilement, especially in light of Ezra and the requirement that Israelites separate from pagan wives (Ezra 9–10). Instead, Paul maintains that the unbelieving spouse and the children of such a union are sanctified and holy because of the presence of the believer.

What is holy is set apart, special, and devoted to God, and thus "what is holy" must not be given "to dogs" (Matt 7:6), because dogs are unclean, and that which is holy must not be defiled. The Jews in Jerusalem seized Paul and almost beat him to death, charging him with bringing an unclean

Gentile into the temple so that he had "defiled this holy place" (Acts 21:28). Food that is eaten at meals "is sanctified by the word of God and by prayer" (1 Tim 4:5). Food is consecrated and set apart—it is pleasing to God—when believers thank God for his goodness in providing it. Finally, we read in Heb 9:13, "If the blood of goats and bulls and the ashes of a young cow, sprinkling those who are defiled, sanctify for the purification of the flesh." Sacrifices ordained by God cleanse, sanctify, and consecrate that which is unclean.

Sanctification in Believers' Lives

When we consider sanctification or holiness in the lives of believers, sanctification can be divided into the temporal categories of (1) definitive or initial sanctification, (2) progressive sanctification, and (3) final or eschatological sanctification. These categories aren't watertight, and in some cases a text may occupy more than one category, or one might argue that some texts belong in one category rather than another. Still, it is helpful to delineate categories for the sake of clarity. And the categories help us see the breadth of God's sanctification of his people.

Definitive Sanctification. In popular circles sanctification is often understood to refer to growth in holiness, and what is often missed is that in quite a few texts the reference is to definitive sanctification, to initial sanctification, instead of progressive sanctification.[3] By definitive sanctification we mean that believers stand before God as holy and perfect, as completely clean because of what God has done for them in Christ. Definitive sanctification overlaps with justification, because such sanctification can't grow or decrease—it is in Christ. This notion is captured nicely by 1 Cor 1:30: "It is from [God] that you are in Christ Jesus, who became wisdom from God for us—our righteousness, sanctification, and redemption." Paul almost certainly refers to definitive sanctification here, for "righteousness" and "redemption" both refer to completed realities. Thus, it is quite likely that sanctification functions the same way: in Christ believers stand before God as holy.

---

[3] On definitive sanctification, see David Peterson, *Possessed by God: A New Testament Theology of Sanctification and Holiness*, NSBT 1 (Grand Rapids: Eerdmans, 1995).

We also see definitive sanctification in 6:11: "Some of you used to be like this. But you were washed, you were sanctified, you were justified in the name of the Lord Jesus Christ and by the Spirit of our God." Paul admonishes the believers at Corinth to live in a godly way, reminding them of who they are in Christ. Baptism symbolizes the cleansing of their sins, and justification signifies that they stand in the right before God. The verb "sanctified" indicates that believers are holy before God. The order of the verbs points to definitive sanctification, for if Paul were speaking of progressive sanctification, he would not put sanctification before justification. Instead, all three terms (washed, sanctified, and justified) refer to the new status that belongs to believers in Christ.

The author of Hebrews, particularly, often teaches definitive sanctification. We read in Heb 2:11, "The one who sanctifies and those who are sanctified all have one Father." The author could be speaking of progressive sanctification, but the way he uses the verb in the letter tilts us toward the idea of definitive sanctification. Jesus sets apart and puts in the realm of the holy those who belong to him. The notion of definitive sanctification is even clearer in 10:10: "By this will, we have been sanctified through the offering of the body of Jesus Christ once for all time." The verb "have been sanctified" (*hēgiasmenoi*) is in the perfect tense, signifying in this context that the work of sanctification is accomplished; this is confirmed by the words "once for all time." The death of Christ, the offering of himself on the cross, has placed believers permanently in the realm of the holy.

A few verses later a similar thought is expressed: "By one offering he has perfected forever those who are sanctified" (v. 14). Jesus's death qualified permanently those who are set apart, those who are consecrated. It is remarkable how often Hebrews connects Christ's death to the sanctification of believers. In what is probably the strongest warning passage in the letter, the author admonishes the readers about turning away from their confession of faith: "How much worse punishment do you think one will deserve who has trampled on the Son of God, who has regarded as profane the blood of the covenant by which he was sanctified, and who has insulted the Spirit of grace?" (v. 29). We see a tension in this verse. On the one hand, believers are sanctified by Jesus's blood (cf. v. 12), so that they are now consecrated to God as his holy ones. On the other hand, if they turn away from Jesus, they will face God's vengeance and anger (vv. 30–31). We will address this tension further in our discussion on preservation and perseverance.

The meaning of some texts is harder to discern. When Paul says that Jesus gave his life for the church "to make her holy, cleansing her with the washing of water by the word" (Eph 5:26), he could be referring to progressive sanctification. The parallel with baptism, however, of being washed with water, suggests that the holiness described here is positional instead of progressive. We also likely see a reference to a decisive setting apart in the statement "We ought to thank God always for you, brothers and sisters loved by the Lord, because from the beginning God has chosen you for salvation through sanctification by the Spirit and through belief in the truth" (2 Thess 2:13). The context centers on election and the initial confession of faith—"belief in the truth"—and thus there are grounds for thinking that sanctification here refers to the definitive setting aside accomplished by the Spirit at conversion.

The same is true in 1 Pet 1:2, which refers to the foreknowledge of the Father, the sprinkling of the blood of the Son, "the sanctifying work of the Spirit," and the obedience of believers. The obedience of believers here is another way of designating their conversion, as the parallels in 1:22 and 3:1 confirm. The sanctifying of the Spirit refers, then, to the setting-apart work that takes place at conversion when believers are sprinkled clean with Jesus's blood and when God's foreknowing and electing work becomes a reality in history (vv. 1–2).

When believers are called a "holy priesthood" (1 Pet 2:5) and a "holy nation" (v. 9), their status before God is in view. The same reality is seen when believers are called "saints" or "holy ones" (Rom 1:7; 1 Cor 1:2; 2 Cor 1:1; Eph 1:1, etc.). Believers are called saints not because they live such godly lives but because they are God's holy ones by virtue of Christ's atoning death on their behalf. The reference in 1 Cor 1:2 is especially interesting, for the Corinthians are said to be "saints" and "sanctified in Christ Jesus." "Sanctified" (*hēgiasmenois*) is in the perfect tense, signifying a completed reality, which is amazing in light of the sins plaguing the Corinthian congregation: divisions, incest, lawsuits, sexual sin, idolatry, refusal by women to submit to authority, drunkenness at the Lord's Supper, a focus on self instead of others in the matter of spiritual gifts, and doubts about the resurrection of the dead. Still, the Corinthians are considered to be sanctified and saints because of their union with Christ, because his holiness is theirs. Finally, Paul's words to the Ephesian elders also refer to definitive sanctification: "Now I commit you to God and to the word of his grace, which is able to build you up and to give you an inheritance among all who are sanctified" (Acts 20:32). "Sanctified" (*hēgiasmenois*) is again in the perfect tense, signifying those who belong to the Lord, who are in the realm of the holy.

Progressive Sanctification. If some have lessened or failed to see the significance of definitive or initial sanctification, the opposite error must also be avoided. We also see clearly in the NT the reality of progressive sanctification, which means that believers are to grow gradually into the likeness of Christ. We could at this point examine everything the NT says about spiritual growth, and such an enterprise would be instructive and fruitful. We would see numerous texts that demonstrate that holiness is progressive. If we engaged in such an enterprise, we would consult all the texts that give clear instructions about spiritual growth. Our purpose here is more limited and we will restrict ourselves to texts that use terms like "sanctify" and "holiness" to show that sanctification is progressive.

Progressive sanctification is present in John 17, where Jesus prays, among other things, that his disciples be preserved until the end, entreating they be kept from apostasy (vv. 11–12, 15). Jesus's prayer for his disciples' sanctification arises in the context of the disciples' perseverance. He prays, "Sanctify them by the truth; your word is truth" (v. 17), and also says, "I sanctify myself for them, so that they also may be sanctified by the truth" (v. 19). Clearly the sanctification is progressive, since it is related to the disciples' enduring to the end, and God's truth, his word, is the means by which sanctification will be carried out.

The importance of growing in holiness and the demand to grow in such holiness is evident in Heb 12:14: "Pursue peace with everyone, and holiness—without it no one will see the Lord." Certainly, holiness is not the same thing as perfection, and it is linked particularly in Hebrews with perseverance, with hanging onto faith until the end. On the other hand, if such holiness is lacking, one won't see the Lord or enjoy the life of the age to come. A few verses prior to verse 14 the author explains to the readers that the Lord is disciplining them as a father does his sons (vv. 5–11), and thus their discipline isn't a sign that the Lord doesn't love them. Quite the contrary: discipline is evidence and confirmation of his love. The connection with holiness is explained in verse 10: "For they disciplined us for a short time based on what seemed good to them, but he does it for our benefit, so that we can share his holiness." Discipline is for the sake of holiness, so that believers will be conformed more and more to the likeness of God.

Peter's admonition in 1 Pet 1:15–16 is well known: "As the one who called you is holy, you also are to be holy in all your conduct; for it is written, 'Be holy, because I am holy.'" Peter picks up here the words of Lev 11:44; 19:2. The holiness mandated for Israel is to be expressed in the church of Jesus Christ. Certainly, Peter refers to progressive holiness in context, for he exhorts the readers not to give way to sinful desires according to their past lives (1 Pet 1:14). The same emphasis on holiness appears in 2 Peter, as at the inception of the letter Peter admonishes the people to live a life of virtue and godliness (2 Pet 1:5–7). As the letter closes, he returns to this theme, reminding his readers of Jesus's coming and of the dissolution of the present world (3:1–10). As Peter begins to conclude the letter he instructs them, "Since all these things are to be dissolved in this way, it is clear what sort of people you should be in holy conduct and godliness" (v. 11). They are to live a new life here and now, a life consecrated to God, a life devoted to what pleases him. Similarly, Zechariah in his song envisions the ideal life as one of goodness, holiness, and righteousness. When God's covenant promises are fulfilled, believers will "serve him without fear in holiness and righteousness in his presence all our days" (Luke 1:74–75).

Romans 6:15–23 reveals that those who are under grace should live like it—they should live transformed and holy lives. Twice holiness is explicitly mentioned. We read in verse 19, "Just as you offered the parts of yourselves as slaves to impurity, and to greater and greater lawlessness, so now offer them as slaves to righteousness, which results in sanctification." The consequence of giving the part of their bodies to righteousness is sanctification. Perhaps Paul has in mind final sanctification here, but it seems evident that a process is at work as well, in which believers are sanctified as they devote themselves to righteousness in everyday life. A few verses later Paul returns to the matter of holiness: "Since you have been set free from sin and have become enslaved to God, you have your fruit, which results in sanctification—and the outcome is eternal life!" (v. 22). Once again the consequence of giving oneself to God is sanctification, and such sanctification leads to eternal life. We see a theme here quite similar to that of Heb 12:14, in that there will not be eternal life without sanctification. Certainly, Paul doesn't think of earning eternal life; he says in the very next verse that it is a gift (Rom 6:23)! The grace that takes hold of human beings transforms them.

The Pauline vision for holiness is summed up in Rom 12:1: "Therefore, brothers and sisters, in view of the mercies of God, I urge you to present your bodies as a living sacrifice, holy and pleasing to God; this is your true worship." Those who are holy are not characterized by their selfish will, but since they are a new creation they give themselves to God. God's intention in electing and choosing believers was the holiness of believers, for he isn't interested only in saving us but also in changing us. "He chose us in him, before the foundation of the world, to be holy and blameless in love before him" (Eph 1:4). Believers, then, are to be committed to and zealous for holiness: "Dear friends, since we have these promises, let us cleanse ourselves from every impurity of the flesh and spirit, bringing holiness to completion in the fear of God" (2 Cor 7:1; cf. 1 Tim 2:15). Doubtless this text refers to progressive sanctification, and such holiness is rooted in God's great new covenant promises and in the strength God supplies within. Such grace animates believers to pursue holiness and remove evil from their lives. The same call to holiness is evident in 1 Thess 4:3, though here the focus is on sexual purity: "This is God's will, your sanctification: that you keep away from sexual immorality." Later in the same paragraph Paul explains, "God has not called us to impurity but to live in holiness" (v. 7). The life that pleases God is one in which believers are devoted to him, consecrated to him, and distinct from the world.

Perhaps a word about the fruit of the Spirit would be helpful here, even if the words "sanctify" or "holiness" are not used (see Gal 5:22–23). We should note at the outset that the fruit ("love, joy, peace, patience, kindness, goodness, faithfulness, gentleness, and self-control") comes from the Spirit. The new life isn't produced in our own strength or from our own resources or by straining with all our might to be good. The fruit is produced as we walk in the Spirit (v. 16), taking step by step at the Spirit's direction. We can say as well that the fruit of the Spirit comes as we are led by the Spirit (v. 18), as we are directed and guided and shaped by the Spirit. The fruit of the Spirit means saying "no" to the works of the flesh (vv. 19–21), but again the power to overcome the flesh's works isn't autonomous. We can only live in such a way because we live by the Spirit and as we march in step with the Spirit (v. 25). To put it another way, we are to sow to the Spirit (6:8), or as Paul says in Eph 5:18 we are to be filled with the Spirit. Living a holy life is supernatural; it is a miracle; it is the work of God in us and through us.

Final Sanctification. Believers are initially and definitively sanctified in Christ when they are converted, but at the same time they pursue progressive sanctification. Believers grow in holiness throughout their lives and become more like Christ. We also must consider final sanctification, or the eschatological perfection of the believer. "Eschatological" signifies that this sanctification will become a reality at the second coming. We could put it this way: at final sanctification the initial sanctification that is ours in Christ becomes a perfect reality in our lives. To put it another way, our progressive sanctification at the eschaton reaches its goal and end, in that we are completely conformed to Christ's character. We see this truth in the language of purification found in 1 John: "Dear friends, we are God's children now, and what we will be has not yet been revealed. We know that when he appears, we will be like him because we will see him as he is. And everyone who has this hope in him purifies himself just as he is pure" (1 John 3:2–3). Believers are to purify themselves now, but they will be perfectly purified and cleansed from sin when Jesus returns. We will be instantaneously transformed into the likeness of Jesus Christ.

Paul prays for the Lord to complete the work of sanctification at Jesus's coming: "May he make your hearts blameless in holiness before our God and Father at the coming of our Lord Jesus with all his saints. Amen" (1 Thess 3:13). This prayer won't be answered in its fullness until Jesus comes, though we must not deny here that Paul also envisions progress in holiness until the day of Jesus's return. We find another prayer at the conclusion of 1 Thessalonians: "Now may the God of peace himself sanctify you completely. And may your whole spirit, soul, and body be kept sound and blameless at the coming of our Lord Jesus Christ. He who calls you is faithful; he will do it" (5:23–24). Paul prays for complete sanctification and holiness, but he contemplates this work being completed and perfected at the second coming of Christ. Paul envisions perfect sanctification not in this life but at Christ's future coming.

We also see the final presentation of the church based on Christ's self-giving love (Eph 5:25–26): "He did this to present the church to himself in splendor, without spot or wrinkle or anything like that, but holy and blameless" (v. 27). The church will be presented as Christ's bride, perfect and without flaw on the last day. Currently the church as the bride of Christ still has spots and wrinkles and flaws, as anyone familiar with the church knows, but the day will come when there will be no imperfection, no blemish, no disfigurement. The work of sanctification will be completed and the church will be Christ's sinless bride. We find the same thought in Col 1:22: "Now he has reconciled you by his physical body through his death, to present you holy, faultless, and blameless before him." Believers through the death of Christ are now reconciled, and they look forward with confidence to the day when they will be presented before God as perfect, without any flaws. The day is coming when we will be all that God has called us to be, and that promise gives us hope, as we struggle and fight against sin now.

Summary

God is holy in his transcendence and in his character. He is unstained or undefiled by any sin or defect; he is separate and distinct from anything in the created world. Sanctification, we have seen from a number of examples, refers to something being consecrated or devoted to God, separated from or distinct from common use. Believers in Jesus Christ are already sanctified or holy in God's eyes positionally. They are saints by virtue of Christ's work on the cross. At the same time, believers are called upon to grow and progress in their holiness as believers. We are conformed more and more to the image of Jesus Christ, a process that will reach its culmination and goal on the last day, when believers are perfected in holiness, transformed so that they are blameless and without fault before God.

Historical Reconnaissance

We remember the annual meeting of the Evangelical Theological Society in 1987 devoted to evangelicals and spirituality. We were startled to listen as evangelicals from various traditions shared their views on the Christian life.

Although they could have emphasized what they had in common with other evangelicals, in keeping with conference expectations, they emphasized their distinctives. The result was five very different views of the Christian life. To avoid the same result, before we describe various views of the Christian life, we will share what they have in common. Each of the five views below is held by evangelicals who believe in the inerrancy of Scripture; the Trinity; the reality of sin; the incarnation, death, resurrection, and second coming of Christ; salvation by grace through faith in Christ; and much more. Nevertheless, the views below differ in emphases. We will summarize sanctification from five viewpoints:[4]

- Lutheran
- Wesleyan
- Keswick
- Pentecostal
- Reformed

Lutheran

The Lutheran view of the Christian life is built around the primacy of justification, its relation to sanctification, the law-gospel dialectic, and Luther's dictum that a Christian is *simul justus et peccator*. Francis Pieper's *Christian Dogmatics* asserts, "In Lutheran theology the article of justification is the central, chief article by which the Christian doctrine and the Christian Church stands and falls. . . . ; it is the apex of all Christian teaching."[5] In these words Luther's tradition remains true to its founder, who wrote concerning justification: "If this article stands, the church stands; if this article collapses, the church collapses."[6] Justification holds such an important place

---

[4] See Melvin E. Dieter, Anthony A. Hoekema, Stanley M. Horton, J. Robertson McQuilkin, and John F. Walvoord, *Five Views on Sanctification* (Grand Rapids: Zondervan, 1996); Donald Alexander, ed., *Christian Spirituality: Five Views on Sanctification* (Downers Grove: IVP, 1989); Kelly M. Kapic, ed., *Sanctification: Explorations in Theology and Practice* (Downers Grove: IVP, 2014).

[5] Francis Pieper, *Christian Dogmatics*, 4 vols. (St. Louis: Concordia, 1953), 2:512–13.

[6] Martin Luther, *What Luther Says: An Anthology*, ed. Ewald M. Plass, 3 vols. (St. Louis: Concordia, 1959), 2:704n5.

in Lutheran dogmatics that critics sometimes claim such dogmatics have no place for sanctification. This is not true, though Lutheranism is very protective of the primacy of justification.

Pieper affirms two principles summarizing the relation between justification and sanctification:

> 1. There is an inseparable connection (*nexus indivulsus*) between justification or faith and sanctification; where there is justification, there is in every case also sanctification. 2. But in this *nexus indivulsus* the cart must not be placed before the horse, that is, sanctification must not be placed before justification, but must be left in its proper place as the consequence and effect of justification.[7]

The key to Lutheran exegesis of both Testaments is the dialectic between law and gospel. In his rediscovery of the gospel, Luther prized the law-gospel distinction. He found in it the way to make sense of all Scripture in light of Paul's message of justification by grace through faith in Christ. Law stands for not only the Ten Commandments but all of Scripture's demands, obligations, threats, warnings, and judgments. The law's demands are impossible for sinners to fulfill (Rom 3:10; 6:23). Even "All our righteous acts are like a polluted garment" (Isa 64:6).

Humans and all their thoughts and actions are tainted by sin, and sin condemns them before a holy God. This is the main function of the law according to Lutheran teaching.

The gospel, however, does not make demands but forgives our sins through Jesus's crucifixion. The gospel even gives faith to poor sinners, that they might be saved. Jesus was our substitute in all he said and did, especially in his death, resurrection, and subsequent victory. And all this is gospel. God delivers to us what Jesus did for us through the church, the sacraments, and the preaching of the Word. The law convicts us of our inability and draws us to Christ, who saves us in the gospel, God's power to salvation (Rom 1:16).

The law-gospel distinction teaches us that the Christian life is not mainly about keeping rules but about receiving God's forgiveness. Every day the law condemns us and Christ forgives us. This is the grand message of

---

[7] Pieper, *Christian Dogmatics*, 7.

the Bible and therefore the grand message of the church upon which the Christian life is based. Any other message diminishes the sinfulness of sin and makes hypocrites or leads to a merit theology that fills its adherents with false pride.

Luther famously defined a Christian as one who is *simul justus et peccator*. A believer in Christ is at one and the same time (*simul*) righteous (*justus*) in God's sight through free justification but also and always a sinner (*peccator*) in himself. Lutheran theologian David Scaer underscores the importance of the word *simul* ("at the same time") in Luther's dictum for the Christian life:

> Luther's concept of *simul justus et peccator* is fundamental for a Lutheran understanding not only of justification but also of sanctification. Before God the person is totally justified and the same person is in himself and sees himself as a sinner. What is important in this understanding is the Latin word *simul*, at the same time, and not in a sequential sense as if one followed the other in point of time. . . . In Lutheran theology justification describes the believer's relationship with God. Sanctification describes the same reality as does justification but describes the justified Christian's relationship to the world and society. Justification and sanctification are not two separate realities, but the same reality viewed from the different perspectives of God and man. From the perspective of God, the reality of the Christian is totally passive and non-contributory as it receives Christ only. From the perspective of the world, the same reality never ceases in its activity and tirelessly performs all good works.[8]

---

[8] David P. Scaer, "Sanctification in Lutheran Theology," *Concordia Theological Quarterly* 49 (April–July 1985): 2–3:181–95, www.ctsfw.net/media/pdfs/scaer sanctificationinlutherantheology.pdf, accessed on 4.4.22. See also Thomas R. Schreiner, "Soundings on *Simul iustus et Peccator:* Evidence in the Pauline Epistles for Our Continuing Problem with Sin" in *Always Reforming: Reflections on Martin Luther and Biblical Studies*, ed. Channing L. Crisler and Robert L. Plummer (Bellingham, WA: Lexham Press, 2021), 126–38.

Wesleyan[9]

John Wesley (1703–1791) not only achieved great success as an evangelist and organizer of discipleship groups but also left his mark as a Christian theologian. His theology was eclectic, combining elements from the Greek fathers, spiritual writers of the Middle Ages, Pietists, the Reformers, and Puritans. As we might expect, therefore, his view of sanctification was also not monochrome.

Wesley basically taught a reformation doctrine of justification, whereby God declares righteous all who trust Jesus as their substitute. Those who respond positively to universal prevenient grace believe in Christ and are born again. Sanctification begins at conversion and is progressive, the result of God's sanctifying grace. To these views Wesley added his doctrine of believers' maturity known as "Christian perfection," "entire sanctification," "holiness," or "second blessing." Wesley thus taught that sanctification was both progressive, beginning at conversion, and instantaneous in Christian perfection.

Sanctification includes the use of spiritual "methods" for which he and his colleagues earned the nickname "Methodists" while students at Oxford. Wesley was influenced in this by Thomas à Kempis, whose *The Imitation of Christ* became a devotional classic. Wesley found that the use of methodical self-discipline was necessary because of "inbred sin" but was insufficient for victory over sin in the Christian life.

Wesley had heard of Christian perfection before he experienced justification by grace through faith in Christ. He had learned of it from the writings of Thomas à Kempis, Bishop Jeremy Taylor, and Wesley's contemporary William Law. Jesus had summarized its goal in the two greatest commandments: "Love the Lord your God with all your heart, with all your soul, and with all your mind. . . . Love your neighbor as yourself" (Matt 22:37, 39). Wesley found it in the Greek fathers as well, especially Clement of Alexandria, and in medieval spiritual writers.

---

[9] We gladly acknowledge help from Thomas A. Noble, "John Wesley as a Theologian: An Introduction." https://didache.nazarene.org/index.php/volume-7-2/, accessed April 5, 2022.

After his rigorous discipline at Oxford and in Georgia failed to bring Christian maturity, Wesley's conversion renewed his expectation of attaining it, but again he failed. He thereby concluded for a time that entire sanctification must be achieved only at death. Nevertheless, he pressed on, seeking Christian perfection and believing that God could bring him to such a wholehearted dedication to God. As he wrote in "A Plain Account of Christian Perfection,"[10] he conceived of this not as sinlessness but as not willfully sinning against God because of overwhelming love for him. In this context, when interpreting 1 John 3:9 ("Whosoever is born of God doth not commit sin," KJV), Wesley defined sin as "a voluntary transgression of a known law." He did acknowledge involuntary transgressions, which we must confess our whole lives, and was grateful that Christ died for all our transgressions, both voluntary and involuntary. Christian perfection, however, concerns voluntary transgressions. Believers will be free from involuntary transgressions only when Christ returns.

In "A Plain Account of Christian Perfection" Wesley emphasized that the grace of God is sufficient to save and to sanctify wholly in this life. When pressed to offer a short definition of Christian perfection, Wesley explained that it consists of "pure love reigning alone in the heart and life—this is the whole of scriptural perfection." Entire sanctification is attained after conversion by many Christians but not all. Once believers attain it, they cease to rebel against God and his commands and instead joyfully obey the one who fills their heart with love for him. Regarding Wesley's long-term creative theological contribution, Thomas Noble wrote, "We should look for it perhaps in the doctrine of the Christian Life." This doctrine contains many elements, one of the most famous of which is the Wesleyan doctrine of entire sanctification.

Wesley influenced his theological heirs in many ways, including bequeathing to them his doctrine of Christian perfection. In one regard, however, the majority broke with him. Whereas Wesley combined progressive sanctification with instantaneous entire sanctification,

---

[10] John Wesley, "A Plain Account of Christian Perfection" in *The Works of John Wesley*, vol. 11, ed. Thomas Jackson (London: Wesleyan Methodist Book Room, 1872), 366–466. https://www.ccel.org/w/wesley/perfection/perfection.html.

Adam Clarke, younger contemporary of Wesley, viewed the matter differently. He writes, "In no part of the Scriptures are we directed to seek holiness *gradatim* ["step by step"]. We are to come to God as well for an instantaneous and complete purification from all sin as for an instantaneous pardon. Neither the *gradatim* pardon not the *seriatim* ["in a series"] purification exists in the Bible."[11]

Kenneth Grider correctly notes, "On this issue of gradual sanctification, the Holiness Movement understood Clarke's view to be scriptural, instead of Wesley's."[12]

Keswick

The annual Keswick Convention has taken place in Keswick, northern England, since 1875. Out of these conferences arose a particular view of sanctification, known as Keswick theology or the Higher Life Movement, that has influenced many. This theology stresses victorious Christian living through the power of the Holy Spirit. Wesleyan teachers exerted influence on the early conferences, including John Wesley himself, John William Fletcher, and Adam Clarke. Over the years many Christian leaders have spoken at Keswick, among them missionaries Hudson Taylor and Amy Carmichael, devotional writer Oswald Chambers, and evangelist Billy Graham. In 2005, Steven Barabas penned the main source for the history and theology of the movement: *So Great Salvation: The History and Message of the Keswick Convention.*[13]

Before noting distinctives of Keswick theology, some of which are controversial, we note that it shares many common evangelical emphases concerning Christian living. It accentuates Christ's lordship and personal holiness and promotes a zeal for missions. It exalts Christ's finished work and

---

[11] J. Kenneth Grider, *A Wesleyan-Holiness Theology* (Kansas City: Beacon Hill, 1994), 398–99, quoting Adam Clarke, *Entire Sanctification* (Louisville: Pentecostal Publishing, n.d.), 38.

[12] Grider, *A Wesleyan-Holiness Theology*, 399.

[13] Steven Barabas, *So Great Salvation: The History and Message of the Keswick Convention* (Eugene, OR: Wipf and Stock, 2005).

justification by faith as the foundation of sanctification. It correctly teaches that not only justification but also sanctification is by grace through faith in Christ. It teaches reliance on the Spirit's power for a life of holiness and love.

According to Keswick theology, the Christian life involves two key crises: justification and sanctification, which ordinarily happen at different times. Justification is by grace through faith in Christ, as the Reformers taught. Sanctification is a later event, occurring after justification, and it too is through faith in Christ. Keswick theology teaches that this second encounter with the Holy Spirit, the second blessing, is necessary for a successful Christian life. The second blessing enables believers in Christ to progress in holiness and the "deeper things" of God. Christians move from justification to sanctification (the second blessing) through surrender and faith.

In fact, to try hard at the Christian life is fruitless. To repeat a slogan, justified believers must "Let go, and let God" to enjoy a victorious Christian life. They must let go of their own efforts at sanctification and let God by the Spirit do it through them. To many this seems like quietism, the view that the key to spirituality is human inactivity and passivity. Critics charge that Keswick teaching discourages believers from doing battle with sin, trusting the Spirit to deal with it instead.

Keswick theology believes that we receive justification and sanctification by faith. We, therefore, receive sanctification by asking God for it. Although Christians receive the Holy Spirit at conversion, they must come to a crisis point of decision and by faith trust the Spirit to enter into the higher life of sanctification. Justification means receiving Christ as Savior; the second work of sanctification means receiving him as Lord. Although this does not lead to sinless perfection in this life, which will occur only in the next life, it should lead to consistent success in overcoming sin in the Christian life.

J. Robertson McQuilkin, who promotes the Keswick view of sanctification, faults "average" Christians for unbelief and too often acting like nonbelievers by not overcoming sin and obeying Christ. His antidote for them is to be the "normal Christian," that is, the one who lives out the Keswick understanding of sanctification:

> The normal Christian is characterized by loving responses to
> ingratitude and indifference, even hostility, and is filled with joy in
> the midst of unhappy circumstances and peace when everything is

going wrong. The normal Christian overcomes in the battle with temptation, consistently obeys the laws of God, and grows in self-control, contentment, humility and courage. Thought processes are so under the control of the Holy Spirit and instructed by Scripture that the normal Christian authentically reflects the attitudes and behavior of Jesus Christ. God has first place in his life, and the welfare of others takes precedence over personal desires. The normal Christian has power not only for godly living but for effective service in the church. Above all, he or she has the joy of constant companionship with the Lord.[14]

Pentecostal[15]

Pentecostalism traces its origins to the first decade of the twentieth century and the ministries of Charles Parham in Topeka, Kansas, and William Seymour in Azusa Street in Los Angeles, California. To understand Pentecostalism, we must become acquainted with the "three waves" of the Holy Spirit. The first wave was classic Pentecostalism, whose roots were just mentioned, which resulted in new denominations such as the Assemblies of God. The second wave was the charismatic movement of the 1960s and 1970s, which influenced mainline Protestant churches and the Roman Catholic Church. It received its name from its emphasis on *charismata*, or miraculous gifts of the Holy Spirit. The third wave began in the 1980s and was characterized by "signs and wonders" that accompanied "power evangelism."

Byron D. Klaus, a respected Pentecostal leader in the Assemblies of God, shares five themes characteristic of classical Pentecostalism: "justification (God's forgiveness of sin), sanctification (freedom from the power of sin), divine healing, the second coming of Christ, and the baptism of the Holy Spirit."[16] Most people consider the last of these to be the defining distinctive

---

[14] *Five Views on Sanctification*, ed. Stanley N. Gundry (Grand Rapids: Zondervan, 1996), 151.

[15] We acknowledge significant help from Gregg Allison, www.thegospelcoalition .org/essay/pentecostal-theology.

[16] Byron D. Klaus, "Why I Am an Evangelical and a Pentecostal," in *Why We Belong: Evangelical Unity and Denominational Diversity*, ed. Anthony L. Chute,

of Pentecostal theology. Because this is regarded as a second blessing after salvation, Pentecostal theology bears some similarity to the Wesleyan second-blessing theology of entire sanctification. However, Wesleyan teaching pertains to "Christian perfection," while the Pentecostal second-blessing teaching concerns God's powerful presence in Christians' lives. Although holiness Pentecostals hold to a three-stage soteriology, with both Pentecostal and Wesleyan second blessings following justification, we will focus on classical Pentecostalism, which does not add Wesleyan entire sanctification to the baptism of the Spirit.

The classical Pentecostal view of the Christian life holds that Holy Spirit baptism is distinguished from initial salvation (viewed as justification or regeneration). Baptism in the Spirit means receiving the Spirit's power for successful Christian living and service. It is important to note that classical Pentecostals regard those who have believed in Jesus to be Christians even if they have not received the baptism of the Holy Spirit. Regeneration is necessary for salvation; Spirit baptism is necessary for vital Christian living and service. Another key note is that classical Pentecostalism insists that the second blessing must be accompanied by speaking in tongues (*glossolalia*) as evidence of Spirit baptism.

Pentecostals' view of the post-conversion baptism of the Spirit indicates that they hold to continuationism with regard to the spiritual gifts, as opposed to cessationism, which holds that the sign gifts ceased with the apostles' writing of the NT. Allison writes of continuationism, "This position holds that the Spirit continues to give to the church all the spiritual gifts (listed in the New Testament as charismata), including the so-called 'sign' or 'miraculous' gifts: word of knowledge, word of wisdom, prophecy, miracles, healings, speaking in tongues, and interpretation of tongues (some would include exorcisms)."[17]

Klaus informs us of Pentecostalism's world and life view:

> To the question of causality that is critical to worldview construction, divine initiative is not just an ideal category but a powerful reality

---

Christopher W. Morgan, and Robert A. Peterson (Wheaton: Crossway, 2013), 156. See also Gordon D. Fee, *Paul, the Spirit, and the People of God* (Grand Rapids: Baker Academic, 1996).

[17] Gregg Allison, "Pentecostal Theology", www.thegospelcoalition.org/essay /pentecostal-theology, accessed May 30, 2023.

for Pentecostalism. The sacred-secular dichotomy that epitomizes modernity is rejected and replaced with an affirmation of the immediate availability of God's power and presence. We see the world through a reality construct in which God is near at hand and provides clear evidence of his powerful presence through his church.[18]

The Pentecostal doctrine of Spirit baptism for power and service combines with an emphasis on Christ's second coming to produce a powerful impetus for world missions. As a result, today Pentecostal and charismatic Christians constitute the second largest group of Christians and the largest body of Protestants in the world. As of 2020, "Globally, there [were] 644 million Christians in the Spirit-Empowered movement, representing 26% of all Christians worldwide."[19]

Reformed

The Reformation of the sixteenth century sparked a biblical revival of the gospel, doctrine, worship and singing, the church, preaching and the sacraments, Bible translation, and the Christian life. The Reformed branch of the Reformation made more changes in doctrine and church life than did the Lutheran and Anglican branches. Like the other views of sanctification treated before this one, John Calvin and his theological heirs held to the biblical view of justification. God the Father declares righteous all who trust his Son as substitute when he imputes Christ's righteousness to them and accepts them as his sons and daughters.

The Reformed view of sanctification holds much in common with the previous four views. It has a high view of Scripture and consequently teaches the doctrines of the Trinity, sin, Christ and his atonement, salvation, the Holy Spirit, the church, and last things. It embraces Luther's doctrine of Christians as *simul justus et peccator* and acknowledges the Lutheran distinction between law and gospel but does not regard it as the hermeneutical key to the Bible. Instead, it traces the biblical storyline of creation, fall,

---

[18] Klaus, "Why I Am an Evangelical and a Pentecostal," 160.

[19] https://www.gordonconwell.edu/center-for-global-christianity/research /global-pentecostalism/, accessed April 11, 2022.

redemption, and consummation and sees in the Abrahamic and new covenants the primary soteriological unity between the Testaments.

The Reformed view parts ways with both Wesleyan and Pentecostal second-blessing views. It rejects Wesley's Christian perfection and instead holds to lifelong progressive sanctification. It also rejects the Pentecostal view of the post-conversion baptism of the Spirit. Instead, it holds that at conversion all believers are baptized by the Spirit into the body of Christ, the church. It appreciates Keswick's emphasis on relying on God's power for holiness but rejects its notion of "letting go." Rather, it points to Scripture's urging believers to expend great energy to fight sin and live for God (e.g., Rom 8:13; Phil 3:12; Col 1:29).

The Reformed doctrine of sanctification distinguishes definitive or initial, progressive or lifelong, and final sanctification. Once for all, God sets apart people to be saints in definitive sanctification. God will confirm them in perfect holiness when Jesus returns. By his Spirit he causes them to grow in progressive sanctification in the present, and this is our concern. *Sola scriptura* is foundational to the Reformed view of the Christian life, for Calvin lectured daily from the Hebrew and Greek texts of the Bible. *Sola gratia* is more than a slogan based on the last two words of Calvin's *Institutes*. Rather it is the ultimate goal of theology and ethics.

Reformed soteriology is trinitarian, emphasizing the Father's role in election, the Son's role in redemption by his blood, and the Spirit's application of salvation in union with Christ. In fact, union is the genius of the Reformed view of sanctification. Union with Christ's death and resurrection entails suffering with him now and glory with him later. The Spirit's role in uniting us to Christ means that believers are genuinely new in Christ, but not totally new. That will happen only when Christ comes again. In the meantime, union with Christ drives the Christian life. We died with the Son of God to the power of sin and were raised with him to newness of life.

In concert with Scripture's storyline, the Reformed view of sanctification focuses on God's conforming believers to Christ's image as the progressive restoration of the image of God marred in the fall. God will perfect Christians in Christ's image when he returns for his people. Now by the Spirit they imitate Christ as they use God's means of grace given to his church: the preaching of the Word, the administration of the sacraments, and prayer.

Evaluation of the Views

The first thing to say in conclusion is the first thing we said at the outset—these five views of sanctification have the most important things in common. This is an important point, for, without it, contrasting the various views of the Christian life tends to distortion by overemphasizing their differences. Therefore, we rejoice that the five views of the Christian life discussed are orthodox in their doctrines of God, sin, salvation, the Holy Spirit, church, and last things. To say this is not to minimize the differences between the views; it is to begin with their common confession of the verities of the evangelical faith.

Nevertheless, there are differences between the five views of the Christian life, and they are substantial. Although all evangelicals owe a debt to Luther for his rediscovery of the gospel, his hesitancy adequately to affirm progressive sanctification lives on in his theological heirs. At the same ETS conference we referenced at the beginning of this section, we heard renowned Lutheran theologian David P. Scaer claim, "There is no progress in the Christian life!" We respectfully disagree and point to 2 Cor 3:18; Eph 4:15, 20–24; Col 1:9–10; 1 Tim 4:12–15; Heb 6:1; 1 Pet 2:2; 2 Pet 1:5–8; 1 John 2:3–6; 3:4–6, 14–18.

We agree with Luther and Calvin on the importance of the doctrine of free justification. With our Lutheran brothers we acknowledge the law-gospel distinction, especially in Paul. But we do not regard it as the key to biblical interpretation, as Lutherans do. We also agree with Luther's description of a Christian as someone who is *simul justus et peccator*, at the same time righteous (in Christ) and a sinner (in practice). But we find this insufficient to describe the *totality* of the Christian life, for that life also involves growth "in the grace and knowledge of our Lord and Savior Jesus Christ" (2 Pet 3:18; cf. the verses cited in the previous paragraph).

We respect John Wesley's life and ministry. We agree with many of his ideas, including that sanctification is a process, against the majority tradition after him that rejected progressive sanctification, starting with Adam Clarke. But we stumble over his teaching on Christian perfection or entire sanctification. We do believe in entire sanctification, but as Paul says it will occur "at the coming of our Lord Jesus Christ" (1 Thess 5:23–24). We admire Wesleyans' desire for holiness and confess that we often fall short of the Lord's command to "Be holy because I am holy" (Lev 11:44–45; 1 Pet 1:16). However, we deny that a state of entire sanctification can be attained in this life.

Keswick follows the basic evangelical theological outline in most areas except for its one distinctive: the second encounter with the Holy Spirit that enables a deeper Christian life. With due respect for godly teachers, we reject this second blessing doctrine as unbiblical. Scripture does not teach us to "Let go and let God." It teaches that we are to rely on God's enabling grace to live for him, but it also calls us not to quietism but to activism in Christian living. We can hardly think of more activist models for the Christian life than soldiers, athletes, and farmers (2 Tim 2:4–6).

We admire the lives and ministries of many of our Pentecostal brothers and sisters in Christ. We rejoice in their spreading the gospel around the globe. However, we are compelled by our understanding of Scripture to reject their second-blessing doctrine. We have known Pentecostal young men paralyzed concerning ministry because they had not "spoken in tongues" as evidence of receiving the Holy Spirit. Paul says that the Corinthians "were all baptized by one Spirit into one body" (1 Cor 12:13) and later in the same chapter asks, "Do all have gifts of healing? Do all speak in tongues? Do all interpret?" (v. 30), where the adverb used requires a negative answer. All had received the Spirit's baptism, but all did not possess any one spiritual gift, including tongue-speaking.

We find Anthony Hoekema's treatment of some of the matters we have discussed compelling. Hoekema rejects the traditional Reformed understanding of the *ordo salutis*, the order of salvation. This is the idea that the various aspects of the application—e.g., regeneration, calling, conversion, justification, adoption, sanctification, perseverance—can all be placed in a logical order. John Frame has shown that this is problematic because of the different senses of "order" in the list (e.g., regeneration stands in a causal relation to the rest, but faith is the means or instrument of justification and adoption, not their cause).[20]

---

[20] John M. Frame, *Systematic Theology: An Introduction to Christian Belief* (Phillipsburg, NJ: P&R, 2013), 936–37.

Further, sanctification, as we have shown, is initial, progressive, and final. It is, then, impossible to put it in only one place in the order.

Instead of viewing the elements of the application of salvation successively, Hoekema urges, "We should think, then, not of an order of salvation with successive steps or stages, but rather of a marvelous work of God's grace—a way of salvation—within which we may distinguish various aspects."[21] Moreover, although these aspects of the application of salvation must be distinguished, they are unified under the heading "union with Christ." All of them are subsets of union. When God joins people spiritually to his Son, he grants them all the blessings of salvation, everything from regeneration and justification to perseverance and glorification.

This discussion has implications for evaluating the second-blessing theologies of Wesleyanism, Keswick theology, and Pentecostalism. These three theologies have two-stage soteriologies: justification followed by a second blessing, whether entire sanctification (Wesleyanism), a deeper-life encounter (Keswick theology), or Holy Spirit baptism (Pentecostalism). In fact, holiness Pentecostals have a three-stage soteriology of justification, entire sanctification, and Holy Spirit baptism. Hoekema concludes:

> Why should these types of soteriology be rejected? We have already seen that a proper understanding of the process of salvation sees the various aspects of that process as simultaneous rather than successive. Advancement in the Christian life should therefore by understood as involving progressive and continuing growth rather than the mounting of specific steps after conversion.[22]

Hoekema sees a further implication with harmful results:

> These soteriologies suggest that there are two types (or three types) of Christians: ordinary ones, sanctified ones, and or Spirit-baptized ones. There is, however, no biblical basis for such a distinction. Further, such a compartmentalization of Christians would seem to open the way for two erroneous and harmful attitudes: depression

---

[21] Hoekema, *Saved by Grace*, 15, (see chap. 3, n. 78).
[22] Hoekema, 18–19.

on the part of those who still think of themselves as being on the lower end of the Christian life, and pride on the part of those who deem themselves to have reached one of the higher levels.[23]

Systematic Formulations

Sanctification and the Trinity

The three Trinitarian persons play roles in sanctification. God the Father treats true believers as his sons by disciplining them. Why? "The Father of spirits" disciplines us "for our benefit, so that we can share his holiness" (Heb 12:9–10). The Son of God "loved the church and gave himself for her to make her holy, cleansing her with the washing of water by the word" (Eph 5:25–26). He will accomplish his goal: "He did this to present the church to himself in splendor, without spot or wrinkle or anything like that, but holy and blameless" (v. 27). The Holy Spirit too takes a part. Paul explains why he, Silvanus, and Timothy give thanks to God for the Thessalonian believers: "We ought to thank God always for you, brothers and sisters loved by the Lord, because from the beginning God has chosen you for salvation through sanctification by the Spirit and through belief in the truth" (2 Thess 2:13). God's means of bringing people to salvation include the Spirit's setting them apart from sin to holiness and faith in the gospel. The whole Trinity, therefore, works to make God's people holy.

Sanctification and Union with Christ

Each aspect of the application of salvation takes place in union with Christ, including sanctification. After listing the fruit of the Spirit, Paul speaks frankly: "Now those who belong to Christ Jesus have crucified the flesh with its passions and desires" (Gal 5:24). Co-crucifixion, union with Christ in his death, is the remedy to sinful living. Paul expands this theme in Romans 6. He is appalled when detractors claim his doctrine of free justification breeds license. They ask, "Should we continue in sin so that grace may multiply?" (v. 1). Paul's answer is "Absolutely not! How can we who died to sin still

---

[23] Hoekema, 19–20.

live in it?" (v. 2). Paul explains that baptism signifies union with Christ in his death and resurrection, which fuel a new life of holiness. Believers died with Christ: "We know that our old self was crucified with him so that the body ruled by sin might be rendered powerless so that we may no longer be enslaved to sin" (v. 6). Union with Christ in his death frees us from sin's tyranny. Believers were also raised with Christ: "Just as Christ was raised from the dead by the glory of the Father, so we too may walk in newness of life" (v. 4). Union with Christ in his mighty resurrection empowers believers to live for God as never before. Paul applies his teaching that union with Christ drives sanctification: "So, you too consider yourselves dead to sin and alive to God in Christ Jesus. Therefore do not let sin reign in your mortal body, so that you obey its desires" (vv. 11–12).

Sanctification and Our Role

God the Holy Spirit is the prime mover in sanctification. He sets us apart from the realm of sin to God's realm of holiness in initial or definitive sanctification. He will confirm us in final and entire sanctification at Christ's return. And he is the major player in progressive sanctification as well. But he is not the only player. When God regenerates us, he liberates our will, previously bound in sin, and enables us to love, serve, and obey him. Part of that is our responsible participation in progressive sanctification under the Spirit's direction and power. When Jesus told his disciples that they must "remain" or "abide" in him in order to produce fruit (John 15:4), he treated them as participants in their growth in practical holiness. After underlining God's sovereign grace in justification, sanctification, and election, Paul writes, "Therefore, brothers and sisters, in view of the mercies of God, I urge you to present your bodies as a living sacrifice, holy and pleasing to God; this is your true worship" (Rom 12:1).

Repeatedly NT writers urge their readers to grow in holiness:

My brothers and sisters, do not show favoritism as you hold on to the faith in our glorious Lord Jesus Christ. (Jas 2:1)

Watch out, brothers and sisters, so that there won't be in any of you an evil, unbelieving heart that turns away from the living God. (Heb 3:12)

Since [the heavens and earth] are to be dissolved in this way, it is clear what sort of people you should be in holy conduct and godliness. (2 Pet 3:10–11)

Dear friend, do not imitate what is evil, but what is good. (3 John 11)

"The time is near. Let the unrighteous go on in unrighteousness; let the filthy still be filthy; let the righteous go on in righteousness; let the holy still be holy." (Rev 22:10–11)

Both God and Christians are active in the Christian life. Paul commands the Philippians, "My dear friends . . . work out your own salvation with fear and trembling" (2:12). In the same sentence Paul gives the reason for this command: "For it is God who is working in you both to will and to work according to his good purpose" (v. 13). Believers are to strive for holiness in the Christian life, knowing that God works within them to give them both incentive and power to live for him.

Sanctification and the Church

Sanctification is both an individual and a communal matter. God makes each of his people holy. He is concerned for every member of the Thessalonian church: "This is God's will, your sanctification: that you keep away from sexual immorality, that each of you knows how to control his own body in holiness and honor, not with lustful passions, like the Gentiles, who don't know God" (1 Thess 4:3–5). Two verses later Paul addresses the church corporately: "God has not called us to impurity but to live in holiness" (v. 7). God wants his people to be holy as individual persons and as his church corporately.

The writer to the Hebrews exhorts his individual readers, "Pursue peace with everyone, and holiness—without it no one will see the Lord. Make sure that no one falls short of the grace of God" (Heb 12:14–15). Shortly before the author reminds individuals that they are to show mutual care for fellow believers: "Let us watch out for one another to provoke love and good works, not neglecting to gather together . . . but encouraging each other, and all the more as you see the day approaching" (10:24–25).

Earlier in the letter the writer addresses individuals and the whole church in a single passage. He twice warns individual persons,

> Since the promise to enter his rest remains, let us beware that none of you be found to have fallen short. (4:1)

> Let us, then, make every effort to enter that rest, so that no one will fall into the same pattern of disobedience. (v. 11)

Then he points the church as a whole to God's mercy and power that enable members to heed these warnings and live for him: "Let us approach the throne of grace with boldness, so that we may receive mercy and find grace to help us in time of need" (v. 16).

Sanctification and Time

Although it is common to reduce sanctification to its present (progressive) aspect, sanctification also pertains to the past and to the future. Sanctification is past: in initial or definitive sanctification the Holy Spirit moves us once and for all from the sphere of sin to that of holiness, and we become saints of God. Sanctification is present, as the Spirit builds practical holiness into God's saints in progressive sanctification. Sanctification is also future: only at Christ's second coming will God confirm his saints in perfect holiness (this is final sanctification).

Surprisingly, Paul calls the struggling Corinthians "those sanctified in Christ Jesus, called as saints" (1 Cor 1:2). The apostle distinguishes between true and false believers. He instructs the church not to accept as believers "anyone who claims to be a brother or sister and is sexually immoral or greedy, an idolater or verbally abusive, a drunkard or a swindler" (5:11). Paul singles out a church member who is "sleeping with his father's wife" (v. 1).

Nevertheless, Paul regards most of the Corinthians as true Christians who need to grow. After listing lifestyles of lost persons, he writes, "And some of you used to be like this. But you were washed, you were sanctified, you were justified in the name of the Lord Jesus Christ and by the Spirit of our God" (6:11). The verbs "washed," "sanctified," and "justified" are all in the past tense (6:11). Initial sanctification is past, as is justification.

God's sanctification of his people is also present. God wants his saints daily to seek his will and pursue godliness, including in their sexuality (1 Thess 4:3–7). The Holy Spirit works holiness in the saints, enabling them to "put off," as one takes off old clothes, ungodly practices and "put on" new, godly ones (Eph 4:20–32). This is progressive sanctification, a major biblical theme, treated by Jesus in Matthew 7, Paul in Galatians 5–6, Peter in 1 Peter 1–2, John in 1 John 1–2, and the author of Hebrews in 3–4, to name only five examples.

Sanctification is also future. The Spirit of God sets us apart to holiness in definitive or initial sanctification. He causes us to grow in applied holiness day by day in progressive sanctification. The Spirit's work is not done, however, until we are "conformed to the image of [God's] Son" (Rom 8:29) in final (entire) sanctification. John's language differs, but he delivers the same message: "We know that when [Christ] appears, we will be like him because we will see him as he is" (1 John 3:2).

At Christ's return he will "present the church to himself in splendor, without spot or wrinkle or anything like that, but holy and blameless" (Eph 5:27). In fact, "The God of peace himself [will] sanctify you completely. . . . Your whole spirit, soul, and body [will] be kept sound and blameless at the coming of our Lord Jesus Christ" (1 Thess 5:23). And in case we had any doubts about this, Paul adds, "He who calls you is faithful; he will do it" (v. 24).

Viewing sanctification as definitive (initial), progressive, and final has advantages. It glorifies God, who performs the work of salvation—in this case, sanctification—from first to last. We are already holy; we grow in holiness; and one day God will make us entirely holy. As said earlier, God's sovereignty in salvation does not minimize our responsibility to live for God but undergirds it. As Paul says, "I labor" to present everyone mature in Christ, "striving with his strength that works powerfully in me" (Col 1:29).

In addition, taking into account sanctification's three tenses of past, present, and future can bring hope to struggling Christians. When tempted to give up, believers can look back to their becoming saints by God's grace. We groan (Rom 8:23) because we have the Holy Spirit, who made us saints and works within us. When overwhelmed with discouragement, we can also look ahead to our final and entire sanctification. Though present circumstances cause us to doubt, we can be confident that God will sanctify us entirely, as he has promised (1 Thess 5:24; Phil 1:6).

Sanctification and Tensions

We do not intend to give the false impression that sanctification is easily understood or easily mastered in life. Forgiven sinners are still sinners, and godly Christians struggle to live consistently for God. Moreover, the fact that sanctification involves tensions complicates matters.

Sanctification Includes Theological and Practical Knowledge

Knowing scriptural teaching on sanctification is necessary but not sufficient. We also need to know how to apply ourselves practically to holiness, as James warns: "Be doers of the word and not hearers only, deceiving yourselves" (Jas 1:22). Studying, learning, and even lecturing on holiness is not enough. We need to learn experientially how to glorify God in family life, work, finances, relating to unsaved people, and much more.

Sanctification Involves God's Sovereignty and Our Responsibility

We must pursue God and holiness within the biblical framework of his absolute control and our responsible participation. God is the Lord of all, and he alone is "the Holy One" (Isa 48:17). His holiness is intrinsic, a very part of his divine nature. All other holiness in the universe—of angels, people, or things—is derived from him. In "divine power" he grants his redeemed people "everything required for life and godliness" (2 Pet 1:3). Our faith in, love for, and obedience to him are reflex actions to his sovereign prevenient grace. As we "walk by the Spirit" (Gal 5:16), the Holy Spirit produces fruit in and though us (vv. 22–23). By God's grace we trust God for holiness while also fighting against sin, going step by step with God, and being thankful.

Sanctification Includes the Positive and the Negative

Living for God involves change. Isaiah Majok Dau puts it plainly:

> Following Jesus is a change process. Following Jesus means enrolling ourselves in the school of change. . . . Following Jesus means answering the Master's beckoning hand that lovingly declares, "Come and follow me and I will make you. . . ." Following him is an

appointment with change, one that makes us what he always wants us to be or become.[24]

This change involves turning from sin and turning to righteousness. God's grace both saves and instructs us: "The grace of God has appeared . . . instructing us to deny godlessness and worldly lusts and to live in a sensible, righteous, and godly way in the present age" (Titus 2:11–12). Sanctification means daily pursuing holiness out of love for Christ while shunning sin out of love for Christ. It means loving Jesus and what he loves and disciplining ourselves to hate what he hates. Jesus makes it plain that loving him means saying yes to obedience and no to disobedience: "If anyone loves me, he will keep my word. My Father will love him, and we will come to him and make our home with him. The one who doesn't love me will not keep my words. The word that you hear is not mine but is from the Father who sent me" (John 14:23–24).

Sanctification Involves the "Already" and the "Not Yet"

We live in between the "already" of Christ's kingdom and the "not yet" of its fullness. His death and resurrection have accomplished "eternal redemption" (Heb 9:12) for everyone who believes in him. However, we long for his return, when he will make all things new. In the meantime, "We all stumble in many ways" (Jas 3:2).

This tension between the "already" and the "not yet" affects everything, including sanctification. The Holy Spirit has set us apart from the realm of sin to that of God, so that we are God's saints. However, sinlessness in thought, word, and deed eludes us now and will come to pass only at the end of the age. Dieumeme Noelliste notes,

Biblically, ethics is shaped and motivated by what God has done in Christ and what he promises to do in the future. The new age longed for in the Old Testament has dawned in Jesus, but it has not

---

[24] Isaiah Majok Dau, "Following Jesus in a World of Suffering," Consultation of the Lausanne Theology Working Group in partnership with the WEA Theological Commission, "Following Jesus in our Broken World," held at Limuru, Kenya, 12–16 February 2007, https://www.lausanne.org/content/lop/following-jesus-in-a-world-of-suffering-and-violence-lop-62-f.

yet been brought to full completion. Biblical ethics, then, is really an interim ethics: it is for those who live between the times (Titus 2:11–14; 2 Pet. 3:13–14).[25]

Noelliste is insightful. This interim season helps clarify our tension in sanctification. We have been definitively sanctified and await full and final sanctification. In the meantime, we know the joys and frustrations of progressive sanctification.

Sanctification Involves the "Indicative" and the "Imperative"

New Testament scholars distinguish between the "indicative" and the "imperative," especially in Paul's epistles. The former, dominated by the indicative mood in Greek, rehearses the mighty acts of God. The latter, which sometimes uses the imperative mood, exhorts the saints to live for God. For example, in Col 3:9–10 Paul writes in the indicative, informing his readers of what God has already done for them: by his grace he enabled them to put off the old clothes of sin and put on the new ones of holiness. In Eph 4:22–24, however, Paul tells them to do the very things he said God already did: take off the old and put on the new.

Scripture thus creates a tension between the indicative and the imperative that impacts the Christian life. The imperative is based on the indicative. The Christian life is not a self-help program. Without the indicatives of Christ's death and resurrection there would be no Christian life. However, to portray the Christian life as passive is a serious mistake. God not only speaks in the indicative; he also addresses his people in the imperative. His free justification results in his telling his people to live for him with their whole hearts.

Sanctification Includes Victory and Struggles

In salvation grace collides with sin, and as a result the Christian life contains not only victories and freedom but also battles and bondage. Paul cries out in frustration at his inability to overcome sin: "What a wretched man I am! Who will rescue me from this body of death?" (Rom 7:24). The same Paul,

---

[25] Dieumeme Noelliste, "Biblical Ethics: An Introduction," in *ESV Global Study Bible* (Wheaton: Crossway, 2012), 1893.

after asking, "Who can separate us from the love of Christ? Can affliction or distress or persecution or famine or nakedness or danger or sword?" (8:35), answers exuberantly: "No, in all these things we are more than conquerors through him who loved us" (v. 37). Victory and defeat, struggle and freedom go hand in hand.

We cannot solve this conundrum perfectly, but we note two important points. First, God knows how to humble his people, and he does so in progressive sanctification. Our failures deflate our pride and overconfidence. Those failures drive us to God's grace. Second, we are saved by grace through faith, and we live the Christian life in the same way. Paul writes of initial salvation, "You are saved by grace through faith, and this is not from yourselves; it is God's gift—not from works, so that no one can boast" (Eph 2:8–9). After Paul experienced many highs and lows living for Christ, God assured him, "My grace is sufficient for you, for my power is perfected in weakness" (2 Cor 12:9).

Living with the Tensions of Sanctification

The tensions are daily realities for all Christians. We bow before God's sovereignty, and we fight to avoid blaming our sins on it. We strive to fulfill our responsibility but then too easily forget our dependence on the Lord. We tend either to overemphasize rejecting the negative or to forget about it in our zeal for the positive. We forget we are "not yet" what we will be and become discouraged at our lack of progress in the Christian life. We sometimes imagine that we have "already" arrived at the end of our journey, only to have our bubble burst by a trustworthy friend. We dwell on the "imperative" to the neglect of the "indicatives" and veer toward legalism. We dwell on the "indicative" to the neglect of the "imperative" and our theology seems too theoretical. We get too high over the victories and too low over repeated struggles and failures.

These tensions highlight Luther's famous dictum that a Christian is a person who is *simul justus et peccator*, at the same time righteous and a sinner. In Christ we are justified by a holy God and accepted by him as his sons and daughters. In ourselves we see too much of the flesh in self-righteousness, jealousy, pride, inconsistency, lack of faith, sinful desires, evil-speaking, and sloth. Unfortunately, there is no simple remedy, no easy way out. We must face the tensions head-on, admit our weakness, and rely repeatedly on God's enabling grace, his strength, his Spirit. We need the church and our brothers and sisters in Christ. We need personal time in the Word and prayer daily. We need to serve God and others. We realize that in one sense we have attained, for God has forgiven us in Christ and given us eternal life. But in another sense, the longer we walk with God, the more we realize our absolute dependence on him for the wisdom, perseverance, and power to live for him with our whole hearts. Thank God that he has given us grace for the journey.

9

Preservation and Perseverance

Preservation is God's keeping his people saved, and perseverance is their continuing to believe the gospel and live for God. Instead of studying words, we begin with key texts in the NT that express these truths, since these doctrines do not depend on particular vocabulary. We could examine the OT as well, but the arrival of the new covenant with Christ's death and resurrection and the gift of the Holy Spirit clarifies in a new and decisive way the scriptural teaching on preservation and perseverance, and thus we will focus on the NT. Indeed, there is so much contained in the NT on these matters that we must be content with a survey.

Exegetical Foundations

Preservation

We saw previously on pages 102–4 that John 6, especially verses 37–40, 44, and 64–65, teach effectual calling. As we examine the text further, we see a connection between effectual calling and the preservation of the saints to the end: "This is the will of him who sent me: that I should lose none of those he has given me but should raise them up on the last day. For this is the will of my Father: that everyone who sees the Son and believes in him will have eternal life, and I will raise him up on the last day" (vv. 39–40). Jesus promises that he won't lose even one of those given to him by the Father, which means that none of those who are called effectually will ever defect from the faith.

Their final preservation is assured because Jesus will finish the work he has begun and raise believers from the dead on the last day. Verse 44 reaffirms the same thought: the Son will raise from the dead on the day of resurrection those who are effectually drawn by the Father.

Jesus identifies himself as the good shepherd of the sheep (John 10) and emphasizes that his sheep hear his voice, that he knows his sheep, and that they follow him (v. 27). He then promises, "I give them eternal life, and they will never perish. No one will snatch them out of my hand. My Father, who has given them to me, is greater than all. No one is able to snatch them out of the Father's hand" (vv. 28–29). The life Jesus gives is "eternal," and by definition such life won't be revoked. If it could be revoked, then the life granted isn't eternal but temporary. The text itself verifies such a reading by affirming that those who are granted "eternal life" "will never perish." Jesus emphasizes the security of believers in that no one will be able to snatch them from his hand or the Father's hand.

In Phil 1:3–8 Paul thanks God for the faith of the Philippians, which is manifested by their concern for Paul. He reminds them of God's promise: "I am sure of this, that he who started a good work in you will carry it on to completion until the day of Christ Jesus" (v. 6). God began the good work in the Philippians by bringing them to faith in Jesus Christ, and what he began he pledges to finish—he will carry out his work to the end, to the "day of Christ Jesus." We should notice the logic of Paul's argument here: what God started he will finish. God doesn't start the good work of salvation and then ask us to finish it autonomously. The same God who won our affections initially will see to it that those affections don't waver to the extent that we ever depart from the Lord.

In Rom 5:9–10 two verses we have looked at earlier when discussing justification come into play. Believers are justified and reconciled through Christ's death and resurrection, and thus believers have assurance of final salvation, confidence that they will not face God's wrath on the last day. It has often been pointed out that hope and assurance are the theme of Romans 5–8 and that such assurance functions as the framework for Romans 5–8, so that Rom 5:1–11 and 8:28–39 center on the believer's confidence before God. We argued in chapter 8 that those who are foreknown, predestined, called, and justified will certainly be glorified (vv. 28–30). As we noted earlier, there is no suggestion that the chain of God's saving work will be broken.

What God began by foreknowing and predestining will certainly be completed by glorification.

Paul celebrates the assurance and confidence of believers in Rom 8:31–39, one of the most comforting texts ever written. Paul teaches that no one can successfully oppose believers, since God has given believers the greatest gift imaginable, his very own Son. Believers have no reason to fear final condemnation, since "God is the one who justifies" (v. 33). No condemnation will be lodged against believers—not because they are perfect in this life but because Christ died for them, is the risen Lord, sits at God's right hand, and intercedes for them based on his atoning sacrifice (vv. 33–34). Finally, nothing will ever separate believers from the love of God and of Jesus Christ (vv. 35–39). Paul contemplates all the terrible things that could separate us from Christ's love before affirming that believers "are more than conquerors through him who loved us" (v. 37). Some think apostasy is possible, arguing that, even though external things can't separate us from Christ's love, our own will may choose to turn away from and forsake the Redeemer. The objection misses the point, for Paul lists the fearsome things that might cause us to abandon the Lord and says they will *not* separate us from Christ's love. Turning away from Christ isn't an abstraction. If anything could provoke such separation it would be the trials and sorrows of life, the very sufferings Paul lists here. Furthermore, when Paul says nothing in creation can remove us from Christ's love, he includes our own human will, since it is part of created reality.

In 2 Thessalonians 2 Paul reflects on unbelievers who are deceived and do not love the truth (vv. 10–12). Believers, on the other hand, can't take credit for their faith since it is God who chose them to be saved and called them to belief through the proclamation of the gospel, and thus they will "obtain the glory of our Lord Jesus Christ" (vv. 13–14). Glory here refers to final salvation, as was noted in our study of glory above. Once again, we see that God's eternal purpose in choosing some for salvation will not be frustrated, for he has appointed what will happen from beginning to end.

The "God is faithful" statements in Paul also assure believers of their preservation until the last day. For instance, we read in 1 Cor 1:8–9, "He [God] will also strengthen you to the end, so that you will be blameless in the day of our Lord Jesus Christ. God is faithful; you were called by him into fellowship with his Son, Jesus Christ our Lord." God promises to fortify

believers until the final day so that, when Jesus comes, they will be blameless
before him. We notice that the promise to be strengthened is given to believers since they are, as the hymn says, "prone to wander." God's faithfulness is
the reason they will be preserved, for the one who initially called them to
faith and into partnership with Christ will not forsake them.

The next reference to God's faithfulness is in 1 Cor 10:13. The place-
ment of the verse is fascinating, for Paul in the same context warns believers
in the strongest terms about the danger of idolatry and the danger of apostasy (cf. vv. 1–12, 14–22). Those who think they stand and who believe they
will never defect must be on their guard so that they don't fall from the faith.
In the midst of these warnings a comforting word is spoken: "No temptation
has come upon you except what is common to humanity. But God is faithful;
he will not allow you to be tempted beyond what you are able, but with the
temptation he will also provide a way out so that you may be able to bear it"
(v. 13). The temptation in context is the temptation to commit apostasy, to
fall away from the Lord. In the midst of the temptation to fall away, God
proves his faithfulness so that believers aren't tempted to the extent that they
fall away and depart from the faith. In the midst of the storm, he keeps them.

We have examined the next "God is faithful" text previously (on pp. 99),
and here we attend to it briefly. "Now may the God of peace himself sanctify
you completely. And may your whole spirit, soul, and body be kept sound
and blameless at the coming of our Lord Jesus Christ. He who calls you is
faithful; he will do it" (1 Thess 5:23–24). Paul prays for sanctification and
blamelessness of believers when Jesus returns. The God who effectually
called them to salvation is faithful, and he will complete what he has started.
He will not abandon them to themselves but will preserve them in the faith.

In 2 Thess 3:2–3 the presence of wicked and devious people is con-
templated, and they are identified as those who don't put their faith in Jesus
Christ. Paul contrasts their situation with believers: "But the Lord is faithful;
he will strengthen and guard you from the evil one" (v. 3). Believers experience the Lord's faithfulness so that he will protect them from the devil. Here
we have a reflection on the Lord's Prayer, in which believers are to pray that
they won't enter temptation but be delivered from the evil one (Matt 6:13).
The devil wants to turn people away from the faith, and he goes about as
a "roaring lion" seeking to devour their faith (1 Pet 5:8). Paul assures his

readers that Satan won't triumph, that he won't quench their faith, and that they will be protected from the evil one's attempt to destroy their faith.

The last reference to God's faithfulness is in 2 Tim 2:13, but we should also look at the saying right before this one: "If we deny him, he will also deny us; if we are faithless, he remains faithful, for he cannot deny himself" (vv. 12–13). Those who deny Jesus will be denied by him before the Father (cf. Matt 10:33). Some argue that the next line communicates the same truth, and, if this is the case, then God is faithful in judging those who deny Jesus. Such a reading is possible, but it is more likely that a different truth is expressed here. Those who deny Jesus, those who commit apostasy, those who turn away from Jesus, will face eternal judgment. But faithlessness isn't the same as apostasy—faithlessness has to do with temporary defection from the faith. Since God's faithfulness elsewhere is always associated with his preserving believers until the end, the same is likely true here. God can't deny himself, which is another way of saying that he can't deny his word. He can't deny his promise to keep believers until the end. If we put the two sayings together, we see the following: those who fully and finally deny Jesus will be denied by him forever, but those who suffer temporary failings of faith will be preserved by them, for he will guard their faith until the end.

Two texts in 1 Peter affirm God's preservation of believers. Peter assures suffering Christians of their end-time inheritance, their final salvation (1 Pet 1:3–9). He affirms that they are "being guarded by God's power through faith for a salvation that is ready to be revealed in the last time" (v. 5). The Lord protects and watches over those who are his so that they will enjoy the fullness of salvation on the last day. Final salvation will be received through persevering faith. Peter teaches that faith is necessary, but such faith is a gift of God and keeps believers to the final day.

The other text relevant to preservation is 1 Pet 5:10: "The God of all grace, who called you to his eternal glory in Christ, will himself restore, establish, strengthen, and support you after you have suffered a little while." The God who effectually called believers to himself is the same God who grants grace and strength so that believers receive "eternal glory," which refers to eschatological inheritance. Peter emphasizes with four verbs that function essentially as synonyms that the God who called them will strengthen and fortify believers until the last day.

The letter of Jude is an impassioned warning about apostasy, about the danger lurking from false teachers in the midst of the church (or churches). The framework for such warnings, the context into which the warnings are tucked, is two remarkable texts on assurance. Jude begins and ends the letter with assurance so that the readers understand that his warnings must be interpreted within the context of the Lord's preserving grace. Believers are identified as those called by God's grace, as recipients of his saving love, and as kept by Jesus Christ (Jude 1). Those whom God has called and set his love upon will be kept by Jesus Christ; the Father and the Son do not work in contrary ways here. The Father called and loves them and Jesus Christ will preserve them. The same theme concludes the letter: "Now to him who is able to protect you from stumbling and to make you stand in the presence of his glory, without blemish and with great joy, to the only God our Savior, through Jesus Christ our Lord, be glory, majesty, power, and authority before all time, now and forever. Amen" (Jude 24–25). When Jude speaks of keeping believers from stumbling, he probably has in mind the main concern in his letter, i.e., admonishing his readers not to be duped by the false teachers and thereby fall away from the gospel. In saying that God is able to keep believers from stumbling, he likely means, in line with verse 1, that God *will keep them from falling away*, and thus they can be assured that they will stand before the Lord with joy and exultation on the last day.

Perseverance

Warning Texts in NT

We have seen the promises that God will preserve until the end the faith of those who belong to him. We also need to observe the many admonitions and warnings about the need to persevere until the end. We will proceed by looking at NT warnings in canonical order. We are not assigning any significance to this order but proceed in this way for practical reasons. Not every writer or book of the NT will be consulted, but we will look at a number of texts to confirm that warnings about the need to persevere permeate the NT.

When Jesus sent out his disciples to proclaim the gospel of the kingdom, he said, "The one who endures to the end will be saved" (Matt 10:22). End-time salvation will be granted only to those who persevere, and they must persevere to the end (cf. 24:13). Notice the text doesn't say that those who are saved will persevere to the end, though that thought is clearly a biblical truth as well. The grammar here is quite different: those who persevere *will be saved*. Similarly, a few verses later in the same discourse Jesus declares, "Whoever denies me before others, I will also deny him before my Father in heaven" (10:33). The warning is real and must be taken seriously. On the one hand, believers are promised final salvation, but, on the other hand, those who deny Jesus will be denied by him before the Father at the final judgment (2 Tim 2:12).

The Lukan explanation of the parable of the four soils illustrates the need for perseverance as well:

> The seed is the word of God. The seed along the path are those who have heard and then the devil comes and takes away the word from their hearts, so that they may not believe and be saved. And the seed on the rock are those who, when they hear, receive the word with joy. Having no root, these believe for a while and fall away in a time of testing. As for the seed that fell among thorns, these are the ones who, when they have heard, go on their way and are choked with worries, riches, and pleasures of life, and produce no mature fruit. But the seed in the good ground—these are the ones who, having heard the word with an honest and good heart, hold on to it and by enduring, produce fruit. (Luke 8:11–15)

The first three soils will not gain an eternal reward. The seed on the path is never received at all. The seed on the rock and the seed among thorns originally germinate and grow, but they eventually die out. They represent those who fall away and don't produce fruit, but the seed on the good ground receives a reward, for it represents those who hold on and endure to the end, proving that they are true disciples. Those who fall away demonstrate that they were not genuine disciples, that their faith was spurious.

A good example of the need for perseverance in the Gospel of John derives from Jesus's parable of the vine and the branches (ch. 15). Believers produce fruit because they are connected to Jesus as the vine, and they must remain in him to produce fruit, for they are unable to do anything apart from him (vv. 4–5). Jesus warns believers in verse 6, "If anyone does not remain in me, he is thrown aside like a branch and he withers. They gather them, throw them into the fire, and they are burned."

Remaining in Jesus is absolutely necessary for life, and those branches that become disconnected are discarded since they are dried up and dead. They are thrown "into the fire" and "burned," which signifies final judgment. The language used is too strong to be restricted to simply losing a reward above and beyond eternal life. The reward here is eternal life itself, since those who are split off from the vine lack life. Can a believer, then, lose eternal life? Those in the Wesleyan tradition answer in the affirmative, saying that this is the only way to take the warning seriously. We propose a different answer that we will explain more fully as we proceed. Warnings like these are the means by which genuine believers are kept from committing apostasy. By taking the warning seriously, believers are kept from falling away.

Prospective Texts in the NT

In Romans 9–11 the destiny of Gentile and especially Jewish believers is considered. The promises made to the Jewish people (Rom 9:6) will not fail, and ultimately "All Israel will be saved" (v. 11:26), which means that there will be a great end-time conversion of the Jewish people. Certainly, many Jews have failed to believe in Christ and will face judgment, and this state of affairs provokes Paul to lament the spiritual state of the Jews in his day. He particularly warns Gentile believers about arrogance and pride regarding their inclusion within the people of God over against the Jews. In verses 17–24 the olive tree represents the people of God, and we are told that the original Jewish branches were broken off and Gentile branches were grafted onto the tree.

It is just here that Paul warns the Gentiles about pride. We pick up Paul's argument and his words to Gentile Christians in verse 19:

> Then you will say, "Branches were broken off so that I might be grafted in." True enough; they were broken off because of unbelief, but you stand by faith. Do not be arrogant, but beware, because if God did not spare the natural branches, he will not spare you either. Therefore, consider God's kindness and severity: severity toward

those who have fallen but God's kindness toward you—if you remain in his kindness. Otherwise you too will be cut off. (vv. 19–22)

The warning here is remarkable for its bracing quality, since Paul says that they will be cut off if they cease believing and trusting in Christ. Gentile believers must not become smug and proud about their inclusion in the people of God. They only "stand by faith," and, if they don't continue to persevere but fall away, they won't be spared either. The warning, as noted earlier, is deadly serious, but it doesn't negate one whit the promises of assurance. The warning becomes the means by which those who truly belong to God are preserved and kept until the end.

In 1 Cor 15:1–4 the Corinthians are reminded of the gospel Paul preached to them, which centers on Christ's death and burial and his resurrection and appearances. The Corinthians were saved by believing in the gospel, but Paul also says that such salvation is conditioned on their perseverance: "if you hold to the message I preached to you" (v. 2). Paul doesn't teach that the Corinthians are saved no matter what they do; they must believe until the end to be saved. We see the same emphasis on perseverance in Galatians. In Gal 5:19–21 Paul lists some of the works of the flesh, and then he warns his readers "that those who practice such things will not inherit the kingdom of God" (v. 21). The Galatians couldn't simply claim that they will receive an inheritance by grace and then give themselves over to evil. Paul makes the same point in 6:8: Those who sow "to the flesh will reap" end-time destruction, but those who sow to the Spirit "will reap eternal life." What one does after conversion is momentous, since those who regularly sow to the flesh won't experience life in the age to come.

Paul's admonition in Col 1:21–23 is most interesting. Paul has just finished setting forth, in what is probably an early Christian hymn, the glory of Christ as Creator and Redeemer (vv. 1:15–20). Paul follows with a warning:

Once you were alienated and hostile in your minds expressed in your evil actions. But now he has reconciled you by his physical body through his death, to present you holy, faultless, and blameless before him—if indeed you remain grounded and steadfast in the faith and are not shifted away from the hope of the gospel that you heard. (vv. 21–23)

Believers are reconciled through Christ's death, but they will be presented blameless before the Father only if they continue in the faith to the end.[1]

Paul's words in 1 Thess 3:1–5 are instructive as he explains why he sent Timothy back to the Thessalonians. He wondered how the Thessalonians were doing since they had encountered trials and persecutions after he left. Paul sent Timothy "to find out about [their] faith, fearing that the tempter had tempted [them] and that our labor might be for nothing" (v. 5). Paul doesn't *assume* that the faith of the Thessalonians was genuine simply because they made an initial profession of faith. He wasn't certain about their status, but one thing is clear: their perseverance in trials would signify the reality of their initial belief.

Hebrews is famous for its warning passages, and admonitions permeate the letter (2:1–4; 3:7–4:11; 5:11–6:12; 10:26–31; 12:25–29). Clearly, space is lacking to investigate these texts in any detail.[2] We must remember that Hebrews is a sermon, an exhortation (13:22), with one main point: its hearers/readers should not fall away. It is thus vital to see that, since the letter has one main point, the warning passages all make the same point. The warnings in the letter should be read synoptically; they mutually inform one another.[3] The warning in 10:26–31 is illustrative. If believers sin "deliberately," if they turn against the gospel of Jesus Christ, there is no forgiveness, no "sacrifice" for their sins (v. 26). If they turn away in such a way, they will be judged and face a fiery judgment (v. 27). Those who sinned under the old covenant were judged on earth with the judgments threatened under the covenant enacted through Moses, but if one tramples on God's Son, considers the blood of the covenant unclean, and insults the Holy Spirit, then such a person will be punished, will face God's vengeance, will face the terrifying prospect of falling into the hands of the living God (vv. 28–31).

---

[1] For further discussion, see Thomas R. Schreiner and Ardel B. Caneday, *The Race Set Before Us: A Biblical Theology of Perseverance and Assurance* (Downers Grove: InterVarsity, 2001), 191–93.

[2] For further discussion, see Thomas R. Schreiner, "Warning and Assurance: Run the Race to the End," in *The Perfect Saviour: Key Themes in Hebrews*, ed. Jonathan Griffiths (Nottingham: InterVarsity, 2012), 89–106.

[3] See for this point and Arminian conclusions, Scot McKnight, "The Warning Passages in Hebrews: A Formal Analysis and Theological Conclusions," *Trinity Journal* 13 (1992): 21–59.

The most controversial text is the warning in Heb 6:4–8. Many in the Reformed tradition claim that the warning is directed to those who are almost Christians.[4] Such a reading, however, should be rejected for several reasons. First, such an interpretation would make the warning passage in chapter 6 different from every other warning in the letter, which are all directed to believers. Second, this reading understands the text to speak of those who have *already fallen away*, and thus the admonition is again read differently from all the other warnings in that it becomes a description of those who *have fallen away* instead of a warning to *avoid falling away*. Such a distinctive reading of the warning is quite improbable. Third, the terms used describe most naturally those who are believers. Those "who were once enlightened" are clearly believers in the only other place we find the same word: after believers were "enlightened," they responded well to discrimination, persecution, and even the stealing of their possessions (Heb 10:32–34). The word "taste," contrary to the "almost Christian" view, doesn't refer merely to sipping God's word, the powers of the coming age, or the heavenly gift (6:4–5), because tasting in Hebrews is used to describe Jesus's death (2:9)—and he did more than sip death! Finally, the author says that they shared in the Holy Spirit (6:4), and sharing in the Spirit is the clearest indication that one is a believer (Gal 3:1–5; Acts 15:7–11). Forms of the word "sharing" are used for sharing "in a heavenly calling" (Heb 3:1), sharing in Christ (v. 14), partaking of milk (5:13), Jesus's sharing in flesh and blood (2:14), and our experiencing discipline (12:8). There is no indication that sharing is somehow substandard or inferior. In every instance full sharing is in view. Exegetically, the author describes believers and warns them about the danger of falling away.

If someone falls away, that person can't be renewed to repentance (Heb 6:4–6). He or she is like ground that has received the blessings of rain but produces no fruit (vv. 7–8). If that happens, the person will be disqualified, "worthless" (*adokimoi*), and cursed (v. 8). The readers must beware of apostasy, of recrucifying the Son of God (v. 6). Some are convinced that such

---

[4] For the best argument for this reading, see Wayne Grudem, "Perseverance of the Saints: A Case Study from Hebrews 6:4–6 and the Other Warning Passages in Hebrews," in *Still Sovereign: Contemporary Perspectives on Election, Foreknowledge, & Grace*, ed. T. R. Schreiner and B. A. Ware (Grand Rapids: Baker, 2000), 133–82.

an interpretation means that those who are believers can apostatize and fall away, but we would argue that the warnings are a means by which the elect are preserved until the end and are always effective in the lives of true Christians. There are actually a number of examples of warnings functioning in this way in the NT. Believers are to *pray* for deliverance from Satan as the evil one (Matt 6:13), but God *promises* they will be delivered from the evil one (2 Thess 3:3). Why should we pray if the Lord promises to protect us from the evil one? The answer is that our prayers are the *means* God uses to preserve us.

Another example comes in Mark 13, where Jesus gives his end-time discourse. In the middle of the discourse he warns his hearers, "Then if anyone tells you, 'See, here is the Messiah! See, there!' do not believe it. For false messiahs and false prophets will arise and will perform signs and wonders to lead astray, if possible, the elect. And you must watch! I have told you everything in advance" (vv. 21–23). A number of different interpretations of this discourse are possible, but we don't need to worry about how to interpret the details here. We can all agree that no one who is identified as a believer will put his faith in a false messiah. By definition a Christian must believe that Jesus is the Messiah! Jesus warns his disciples to be alert and watchful in the strongest terms in this text. In fact, the discourse concludes with these words: "What I say to you, I say to everyone: Be alert!" (v. 37). The warning is bracing and strong, and yet Jesus says in the midst of the warning that it isn't possible for the elect to be led astray. Some might be tempted to say that the warning is beside the point if the elect can't be led astray, concluding that the elect don't need a warning if they can't be led astray. Such a reading fails because it doesn't see that the elect are kept safe from apostasy *by heeding the warning*, and thus the warning becomes the means by which the elect persevere until the end.

We find the same pattern in Acts 27, where we read the thrilling narrative of Paul's shipwreck and deliverance. In the midst of the storm Paul assures those on board that every single one of them will live, that not a single life on the ship will be lost (vv. 21–25). When we come to the end of the account, the promise given to Paul has become a reality: all 276 of those on the ship make it safely to land (vv. 39–44). And yet in the middle of the text, after Paul received the promise that every single person would live, we come across what might seem to be surprising words from the apostle.

"Some sailors tried to escape from the ship; they had let down the skiff into the sea, pretending that they were going to put out anchors from the bow. Paul said to the centurion and the soldiers, 'Unless these men stay in the ship, you cannot be saved.' Then the soldiers cut the ropes holding the skiff and let it drop away" (vv. 30–32). Paul has already received the promise that every single person would live, and yet he warns that if the sailors of the ship got away on the skiff, then the centurion and soldiers would lose their lives! Paul isn't joking but is deadly serious, for the sailors are needed to guide the ship. The same Paul who made a promise also gives a warning, and the two aren't incompatible, for the warning is the means by which the promise given becomes a reality.

The letters of 2 Peter and Jude are very similar in many ways. In both letters the readers are warned about the danger of false teachers. Peter begins by emphasizing the godly virtues that must be practiced by believers (2 Pet 1:5–7). He explains why these virtues are so important: Those who practice these qualities show their saving knowledge of Jesus is fruitful and useful (v. 8). Believers must confirm their "calling and election" by practicing these godly qualities (v. 10). When Peter says that those who practice such virtues won't "stumble", he means they won't fall away—they will be preserved from apostasy.[5] Those who enter the kingdom are those who practice these virtues. Jude teaches the same truth when he exhorts his readers to "keep yourselves in the love of God" (Jude 21). We saw earlier in Jude that God promises to preserve and keep those who belong to him (vv. 1, 24–25), but verse 21 shifts the emphasis to the responsibility of believers to keep themselves in God's love. God promises to keep believers so that they don't fall away, but at the same time believers are enjoined to remain in God's love.

The book of Revelation was written to churches that were being persecuted. Some of them were becoming lackadaisical in their faith. John writes so that believers will endure and be faithful (Rev 13:10; 14:12). We see this especially in the repeated calls to conquer and overcome (2:7, 11, 17, 26; 3:5, 12, 21; 21:7). We will limit ourselves to three statements. In 2:7 Jesus promises the church at Ephesus, "To the one who conquers, I will give the right to eat from the tree of life, which is in the paradise of God." Overcoming and

---

[5] Most commentators agree. See Richard Bauckham, *2 Peter, Jude* WBC (Waco, TX: Word, 1983), 191.

conquering aren't optional. Those who don't overcome won't eat of the tree of life and won't enter paradise. Overcoming is a matter of life and death, as is clear also in verse 11: "The one who conquers will never be harmed by the second death." The second death is the lake of fire, as John explicitly says in 20:14; 21:8. Those who don't overcome and conquer, then, will end up in the lake of fire. The last example is taken from verse 7: "The one who conquers will inherit these things, and I will be his God, and he will be my son." God will be the God of those who overcome, but those who don't conquer are on the outside of the heavenly city and will experience the second death (v. 8). Believers are warned that they must conquer to obtain life and to avoid the lake of fire.

Retrospective Texts in the NT

The warning passages in the NT are *prospective*, warning believers about the future consequences that would occur if they fell away. It is crucial to understand, however, that we also find *retrospective* texts, which look back on those who have fallen away. We will consider briefly several of these texts here.

The first letter of John was written to believers reeling from the departure of some from their midst. It seems that those who left had set up a separate church, and their defection caused those remaining to wonder if they themselves truly belonged to the Lord. John's primary purpose was to assure believers that they truly belonged to God (e.g., 1 John 2:12–14, 20–21, 24–27; 3:1–2, 14, 19–22; 5:13). Those who remained were in the right, while those who left had strayed from the one true God. John helps believers think about those who had left the community: "They went out from us, but they did not belong to us; for if they had belonged to us, they would have remained with us. However, they went out so that it might be made clear that none of them belongs to us" (2:19). Some in the church initially gave every evidence of being believers. But eventually they left the church and established another church, and they did not confess Jesus as the historical Christ (vv. 22–23; 4:1–3; 5:6–12). The departure of these people demonstrated that they never truly belonged to God. John doesn't say that "they *no longer* belong to us" but that "they did not belong to us." If their faith were genuine, they would have persevered until the end—"they would have remained with us," as John says, but their leaving proved they weren't truly Christians. Looking back *retrospectively*, we see that those who departed never truly knew God.

Another fascinating text surfaces in 1 Cor 11:17–34, addressing divisions at the Lord's Supper. The rich were apparently hoarding and gorging on food and wine, while the poor weren't getting enough food. Paul was scandalized by such a gross abuse of the Lord's Supper. Tucked into this discussion is a comment about the benefit of such divisions: "It is necessary that there be factions among you, so that those who are approved may be recognized among you" (v. 19). The words "it is necessary" (*dei*) signify divine necessity, i.e., God's purposes and intentions. The word "approved" (*dokimoi*) signifies those who truly belong to God (2 Cor 10:18; 13:7; 2 Tim 2:15), while "unapproved" or "disqualified" (*adokimoi*) refers to those who aren't truly believers (Rom 1:28; 1 Cor 9:27; 2 Cor 13:5, 6, 7; 2 Tim 3:8; Titus 1:16; Heb 6:8). The Lord used the divisions in the church to disclose those who were believers and those who were false. Of course, we can discern who is true and false only retrospectively. It is hardly evident who is genuine from the beginning. The use of "approved" signifies that those who are shown to be false were never believers in the first place. It is not as if they lost their faith. On the contrary, there were some in the church who were not authentic from the outset.

Another fascinating text in this regard is 2 Timothy 2, where Paul discusses the false teaching spreading "like gangrene" via Hymenaeus and Philetus, among others (v. 17). These men maintained that the resurrection was a past reality, and as a consequence they were "ruining the faith of some" (v. 18). This ruination of the faith of some might suggest that some had lost their salvation, but Paul corrects that misapprehension immediately: "Nevertheless, God's solid foundation stands firm, bearing this inscription: 'The Lord knows those who are his,' and let everyone who calls on the name of the Lord turn away from wickedness" (v. 19). Paul alludes to the narrative in Numbers 16, in which Dathan, Abiram, and Korah and his followers rebelled against the authority of Moses and Aaron. The text reveals, with the earth's swallowing up those in rebellion, those who truly belonged to the Lord. Paul makes the same point here: When the faith of some is ruined, it becomes clear who really belongs to the Lord. The Lord knows those who are his from the beginning, and those who fall away reveal that they didn't truly belong to the Lord. There is no reason for fear, therefore, because no one who truly belongs to the Lord falls away. The Lord knows all along those who are truly his.

The final text is from the Gospel of Matthew: "Not everyone who says to me, 'Lord, Lord,' will enter the kingdom of heaven, but only the one who does the will of my Father in heaven. On that day many will say to me, 'Lord, Lord, didn't we prophesy in your name, drive out demons in your name, and do many miracles in your name?' Then I will announce to them, 'I never knew you. Depart from me, you lawbreakers!'" (Matt 7:21–23). Some appear to be believers since they prophesy, exorcise demons, and do miracles in Jesus's name, but their lack of obedience reveals that they don't belong to him. It is instructive that Jesus does not say that they had lost what they once had. Instead, he says, "I *never* knew you," which shows that, despite outward appearances, those who lived lawlessly were never true believers. In retrospect, it is apparent who truly belongs to the Lord.

Summary

We have made three points in this section. First, those whom God has chosen and elected will never fall away. Those whom God has foreknown, predestined, called, and justified will certainly be glorified. Nothing will separate believers from Christ's love, and God will complete the good work he has begun. The eternal life he gives is by its very nature eternal, and thus it can never be revoked. Second, we find warnings and admonitions repeatedly that threaten believers with final judgment if they fall away. Such warnings aren't the exception but the rule, showing them to be a constituent part of the gospel. The warnings, however, don't cancel the promises of final salvation. Final salvation is given to those who heed the warnings, to those who take them seriously, for the warnings are the means God uses to preserve his elect from eternal harm. Third, the warnings are *prospective*, admonishing believers about the danger of falling away. We also observe *retrospective* texts in the NT, and we discover in these instances that there are some who were part of the church who have fallen away. The retrospective texts, however, clarify that those who fell away were never truly believers in Jesus Christ. They appeared to be genuine Christians, but their apostasy indicates that their faith was not genuine.

Systematic Formulations

Traditionally, the topics treated in this chapter have gone under the heading "the perseverance of the saints." That tag is ambiguous, however, because it covers two elements: God's perseverance *with* his saints, his keeping them saved, and the perseverance *of* the saints proper. We will label the first "preservation" and the second "perseverance." In addition, we will treat two other topics that interface with them: assurance and apostasy. Assurance is confidence of final salvation, while apostasy is defection from a faith previously confessed.[6] After handling these four doctrines in turn, we will attempt to systematize them.

Preservation

We have studied many texts that teach preservation, the truth that God keeps to the end the people he has saved. Here we present theological arguments for preservation, bolstered by more exegesis.

- The Trinity's Roles
- God's Attributes
- Christ's Work

The Trinity's Roles

Scripture teaches that each of the Trinitarian persons is active in preserving the people of God for final salvation.

The *Father* plays a significant role in preservation. We see this in John's Gospel. Jesus in his bread of life discourse teaches that every person whom the Father has chosen will believe in Jesus, and he will keep them saved. Jesus then explains the Father's will:

> "I have come down from heaven, not to do my own will, but the will of him who sent me. This is the will of him who sent me: that I should lose none of those he has given me but should raise them up on the last day. For this is the will of my Father: that everyone who sees the Son and believes in him will have eternal life, and I will raise him up on the last day." (John 6:38–40)

---

[6] For more on these themes, see Robert A. Peterson, *Our Secure Salvation: Preservation and Apostasy*, EBT (Phillipsburg, NJ: P&R, 2009).

Speaking as the good shepherd, who loves his sheep and dies for them, Jesus explains that eternal life is his gift to them. They will not experience God's wrath, for they are safe in Jesus's hand (John 10:28–29). He then adds, "My Father, who has given them to me, is greater than all. No one is able to snatch them out of the Father's hand" (v. 29). The Father is greater than the incarnate Son, and believers are safe in the Father's powerful hand, his working to preserve them.

As we saw in numerous passages treated in the exegetical section, Paul also presents the Father as keeping the saints saved. The apostle begins Romans 8 with such a statement: "Therefore, there is now no condemnation for those in Christ Jesus" (Rom 8:1). The Father (along with the Son) is the judge on the last day, but he will not condemn those united to his Son. To the contrary, the Father will justify them before humans and angels at the Last Judgment.

The judgments on believers because of abuses at the Lord's Supper are commonly misunderstood. Paul says that those partaking unworthily of the Supper are guilty and that partakers, therefore, should examine themselves (1 Cor 11:27–28). Anyone who partakes "without recognizing the body, eats and drinks judgment on himself" (v. 29). Paul tells us what is involved in this judgment: "Many are sick and ill among you, and many have fallen asleep" (v. 30). These are temporal judgments of weakness, illness, or premature death. If God's people "properly judged [them]selves," God would spare them those judgments (v. 31). But even if they failed, they would experience temporal rather than eternal judgment: "But when we are judged by the Lord, we are disciplined, so that we may not be condemned with the world" (v. 32). Ironically, then, Corinthian abuses at the Lord's Table lead to a preservation passage, teaching that the Father spares his children eternal punishment when he visits them with temporal punishments.

The *Son* plays a prominent role in preserving God's people, as we saw in John 6. There Jesus pledges to "never cast out" any that the Father gives to him (v. 37). Three times Jesus says that he will "raise them [or "him"] up on the last day" (vv. 39, 40, 44). Along with the Father, the Son actively preserves the sheep. Jesus gives his people the gift of eternal life, states that they will never perish categorically,[7] and says no one can take them from

---

[7] Daniel B. Wallace, *Greek Grammar Beyond the Basics* (Grand Rapids: Zondervan, 1997), calls the emphatic negation present in John 10:28 "the strongest way to negate something in Greek" (468).

his and the Father's strong arms (John 10:28–29). In fact, when Jesus says "I and the Father are one" (v. 30), he means one in preserving the sheep for final salvation.

Three times Jesus affirms his preservation of the people of God in his high priestly prayer. First, Jesus, returning to his heavenly Father, asks him to protect and unify personally those the Father gave him out of the world (John 17:9, 11). "While I was with them, I was protecting them by your name that you have given me. I guarded them and not one of them is lost, except the son of destruction, so that the Scripture may be fulfilled" (John 17:12). Jesus preserved all the Father gave him, which excludes Judas, who was not a true believer.

Second, shortly thereafter Jesus prays to the Father: "I am not praying that you take them out of the world but that you protect them from the evil one" (v. 15). Jesus, who kept God's people saved on earth, commits them to the Father's care when Jesus returns to him.

Third, Jesus asks the Father to take the elect to heaven so they can be with Jesus and see his glory: "Father, I want those you have given me to be with me where I am, so that they will see my glory, which you have given me because you loved me before the world's foundation" (v. 24). Although John's eschatology is primarily realized, his Gospel does contain futuristic elements (cf. 5:28–29; 14:2–3), as it does here. Carson is right:

> [This is] an unambiguous reference to v. 5, where Jesus prays to be restored to the glory that he had with the Father before the world began. . . . The glory that his followers will see is his glory as God, the glory he enjoyed before his mission because of the Father's love for him. . . . Presumably, those who share, with the Son, the delight of being loved by the Father (v. 23), share also the glory to which the Son is restored in consequence of his triumphant death/exaltation.[8]

First John also testifies to Jesus's keeping believers saved: "We know that everyone who has been born of God does not sin, but the one who is born of God keeps him, and the evil one does not touch him" (1 John 5:18). John distinguishes between each one "who has been born," or regenerated,

---

[8] D. A. Carson, *The Gospel according to John*, PNTC (Grand Rapids: Eerdmans, 1991), 569–70.

"of God" and "the one who is born of God," namely, the unique Son of God. No one born again lives a life of sin, but the eternal Son become incarnate "keeps" him so that the devil cannot fatally harm him. Yarbrough, alluding to the good shepherd's keeping his sheep in John 10, deserves quotation: "In 1 John 5:18, John draws on this image of Christ protecting and preserving the life and soul of the one who trusts in him because this one has been born of God (cf. 5:1; Jude 1)."[9]

The *Holy Spirit* too plays an important role in preservation. Paul speaks three times of God's sealing of believers (in Eph 1:13; 4:30; 2 Cor 1:22). In the last passage Paul indicates, by distinguishing "God" from "Christ" (v. 21) and "the Spirit" (v. 22), that the Father is the one who performs the sealing. In the first passage the Father, indicated by the divine passive, seals believers "in him," that is, in Christ. God seals us in union with his Son, indicating the permanence of union with Christ.

In all three texts the Holy Spirit is mentioned:

> In him you also were sealed with the promised Holy Spirit when you heard the word of truth, the gospel of your salvation, and when you believed. The Holy Spirit is the down payment of our inheritance, until the redemption of the possession, to the praise of his glory. (Eph 1:13–14)

> Don't grieve God's Holy Spirit. You were sealed by him for the day of redemption. (Eph 4:30)

> Now it is God who strengthens us together with you in Christ, and who has anointed us. He has also put his seal on us and given us the Spirit in our hearts as a down payment. (2 Cor 1:21–22)

In all three passages the seal is the Holy Spirit.[10] The second text is better translated, "You were sealed with him," for we were sealed by the Father, not the Spirit. The Father seals us with the Spirit, who is God's seal on believers. In this role the Spirit marks us as God's own and, more importantly,

---

[9] Robert W. Yarbrough, *1–3 John*, BECNT (Grand Rapids: Baker, 2008), 316.

[10] This is implied in 2 Cor 1:22, where the text refers to the Spirit three times but uses his name only the third time: God "anointed" us with the Spirit, God's "seal" is the Spirit, and God gave us "the Spirit."

preserves us for salvation on the last day. Paul is explicit: the Father sealed us (divine passive again) "for the day of redemption" (Eph 4:30). The first and last texts above call the Spirit the "down payment" of our inheritance, another reference to the Spirit's role in keeping us saved.

These titles of the Spirit reflect Paul's already/not yet theology. Already the Spirit as God's seal marks us as God's own people and points to the "day of redemption," when we will enjoy salvation in its fullness. Already God has given believers the Spirit as a "down payment," which, as Baugh explains, "will be consummated in the future. This inheritance centers on his people's resurrection in the new creation."[11]

God's Attributes

Another vantage point on preservation is the attributes of God. Scripture portrays God's sovereignty, justice, power, faithfulness, and love as functioning in the preservation of God's own. Paul regards the *sovereignty of God* as the basis of believers' confidence of final glory:

> We know that all things work together for the good of those who love God, who are called according to his purpose. For those he foreknew he also predestined to be conformed to the image of his Son, so that he would be the firstborn among many brothers and sisters. And those he predestined, he also called; and those he called, he also justified; and those he justified, he also glorified. (Rom 8:28–30)

God freely causes everything that comes into the lives of those who love him (his people)—even suffering—to work for their ultimate good. Paul strengthens this statement by affirming that God has acted for our greatest good by planning and accomplishing our salvation from beginning to end (in vv. 29–30). God foreloved, chose, summoned, declared righteous, and glorified his people. Although glorification won't occur until the end, the apostle describes it using the same past tense he has used to describe the past aspects of salvation. God's people are already as good as glorified.

Moo captures the strong accents on God's sovereignty undergirding believers' hope of glory:

---

[11] S. M. Baugh, *Ephesians*, Evangelical Exegetical Commentary (Bellingham, WA: Lexham Press, 2016), 100.

It is because this is God's plan for us who are called and who, thereby, love God, that we can be certain that all things will contribute toward "good" [in v. 28]—the realization of this plan in each of our cases. . . . The realization of God's "purpose" [v. 28] in individual believers is the bedrock of "the hope of glory." . . . Paul is looking at the believer's glorification [v. 30] from the standpoint of God, who has already decreed that it should take place. While not yet experienced, the divine decision to glorify those who have been justified has already been made; the issue has been settled. Here Paul touches on the ultimate source of the assurance that Christians enjoy, and with it he brings to a triumphant climax his celebration of the "no condemnation" [v. 1] that applies to every person in Christ.[12]

Paul also presents *God's justice* as actively keeping Christians safe in Christ: "Who shall bring any charge against God's elect? It is God who justifies. Who is to condemn? Christ Jesus is the one who died—more than that, who was raised—who is at the right hand of God, who indeed is interceding for us" (Rom 8:33–34 ESV). Paul uses rhetorical questions to underline the truth. The enemies of God and his people—Satan, demons, and human rebels—bring many accusations of guilt. Paul's point is that none of these charges will stick, because our case has already gone to the supreme court of the universe, and the judge, almighty God, has declared us righteous. No one will ever reverse his verdict (v. 33).

The same truth is conveyed in verse 34. After Paul's rhetorical question "Who is to condemn?" he mentions "Christ Jesus." To follow Paul's argument we need to know that the Father and the Son are each the judge in half of Scripture's last-judgment passages, respectively. So Paul could have answered his question by saying, "Christ Jesus will condemn." Instead, he says that Christ died, was raised, sits at God's right hand, and prays for us. His meaning is clear: the Son, the judge of all the earth, will not condemn us but save us. Christ Jesus, the judge, is our Savior. Once more God's justice sustains our salvation.

God's power is another divine quality that keeps us in the faith. We have already seen that Jesus affirms his power to keep his sheep safe in his hand.

---

[12] Moo, *The Epistle to the Romans*, 531, 536 (see chap. 2, n. 62).

He gives them the gift of never-ending life, affirms they will never go to hell, and then says, "No one will snatch them out of my hand" (John 10:28). Carson mentions "eternal life" and then hits the nail on the head: "The focus is not on the power of the life itself, but on Jesus' power: *no-one can snatch them out of my hand*, not the marauding wolf (v. 12), not the thieves and robbers (vv. 1, 8), not anyone. . . . The ultimate security of Jesus' sheep rests with the good shepherd."[13]

God's faithfulness preserves his people. The exegetical section treated four statements of God's faithfulness:

> He will also strengthen you to the end, so that you will be blameless in the day of our Lord Jesus Christ. God is faithful; you were called by him into fellowship with his Son, Jesus Christ our Lord. (1 Cor 1:8–9)

> Now may the God of peace himself sanctify you completely. And may your whole spirit, soul, and body be kept sound and blameless at the coming of our Lord Jesus Christ. He who calls you is faithful; he will do it. (1 Thess 5:23–24)

> The Lord is faithful; he will strengthen you and guard you from the evil one. (2 Thess 3:3)

> If we are faithless, he remains faithful, for he cannot deny himself. (2 Tim 2:13)

We add a fifth passage on God's faithfulness to this list. It does not contain the words "God is faithful" but nevertheless is a powerful witness to that truth. The writer to the Hebrews cites Gen 22:17 as evidence of the reliability of God's promises: "I will indeed bless you, and I will greatly multiply you" (Heb 6:14). After Abraham was willing to sacrifice Isaac, God repeated his earlier promise and added to it an oath. Why would almighty God do such a thing?

> When God desired to show more convincingly to the heirs of the promise the unchangeable character of his purpose, he guaranteed it with an oath, so that by two unchangeable things, in which it is impossible for God to lie, we who have fled for refuge might have

---

[13] Carson, *The Gospel according to John*, 393.

strong encouragement to hold fast to the hope set before us. (Heb 6:17–18 ESV)

God's oath-taking underscores the fact that his divine attributes—in this case faithfulness—bind him to his word. God will not, indeed cannot, go back on his word, for he gave it and "guaranteed it with an oath" (v. 17). His promise to Abraham is irrevocable. That is clear, but it is not immediately evident how God's promise to bless and multiply faithful Abraham brings "strong encouragement to hold fast to the hope set before" Hebrews' readers (v. 18).

The context urges the readers to "be imitators of those who inherit the promises through faith and perseverance" (v. 12) and then sets forth father Abraham as a prime example of that very thing: "After waiting patiently, Abraham obtained the promise" (v. 15).

So the question remains: how does God's promise to Abraham encourage Hebrews' readers to persevere in faith? Lane provides the best answer:

> The focus of the exposition shifts sharply from the patriarch to Christians, who are designated . . . "the heirs of the promise" (cf. v. 12). As those who have inherited the promises through Christ, they are to appreciate the relevance of the biblical account to them. What is recorded in Scripture is intended to strengthen them in their conviction that God's purpose for them is also unalterable. . . . In view of the context and the focus on the Christian community in vv. 17–18 it would appear to be proper to regard the promise given to Abraham and confirmed with an oath as the type that is given to the community of the new covenant in Christ.[14]

God stooped to take an oath that underlined his resolve to do what he had promised Abraham. God's promise to him fortifies our confidence, as Abraham's spiritual heirs, that he will fulfill his new covenant promises to us. God is faithful, and his promise and oath give believers a sure hope. Indeed, this hope is "a sure and steadfast anchor of the soul, a hope that enters into the inner place behind the curtain, where Jesus has gone as a forerunner on our behalf" (Heb 6:19–20). God provides more evidence of his faithfulness to preserve his people when he tells of Jesus, our great high priest who

---

[14] William L. Lane, *Hebrews 1–8*, WBC (Dallas: Word, 1991), 152.

gave himself to save us and now appears in the very presence of God on our behalf. God preserves us because he is faithful.

God's love preserves believers for final salvation. The *textus classicus* on this theme is Rom 8:35–39. We have treated this passage in the exegetical section and add a few comments here. Paul asks rhetorically what can separate Christians from Christ's love. He then enumerates seven possible answers before concluding that nothing at all can do so. The last element in the series, "sword," stands for death by execution, and even that cannot frustrate God's love in his Son for his people. As stated previously, attempting to square the possibility of apostasy with Paul's words here does not work: "For I am persuaded that neither death nor life, nor angels nor rulers, nor things present nor things to come, nor powers, nor height nor depth, nor any other created thing will be able to separate us from the love of God that is in Christ Jesus our Lord" (vv. 38–39). Paul uses comprehensive couplets: everything is included in someone's "death" and "life." "Things present" and "things to come" covers everything, for even the most meager doctrine of salvation includes things past. As a last hurrah Paul mentions "any other created thing [that would] be able to separate us from the love of God that is in Christ Jesus our Lord" (v. 39). This includes believers and their failures. Because of the Trinity's love we are safe in Christ.

Christ's Work

Scripture connects Christ's saving work to our preservation. Because of what Jesus did to save us, we are safe in him. Our preservation is grounded in his cross, empty tomb, intercession, and return. Preservation is grounded in *Jesus's crucifixion*. Paul expresses this truth when he compares the two Adams: "Just as through one man's disobedience the many were made sinners, so also through the one man's obedience the many will be made righteous" (Rom 5:19). Adam's primal sin caused "many," over against the one Adam, to be "made sinners." Adam's disobedience caused all his race to become sinners in God's sight. Parallel to Adam's sin, Christ's "becoming obedient to the point of death—even to death on a cross" (Phil 2:8) is the basis of the justification of all his people. Paul uses the future tense "will be made righteous" (Rom 5:19) to show that Christ's work accomplishes justification now and forever. God will declare believers righteous before humans and angels at the Last Judgment because Christ our Savior died to justify us.

Paul teaches the same truth in different words later in Romans:

> There is now no condemnation for those in Christ Jesus, because
> the law of the Spirit of life in Christ Jesus has set you free from
> the law of sin and death. For what the law could not do since it
> was weakened by the flesh, God did. He condemned sin in the
> flesh by sending his own Son in the likeness of sinful flesh as a
> sin offering, in order that the law's requirement would be fulfilled
> in us who do not walk according to the flesh but according to the
> Spirit. (Rom 8:1–4)

Though the law was unable to rescue the lost because people could not keep
it, God rescued them in Christ. God sent his incarnate Son to be a sin offering to "condemn sin in the flesh" (v. 3). Christ died in our place, taking the
condemnation that we lawbreakers deserved, and as a result "there is now no
condemnation for" us believers (v. 1).[15] Jesus's death on the cross saves us and
keeps us saved.

Preservation is grounded in *Jesus's resurrection*. Reconciliation is Christ's
saving work viewed as that which overcomes our enmity with God, thereby
making peace between us. It is attributed to Christ's death alone in every
passage except one: "If, while we were enemies, we were reconciled to God
through the death of his Son, then how much more, having been reconciled,
will we be saved by his life" (Rom 5:10). Paul mentions both "Christ's death"
and "his life." Does he thereby divide Christ's accomplishment of reconciliation? No. Rather, he intends for us to understand that Christ's death and
resurrection together constitute his saving work (cf. Rom 4:25; 6:5; 1 Cor
15:3–4). The one who died to reconcile God's people lives forever to keep
them reconciled.

Hebrews' warning passages are well known. Not as well-known are its
preservation passages in 6:17–20 and 7:23–25. We have studied the former
and now turn attention to the latter:

> Many have become Levitical priests, since they are prevented by
> death from remaining in office. But because he remains forever, he

---

[15] Moo, *The Epistle to the Romans*, 481; Judith M. Gundry Volf, *Paul and
Perseverance: Staying in and Falling Away* (Louisville: John Knox, 1990), 68.

holds his priesthood permanently. Therefore, he is able to save completely those who come to God through him, since he always lives to intercede for them. (Heb 7:23–25)

Unlike the Levitical priests, who served until death and were replaced by a descendent, Jesus Christ, as the crucified and risen one, has "the power of an indestructible life" (Heb 7:16). Therefore he "remains" a priest "forever," because he arose from the dead and "holds his priesthood permanently" (7:24). This has great practical import for his people: "Therefore, he is able to save completely those who come to God through him, since he always lives to intercede for them" (v. 25). The risen Christ is our great high priest and as such has no successors. He saves "completely," which has often been taken in a temporal sense to mean "forever" (NASB) and sometimes in a qualitative sense as "completely" (NIV) but probably means "absolutely," which encompasses both meanings, as Lane argues.[16] Jesus's death and resurrection are the basis of God's preservation of his saints.

Preservation is grounded in *Jesus's intercession*. The passage just studied does double duty. It shows that both Jesus's resurrection and his intercession save. Christ saves believers absolutely, "since he always lives to intercede for them" (Heb 7:25). Our great high priest's prayers keep us safe as he appears in God's presence for us: "The Son's indissoluble life is the basis of his uninterrupted priestly intercession."[17]

Jesus predicts his intercessory ministry in Luke's Gospel. Jesus tells the disciples that Satan (after moving Judas to betray Jesus) wants to prove the others to be frauds too. Jesus tells Peter, "But I have prayed for you, Simon, that your faith may not fail. And when you have turned back, strengthen your brothers" (Luke 22:32). Peter balks and professes his undying loyalty to Jesus, even unto death. In reply Jesus predicts Peter's three denials (vv. 33–34). Jesus's intercessory prayer for Peter keeps his faith from utterly failing after these three denials (cf. John 21:15–19).

We have already seen that Jesus prays three times for the Eleven in his high priestly prayer:

---

[16] Lane, *Hebrews 1–8*, 176, 189.
[17] Lane, 191.

"Holy Father, protect them by your name that you have given me, so that they may be one as we are one." (John 17:11)

"I am not praying that you take them out of the world but that you protect them from the evil one." (17:15)

"Father, I want those you have given me to be with me where I am, so that they will see my glory, which you have given me because you loved me before the world's foundation." (17:24)

We have also seen that Jesus will not condemn his people but, on the contrary, dies, rises, and intercedes for them (Rom 8:34). In the Gospels and Epistles, then, we learn that Jesus intercedes on behalf of his people to preserve them in the faith.

Preservation is grounded in *Jesus's return*. The apostle John records Jesus's heartening words:

"Don't let your heart be troubled. Believe in God; believe also in me. In my Father's house are many rooms. If it were not so, would I have told you that I am going to prepare a place for you? If I go away and prepare a place for you, I will come again and take you to myself, so that where I am you may be also." (John 14:1–3)

Jesus promises to come again to take his people to the Father in heaven. Jesus wants those who believe in the Father and him to anticipate being welcomed by the Father. The immediately preceding context of these verses strengthens the idea of preservation here, for Jesus's comforting words in 14:2–3 are to be seen in light of his prediction of Peter's three denials (13:37–38). Peter will falter, but Jesus assures the Eleven (Judas had gone out to betray him, vv. 28–30) that they belong to the Father and have places in his heavenly home.

Peter paints a different picture that teaches the same truth: "With your minds ready for action, be sober-minded and set your hope completely on the grace to be brought to you at the revelation of Jesus Christ" (1 Pet 1:13). Peter enjoins preparedness and moral sobriety as he points his readers to the second coming. The "revelation of Jesus Christ" will feature a great outpouring of God's grace on his people. "Grace" here stands for the consummation of salvation. It involves God's preservation of his people, for they will not fail to receive ultimate redemption. Kistemaker speaks wisely:

When Jesus returns at the appointed time, he will bring to his followers the fulfillment of their salvation. When he appears, his redemptive work will be realized in all the believers. He grants them full salvation through deliverance from sin, glorification of body and soul, and the knowledge that he will be in their midst forever.[18]

We have summarized the biblical teaching on God's preservation of his saints. The roles of the Trinitarian persons, the attributes of God, and Christ's saving work combine to secure the final salvation of all who truly believe in Jesus. Calvin encourages believers with this truth:

> Whenever we hear of Christ as armed with eternal power, let us remember that the perpetuity of the church is secure in this protection. . . . Hence it follows that the devil, with all the resources of the world, can never destroy the church, founded as it is on the eternal throne of Christ. . . . In like manner, Christ enriches his people with all things necessary for the eternal salvation of souls and fortifies them with courage to stand unconquerable against all the assaults of spiritual enemies. . . . Our King will never leave us destitute, but will provide for our needs until, our warfare ended, we are called to triumph.[19]

Perseverance

God's preservation of his saints is correlative to their perseverance. Because he keeps them, they continue in the faith. This underscores divine sovereignty in salvation. Scripture also teaches genuine human responsibility, and this means that believers *must* persevere to be finally saved. Every part of the NT teaches the necessity of perseverance for final salvation:

> "The one who endures to the end will be saved." (Matt 24:13)

---

[18] Simon J. Kistemaker, *Peter and Jude*, NTC (Grand Rapids: Baker, 1987), 59.

[19] John Calvin, *Institutes of the Christian Religion*, ed. John T. McNeill, trans. Ford Lewis Battles, 2 vols. (Philadelphia: Westminster, 1960), 2.15.3–4 (1:497, 498, 499).

After they had preached the gospel in that town and made many disciples, they returned to Lystra, to Iconium, and to Antioch, strengthening the disciples by encouraging them to continue in the faith and by telling them, "It is necessary to go through many hardships to enter the kingdom of God." (Acts 14:21–22)

You need endurance, so that after you have done God's will, you may receive what was promised. (Heb 10:36)

"This calls for endurance from the saints, who keep God's commands and their faith in Jesus." (Rev 14:12)

God's people must continue in at least three ways:

- Trusting Christ
- Loving Others
- Pursing Holiness

Believers Must Continue to Trust Christ

The Bible teaches that making an initial profession of faith in Christ is insufficient. True believers persevere to the end in trusting Jesus. After Jesus delivered difficult words concerning eating his flesh and drinking his blood, "From that moment many of his disciples turned back and no longer accompanied him" (John 6:66). Obviously "disciples" is used here in a broad sense. Some who followed Jesus because he multiplied the bread and fish were offended by his strong words and followed him no longer. Jesus then asks his twelve disciples: "You don't want to go away too, do you?" (v. 67). He encourages his disciples (the word is now used in a narrow sense) to profess their intention of continuing to follow him. Peter, their leader, does so: "Lord, to whom will we go? You have the words of eternal life. We have come to believe and know that you are the Holy One of God" (vv. 68–69). We love Peter's answer. He does not profess to understand all mysteries concerning the Son of God. He, on behalf of his fellows, professes faith in Christ and the futility of going anywhere else to learn about eternal life.

Paul too teaches the necessity of perseverance in faith. After affirming Christ's preeminence in creation and redemption (Col 1:15–18), Paul presents him as God incarnate and as reconciler of the whole creation (vv.

19–20). He then applies the latter truth to his readers. Their sinful lives had estranged them from God, but Christ reconciled them to God by dying in their place, and he will present them sinless before God (vv. 21–22). As noted in the exegetical section, Paul adds a proviso: "If indeed you remain grounded and steadfast in the faith and are not shifted away from the hope of the gospel that you heard" (v. 23). The Colossians must continue to trust Christ as Lord and Savior to be finally saved. Saving faith involves more than an initial profession; it also involves perseverance to the end.

The writer to the Hebrews views the Christian life not as a sprint but as a long-distance race. Urged on by the heroes and heroines of faith of chapter 11, the readers must not be distracted by persecution and their own sin but must instead "run with endurance the race that lies before" them (Heb 12:1). Their ultimate focus must remain on "Jesus, the pioneer and perfecter of our faith, who for the joy that was set before him endured the cross, despising the shame, and sat down at the right hand of the throne of God" (v. 2). Although they will never suffer as Jesus did, God calls them to imitate him in enduring unjust suffering for God's glory and the promise of joy. An eternal reward awaits Hebrews' readers if they do "not grow weary or fainthearted" (v. 3 ESV). Indeed, the writer expects them to persevere even to the point of dying for Christ (v. 4). Professed believers must endure in faith, and true believers do.

Believers Must Continue to Love Others

Commands and exhortations for believers to love one another are commonplace in the NT:

> [Jesus] said to him, "'Love the Lord your God with all your heart, with all your soul, and with all your mind.' This is the greatest and most important command. The second is like it: 'Love your neighbor as yourself.'" (Matt 22:37–39)

> [Jesus said,] "This is my command: Love one another as I have loved you." (John 15:12)

> Love one another deeply as brothers and sisters. (Rom 12:10)

> Let brotherly love continue. (Heb 13:1)

We will explore three passages that teach that Christians must love one another. First, Jesus raises the OT's command to love one's neighbor as one-self (Lev 19:18) to a new level: "I give you a new command: Love one another. Just as I have loved you, you are also to love one another. By this everyone will know that you are my disciples, if you love one another" (John 13:34–35). The command to love one's neighbor is strengthened Christologically. Christ's display of love in his cross becomes the goal, incentive, and measure of our love for other Christians. It is our goal, and who can claim to have reached it? It thus humbles us and drives us to God's enabling grace to live the Christian life. Christ's love is our incentive; it is an inexhaustible fuel motivating us to love even the unlovely. And it is the highest measure of love. The gauge of loving others is not simply love for self but Christ's love for us. We love others as Jesus loved us, that is, freely, sacrificially, unselfishly. This is the Lord's command; if people truly loved like this, it would indeed set them apart from those who don't know Christ. Love is obligatory for those loved and saved by Christ.

Second, Peter prizes brotherly love: "Since you have purified yourselves by your obedience to the truth, so that you show sincere brotherly love for each other, from a pure heart love one another constantly" (1 Pet 1:22). Peter means that, because his readers have obeyed the gospel (which is a com-mand) and trusted Christ as Savior, thereby experiencing the cleansing of sins, they are to demonstrate love. This is *philadelphia*, or brotherly love, occurring only here and in Rom 12:10; 1 Thess 4:9; Heb 13:1; 2 Pet 1:7 in the NT. After stating that the goal of his readers' conversion is to show love, Peter commands them to "love one another constantly." This is a call to deepen and increase their love for each another. Davids is correct: "Loving fellow-Christians is obviously no minor issue, but a central concern of both our author and the whole New Testament."[20] Further, the next verse informs us of the power that enables this love—the new life that comes from being "born again . . . through the living and enduring word of God" (1 Pet 1:23). True believers persevere in love.

Third, 1 John is clearest on the necessity of the saints' continuing in love. John sets this forth in both negative and positive terms. Speaking negatively,

---

[20] Peter H. Davids, *The First Epistle of Peter*, NICNT (Grand Rapids: Eerdmans, 1990), 77.

he writes, "The one who does not love remains in death. Everyone who hates his brother or sister is a murderer, and you know that no murderer has eternal life residing in him" (1 John 3:14–15). A lack of love for fellow believers is a bad sign, suggesting a lack of regeneration. Further, John asks, "If anyone has this world's goods and sees a fellow believer in need but withholds compassion from him—how does God's love reside in him?" (v. 17). John concludes, "Little children, let us not love in word or speech, but in action and in truth" (v. 18).

In a later passage John continues to issue warnings concerning a lack of love:

> The one who does not love does not know God, because God is love. (1 John 4:8)

> If anyone says, "I love God," and yet hates his brother or sister, he is a liar. For the person who does not love his brother or sister whom he has seen cannot love God whom he has not seen. (v. 20)

Now John's accent is positive: "Dear friends, let us love one another, because love is from God, and everyone who loves has been born of God and knows God" (4:7). God showed his love to us by sending his unique Son to become incarnate, to love us, and "to be the propitiation for our sins" (v. 10 ESV). Once again, Christ's atoning love is our example: "Dear friends, if God loved us in this way, we also must love one another. . . . We love because he first loved us" (vv. 11, 19). Christians' persevering in love is not a mere option but a command, for "We have this command from him: The one who loves God must also love his brother and sister" (v. 21).

Believers Must Continue to Pursue Holiness

Christians must persevere in holiness if they are to be finally saved. Salvation is by faith, not by pursuing holiness. But true saving faith "works"; it produces good works. "In Christ Jesus neither circumcision nor uncircumcision accomplishes anything; what matters is faith working through love" (Gal 5:6).

We will see this truth in four passages. The first is Paul's most famous faith-and-works text: "You are saved by grace through faith, and this is not from yourselves; it is God's gift—not from works, so that no one can boast. For we are his workmanship, created in Christ Jesus for good works, which God prepared ahead of time or us to do" (Eph 2:8–10). Salvation is "by grace through faith" and "is God's gift" from beginning to end. Justification is not "from works," for, if it were, those saved would have reason for boasting. But that is not the case: "Where, then, is boasting? It is excluded. By what kind of law? By one of works? No, on the contrary, by a law of faith. For we conclude that a person is justified by faith apart from the works of the law" (Rom 3:27–28).

So then, does salvation have anything to do with works? Salvation is not based on works, but true salvation results in good works: "For we are his workmanship, created in Christ Jesus for good works, which God prepared ahead of time for us to do" (Eph 2:10). Believers are already a part of God's new creation (2 Cor 5:17), which will appear fully only in the new earth. In the meantime, God has re-created us in Christ to do good works. In fact, God has prepared these works ahead of time for us to do. This is why Christians feel God's pleasure in doing his will. True believers persevere in holiness, for doing so is as much God's will as is free salvation.

Second, Paul again insists that justification is not based on works but inevitably leads to good works. Regeneration and justification do not involve human achievement but are all of God's grace:

> When the kindness of God our Savior and his love for mankind appeared, he saved us—not by works of righteousness that we had done, but according to his mercy—through the washing of regeneration and renewal by the Holy Spirit. He poured out his Spirit on us abundantly through Jesus Christ our Savior so that, having been justified by his grace, we may become heirs with the hope of eternal life. (Titus 3:4–7)

Salvation is due not to our "works of righteousness" but to God's "kindness," "love," "mercy," and "grace." As a result, we are saved, that is, regenerated, justified, and heirs of eternal life. Paul could not be clearer that salvation is not by works but by faith. At the same time he is also clear that free justification results in a godly life. Immediately following the verses above we read, "This saying is trustworthy. I want you to insist on these things, so that those who have believed God might be careful to devote themselves to good works. These are good and profitable for everyone" (v. 8).

Yarbrough highlights the importance for Paul of good works in the Christian life:

"These things" [in v. 8] are the good works that Paul is urging Titus to make sure that the Cretan believers set a high premium on. Their behavior will benefit not only those performing such actions but also those in the world, to whom God calls the church to witness. "For everyone" is "for people" (*tois anthrōpois*), an expression inclusive of everyone. . . . Those whom the church might be tempted to despise (v. 3) are among those Paul calls on Christians to bless by their stellar comportment in society (vv. 1–2).[21]

Third is a text in Hebrews that shows believers must persevere in holiness. Following the passage that enjoins readers to endure persecution as divine discipline, the writer exhorts, "Pursue peace with everyone, and holiness—without it no one will see the Lord" (Heb 12:14). Hebrews commands readers to seek peace with everyone. The author puts "peace" in the emphatic first position. In context this refers to peace within the community of faith. "Pursue" is a strong verb and communicates active effort on the readers' part with regard to harmony and holiness.

The readers are commanded to pursue holiness and warned that those who lack it will fail to experience the beatific vision, the eschatological seeing of God that fills beholders with joy. Bruce is accurate:

"The sanctification without which no man shall see the Lord" is, as the words themselves make plain, no optional extra in the Christian life but something that belongs to its essence. It is the pure in heart, and none but they, who shall see God (Matt 5:8). Here, as in verse 10, it is practical holiness of life that is meant, the converse of those things against which a warning is uttered in the verses which follow.[22]

---

[21] Yarbrough, *The Letters to Timothy and Titus*, PNTC (Grand Rapids: Eerdmans, 2018), 552. Earlier in the epistle Paul had promoted Christian good works: "[Christ] gave himself for us to redeem us from all lawlessness and to cleanse for himself a people for his own possession, eager to do good works" (2:14); "Remind them . . . to be ready for every good work" (3:1).

[22] F. F. Bruce, *The Epistle to the Hebrews*, NICNT (Grand Rapids: Eerdmans, 1964), 364. Lane holds that "holiness" is not ethical in Hebrews and that the writer here urges readers "to hold firmly the gift of Christ through which believers have been made holy"; William L. Lane, *Hebrews 9–13*, WBC (Dallas: Word, 1991), 450.

Believers must persevere to the end in holiness to enter the final kingdom of heaven. The next passage teaches us that this holiness is not sinless perfection but involves confession of sin.

Fourth, 1 John adds balance to the study of perseverance in holiness. It emphasizes as strongly as anywhere in Scripture the necessity of such perseverance for salvation:

> This is the message we have heard from him and declare to you: God is light, and there is absolutely no darkness in him. If we say, "We have fellowship with him," and yet we walk in darkness, we are lying and are not practicing the truth. (1 John 1:5–6)

> This is how we know that we know him: if we keep his commands. The one who says, "I have come to know him," and yet doesn't keep his commands, is a liar, and the truth is not in him. But whoever keeps his word, truly in him the love of God is made complete. (2:3–5)

> If you know that he is righteous, you know this as well: Everyone who does what is right has been born of him. (2:29)

> Everyone who remains in him does not sin; everyone who sins has not seen him or known him. Little children, let no one deceive you. The one who does what is right is righteous, just as he is righteous. The one who commits sin is of the devil, for the devil has sinned from the beginning. . . . This is how God's children and the devil's children become obvious. Whoever does not do what is right is not of God, especially the one who does not love his brother or sister. (3:6–8, 10)

First John thus places great emphasis on believers' living out the faith they profess. In the passages cited this involves saying no to sin and yes to holiness. In fact, it is possible to interpret the passages above as teaching that Christians never sin. Such an interpretation would be wrong, however, based on 1 John 1:5–2:2. Basic to the whole passage is verse 5: "God is light, and there is absolutely no darkness in him." God's holiness is absolute, and certain implications follow from that fact.

> If we say, "We have fellowship with him," and yet we walk in darkness, we are lying and are not practicing the truth. If we walk in

the light as he himself is in the light, we have fellowship with one another, and the blood of Jesus his Son cleanses us from all sin. If we say, "We have no sin," we are deceiving ourselves, and the truth is not in us. If we confess our sins, he is faithful and righteous to forgive us our sins and to cleanse us from all unrighteousness. If we say, "We have not sinned," we make him a liar, and his word is not in us.

My little children, I am writing you these things so that you may not sin. But if anyone does sin, we have an advocate with the Father—Jesus Christ the righteous one. (1:6–2:1)

These verses alternate between 1) statements that deny sin theoretically or practically and 2) statements that admit sin or commend a holy life:

> 1:6: a statement that denies sin practically
>> 1:7: a statement that commends a holy life
> 1:8: a statement that denies sin theoretically
>> 1:9: a statement that admits sin
> 1:10: a statement that denies sin practically
>> 2:1: a statement that commends a holy life and admits sin

These statements accomplish a number of things. They show that God hates sin in the lives of his people. He commands them to be holy as he is holy (cf. Lev 11:44; 19:2; 1 Pet 1:16). Holiness is not optional but rather an integral part of what it means to be a believer. It is possible for Christians to deny sin theoretically or practically, both of which are disastrous. Omitted from the list above are statements in the passage regarding God's grace, Christ's cross, and forgiveness. Even if to the best of their knowledge Christians are not sinning, they do not save themselves, but Christ's atonement avails for them: "The blood of Jesus his Son cleanses us from all sin" (1 John 1:7). When they do confess their sins, God is "faithful and righteous to forgive us our sins and to cleanse us from all unrighteousness" (v. 9). Even when believers stumble and fall, they have an "advocate with the Father—Jesus Christ the righteous one" (2:1), who made propitiation for all who believe (v. 2).

Thus 1 John 1:6–2:1 qualifies interpretation of the apparently perfectionist texts in the epistle. Key aspects of perseverance in holiness include acknowledging sin both theoretically and practically, confessing sin as a normal part of the Christian life, and relying on God's grace and Christ's atoning sacrifice to save and keep us.

Assurance

God's preservation of his saints and their perseverance in faith, love, and holiness affect other doctrines, including assurance and apostasy. We will briefly treat these in turn. Assurance is confidence of eternal salvation. God graciously assures his people by three primary means: the promises of salvation in his Word, the internal witness of the Holy Spirit, and spiritual growth in the lives of his people.[23]

Assurance through the Word

Gospel promises belong here. For example: "God loved the world in this way: He gave his one and only Son, so that everyone who believes in him will not perish but have eternal life" (John 3:16). When people trust the Son to give them eternal life, they gain confidence of salvation. God's reliable Word is the fundamental source of assurance for all who believe its saving message.

First John grounds assurance in faith in Christ: "This is the testimony: God has given us eternal life, and this life is in his Son. The one who has the Son has life. The one who does not have the Son of God does not have life" (1 John 5:11–12). John distinguishes between the "haves" and the "have nots." His distinction is not based on having beauty, brains, or brawn, three things we highly value. Rather, his distinction is based on having Christ as Savior by grace through faith. God assures of eternal life those who "have" the Son of God.

The preservation passages that we studied likewise teach that God grants assurance to his people via his Word. For instance:

"I give [my sheep] eternal life, and they will never perish." (John 10:28)

There is now no condemnation for those in Christ Jesus. (Rom 8:1)

---

[23] For more on assurance, see Robert A. Peterson, *The Assurance of Salvation: Biblical Hope for Our Struggles* (Grand Rapids: Zondervan, 2019).

I am persuaded that neither death nor life, nor angels nor rulers, nor things present nor things to come, nor powers, nor height nor depth, nor any other created thing will be able to separate us from the love of God that is in Christ Jesus our Lord. (vv. 38–39)

He holds his priesthood permanently, because he continues forever. Consequently, he is able to save to the uttermost those who draw near to God through him, since he always lives to make intercession for them. (Heb 7:24–25)

Assurance through the Spirit

Although the Word of God is the primary way in which God assures his own, it is not the only way. God also grants confidence of final salvation by his Spirit's working within believers. Romans is the primary witness to this truth, but 1 John also testifies:

This is how we know that we remain in him and he in us: He has given us of his Spirit. (1 John 4:13)

The way we know that he remains in us is from the Spirit he has given us. (1 John 3:24)

Jesus Christ—he is the one who came by water and blood, not by water only, but by water and by blood. And the Spirit is the one who testifies, because the Spirit is the truth. For there are three that testify: the Spirit, the water, and the blood—and these three are in agreement. If we accept human testimony, God's testimony is greater, because it is God's testimony that he has given about his Son. The one who believes in the Son of God has this testimony within himself. (1 John 5:6–10)

The first two texts merely state that the Holy Spirit plays a role in believers' knowing that they are united to Christ. The third text includes the Spirit among the three witnesses to Jesus. John places signposts at the beginning and end of Jesus's life: "water" (Jesus's baptism) and "blood" (his crucifixion). The Spirit bears witness to these historical markers. Like the Father (John 17:17) and the Son (14:6), the Spirit is "the truth" (1 John 5:6). For people to be saved, they must believe God's witness concerning Jesus. When someone does so, he has "this testimony within himself" because of the Spirit's witness in his heart (v. 10).

Romans offers the two most outstanding passages concerning the Holy Spirit's inner witness to assurance. Paul extols the hope of final salvation that believers enjoy because Christ has reconciled them to God. Their hope rests on God's word and his working in their lives (Rom 5:1–4). Christians need not worry if their hope is secure, as Paul explains: "This hope will not disappoint us, because God's love has been poured out in our hearts through the Holy Spirit who was given to us" (Rom 5:5). The Spirit assures us inwardly that God loves us. He thus complements assurance given through the word. The word and Spirit work together to strengthen believers' confidence that God loves them and will keep them saved until the end.

The *textus classicus* on the internal witness of the Holy Spirit is Rom 8:16. The context deals with God's adoption of believers. God's children are identifiable, "For all those led by God's Spirit are God's sons" (v. 14). The Father delivers his children from fear when he gives them the Holy Spirit. This is because "the Spirit of adoption" enables them to cry out, "Abba, Father!" (v. 15). "Abba" is not baby talk but is a children's term of endearment for one's father. The term "cry out" carries with it emotional intensity.[24]

The Spirit not only empowers lost persons to call God "Father" in truth, but he also assures believers inwardly of the Father's love: "The Spirit himself testifies together with our spirit that we are God's children" (v. 16). God assures his children of his love outwardly by making promises to them in his Word. He also assures them inwardly by virtue of the Holy Spirit's bearing witness with their human spirits that God is their Father and that they are his beloved children. Because they are children, they are also "heirs of God and coheirs with Christ" if their faith is genuine. Those who trust Christ as Lord and Savior and are united in suffering to him in his death will be united with him in glorification also (v. 17).

---

[24] As indicated by ESV, NASB, and CSB, punctuating the sentence with an exclamation point.

God ministers to both the head and the heart. Many evangelicals in their zeal to give Scripture the utmost place in their faith minimize the heart, as Moo, referring to the verb in verse 16, observes:

> In using the verb "crying out," Paul stresses that our awareness of God as Father comes not from rational consideration nor from external testimony alone but from a truth deeply felt and intensely experienced. If some Christians err in basing their assurance of salvation on feelings alone, many others err in basing it on facts and arguments alone. Indeed, what Paul says here calls into question whether one can have a genuine experience of God's Spirit of adoption without it affecting the emotions.[25]

Assurance through Spiritual Growth

God blesses his own with assurance via the promises of preservation in his Word, his Spirit's testimony in their hearts, and his working in their lives. We will investigate this last point with the help of three passages.

First, Luke 8:11–15, which we previously discussed, distinguishes inadequate from adequate reception of the Word of God. Jesus told the parable of the sower and his seed. Some seed fell along the path, and birds ate it. Some fell on rock, where it sprouted but withered without moisture. Some fell among thorns, which choked it. The seed is the Word of God, and the first three types of soil are hearers of the Word who do not truly receive the Word so as to produce lasting fruit. Only the last type of soil represents true believers, as Jesus describes them: "The seed in the good ground— these are the ones who, having heard the word with an honest and good heart, hold on to it and by enduring, produce fruit" (v. 15). The assurance of Jesus's followers who were growing in their faith would increase as they heard these words.

Second is Peter's challenge to his readers to pursue godly lives. He reminds them of God's provision by his power and Word of "everything required for life and godliness" (2 Pet 1:3–4). He then exhorts them, "Make every effort to supplement your faith with goodness, goodness with knowledge, knowledge with self-control, self-control with endurance, endurance

---

[25] Moo, *The Epistle to the Romans*, 502.

with godliness, godliness with brotherly affection, and brotherly affection with love" (vv. 5–7). Peter promises his readers usefulness and fruitfulness if they are growing in these qualities (v. 8). Moreover, someone lacking in these qualities gives evidence of being unsaved (v. 9).

Most important for our purposes are Peter's next words: "Therefore, brothers and sisters, make every effort to confirm your calling and election, because if you do these things you will never stumble. For in this way, entry into the eternal kingdom of our Lord and Savior Jesus Christ will be richly provided for you" (vv. 10–11). Their calling is God's effectively summoning them to Christ through the gospel. Their election is God's having chosen them for salvation before the foundation of the world. Of course, their calling and election are known to God, who elected and called them. Peter prays that his readers' confidence that God has chosen and called them might increase. He puts calling before election because that is how they came to know the Lord. They did not reason their way to God's election of them. Rather, they believed the gospel when God effectively called them. It is by their calling that they came to know their election (cf. 1 Thess 1:4–5). Harvey and Towner capture Peter's message to his readers: "He holds before us the promise that by pursuing such growth they will confirm the reality of their place among God's chosen people (v. 10), avoid damaging spiritual reverses (v. 10), and enrich their capacity to enjoy the glories of eternal life (v. 11)."[26] So, God's people strengthen their assurance as they pursue God and the qualities of life he desires for them.

Third, 1 John powerfully bears witness to the fact that God connects assurance to growth in obedience to him. As is his custom, John teaches this truth both positively and negatively:

> This is how we know that we know him: if we keep his commands. The one who says, "I have come to know him," and yet doesn't keep his commands, is a liar, and the truth is not in him. But whoever keeps his word, truly in him the love of God is made complete. This is how we know we are in him: The one who says he remains in him should walk just as he walked. (1 John 2:3–6)

---

[26] Robert Harvey and Philip H. Towner, *2 Peter & Jude* (Downers Grove: InterVarsity, 2009), 51.

Positively, by keeping God's commands Christians gain assurance of knowing him (v. 3). Conversely, claiming to know him while disobeying his commands is a very bad sign (v. 4). Positively again, God's love attains its goal in believers when they obey his Word and thereby strengthen their assurance (v. 5). In sum, those who claim to be in union with Christ must live following his example (v. 6).

Our emphasis on assurance through spiritual growth can be misunderstood. At no point is the Christian life a self-help program. Believers are active throughout and must persevere in faith, love, and holiness to be saved in the end. But they are not independently active. God works in and through his children every step of the way, including in spiritual growth. We really grow by grace through faith, but God enables that growth. We see this for each of the Trinitarian persons. We "work out [our] own salvation with fear and trembling. For it is God [the Father] who is working in [us] both to will and to work according to his good purpose" (Phil 2:12–13). We abide in the true vine, which is Christ, but he reminds us, "You can do nothing without me" (John 15:5). We "walk by the Spirit" (Gal 5:16; cf. v. 25), but the fruit that we bear is the "fruit of the Spirit" (v. 22).

Moo summarizes the fact that assurance is based in part on our pursuing holiness: "Paul insists that what God has done for us in Christ is the sole and final grounds for our eternal life at the same time as he insists on the indispensability of holy living as the precondition for attaining that life."[27]

One Passage Combines the Three Means of Assurance

God is good to his children! He not only saves them by grace through faith; he also assures them that he is theirs and they are his. He does so in three ways, primarily by promising them salvation in his Word and also by assuring them within by his Spirit and producing spiritual growth in their lives. Remarkably, Paul in Rom 5:1–5, 10 combines these three means of assurance.

On the basis of Scripture Paul gives his readers confidence of their justification and reconciliation. God declared them righteous when they trusted in Christ (Rom 5:1). Though they were God's enemies, he reconciled them

---

[27] Moo, *The Epistle to the Romans*, 495.

to himself through Christ's cross. It follows then, that "much more, having been reconciled, will [they] be saved by his life" (v. 10). The Bible affirms final salvation for God's people, thereby assuring them.

As we have seen, the Holy Spirit also plays a part in confirming Christians' hope of future glory: "This hope will not disappoint us, because God's love has been poured out in our hearts through the Holy Spirit who was given to us" (v. 5). The Spirit assures us within that God our Father loves us and will keep us saved.

God's working in our lives also reinforces assurance. Because of God's promise of heaven, believers rejoice "in the hope of the glory of God" (v. 2). "And not only that, but we also boast in our afflictions, because we know that affliction produces endurance, endurance produces proven character, and proven character produces hope" (vv. 3–4). Here Paul teaches that God assures us by changing our lives. Paul links a chain: affliction → endurance → proven character → hope. When Christians respond to affliction in a God-honoring manner, God builds endurance into them. As they continue to do so, God changes their character so that they become steady persons. And, when they see God at work in them in these ways, it strengthens their assurance. Observing God at work in the here and now bolsters our confidence of his working in the future. "God's working in what we can see produces hope for what we cannot see."[28]

Romans 5, then, portrays God's word, the Spirit's inner witness, and changed lives as ways in which God assures believers of their heavenly hope.

Apostasy

Assurance and apostasy are theological topics related to preservation and perseverance. Having treated the former, we turn to the latter. Apostasy is departure from a previously professed faith in Christ. Scripture contains warnings of apostasy. However, warnings have multiple functions:[29]

---

[28] Peterson, *The Assurance of Salvation*, 158.

[29] This material is adapted from Peterson, *Our Secure Salvation*, 204–5, (see chap. 9, n. 174).

To differentiate true from false believers: Matt 7:16–23; Luke 8:4–15; John 15:1–8; Acts 8:13, 20–24; Rom 8:13;

To uncover deficient faith: John 2:23–25; 1 Tim 1:3–7, 18–20; 2 Tim 2:11–13;

To warn against refusing the gospel: Matt 10:33; 1 Tim 4:1–5; 2 Tim 2:17–19;

To unmask unsaved persons who seem to be saved: 1 Tim 5:8; 11–12; 2 Pet 2:20–22; 1 John 5:16–17; Rev 22:18–19;

To show God's hatred of sin: Acts 5:5, 10; Jas 5:19–20;

To warn of disqualification from office: 1 Cor 9:27;[30]

To warn of temporal judgments: 1 Cor 11:32;

To emphasize the need for perseverance: Col 1:23; Heb 6:4–8; 10:26–38.

The NT warns of the danger of apostasy for those who claim to know Christ:

"Then they will hand you over to be persecuted, and they will kill you. You will be hated by all nations because of my name. Then many will fall away, betray one another, and hate one another." (Matt 24:9–10)

The Spirit explicitly says that in later times some will depart from the faith, paying attention to deceitful spirits and the teachings of demons. (1 Tim 4:1)

Watch out, brothers and sisters, so that there won't be in any of you an evil, unbelieving heart that turns away from the living God. (Heb 3:12)

They went out from us, but they did not belong to us; for if they had belonged to us, they would have remained with us. (1 John 2:19)

---

[30] For exegesis supporting this view, see Volf, *Paul and Perseverance*, 233, 236.

Scripture's witness to apostasy raises an important question: How do we systematize the Bible's teachings on preservation, perseverance, assurance, and apostasy?[31]

Systematizing Preservation, Perseverance, Assurance, and Apostasy

The Bible does not provide a complete systematic theology, but it partially systematizes certain doctrines. It does this for preservation and apostasy.

Scripture Relates Preservation and Perseverance

God's Word teaches that God preserves his people—he keeps them so they do not fall away from the faith totally and finally. Scripture also teaches that God's people must persevere in faith, love, and holiness to attain final salvation. How can we correlate these two truths? We cannot perfectly correlate them, for they are a subset of the biblically revealed mystery of God's sovereignty and human responsibility. There are three big biblical mysteries, the first two of which are essential to the Christian faith. The first mystery is that of the Trinity. Scripture reveals that there is one God who has eternally existed in three persons as Father, Son, and Holy Spirit. The second mystery is that of Christ's two natures. Scripture teaches that the eternal Son of God became a human being in Jesus of Nazareth with the result that he is the God-man, with both divine and human natures united in one person.

The Bible also teaches a third mysterious truth—that of divine sovereignty and human responsibility. We maintain a compatibilist view of sovereignty and responsibility. Both are taught in Scripture and are therefore true, although we cannot fully understand how they fit together. Hence it is a mystery.

The Word of God reveals that God is the sovereign One who controls all his creatures and all they do (Ps 33:10–11; Isa 14:26–27; Rom 11:36; Eph 1:11). Scripture also reveals that humans are responsible to God for their thoughts, words, and deeds (Josh 24:15; Ezek 18:20; Rom 14:11–12; 1 Pet 4:4–5). Daily we make real choices, and it matters whether we believe in Christ (John 3:17–18) and whether we preach the gospel (1 Cor 9:22).

---

[31] This section owes a debt to Peterson, *Our Secure Salvation*, 205–7.

God's Preservation Causes Our Perseverance

Scripture presents divine sovereignty and human responsibility in a dynamic interplay that we do not comprehend perfectly. We can, however, explore two biblical truths that shed light on that interplay. Preservation causes perseverance, and perseverance is a fruit of preservation. First, they stand in a cause-and-effect relationship. God's preservation of his people causes their perseverance. His sovereign grace saves and keeps believers.

In Paul's tussles with the Corinthian church, he repeatedly addresses them regarding human responsibility, accountability, and culpability. He corrects them in many matters of theology and ethics and urges them to persevere (1 Cor 1:10–13; 3:1–4; 4:14; 5:1–2; 6:1–8; 10:14, 20–22; 11:17–22, 30; 15:12, 33–34). Paul enjoins their perseverance and at the same time begins his letter with a strong statement of God's preservation of the struggling saints in Corinth. We mentioned this previously and draw out implications now. After words of salutation Paul writes,

> I always thank my God for you because of the grace of God given to you in Christ Jesus, that you were enriched in him in every way, in all speech and all knowledge. In this way, the testimony about Christ was confirmed among you, so that you do not lack any spiritual gift as you eagerly wait for the revelation of our Lord Jesus Christ. He will also strengthen you to the end, so that you will be blameless in the day of our Lord Jesus Christ. God is faithful; you were called by him into fellowship with his Son, Jesus Christ our Lord. (1 Cor 1:4–9)

Paul thanks God for conferring gifts and blessings richly upon the Corinthian congregation (vv. 4–7). The apostle is confident that Christ will "sustain [them] to the end" (v. 8, ESV). Moreover, he will sustain them "guiltless in the day of our Lord Jesus Christ" (v. 8, ESV). Commenting on the word "guiltless," Thiselton stresses, "The primary emphasis falls upon the verdictive nature of the word. God pronounces a verdict; issues of human moral conditions remain secondary."[32] Paul means that the present

---

[32] Anthony C. Thiselton, *The First Epistle to the Corinthians*, NIGTC (Grand Rapids: Eerdmans, 2000), 102.

announcement of justification by grace through faith in Christ will not be revoked but will be proclaimed at the Last Judgment, when Christ returns.

Paul's strong words of God's preservation are all the more noteworthy given the spiritual condition of the Corinthians, as Fee points out: "What is remarkable is that Paul should express such confidence about a community whose current behavior is anything but blameless and whom on several occasions he must exhort with the strongest kinds of warning."[33] What is the basis of Paul's confidence of their spiritual security? The fact that "God is faithful; you were called by him into fellowship with his Son, Jesus Christ our Lord" (v. 9). Again Fee deserves quotation:

> The secret, of course, lies in the subject of the verb, "he" (= God). If Paul's confidence lay in the Corinthians themselves, then he is in trouble. But just as in later passages (5:6–8 and 6:10–11), in Paul's theology the indicative (God's prior action of grace) always precedes the imperative (their obedience as response to grace) and is the ground of his confidence.[34]

Paul thus begins 1 Corinthians with a bold statement of preservation before he issues numerous corrections to the immature congregation. His confidence that God will keep the Corinthians does not prevent his admonitions to them. As we stressed in the exegetical section, the admonitions serve in part as one of God's means of preserving his saints. In addition, the dire need of the Corinthians for reprimand does not cause Paul to doubt whether the majority of their number are true believers (see 5:11; 2 Cor 13:5), who by God's grace will finally be saved.

First Thessalonians also demonstrates the dynamic interplay between exhortations to persevere and statements of preservation. Paul commends the Thessalonians for their love and urges them to persevere in it: "About brotherly love: You don't need me to write you because you yourselves are taught by God to love one another. In fact, you are doing this toward all the brothers and sisters in the entire region of Macedonia. But we encourage you, brothers and sisters, to do this even more" (4:9–10; cf. 5:15). It is

---

[33] Gordon D. Fee, *The First Epistle to the Corinthians*, rev. ed., NICNT (Grand Rapids: Eerdmans, 2014), 42.

[34] Fee, *The First Epistle to the Corinthians*, 42.

the same for holiness. Paul recognizes the Thessalonians' pursuit of holiness while urging them to persevere in it:

> Brothers and sisters, we ask and encourage you in the Lord Jesus, that as you have received instruction from us on how you should live and please God—as you are doing—do this even more. For you know what commands we gave you through the Lord Jesus. For this is God's will, your sanctification: that you keep away from sexual immorality. (4:1–3; cf. 5:6)

After admonitions to persevere in love and holiness Paul ends the letter with a wish-prayer that God would sanctify the Thessalonians entirely when Jesus comes again. He immediately follows this with assurance that God will accomplish that very thing: "Now may the God of peace himself sanctify you completely. And may your whole spirit, soul, and body be kept sound and blameless at the coming of our Lord Jesus Christ. He who calls you is faithful; he will do it" (5:23–24).

God's faithfulness to keep his people saved assures the Thessalonian believers' entire sanctification when Jesus returns. Paul views this truth as compatible with his words urging them to love and godliness. The exhortations to persevere do not compromise God's sovereign preservation; instead, they undergird the saints' perseverance.

Paul expresses the same ideas in his letter to the Philippians. First, he exhorts them, "My dear friends, just as you have always obeyed, so now, not only in my presence but even more in my absence, work out your own salvation with fear and trembling" (Phil 2:12). Then he assures them, "For it is God who is working in you both to will and to work according to his good purpose" (v. 13). Perseverance is necessary for salvation, and God's preservation stands behind it. God gives his people incentive and energy to persevere. And, as we have seen, the saints' perseverance is one means God uses to preserve them in the faith.

Paul's life illustrates the dynamic interplay between divine sovereignty and human responsibility. He works hard to fulfill his apostolic ministry of presenting redeemed sinners as mature in Christ (Col 1:28). Yet he does not rely on his own resources: "I labor for this, striving with his strength that works powerfully in me" (v. 29). Preservation is the cause of perseverance, and perseverance is a fruit of preservation, as we will see next.

Our Perseverance Is a Fruit of Preservation

If we begin with God, we note that he preserves his people; his preservation is the ultimate cause of our perseverance. If we begin with humans, we note that God's preservation bears fruit in our lives, including perseverance. Thus, our perseverance is a confirmation of his keeping us. Many passages confirm this. Jesus spoke of false prophets and twice warned, "You'll recognize them by their fruit" (Matt 7:16, 20). False disciples perform impressive deeds, including prophesying, casting out demons, and doing miracles in Jesus's name. However, at his second coming Jesus will banish them from his presence, for he never "knew" them with saving knowledge (v. 23). They were "lawbreakers," whose fruit revealed a lack of salvation (v. 23). Genuine salvation shows up in the "good fruit" (v. 17) of faith, love, and holiness. Of course, this fruit is not perfect in this life, but it is real. Christians are not totally new but are genuinely new.

Jesus points to evidence of regeneration: "Every good tree produces good fruit, but a bad tree produces bad fruit. A good tree can't produce bad fruit; neither can a bad tree produce good fruit. Every tree that doesn't produce good fruit is cut down and thrown into the fire" (Matt 7:17–19). Fruitlessness indicates a lack of salvation, whereas fruitfulness indicates the presence of salvation.

Jesus teaches the same truths when he speaks of himself as the true vine and followers as branches (John 15:1–8). He contrasts fruitless and fruitful branches and their respective fates: "Every branch in me that does not produce fruit he removes, and he prunes every branch that produces fruit so that it will produce more fruit" (v. 2). Jesus explains further in verses 5–6: "The one who remains in me and I in him produces much fruit, because you can do nothing without me. If anyone does not remain in me, he is thrown aside like a branch and he withers. They gather them, throw them into the fire, and they are burned." The imagery depicts hellfire.

Fruitfulness shows the reality of salvation: "My Father is glorified by this: that you produce much fruit and prove to be my disciples" (v. 8). Samuel Ngewa notes, "By bearing fruit, the disciples will both glorify God the Father and prove their discipleship."[35] Scripture consistently regards fruit as a sign

---

[35] Samuel Ngewa, "John," *Africa Bible Commentary*, ed. Tokunboh Adeyemo (Grand Rapids: Zondervan, 2006), 1285.

of salvation and the absence of fruit as a sign of the lack of salvation. Paul repeatedly condemns false teachers for both their theological errors and their lives. He summarizes, "They claim to know God, but they deny him by their works" (Titus 1:16). Believers vary in degrees of fruitfulness. Indeed, as Jesus taught in the parable of the sower, "The one sown on the good ground—this is one who hears and understands the word, who does produce fruit and yields: some a hundred, some sixty, some thirty times what was sown" (Matt 13:23). Genuine believers persevere, but unbelievers do not.

Scripture Itself Relates Preservation, Perseverance, Assurance, and Apostasy

In New Testament books: The Bible brings together preservation, perseverance, and apostasy in a way that helps us understand them and their interrelation. The same NT books teach all three doctrines, as the chart below indicates:

Preservation	Perseverance	Apostasy
Luke 22:31–32	Luke 8:4–15	Luke 21:16–19
John 6:37–44; 10:26–30	John 15:1–8	John 13:21–30
Rom 5:9–10; 8:31–39	Rom 8:13	Rom 11:17–21
1 Cor 1:8–9; 11:27–32	1 Cor 9:24–27	1 Cor 5:1–4
Heb 6:13–20; 7:23–25	Heb 10:36	Heb 3:14; 10:26–29
1 John 5:18	1 John 5:16–17	1 John 2:19

New Testament writers spoke of God's preservation, saints' perseverance, and apostasy without fear of contradiction. They believed that God kept his people safe and also believed that believers must continue to the end in faith, love, and holiness, and that some people defect from the faith. Unless we would accuse them of contradicting themselves, which we would not, the NT writers did not intend the necessity of perseverance and the warnings of apostasy to cancel the truth of preservation. They did not intend the truth of preservation to lessen the need for believers to persevere. They also did not intend their teaching of preservation to nullify the warnings of apostasy.

We cannot correlate these three doctrines perfectly. Preservation is the cause of perseverance, and perseverance is one evidence of preservation. Previous study has shown that, although scriptural warnings have many purposes, a primary one is to distinguish true from false believers.[36] As stated before, apostolic urgings for the saints to persevere and warnings of apostasy are among the means God uses to preserve his people. Nevertheless, we bow to the mystery of divine sovereignty and human responsibility and cannot explain their dynamic interplay completely.

One passage in particular integrates perseverance and apostasy:

> Children, it is the last hour. And as you have heard that antichrist is coming, even now many antichrists have come. By this we know that it is the last hour. They went out from us, but they did not belong to us; for if they had belonged to us, they would have remained with us. However, they went out so that it might be made clear that none of them belongs to us. (1 John 2:18–19)

The theme of "antichrist" shares with many biblical themes the feature of being "already" and "not yet." The end-time antichrist figure has not yet appeared, but John could say that already in the first century "many antichrists have come" (v. 18). John identifies them with the false teachers who had attended the Johannine churches. They outwardly belonged to Christ and his people but did not belong in a deeper sense. They outwardly appeared to be Christians, but their apostasy revealed them to be false believers (v. 19). John's words are telling: "If they had belonged to us, they would have remained with us" (v. 19). Genuine believers persevere; they do not apostatize. Those who apostatize reveal they were never genuine believers.

In one New Testament passage: Hebrews 6:1–20 ties together preservation, perseverance, assurance, and apostasy. Here is the big picture:

Exhortation to persevere (6:1–3)
    Strong warning of apostasy (vv. 4–6)
        Assurance that the majority of readers are saved (vv. 7–10)
    Exhortation to persevere to strengthen assurance (vv. 11–12)
        Strong assurance of preservation (vv. 13–20)

After a rebuke of their spiritual immaturity (5:11–14), the writer exhorts the readers to perseverance in 6:1–3: "Therefore, let us leave the elementary teaching about Christ and go on to maturity" (v. 1). There follows as strong

---

[36] See Peterson, *Our Secure Salvation*, 204.

a warning of apostasy as there is in Scripture: "For it is impossible to renew to repentance those who" experienced great spiritual blessings "and who have fallen away. This is because, to their own harm, they are recrucifying the Son of God and holding him up to contempt" (vv. 4–6). Next the writer offers an illustration of two kinds of land. Both receive the rain of God's blessing, and the first produces good vegetation, which God blesses. But the second produces only thorns and thistles and is thus worthless, so God is ready to curse and burn it (vv. 7–8). The two types of land represent true and false believers, respectively. The writer wants his readers to identify with the first type of land and to persevere.

After the strong warning and discriminating illustration, the writer offers the majority of his readers encouraging words in verses 9–10: "Even though we are speaking this way, dearly loved friends, in your case we are confident of things that are better and that pertain to salvation" (v. 9). He warns the whole congregation of apostasy, knowing that some are contemplating it, while he remains confident of the majority's salvation and perseverance.[37] Again he exhorts them to persevere, so as to increase their assurance: "Now we desire each of you to demonstrate the same diligence for the full assurance of your hope until the end, so that you won't become lazy but will be imitators of those who inherit the promises through faith and perseverance" (vv. 11–12).

Often neglected, the next eight verses make a strong case for God's preservation of his saints. A previous work summarizes the arguments, showing that God guarantees believers' final salvation by:

1. promising it (v. 13),
2. confirming the promise with an oath (v. 14),
3. labeling his resolve "unchangeable" (v. 17),
4. reminding us of his veracity (v. 18),
5. calling our hope of salvation an "anchor of the soul" (v. 19),
6. three times describing this anchor as utterly reliable (v. 19),
7. teaching that Christ our forerunner has already entered heaven for us (vv. 19–20), and
8. affirming the eternity of Christ's priesthood (v. 20).[38]

---

[37] Those whom God has chosen ultimately heed the warnings and are thus saved. The warnings are one means by which they are preserved until the end.

[38] Peterson, *Our Secure Salvation*, 88.

The author to the Hebrews correlates the four doctrines to minister to his readers. In doing so he increases our understanding. Placing preservation last and treating it extensively underscores the fact that genuine believers cannot fall away. God preserves his people for final salvation. The author regards exhortations to persevere and warnings of apostasy as compatible with preservation. As a pastor he knows churches are a mixture of believers and unbelievers. Every church member needs encouragement and admonition to persevere in faith, love, and holiness. Some need the strong medicine of God's Word to awaken them from the illness of spiritual lethargy. Christians need a robust assurance that comes from God's promises, the Spirit's ministry within, and their walking with him. Church leaders must love their flock faithfully by exhorting them to continue in the faith, warning them of the danger of apostasy, and encouraging the majority to live in assurance.

Conclusion

As we have seen, God is the beginning, middle, and end of our salvation. God's grace begins it (Eph 1:3–14; 2:1–10; Titus 3:4–7) and will complete it (Phil 1:6; Rom 8:18–39; 1 Pet 1:3–5). We will "persevere in holiness because God perseveres in grace."[39]

And in the meantime, God's grace provides the fuel for our spiritual journey. Charles Spurgeon said it well: "Between here and heaven, every minute that the Christian lives will be a minute of grace."[40] When we are in need, God's grace gives us boldness: "Let us then with confidence draw near to the throne of grace, that we may receive mercy and find grace to help in time of need" (Heb 4:16). When we are in sin, God's grace fosters our repentance and promotes our holiness: "The grace of God has appeared, bringing salvation to all people, training us to renounce ungodliness and worldly passions, and to live self-controlled, upright, and godly lives in the present age" (Titus 2:11–12). When we need strength to keep on serving God, God's

---

[39] Charles H. Spurgeon, *All of Grace*, Read and Reflect with the Classics (reprint; Nashville: B&H, 2017), 162.

[40] Spurgeon, "The Tenses" (No. 2718), sermon preached May 13, 1880, accessed November 27, 2017; https://www.ccel.org/ccel/spurgeon/sermons47.xi.html.

grace enables us, as Paul testifies: "I worked harder than any of them, though it was not I, but the grace of God that is with me" (1 Cor 15:10 ESV). When we are tired and weak, God's grace fortifies us, as Paul attests: "My grace is sufficient for you, for my power is perfected in weakness" (2 Cor 12:9).[41] When we forget who we are in Christ, God's grace reminds us, as Geoffrey Thomas explains:

> God has joined us to Christ. We are no longer standing under what Adam deserves, and I no longer stand under what I deserve, but God has caused us to stand under what Christ deserves. God's grace places us under the eloquence of his blood. He places us under all the adequacy of that sacrifice. God places us in the full deserving of our Lord's obedience and righteousness. He causes us to stand under the total logic of his atonement, so that there is now no condemnation for us who are in Christ Jesus. Your conscience has no right to condemn you, and death has no right to terrorize you, and hell has no right to stand up before you because there is now no condemnation whatsoever. Why? Because you were and are in Christ Jesus. You stand in his merit, and you stand in his righteous obedience in all its glory, because that is what God did when he gave you to his Son Jesus Christ and joined you to him forever. Your life stands under all the implications of how Christ lived and how he died. You stand in the logic of Calvary and the glory of the shed blood. You stand in the righteous life of Christ the blameless Son of God. God has united us to Jesus Christ his Son.[42]

---

[41] For more, see Christopher W. Morgan and Justin L. McLendon, "A Trajectory of Spirituality," *Biblical Spirituality*, Theology in Community, ed. Christopher W. Morgan (Wheaton: Crossway, 2019), 51–53.

[42] Geoffrey Thomas, sermon, "But God," preached May 2, 2004, accessed September 19, 2022, http://geoffthomas.org/index.php/gtsermons/24-7-but-god/; I owe this reference to John Mahony, unpublished notes and "Purchased Grace," Christian Ministries Lectures, California Baptist University, February 23, 2016; https://calbaptist.edu/school-of-christian-ministries/lecture-series; https://vimeo.com/158992886.

10

Eternal Life and Glorification

This book focuses on the application of salvation, but it is important to place it in its theological context. For that reason we put election before the application of salvation and eternal life and glorification after it. The application of salvation takes place in history. In time and space God calls, regenerates, converts, justifies, adopts, sanctifies, and preserves his people. However, God's plan of salvation is larger than redemptive history. It is rooted in eternity past, where God chose a people for himself and planned to join them to his Son (Eph 1:4; 2 Tim 1:9). It culminates in eternity future, when God's people will be glorified and enjoy eternal life in its fullness (1 Cor 15:42–44; Titus 3:6–7). Here we treat the themes of eternal life and glorification.

Scripture sometimes ties life and glory together:

[God] will repay each one according to his works: eternal life to those [justified by his grace] who by persistence in doing good seek glory, honor, and immortality. (Rom 2:6–7)

When Christ, who is your life, appears, then you also will appear with him in glory. (Col 3:4)

His divine power has given us everything required for life and godliness through the knowledge of him who called us by his own glory and goodness. (2 Pet 1:3)

Eternal Life

Exegetical Foundations

Eternal Life in the Old Testament

The OT uses the phrase "eternal life" only once (Dan 12:2) but refers often to life, primarily focusing on life in this world. Early on in Scripture, however, we encounter the "tree of life" (Gen 2:9; 3:22, 24), with life promised to Adam and Eve if they refrained from eating of the tree of the knowledge of good and evil. Of course, they ate from the forbidden tree and experienced the death of which they were warned (Gen 2:17). The roll call of death in Genesis 5—"then he died"—certifies that human beings forfeited life by their disobedience. The impact of human sin, the overwhelming scourge of death, is evident in the flood, which was the judgment for human rebellion and depravity (Genesis 6–9). That the tree of life had spiritual significance beyond mere physical life is borne out by its reappearance in the last book of Scripture (Rev 2:7; 22:2, 14, 19).

The word "life" isn't prominent in the covenant with Abraham, but surely the blessing promised to Abraham, Isaac, and Jacob (Gen 12:2–3; 22:17–18; 26:3–4; 27:29; 28:24) was intended to undo the curse, which reached its zenith in the death, physical and spiritual, imposed upon human beings. The covenant with Israel enacted on Mount Sinai is in some ways like the command given to Adam, for the Lord promises "life" in the land if the people keep his commands (Lev 18:5; Deut 4:1, 40; 5:33; 8:1; 11:8–9). Israel is implored to choose life by loving the Lord and keeping his commands (30:15–20). Ezekiel 18 stresses that those who repent from evil and turn to the Lord will live. But, as the OT story unfolded, Israel disobeyed the covenant, violated the Lord's stipulations, and suffered the curses of the covenant (Lev 26; Deut 27–28). They were ejected from the land and experienced death instead of life. When the OT refers to life, the referent is typically life in the land or the experience of good life on earth. When NT writers refer to OT texts that refer to life (e.g., Lev 18:5 in Rom 10:5 and Gal 3:12), such life is often used typologically of eternal life.

Some texts in the OT, however, refer to the resurrection and therefore to hope for life in the future:

When he has swallowed up death once and for all, the Lord God will wipe away the tears from every face and remove his people's disgrace from the whole earth, for the Lord has spoken. (Isa 25:8)

Your dead will live; their bodies will rise. Awake and sing, you who dwell in the dust! For you will be covered with the morning dew, and the earth will bring out the departed spirits. (26:19)

I prophesied as I had been commanded. While I was prophesying, there was a noise, a rattling sound, and the bones came together, bone to bone. As I looked, tendons appeared on them, flesh grew, and skin covered them, but there was no breath in them. He said to me, "Prophesy to the breath, prophesy, son of man. Say to it: This is what Lord God says: Breath, come from the four winds and breathe into these slain so that they may live!" So I prophesied as he commanded me; the breath entered them, and they came to life and stood on their feet, a vast army. Then he said to me, "Son of man, these bones are the whole house of Israel. Look how they say, 'Our bones are dried up, and our hope has perished; we are cut off.' Therefore, prophesy and say to them, 'This is what the Lord God says: I am going to open your graves and bring you up from them, my people, and lead you into the land of Israel. You will know that I am the Lord, my people, when I open your graves and bring you up from them. I will put my Spirit in you, and you will live, and I will settle you in your own land. Then you will know that I am the Lord. I have spoken, and I will do it. This is the declaration of the Lord.'" (Ezek 37:7–14)

Come, let's return to the Lord. For he has torn us, and he will heal us; he has wounded us, and he will bind up our wounds. He will revive us after two days, and on the third day he will raise us up so we can live in his presence. Let's strive to know the Lord. His appearance is as sure as the dawn. He will come to us like the rain, like the spring showers that water the land. (Hos 6:1–3)

The OT focuses on life in this world. Nevertheless, we adduce other texts for future hope in the OT. We think especially of two streams of evidence in the Psalms. One such stream is the use of the word "life" to point to life beyond the present one:

> Surely goodness and mercy shall follow me all the days of my life, and I shall dwell in the house of the Lord forever. (23:6 ESV)

> My heart is glad and my whole being rejoices; my body also rests securely. For you will not abandon me to Sheol; you will not allow your faithful one to see decay. You reveal the path of life to me; in your presence is abundant joy; at your right hand are eternal pleasures. (16:9–11)

> It is like the dew of Hermon falling on the mountains of Zion. For there the Lord has appointed the blessing—life forevermore. (133:3)

Another evidence of future life is the fact that some psalms use the word "forever" in a way that anticipates future life:

> You give him blessings forever; you cheer him with joy in your presence. For the king relies on the Lord; through the faithful love of the Most High he is not shaken. (21:6–7)

> The Lord is the strength of his people; he is a stronghold of salvation for his anointed. Save your people, bless your possession, shepherd them, and carry them forever. (28:8–9)

> Lead me to a rock that is high above me, for you have been a refuge for me, a strong tower in the face of the enemy. I will dwell in your tent forever and take refuge under the shelter of your wings. (61:2–4)

> I am always with you; you hold my right hand. You guide me with your counsel, and afterward you will take me up in glory. Who do I have in heaven but you? And I desire nothing on earth but you. My flesh and my heart may fail, but God is the strength of my heart, my portion forever. (73:23–26)

We conclude our OT survey where we began, by pointing out that the only text that speaks specifically of eternal life is Dan 12:2: "Many who sleep in the dust of the earth will awake, some to eternal life, and some to disgrace and eternal contempt." Eternal life here is associated with the resurrection from the dead, to life beyond this life, to life beyond death.

Eternal Life in the Synoptics

Eternal life is the life of the age to come; it is the life believers will enjoy with God forever. The Scriptures use the term "eternal life" (*aiōnios zōē*) and often use "life" (*zōē*) as a shorthand. When the Synoptics use the term "eternal life," they refer to a future reality, unending life in the age to come. Jesus demonstrates this when he answers the disciples' question concerning their place in heaven. Jesus explains that "in the renewal of all things, when the Son of Man sits on his glorious throne" (Matt 19:28), God will reward his faithful people. In fact, Jesus taught:

> "There is no one who has left house or brothers or sisters or mother or father or children or fields for my sake and for the sake of the gospel, who will not receive a hundred times more, now at this time—houses, brothers and sisters, mothers and children, and fields, with persecutions—and eternal life in the age to come." (Mark 10:29–30; cf. Luke 18:29–30)

In one of Scripture's most important verses on eternal destinies, Jesus powerfully connects eternity to the fates of human beings. Speaking of the lost and saved, respectively, Jesus declares, "They will go away into eternal punishment, but the righteous into eternal life" (Matt 25:46). Jesus uses the same adjective, "eternal," to describe the destinies of the wicked and of the righteous. Augustine draws an inexorable conclusion: "Hence, because the eternal life of the saints will be endless, the eternal punishment also for those condemned to it, will assuredly have no end."[1]

Jesus solemnly asserts, "Whoever blasphemes against the Holy Spirit never has forgiveness, but is guilty of an eternal sin" (Mark 3:29). James Edwards explains that this is not "an indefinable offense against God, but a specific misjudgment that Jesus is motivated by evil rather than by good,

---

[1] Robert A. Peterson, *Hell on Trial: The Case for Eternal Punishment* (Phillipsburg, NJ: P&R), 46, quoting Augustine, *The City of God* 21:23–24.

that he is empowered by the devil rather than by God." Edwards accurately defines "eternal": "Such sin is called 'an eternal sin' (v. 29), that is, a sin with an eternal consequence."[2]

The Synoptics emphasize the cost and commitment necessary to gain life. The gate to life is narrow and restricted, and its road is one less traveled and difficult (Matt 7:14). One must cut off any bodily members or gouge out eyes if they hinder one from obtaining life (18:8–9; Mark 9:45, 47). Of course, Jesus does not hereby teach bodily mutilation, but he does stress that severe restrictions are sometimes necessary in order to avoid sinning. The rich ruler asked Jesus how he could obtain "eternal life" (Matt 19:16; Mark 10:17; Luke 18:18). Jesus instructed him that he must sell all his possessions and become Jesus's disciple (Matt 19:21; Mark 10:21; Luke 18:22). Such a radical transformation is only possible with God (Matt 19:26; Mark 10:27; Luke 18:27)!

Those who forsake all for Jesus will experience eternal life (Mark 10:30; Luke 18:30). So too, in Jesus's teaching about the sheep and goats (Matt 25:31–46) the sheep are those who feed their brothers and sisters in Christ who are hungry, care for them when they are rejected, clothe them when they are naked, nurture them when they are sick, or visit them in prison (vv. 35–36). Those who live in such a way will enjoy "eternal life" (v. 46). The one who obtains eternal life truly loves his neighbor (Luke 10:25–37).

We include the two uses of "eternal life" in Acts here as well since Luke wrote both the Gospel of Luke and Acts. We find them after Paul's sermon on his first missionary journey when he proclaimed the gospel in the synagogue in Pisidian Antioch. Many Jews, though not all, rejected the gospel, and Paul and Barnabas stated that they would bring their message to the Gentiles since the Jews had rejected it "and judge[d] yourselves unworthy of eternal life" (Acts 13:46). The Gentiles responded to this turn of affairs joyfully and "honored the word of the Lord, and all who had been appointed to eternal life believed" (v. 48).

We make two observations about eternal life from this verse. First, the focus is on the future—eternal life is something believers will enjoy eschatologically. Second, eternal life is given to those who believe, to those whom

---

[2] James R. Edwards, *The Gospel according to Mark*, PNTC (Grand Rapids: Eerdmans, 2002), 122, 123.

God ordained to believe. The reference to belief is instructive, since some examples seen thus far emphasize the commitment to Jesus necessary to obtain eternal life.

Eternal Life in the Johannine Literature

John is the theologian of life and eternal life, using the term far more than any other writer in the NT.[3] What is also striking in John is that eternal life refers typically to life that believers enjoy now. We saw in the Synoptics that eternal life is future, referring to the day when God's people will obtain a final reward. John, however, stresses that the life of the age to come already belongs to believers. The most famous verse in his Gospel contains its first reference to eternal life: "God loved the world in this way: He gave his one and only Son, so that everyone who believes in him will not perish but have eternal life" (John 3:16). Here eternal life could be entirely future, but, if we look at John's usage elsewhere, such an interpretation is doubtful. The next reference to eternal life makes the point: "The one who believes in the Son has eternal life, but the one who rejects the Son will not see life; instead, the wrath of God remains on him" (v. 36). Those who believe in the Son have eternal life now, as the present-tense verb "has" (*echei*) testifies. On the other hand, those who refuse to obey the Son will not experience life in the age to come—and God's wrath is their portion even now.

John has often been designated the theologian of realized eschatology, and we see this very clearly with reference to eternal life in John 5:24: "Truly I tell you, anyone who hears my word and believes him who sent me has eternal life and will not come under judgment but has passed from death to life." Once again we find the present-tense "has," signifying that eternal life is the present possession of those who put their trust in the Father who sent the Son. The conclusion of the verse underlines this truth: believers have already passed "from death to life." The verb "has passed" (*metabebēken*) is

---

[3] For this theme in John, see C. H. Dodd, *The Interpretation of the Fourth Gospel* (Cambridge: Cambridge University Press, 1953), 144–50; George Eldon Ladd, *A Theology of the New Testament*, rev. ed., ed. D. A. Hagner (Grand Rapids: Eerdmans 1993), 290–305.

perfect tense, showing that death is relegated to the past and that life is an existing reality. The life of the age to come has invaded the present evil age, and believers now enjoy such life. As Jesus says, the hour "is now here" when the spiritually dead will hear the Son of God's voice, and when they hear they will "live" (v. 25). John isn't saying that they will live in the future. His point is that those who are dead enter life *now*, before the day of the final resurrection.

Although John emphasizes realized eschatology, he does not neglect consistent eschatology, that is, future eschatology. Such is the case in John 5:28–29: "Do not be amazed at this, because a time is coming when all who are in the graves will hear his voice and come out—those who have done good things, to the resurrection of life, but those who have done wicked things, to the resurrection of condemnation." These verses refer to the end of the age, when God (here God the Son) will raise the dead to eternal life or eternal hell.

Jesus identifies himself as the bread of life (John 6:35, 48), promising eternal life to those who believe in him (vv. 27, 33, 40, 51, 58). The "one who believes has [*echei*] eternal life" now (v. 47), and Jesus makes the same point later in the discourse: "The one who eats my flesh and drinks my blood has eternal life, and I will raise him up on the last day" (v. 54). Eating and drinking are vivid metaphors that describe believing, and those who drink of Jesus and feed upon him enjoy eternal life now.

When Jesus interacts with Martha on the occasion in which he raises Lazarus from the dead, we find a similar theme. Jesus tells Martha, "I am the resurrection and the life. The one who believes in me, even if he dies, will live. Everyone who lives and believes in me will never die. Do you believe this?" (11:25–26). Eternal life isn't abstract; it isn't a thing or quality that believers somehow find. Instead, Jesus himself is the resurrection and the life; he himself is the life of the age to come. Consequently, those who believe in Jesus will live (be raised from the dead!) even if they die. On the other hand, "The one who lives and believes in me will never die." When Jesus describes "the one who lives," he doesn't refer to the one who lives physically; he refers to one who enjoys eternal life now. And if eternal life is a present possession, then that person will never die even if he dies! In other words, eternal life conquers death. John actually wrote his Gospel so that people by believing in Jesus as the Messiah and the Son of God would experience such life (20:30–31)—or, as he puts it in 17:3, eternal life consists in knowing God and knowing his Son.

First John also emphasizes the present possession of life. The message John proclaimed, the promise he heralded, was eternal life (1 John 1:2; 2:25). Such eternal life is granted to believers in Jesus as the Son of God (5:11), and one purpose for the letter is so that believers will know now that they have eternal life (v. 13). John wants believers to be assured of their status as children of God (3:1–3), so that they live with confidence and without fear (2:28; 3:19–21; 4:17–18). The present possession of life is emphasized: "We know that we have passed from death to life because we love our brothers and sisters. The one who does not love remains in death" (3:14). John uses the same verb, "have passed" (*metabebēkamen*), he used in John 5:24, and both verbs are in the perfect tense to teach that believers enjoy eternal life now. The same truth is communicated in 1 John 5:12: "The one who has the Son has life. The one who does not have the Son of God does not have life." The present-tense verb "has" leaves no doubt that believers who by faith belong to the Son of God enjoy eternal life now.

We add one final note. John's emphasis on realized eschatology, his teaching that we already enjoy eternal life, has led some scholars to claim that there is no future eschatology in John.[4] Certainly the accent in the Gospel and the first epistle is on realized eschatology, but it would be a mistake to conclude that there is no future eschatology in John. We have already seen a future eschatology very clearly in John 5:28–29. John envisions a day of resurrection, of physical resurrection of both the just and the unjust, and that day will only come after death. Rudolf Bultmann was so committed to realized eschatology in John that he dismissed these verses as later glosses. Such a gambit should be rejected, for there is no evidence for such glosses, and such a move is an example of excluding evidence unfavorable to one's thesis. We should interpret John in all his complexity instead of straitjacketing him to fit our theory.

Moreover, twice John combines both realized and future eschatology in a single passage. He alerts us to the fact that he is doing so by his language.

---

[4] See Rudolf Bultmann, *The Gospel of John: A Commentary*, trans. G. R. Beasley-Murray (Philadelphia: Westminster, 1971), 261. He also argues that an editor added references to being raised on the last day in John 6:39, 40, 44 (p. 219).

He distinguishes "an hour" (or time) that "is coming" from one that "is coming *and is now here.*" We have already considered John 5, where Jesus teaches that "an hour is coming, and is now here" (v. 25) when God moves believers from spiritual death to spiritual life (v. 24). The result is that they already possess eternal life. A few verses later Jesus points to the future when he predicts his raising the dead on the last day. There he omits the words "and is now here" and instead simply says "a time is coming" when he will raise the dead by his word (vv. 28–29). Future eschatology is thus not absent from John, but it is far from his main accent, which is plainly on realized eschatology, the present fulfilment of God's promises.

Eternal Life in Pauline Literature

When we turn to Paul, we find that he uses the term "eternal life" quite differently than John. In Paul the term is in large measure eschatological, denoting life in the future age to come. For instance, in Romans 2 Paul considers the final judgment, stressing that there will be judgment for those who disobey and refuse to repent (vv. 4–6, 8–9). On the other hand, those who persevere in doing good works will experience eschatological reward, including glory, honor, immortality, and peace (vv. 7, 10). Included in these blessings is "eternal life" (v. 7), which is obviously an end-time gift in this context.

Another clear text is Gal 6:8, where those who sow to the flesh "will reap destruction" but those who sow to the Spirit "will reap eternal life." "Sowing" and "reaping" pick up a common experience of agricultural life, where there is a temporal interval between present activity and future reward. Believers sow to the Spirit now, and in the future they will reap an end-time reward—eternal life. We see the same kind of connection in Rom 8:6: "The mind-set of the flesh is death, but the mind-set of the Spirit is life and peace." Death is the consequence of pursuing the flesh, but "life," which is certainly eternal life here, is the result of following the Spirit. Since death is contrasted with eternal life, the latter is almost certainly eschatological.

We see the eschatological nature of eternal life in Titus 3:7 as well, where Paul celebrates justification by grace, with its result that "We may become heirs with the hope of eternal life." "Heirs" and "hope" both point to eternal life as an eschatological gift. Similarly, Paul in 1:2 speaks of the "hope of eternal life," assuring his readers that their hope will become a reality, since

God can't lie. The future nature of life is evident also in the phrase "promise of life" (2 Tim 1:1).

In a number of texts eternal life is explained as an outcome or result, and in these cases the future envisioned is certainly eschatological. For example, sin reigns "in death," but in Jesus Christ grace also reigns, and the result is "eternal life" (Rom 5:21). Those who are liberated from sin are sanctified, "and the outcome [*telos*] is eternal life." One of the most well-known contrasts can be seen in 6:23: "The wages of sin is death, but the gift of God is eternal life in Christ Jesus our Lord." "Wages" and "death" anticipate the future, when sinners will receive the recompense for their sin, and "eternal life" is the future gift for those who belong to Christ Jesus. Eternal life is given to those who put their faith in Christ (1 Tim 1:16).

While Paul's great emphasis is on eternal life in the future, he also hints at a present sense of eternal life. Paul contrasts the two Adams:

> If by the one man's trespass, death reigned through that one man, how much more will those who receive the overflow of grace and the gift of righteousness reign in life through the one man, Jesus Christ. So then, as through one trespass there is condemnation for everyone, so also through one righteous act there is justification leading to life for everyone. (Rom 5:17–18)

Doubtless, "justification leading to life" (v. 18) describes eschatological life. But what about believers' reigning "in life" through Christ (v. 17)? Is that totally future? Moo suggests otherwise: "Because Paul uses a future verb to depict the reigning of those who receive the gift, most think that the reference must be to the eschatological future. But without denying that this is involved, and may even be the primary emphasis, it may be that this 'reigning in life' begins with the reception of the gift of righteousness."[5] Perhaps this should not surprise us, for "the Spirit is life" (Rom 8:10 ESV), and the "newness of life" (6:4) he brings is life of the age to come experienced now.

Twice in 1 Timothy, Paul exhorts readers to "take hold of eternal life" (1 Tim 6:12, 19). The first text, in which Paul advises Timothy, bears quotation: "Fight the good fight of the faith. *Take hold of eternal life* to which you were called and about which you have made a good confession in the

---

[5] Moo, *The Epistle to the Romans*, 340 (see chap. 2, n. 62).

presence of many witnesses" (emphasis added). Paul thus speaks of taking hold of eternal life now, as Yarbrough explains: "This is not merely a duration of life in the age to come but a quality of life in the present age. 'Take hold' (*epilabou*) means to fully appropriate."[6]

We conclude that although Paul is primarily a theologian of "not-yet" life, the "already" aspect of eternal life is not absent from his writings.

Summary

In the OT, "life" typically refers to physical life and blessing, though the phrase "eternal life" occurs in Dan 12:2. Other texts also foreshadow NT teaching, especially those that predict the resurrection of the dead and some psalms that use the words "life" or "forever." New Testament writers sometimes used OT words for physical life typologically of life in the age to come. Outside of the Johannine writings, eternal life in the NT mostly looks forward to the eschaton, to life in the age to come, when believers will enjoy life forever with God in and through Jesus Christ. We see this eschatological emphasis in Jude 21: "Keep yourselves in the love of God, waiting expectantly for the mercy of our Lord Jesus Christ for eternal life." Believers wait for the mercy that will be poured on them on the last day, and the reward will be "eternal life" on that day. John, however, stresses that believers enjoy eternal life now during this present evil age. The gift of the end time has already penetrated this current age. Such life will be consummated at the resurrection, but believers can be assured now that they possess eternal life. The eschaton has invaded this age; the life of the future is given to those who trust in Jesus Christ, to those who follow him as his disciples in profession and life.

Glorification

Eternal life and glorification are closely related, which is why we study them together. We will show that glorification is almost always future, and eternal life, though future, refers to the present more than "glory" does. The words

---

[6] Robert W. Yarbrough, *The Letters to Timothy and Titus*, PNTC (Grand Rapids: Eerdmans, 2018), 324.

"glory" (*doxa*) and "glorify" (*doxazō*) both occur often in the Scriptures, but our purpose isn't to study these terms in general but to consider places that speak of God's sharing his glory with believers in glorification. We narrow our search to focus on 1 Peter, Hebrews, and Paul.

Exegetical Foundations

Future Glory in 1 Peter and Hebrews

On several occasions Peter reflects on the glory to be given to believers. The churches to which Peter wrote were suffering and facing difficulties. Peter lifts their eyes heavenward, pointing them to the future and reminding them that through enduring trials they will experience "praise, glory, and honor at the revelation of Jesus Christ" (1 Pet 1:7). The suffering is painful, but Peter motivates believers by reminding them of their future reward, of the splendor and beauty awaiting them. Elders in the congregation have a particular responsibility as shepherds of the flock, and Peter exhorts them in light of the "sufferings of Christ" and, of course, their own sufferings. They will share as well "in the glory about to be revealed" (5:1). The glory that will be theirs is hidden now but will be unveiled and unfurled on the last day. The same thought is reaffirmed in verse 4. The elders are shepherds of the flock, but Jesus Christ is the "chief Shepherd," and when he returns the elders "will receive the unfading crown of glory." This crown *is* glory, and the expression is another way of describing eternal life. Sufferings are short-lived, but glory is forever, and this glory won't wane but will continue to burn brightly forever.

This glory isn't restricted to leaders, however, as Peter makes clear in one of the concluding verses of the letter: "The God of all grace, who called you to his eternal glory in Christ, will himself restore, establish, strengthen, and support you after you have suffered a little while" (1 Pet 5:10). Glory is the destiny of all believers, and the God who called them to eschatological and everlasting glory and who will strengthen them in all their sufferings will also see to it by his grace that they receive what is promised. This forms an *inclusio* in the letter, as the sufferings and pressures of believers at both the beginning of the letter (1:7) and its end (5:10) are answered by the assurance of eschatological glory.

Hebrews includes only one reference to eschatological glory, but the context is quite significant. The author argues in chapter 1 and particularly in chapter 2 that human beings are superior to angels. He cites Psalm 8 to confirm that God intended human beings to rule the world as God's viceregents (Heb 2:5–9). The rule believers were intended to exercise is theirs only through Jesus's becoming a man and suffering the curse of death (vv. 10–18). In this way he triumphed over the devil and freed human beings from fear of and slavery to death. God's purpose "in bringing sons and daughters to glory" (v. 10) is achieved through Jesus's suffering. The glory promised is eschatological, since it includes victory over death, which belongs to believers in principle now but will be theirs fully on the day of resurrection, on the day they shine with radiant and splendid glory.

Future Glory in Pauline Literature

Paul also reminds readers in his various letters of the glory to be theirs. We see the eschatological character of glory in Romans 2, where God's impartial judgment of all is featured: those who do what is good will experience eternal life, while those who do what is evil will face end-time judgment (Rom 2:7–10). Those who are justified freely by God's grace and persist in doing what is good, those who "seek glory, honor, and immortality," will be granted eternal life (v. 7). "Glory, honor, and immortality" is another way of describing eternal life. The same truth is reaffirmed in verse 10: those who pursue goodness will enjoy "glory, honor, and peace." We all recognize that those who please God may not be honored and blessed in this life, but Paul casts his eye toward the future and holds before his readers the end-time joys that will be theirs, a future that is radiant and splendid and beautiful.

We saw in 1 Peter that those whom God called he will also glorify (1 Pet 5:10). We see this same emphasis in Paul. For instance, in Romans 9 Paul reflects on God's promises, assuring the readers that God is faithful, that he will fulfill what he has pledged (v. 6), whether in the lives of Jews or of Gentiles. God's promises can't be derailed, for they depend upon his sovereign grace, wise purpose, and unalterable will. God both hardens and shows mercy, and no one will ultimately resist his will (vv. 15–19). He has the right to save and to judge, and some are "objects of mercy" while others are "objects of wrath" (vv. 22–23). The objects of wrath will experience eschatological destruction, while conversely God has "prepared . . . for glory" those who will know his mercy (v. 23). "Glory" here is the antonym of "destruction" and thus refers clearly to the end-time beauty and splendor that is the certain portion of those whom God has chosen.

If we back up into Romans 8, we see that chapter's emphasis concerning glory is present in Romans 9 as well. The conclusion of chapter 8 rings with assurance and joy as believers are comforted with the certain hope promised to those in Christ Jesus. God will grant them everything they need in Christ (Rom 8:31–32), and they can be confident that they will not be condemned but will be declared righteous at the Last Judgment (vv. 1, 33–34). Indeed, nothing whatsoever can separate them from the love of Christ (vv. 35–39). Because all things work together to make them like Christ (vv. 28–29), they are filled with joy. The foundation for all things working together for good is what William Perkins called the golden chain: Paul begins with God's foreknowing and goes on to say in verse 30, "And those he predestined, he also called; and those he called, he also justified; and those he justified, he also glorified." God's work began in eternity past and extends to eternity future. In the past he foreknew and predestined those who would be his, and then he called them in history through the proclamation of the gospel. As those who were effectually called, they believed and thus were justified. And all those who were justified will also be glorified, that is, they will obtain the eschatological reward.

The aorist tense of "glorified" (*edoxasen*) certifies the work will certainly be completed. There has been some pushback in recent years to reading the tense this way, and rightly so, since the aorist tense doesn't necessarily denote past time, and the newer studies provoke us to be careful when appealing to the tense of a Greek verb. Still, the series of aorist verbs is probably significant here, and we certainly begin with past realities, since Paul refers to God's foreknowing and predestining work. The use of the aorist tense, then, with a string of aorist verbs that have to do with the past helps us interpret the aorist tense of "glorified." The older interpreters are probably correct: Paul assures his readers that glorification is certain. Some interpreters argue that glorification has an already-but-not-yet dimension, so that glorification is both present and future. Such a reading is possible, but it seems that Paul uses glorification mainly of future glory, and the evidence for an already-but-not-yet understanding here isn't compelling.

God began the salvation process, and he will complete it (cf. Phil 1:6). The reading proposed here is confirmed by 2 Thess 2:14: "He called you to this through our gospel, so that you might obtain the glory of our Lord Jesus Christ." We remember that the call in Paul is compelling and effective, and in that sense, it is ultimately irresistible. Initial resistance will be overcome by God's efficacious grace, and those whom he called will also experience eschatological glory. Such a scenario makes sense. It would be strange indeed if God called people to faith but then their faith collapsed so that they didn't make it to the end. Those who are called will also receive glory on the last day. Similarly, Paul speaks of God's wisdom, which was "predestined before the ages for our glory" (1 Cor 2:7). Wisdom here isn't some abstract philosophical matter but has to do with Christ and him crucified, which is the wisdom that leads to salvation (1:18–25). What God has predestined—our glory!—will certainly be achieved.

Believers, then, look forward to the glory that will be theirs. When Jesus returns, believers will glorify and honor him, and they in turn will be glorified in him (2 Thess 1:12). As Paul says in Col 3:4, "When Christ, who is your life, appears, then you also will appear with him in glory." The glory given is hidden now but will be manifested when Jesus comes. Glory is hoped for and anticipated but not yet possessed. Yes, Paul says we are changed "from glory to glory" even now (2 Cor 3:18), but when he speaks of glorification, he typically has in mind the complete glorification and splendor and radiance and perfection—our being conformed to God's character—that will be ours on the last day. The hope, the sure confidence, that we will receive the glory that comes from God (Rom 5:2) gives believers strength to endure present trials. Since Paul speaks of "hope," it is clear that the glory is future and not presently ours. The whole purpose of Paul's ministry is designed to bring salvation and "eternal glory" to the elect (2 Tim 2:10; cf. Eph 3:13). Thus, we have another hint that election secures the final glory of believers.

The glory promised gives ballast and strength when trials, afflictions, and sufferings come. Believers are "heirs of God and coheirs with Christ"—suffering comes first, then glory (Rom 8:17). The eschatological character of glory is quite clear here. Now believers are not glorified but suffer, which fits with verse 18 as well: "I consider that the sufferings of this present time are not worth comparing with the glory that is going to be revealed to us." Suffering is worth it, even intense suffering, though it may seem overwhelming. The glory to come hasn't been disclosed to us, which shows again that it is escha-tological. A curtain hides from us what the glory will be, but we know it will be stunning and amazing, and thus every pain will be worth enduring. Second Corinthians 4:17 voices the same thought: "Our momentary light affliction is producing for us an absolutely incomparable eternal weight of glory." Paul isn't teaching us that our sufferings are light and inconsequential. They often feel weighty and unbelievably heavy, but, when we experience the glory that is coming and look back, we will say that all our sufferings were worth it. Paul motivates believers to endure, encouraging them in their suf-fering with the promise of the indescribable beauty awaiting them.

God's Glory and the Creation

Paul teaches that God's glory will extend to the creation. The creation was affected by the fall and needed to be made right. The work of Christ is so effective and superb that it accomplished more than we often realize. Not only did it defeat our foes and redeem God's people individually and cor-porately, but it also delivered the creation. Paul teaches this in at least two passages. First, "God was pleased to have all his fullness dwell in [Christ], and through him to reconcile everything to himself, whether things on earth or things in heaven, by making peace through his blood, shed on the cross" (Col 1:19–20).

The second passage presents Christ's redemption of creation:

> I consider that the sufferings of this present time are not worth comparing with the glory that is going to be revealed to us. For the creation eagerly waits with anticipation for God's sons to be revealed. For the creation was subjected to futility—not willingly, but because of him who subjected it—in the hope that the creation itself will also be set free from the bondage to decay into the glori-ous freedom of God's children. For we know that the whole creation has been groaning together with labor pains until now. Not only that, but we ourselves who have the Spirit as the firstfruits—we also groan within ourselves, eagerly waiting for adoption, the redemp-tion of our bodies. (Rom 8:18–23)

Paul here presents believers as a microcosm of the macrocosm, the whole creation. God will reveal great glory to and in us in our resurrection, "the redemption of our bodies" (v. 23). The creation personified, moreover, longs for that day, for our revelation in glory will mean creation's freedom from "the bondage to decay" into participation in "the glorious freedom of God's children" (v. 21). Then the words of Rev 22:3 will apply: "There will no longer be any curse." In the meantime believers, the creation personified, and even the Holy Spirit "groan" in our present struggles, eagerly waiting for final redemption (Rom 8:22, 23, 26). When we put our present sufferings up against our future glory, there is no comparison (v. 18). As Paul says elsewhere, "Our momentary light affliction is producing for us an absolutely incomparable eternal weight of glory" (2 Cor 4:17).

Present Glory Too

We must not allow Paul's overwhelming emphasis on future glory to obscure a place where he teaches that God gives glory to his people in this life. The key text here is 2 Cor 3:18: "We all, with unveiled faces, are looking as in a mirror at the glory of the Lord and are being transformed into the same image from glory to glory; this is from the Lord who is the Spirit." Vocabulary counts are not a sure guide to exegesis, but 2 Cor 3:7–18, whose thirteen references to "glory" are the highest of any Pauline passage, is a key text on that theme. Paul begins verse 18 with "we all," in contrast to God's dealings with Moses (Exod 34:34). Unlike OT saints, NT believers have access to God's presence. Unlike Moses, the mediator of the old covenant, we do not wear a veil as we behold Christ's glory. Although there is debate, it seems that Paul's words should be rendered "behold" or "look as in a mirror" rather than "reflect as in a mirror."[7] Paul explains that "the light of the knowledge of the glory of God" is seen "in the face of Jesus Christ" (2 Cor 4:6).

We see God's glory in "the gospel of the glory of Christ, who is the image of God" (2 Cor 4:4). Adam and Eve were created in the image of God, which was tarnished in the fall but is restored progressively in Christ, the true image of God, and will be perfected when Jesus returns (1 Cor 15:49). Paul declares that Christians "are being transformed into the same image from one degree of glory to another" (2 Cor 3:18 ESV), or, more literally, "from glory to glory." But this glorious description does not seem to square

---

[7] CSB, ESV, NASB.

with anyone's Christian life. How have scholars handled this problem? A Lutheran approach, illustrated by Seifrid, says that Paul does not speak of "movement from one degree of glory to another. . . . It is not a moral quality within them but God's favor and comfort given to those in need and distress, including the distress of their sin and rebellion."[8] This view holds that "glory to glory" speaks of justification, not progressive sanctification. Barnett, Garland, Harris, and Martin disagree, and they persuade us, as do the ESV, NIV, NASB, and NRSVA.[9] This is a difficult description of the Christian life, and we can understand in part by noting that the Holy Spirit produces this glory: "This is from the Lord who is the Spirit" (v. 18). In fact, the Spirit appears six times in the context (vv. 3, 6, 8, 17).

Therefore, unlike Paul's common "not-yet" emphasis on glory, 2 Cor 3:18 teaches that "already" the Spirit works in believers so that they increase progressively in glory until the return of Christ, when he will transform our current bodies into a glorious one like his, a topic to which we now turn.

Resurrection Glory

Although there is continuity between our present bodies and our resurrection bodies, Phil 3:20–21 highlights the discontinuity between the two: "Our citizenship is in heaven, and we eagerly wait for a Savior from there, the Lord Jesus Christ. He will transform the body of our humble condition into the likeness of his glorious body, by the power that enables him to subject everything to himself." The all-powerful Christ will fit our current bodies for eternal life on the new earth. The key concept is transformation: Christ will transform (change) our present bodies to be like his glorious resurrection body.

In 1 Corinthians 15 Paul draws vivid contrasts between our present and resurrection bodies. The former is characterized by "corruption," "dishonor," and "weakness," as befits "natural" bodies belonging to this age (vv. 42–44). The latter are characterized by "incorruption," "glory," and "power," as befits

---

[8] Mark A. Seifrid, *The Second Letter to the Corinthians*, PNTC (Grand Rapids: Eerdmans, 2014), 183.

[9] Paul Barnett, *The Second Epistle to the Corinthians*, NICNT (Grand Rapids: Eerdmans, 1997), 207–8; David E. Garland, *2 Corinthians* (Nashville: B&H, 1999), 200–201; Murray J. Harris, *The Second Epistle to the Corinthians*, NIGTC (Grand Rapids: Eerdmans, 2005), 316; and Ralph P. Martin, *2 Corinthians*, 2nd ed, WBC (Grand Rapids: Zondervan, 2014), 72.

"spiritual" bodies (bodies controlled by the Holy Spirit) belonging to the age to come (vv. 42–44). Paul summarizes: "This corruptible body must be clothed with incorruptibility, and this mortal body must be clothed with immortality" (v. 53). Our present bodies get ill and grow old, they are dishonored in burial, they exhibit weakness with age, and because of the fall they eventually die. By contrast, our resurrected bodies will not become ill or grow old but will be glorious and powerful, reflecting "the image of the man of heaven," Christ (v. 49). Our bodies will be also "spiritual" (v. 44), not incorporeal but dominated by the Spirit, who will fit them for eternal life on the new earth. Thus, believers' bodies will share in the glory of Christ and the age to come.

Christ and Glory

Jesus Christ is central to the revelation of the glory of God. Repeatedly Paul uses "glory" to depict the inheritance of the sons and daughters of the living God. It is critical for us to realize that this future glory is inseparable from Jesus Christ, our Redeemer. The unregenerate rulers of the present world did not know "Christ Jesus, who became wisdom from God for us—our righteousness, sanctification, and redemption" (1 Cor 1:30). Moreover, this wisdom was not an afterthought on God's part but was "a wisdom God predestined before the ages for our glory" (1 Cor 2:7). This world's rulers thought they were wise but displayed their ignorance of God's true wisdom: "None of the rulers of this age knew this wisdom, because if they had known it, they would not have crucified the Lord of glory" (v. 8). Jesus is the "Lord of glory," the "glorious Lord."

The link between the Lord Jesus and God's wisdom and glory is intimate. Paul prays for the Colossians, whom he has never met. He wants "their hearts to be encouraged and joined together in love, so that they may have all the riches of complete understanding and have the knowledge of God's mystery—Christ. In him are hidden all the treasures of wisdom and knowledge" (Col 2:2–3). Indeed, Christ is so tied to believers' hope of final glory that Paul's goal is "to make known among the Gentiles the glorious wealth of this mystery, which is Christ in you, the hope of glory" (Col 1:27).

Believers are so united to Christ in salvation that, when he comes again, so will they in a sense: "When Christ, who is your life, appears, then you also will appear with him in glory" (Col 3:4). Both Christ and his people have an "appearing." Our union with Christ is so permanent that our full identity will be revealed only when he returns for us. His return will reveal not only his full identity but ours as well. God the Father "calls [believers] into his own kingdom and glory" (1 Thess 2:12), and they will not fail to attain those lofty goals. In fact, God will enable us to obtain the "glory of our Lord Jesus Christ" (2 Thess 2:14). Here again Paul equates our salvation and Christ's glory. Christ and glory are correlative.

Salvation and God's Glory

Paul praises the Trinity for salvation: the Father elects us, the Son redeems us, and the Spirit is God's seal on us (Eph 1:3–14). Paul uses comprehensive language: "Blessed is the God and Father of our Lord Jesus Christ, who has blessed us with every spiritual blessing in the heavens in Christ" (v. 3). "Every spiritual blessing" includes election, adoption, redemption, forgiveness, reconciliation, an inheritance, sealing, and more. God the Father plans all of these things, accomplishes them all through Christ's death and resurrection, and applies them through our union with Christ. Repeatedly Paul adds a sweet refrain: "to the praise of his glorious grace" (v. 6), "praise to his glory" (v. 12), "to the praise of his glory" (v. 14). We must not miss Paul's point: the final goal of our salvation is not even salvation but the praise of God's glory for such a great salvation.

Summary

Glorification in the New Testament is chiefly a future blessing, though one passage shows it to be a present one too (2 Cor 3:18). Nevertheless, believers don't now possess the full glory that will be theirs when Christ returns. The promise of glory encourages believers during present sufferings, reminding them of the splendor and beauty awaiting them. Glory is guaranteed for those who are foreknown, predestined, called, and justified. Those whom God has called will certainly receive eternal glory, since the God who called them will strengthen them to the end. And the ultimate end of believers' glorification is that God might be eternally praised for lavishing such grace on them.

Systematic Formulations

Restored to Glory

We were created in the image of God to worship and display God, but we all refused to acknowledge God's glory and instead sought our own. Through this we forfeited the glory God intended for us as his image-bearers. By his grace and through union with Christ the perfect image, however, God saves us, restoring us as full image-bearers to participate in and reflect the glory we longed for the whole time. Thus we are recipients of glory, are undergoing transformation through glory, and will be sharers of glory. Our salvation is not merely from sin but is also unto glory. We who exchanged the glory of God for idols, we who rebelled against God's glory, have been, are being, and will be completely transformed by the very glory we despised and rejected (Rom 1:18–31; 3:23; 8:28–30; 9:23; 2 Cor 3:18).

Characterized by Glory, Past, Present, and Future

Our glory in Christ is past, present, and future. We have already been given glory, as Jesus states: "I have given them the glory you have given me, so that they may be one as we are one" (John 17:22). We are being transformed from glory to glory, as Paul expresses: "We all, with unveiled faces, are looking as in a mirror at the glory of the Lord and are being transformed into the same image from glory to glory; this is from the Lord who is the Spirit" (2 Cor 3:18). And we await glory, as Paul describes: "We boast in the hope of the glory of God" (Rom 5:2). Our future glorification follows Christ's glorious return (Titus 2:13; 1 Pet 4:13) and is coupled to the renewal of the cosmos (Rom 8:19–23; 2 Pet 3:13). All of us as God's people, both the living and the resurrected dead, will be glorified together (1 Thess 4:15–18; 1 Cor 15:51–52).

Conformed to Christ's Image

The image of God, in which we were created (Gen 1:26–27), still exists in our being. Its function was tarnished in the fall but is restored gradually in

Christ (Col 3:9–10; Eph 4:22–24). It will be perfected only when Christ, the true image (2 Cor 4:4; Col 1:15), powerfully conforms us to his image in resurrection: "He will transform the body of our humble condition into the likeness of his glorious body, by the power that enables him to subject everything to himself" (Phil 3:21). Ferguson points out, "The image and image-bearers are one in Spirit to the end, so that when Christ appears in glory image-bearers are one with him in that glory (Col 3:4). We are raised in Christ, with Christ, by Christ, to be like Christ."[10] In the meantime we know "Christ in [us], the hope of glory" (Col 1:27).

Participation in Christ's Glory

Paul writes, "I consider that the sufferings of this present time are not worth comparing with the glory that is going to be revealed to us" (Rom 8:18). Astoundingly, glorification means resurrected saints' seeing Christ's glory and being transformed by it, so as to partake of it. God will produce "for us an absolutely incomparable eternal weight of glory" (2 Cor 4:17). In answer to Jesus's prayer, we will see his glory (John 17:24), and that vision will transform us (Phil 3:21; 1 John 3:2) so that we will actually partake of his glory (1 Pet 5:2). God has "prepared [us] beforehand for glory" (Rom 9:23) from the beginning, and by his grace he will bring his "many sons to glory" (Heb 2:10) in the end.

Alive with Glorified Bodies

Though at death our spirits are "made perfect" (Heb 12:23), glorification involves our *bodies'* being redeemed (Rom 8:23). There will be continuity between our present bodies and our resurrection bodies (v. 11), but there will also be discontinuity, for our new bodies will be imperishable, glorious, powerful, and immortal (1 Cor 15:42–54). They will be both physical and "spiritual" (v. 44), ruled by the Spirit.

---

[10] Sinclair B. Ferguson, *The Holy Spirit*, CCT (Downers Grove: InterVarsity, 1996), 251.

Dwelling in a Renewed Creation

As believers, we are a microcosm of the final redemption of the cosmos, the macrocosm: "The creation itself will also be set free from the bondage of corruption into the glorious freedom of God's children" (Rom 8:21). God will fulfill his purposes for his creation by delivering it from the curse (Rev 22:3) and perfecting us (1 Thess 5:23) and it (2 Pet 3:13). Ferguson puts it well: "The consummation of this glorification awaits the eschaton and the Spirit's ministry in the resurrection. Here, too, the pattern of his working is: as in Christ, so in believers and, by implication, in the universe."[11]

---

[11] Ferguson, 249.

Salvation and Theological Themes

We have explored ten aspects of salvation exegetically and theologically: union with Christ, election, calling, regeneration, conversion, justification, adoption, sanctification, perseverance, and eternal life and glorification. Theologians distinguish the Father's planning of salvation before creation (election), the Son's accomplishing of salvation in his death and resurrection in the first century AD, the Holy Spirit's ongoing application of salvation (union with Christ, and everything else from calling to present glorification in the list above), and the consummation of salvation in resurrection on the new earth (including eternal life and future glorification). This chart summarizes our conclusions concerning the application of salvation:

The Application of Salvation

Aspect	Need	Description	Scripture
Union with Christ	Separation	God joins us to Christ	Eph 1:3–14
Calling	Hearing	God enables us to hear	2 Tim 1:9
Regeneration	Death	God makes us alive	Eph 2:1–5
Conversion	Lostness	We turn from sin to Christ	Acts 20:21

Justification	Condemnation	God declares us righteous	Gal 2:15–16
Adoption	Slavery	God brings us into his family	Gal 3:26
Sanctification	Uncleanness	God makes us holy	Eph 5:25–27
Preservation	Unfaithfulness	God keeps us saved	Rom 8:28–39
Glorification	Shame	God gives us his glory	2 Cor 3:18

The traditional Reformed understanding of the *ordo salutis*, the order of salvation, holds that these aspects of salvation can be placed in a logical order.[1] John Murray's view of the *ordo salutis* is representative, and many have found it convincing. He urged:

> When we think of the application of redemption we must not think of it as one simple and indivisible act. It comprises a series of acts and processes. . . . There are good and conclusive reasons for thinking that the various actions of the application of salvation . . . take place in a certain order, and that order has been established by divine appointment, wisdom, and grace.[2]

Murray was convinced that Scripture "clearly implied an order or arrangement in the various steps of the application of redemption." He adduced John 3:3, 5; 1 John 3:9; John 1:12; Eph 1:13; and especially Rom 8:28–30 as evidence of this. After discussion of the particulars he concluded, "The order in the application of redemption is found to be, calling, regeneration, faith and repentance, justification, adoption, sanctification, perseverance, glorification."[3]

Although many Reformed theologians accepted Murray's thesis, with some tinkering with the specifics of his sequence, recently some have

---

[1] See our prior discussion of this issue and its application to sanctification on pp. 250–51.

[2] John Murray, *Redemption Accomplished and Applied* (Grand Rapids: Eerdmans, 1955), 79–80.

[3] Murray, 87.

criticized his approach. John Frame argued that there are different senses of "order" in the list of doctrines, which brings the whole idea into question.[4] Furthermore, to cite one example, we found sanctification to be initial, progressive, and final, and we therefore cannot place it in only one slot in an order of salvation.

We have benefitted from Hoekema's evaluation of the traditional *ordo salutis*.[5] As we showed previously, he rejects Murray's idea of a series of steps in the application of salvation. Further, Hoekema rejects Murray's rejection of salvation as "one simple and indivisible act" and maintains that the various aspects of salvation are indeed unified under the concept of union with Christ. Instead of attempting to list the various aspects of salvation in logical order, Hoekema maintains, "The process of salvation ought not to be understood as a series of successive experiences. . . . Rather, [it] ought to be understood as a unitary experience involving various aspects which begin and continue simultaneously: "New Life" (regeneration), "New Direction" (conversion), "New Status" (justification), "Progressive Newness" (sanctification), and "Persistent Newness" (perseverance).[6]

We agree with both Murray and Hoekema that the various doctrines that constitute the application of salvation should be distinguished, and so we have devoted separate chapters to them. However, we side with Hoekema concerning the priority of union with Christ and the inadvisability of formulating a strict logical order for the doctrines. Indeed, at the end of the day, we think Frame is right in arguing that the "order" in the various presentations of an *ordo salutis* is best understood as a pedagogical order, an arrangement that is somewhat helpful in teaching the doctrines and their interrelation.[7]

We now turn our attention from exegesis and systematic theology to biblical theology. We attempt to harmonize these ten aspects of salvation under biblical-theological themes:

---

[4] John M. Frame, *Systematic Theology: An Introduction to Christian Belief* (Phillipsburg, NJ: P&R, 2013), 936–37. Frame finds in Scripture various orders, including temporal, causal, conditional, and pedagogical ones. In Rom 8:29–30 he does not see one consistent kind of order of the aspects of salvation but various orders and priorities: temporal, causal, instrumental, and legal-forensic.

[5] Hoekema, *Saved by Grace*, 11–27 (see chap. 3, n. 78).

[6] Hoekema, 16.

[7] Frame, *Systematic Theology*, 937.

Salvation and the Trinity

The one God has eternally existed in three persons: Father, Son, and Holy Spirit. These three persons are distinct but never separated. In Augustine's summary of Christian doctrine, he made a classic statement concerning the Godhead:

> It is better to say that this Trinity is one God and that "of him, and by him, and in him are all things." Thus there are the Father, the Son, and the Holy Spirit, and each is God, and at the same time all are one God; and each of them is a full substance, and at the same time all are one substance. The Father is neither the Son nor the Holy Spirit; the Son is neither the Father nor the Holy Spirit; the Holy Spirit is neither the Father nor the Son. But the Father is the Father uniquely; the Son is the Son uniquely; and the Holy Spirit is the Holy Spirit uniquely. All three have the same eternity, the same immutability, the same majesty, and the same power.[8]

Further, the Trinitarian persons mutually indwell each other so that each is fully God. Many aspects of the doctrine of salvation feature the Trinity.

Election

God the Father is the author of election in every place but one in Scripture. For example, "Blessed is the God and Father of our Lord Jesus Christ, who has blessed us with every spiritual blessing in the heavens in Christ. For he chose us in him, before the foundation of the world, to be holy and

---

[8] Augustine, *On Christian Doctrine*, trans. D. W. Robertson Jr., Library of Liberal Arts (Indianapolis: Bobbs-Merrill, 1958), 10.

blameless" (Eph 1:3–4). The one exception is John 15:16, 19, which presents Jesus as the author of election: "You did not choose me, but I chose you. I appointed you to go and produce fruit and that your fruit should remain. . . . If you were of the world, the world would love you as its own. However, because you are not of the world, but I have chosen you out of it, the world hates you."

Union with Christ

The persons of the Trinity are involved in union with Christ. The Father planned union with Christ. We see this in two of Scripture's passages treating election:

> God and Father of our Lord Jesus Christ. . . . chose us in him, before the foundation of the world. (Eph 1:3–4)

> [God] has saved us and called us with a holy calling, not according to our works, but according to his own purpose and grace, which was given to us in Christ Jesus before time began. (2 Tim 1:9)

God the Father not only chose us before creation, but he chose us *in Christ* (Eph 1:4), that is, in prospect of uniting us to Christ so that we would experience the salvation he planned. The second text uses the divine passive to speak of the Father. Salvation is based not on our works but on his purpose and grace, which he planned to give us before time *in Christ*.

Of course union with Christ involves Christ! We are joined to him by grace through faith in salvation. We participate in his story: we died with him (Gal 2:20), were raised with him (Rom 6:4–8), ascended and sat down in heaven with him (Eph 2:6), and even come again with him (Col 3:4). We receive all his saving benefits in union with him.

The Holy Spirit also plays a part, for he unites us to Christ. Paul declares, "We were all baptized by one Spirit into one body—whether Jews or Greeks, whether slaves or free" (1 Cor 12:13). As a result, "If anyone does not have the Spirit of Christ, he does not belong to him" (Rom 8:9).

It is fruitful to consider union with Christ temporally. As we have seen, the Father planned to join us to the Son in eternity past. The fruits of union will be fully revealed only in the eschaton. Union with Christ has large repercussions in the present too, for present union with Christ is identical with indwelling. The Trinity indwells believers, including the Father (in two texts), the Son (in six texts), and the Holy Spirit (in eight texts). Unending praise is due the Holy Trinity for uniting us to Christ (Eph 1:6, 12, 14).

Regeneration

Each person of the Trinity plays a role in the regeneration of individual believers who make up the church. God the Father's role was planning, as Peter explains: "Blessed be the God and Father of our Lord Jesus Christ. Because of his great mercy he has given us new birth" (1 Pet 1:3). In mercy the Father caused us to be born again, and for that he is worthy of much praise.

The Son's role is providing the power for regeneration by his resurrection (v. 3). On account of his great mercy the Father "has given us new birth into a living hope through the resurrection of Jesus Christ from the dead" (v. 3). Jesus's death and resurrection are correlative, which is why Paul includes both in his summary of the gospel (1 Cor 15:3–4). In his farewell discourses Jesus asserts, "Because I live, you will live too" (John 14:19). The risen Lord empowers our regeneration.

The Spirit's role is to effect regeneration by causing us to be born again. Jesus remarked, "The wind blows where it pleases, and you hear its sound, but you don't know where it comes from or where it is going. So it is with everyone born of the Spirit" (John 3:8). The Father loved us and "saved us—not by works of righteousness that we had done, but according to his mercy—through the washing of regeneration and renewal by the Holy Spirit" (Titus 3:5).

The Trinity not only gives us new life now, but the three persons also will raise us from the dead on the last day to eternal life on the new earth:

The Father: "He who raised Christ from the dead will also bring your mortal bodies to life" (Rom 8:11).

The Son: "This is the will of my Father: that everyone who sees the Son and believes in him will have eternal life, and I will raise him up on the last day" (John 6:40).

The Holy Spirit: "If the Spirit of him who raised Jesus from the dead lives in you, then he who raised Christ from the dead will also

bring your mortal bodies to life through his Spirit who lives in you"
(Rom 8:11).

The Trinity gives us new life now in regeneration and forever in resurrection and therefore deserves our worship.

Justification

God the Father, God the Son, and God the Holy Spirit all play roles in
our justification. The Father is the judge who justly pronounces a guilty
verdict on all unbelievers. Paul speaks of people outside of Christ: "We
have already charged that both Jews and Greeks are all under sin" (Rom
3:9). Is salvation by law-keeping possible? The apostle answers: "We know
that whatever the law says, it speaks to those who are subject to the law, so
that every mouth may be shut and the whole world may become subject
to God's judgment" (v. 19). Thankfully God, "who justifies the ungodly,"
pronounces another verdict on all who trust Christ for salvation: "What
does the Scripture say? Abraham believed God, and it was credited to him
for righteousness. Now to the one who works, pay is not credited as a gift,
but as something owed. But to the one who does not work, but believes
on him who justifies the ungodly, his faith is credited for righteousness"
(Rom 4:3–5).

The Father is the judge who justifies believers. He does so on the basis
of the Son's work, for "He was delivered up for our trespasses and raised for
our justification" (Rom 3:25). Jesus's atoning death averts God's wrath from
us (3:25–26) and obtains rightness that we lack (5:18–19).

Although it is not commonly recognized, the Holy Spirit also plays a
role in justification, for he enables us to believe in Jesus. Paul writes, "You
were washed, you were sanctified, you were justified in the name of the Lord
Jesus Christ and by the Spirit of our God" (1 Cor 6:11).

Adoption

Again we see the Trinity involved in our salvation, this time under a family
metaphor. The Father adopts us on the basis of the Son's atoning work, and
the Spirit enables us to believe in Christ. The Father not only "predestined us

to be adopted as sons" (Eph 1:5) but accepted us former slaves into his family as adult sons or daughters (Gal 4:4–5; 2 Cor 6:18). The Son is our Redeemer, who delivers all who trust him. Christ "redeemed" us by sacrificing his "precious blood." After saying that lawbreakers are under the curse (penalty) of the law, Paul speaks of deliverance: "Christ redeemed us from the curse of the law by becoming a curse for us, because it is written, 'Cursed is everyone who is hung on a tree'" (Gal 3:13).

When the Trinity turns children of the devil into children of God (1 John 3:10), the Holy Spirit is active too. The Spirit of adoption loved us and enabled us to believe in Christ: "You received the Spirit of adoption, by whom we cry out, '*Abba*, Father!'" (Rom 8:15). The Spirit also bears witness in our hearts "that we are God's children" (v. 16).

Sanctification

The Holy Trinity sanctifies the people of God. In definitive sanctification the Father calls "saints" (1 Cor 1:2) us who formerly were unclean. In progressive sanctification he loves and disciplines us to make us holy (Heb 12:5–10). In final sanctification the Father will faithfully "sanctify [us] completely . . . at the coming of our Lord Jesus Christ" (1 Thess 5:23; cf. v. 24).

The Son "loved the church and gave himself for her to make her holy, cleansing her with the washing of water by the word" (Eph 5:25–26). This text probably views sanctification globally, encompassing initial (definitive) to final sanctification, when Christ will present the church to himself in moral perfection (v. 27).

The Holy Spirit also plays a role: "From the beginning God has chosen you for salvation through sanctification by the Spirit and through belief in the truth" (2 Thess 2:13). This is initial sanctification because it is combined with belief in the gospel. It's the same for Peter's salutation, which tells of people saved by "the sanctifying work of the Spirit, to be obedient and to be sprinkled with the blood of Jesus Christ" (1 Pet 1:2). Peter notes that sanctification leads to being "obedient" to the gospel (cf. 4:17), so this must refer to initial sanctification. Paul articulates the Spirit's activity in progressive sanctification in Rom 4:19; 8:12–13 and in final sanctification in 15:16.

Preservation

The Trinity saves us and keeps us saved. God the Father chose people for salvation, including the Colossian believers, who are among "God's chosen ones, holy and dearly loved" (Col 3:12). Paul tells how we can know that the Father chose someone: "We know, brothers and sisters loved by God, that he has chosen you, because our gospel did not come to you in word only, but also in power, in the Holy Spirit, and with full assurance" (1 Thess 1:4–5).

The Son saved us by his death and resurrection (John 10:11, 17) and preserves us:

"I have come down from heaven, not to do my own will, but the will of him who sent me. This is the will of him who sent me: that I should lose none of those he has given me but should raise them up on the last day. For this is the will of my Father: that everyone who sees the Son and believes in him will have eternal life, and I will raise him up on the last day." (John 6:38–40)

The Spirit also plays a significant role: "In him you also were sealed with the promised Holy Spirit when you heard the word of truth, the gospel of your salvation, and when you believed. The Holy Spirit is the down payment of our inheritance, until the redemption of the possession, to the praise of his glory" (Eph 1:13–14). The Spirit is both the seal (Eph 1:13; 4:30; 2 Cor 1:22) and down payment, guaranteeing our salvation "for the day of redemption" (Eph 4:30).

Eternal Life and Glorification

Although it is little recognized, the three persons of the Trinity are also active in enabling believers to attain the final glory of salvation. Paul had encouraged the Thessalonians to "walk worthy of God, who calls [them] into his own kingdom and glory" (1 Thess 2:12). Moreover, "The glory of God illuminates the new Jerusalem, and its lamp is the Lamb" (Rev 21:23).

Not only does the Son ("the Lamb") illumine the holy city, but in his second advent he also "will transform the body of our humble condition into the likeness of his glorious body, by the power that enables him to subject everything to himself" (Phil 3:20–21). As a result, we will "obtain the glory of our Lord Jesus Christ" (2 Thess 2:14).

The Holy Spirit both transforms us "from glory to glory" now and will raise us in glory on the last day. The former appears in 2 Cor 3:18: "We all, with unveiled faces, are looking as in a mirror at the glory of the Lord and are being transformed into the same image from glory to glory; this is from the Lord who is the Spirit." Paul indicates the latter when he describes our resurrection bodies as those that are "raised a spiritual body" (1 Cor 15:44). Ciampa and Rosner summarize: "Our resurrection experience could not be anything other than an existence in which the Spirit has full sway and through which the Spirit is fully manifest in and through us as it is in Christ himself."[9]

Again and again, then, we see the Trinity's grace and power manifested in the salvation of its people, whether Scripture presents that salvation as election, union with Christ, regeneration, justification, adoption, sanctification, preservation, or glorification. The Father plans salvation, the Son does the work to accomplish it, and the Spirit applies salvation to believers. *Soli Deo gloria*!

Salvation as Individual, Corporate, and Cosmic

Election

God saves individual believers, the church, and the creation. The OT's picture of election is largely the corporate election of Israel, although not all ethnic Israel is spiritual Israel. The NT emphasizes the corporate election of the church while also teaching individual election. Three texts that personify churches as a woman teach corporate election: 1 Pet 5:13; 2 John 1, 13. The woman "in Babylon, chosen" (1 Pet 5:13), the "elect lady" (2 John 1), and her "elect sister" (v. 13) are references to the corporate election of churches.

Paul is the principal author on election, and, since he wrote epistles chiefly to churches, he speaks of election mainly in the plural. He speaks

---

[9] Roy E. Ciampa and Brian S. Rosner, *The First Letter to the Corinthians*, PNTC (Grand Rapids: Eerdmans, 2010), 818.

of individual election in Romans 9, where he quotes the OT to teach God's sovereignty: "What should we say then? Is there injustice with God? Absolutely not! For he tells Moses, 'I will show mercy to whom I will show mercy, and I will have compassion on whom I will have compassion'" (vv. 14–15). He applies that passage: "So then, he has mercy on whom he wants to have mercy and he hardens whom he wants to harden" (v. 18). The four uses of the word "whom" (in vv. 15, 18) are all singular, showing individual election. Paul teaches corporate election of the church, identifying "objects of mercy that [God] prepared beforehand for glory" with called Jews and Gentiles (vv. 23, 24).

Along with corporate election, the Gospels teach individual election also. Jesus does so in Matthew: "No one knows the Son except the Father, and no one knows the Father except the Son and anyone to whom the Son chooses to reveal him" (Matt 11:27). John teaches individual election when Jesus speaks of the Father's giving people to the Son (note our italics):

> "*Everyone* the Father gives me will come to me, and *the one* who comes to me I will never cast out." (John 6:37)

> "This is the will of him who sent me: that I should lose *none* of those he has given me but should raise them up on the last day." (v. 39)

Acts mentions election twice, once of corporate election (Acts 18:9–10) and once of individual election (in 13:48). Paul begins to preach the good news to the Gentiles, rather than the Jews, and "When the Gentiles heard [the gospel], they rejoiced and honored the word of the Lord, and all who had been appointed to eternal life believed" (13:48). God's appointment to life issues forth in saving faith.

The NT thus speaks of both corporate and individual election but not of cosmic election. It is important to remember that Scripture joins the individual and the corporate; we cannot have a corporate entity without individuals.

Union with Christ

Union with Christ, the most comprehensive way of referring to the application of salvation, is individual, corporate, and cosmic. Although the NT's main focus is corporate, it also teaches that God joins individuals to Christ.

Paul, in condemning Corinthian men's use of prostitutes, teaches the intimacy of union with Christ (1 Cor 6:15–17). Believers belong to Christ, and their bodies "are a part of Christ's body" (v. 15). In this context Paul says, "Anyone joined to the Lord is one spirit with him" (v. 17).

Paul sometimes speaks of his own union with Christ:

> I have been crucified with Christ, and I no longer live, but Christ lives in me. The life I now live in the body, I live by faith in the Son of God, who loved me and gave himself for me. (Gal 2:20)

> Because of [Christ] I have suffered the loss of all things and consider them as dung, so that I may gain Christ and be found in him, not having a righteousness of my own from the law, but one that is through faith in Christ—the righteousness from God based on faith. (Phil 3:8–9)

Again, because Paul wrote letters mainly to churches, most often he speaks of the church as united to Christ. As a result of the Son of God's work of reconciliation, Paul tells believing Gentiles, "Now in Christ Jesus, you who were far away have been brought near by the blood of Christ" (Eph 2:13). As a result, we believers "have access in one Spirit to the Father" and "are no longer foreigners and strangers, but fellow citizens with the saints, and members of God's household" (vv. 18–19). Paul's well-known words connecting union with Christ to his death and resurrection are addressed to the church in Rome and are therefore communal. Believers died with Christ (Rom 6:3–8) and were raised with him (vv. 4–8).

In at least one passage Paul teaches cosmic union with Christ. After speaking of Christ's work of redemption he discusses God's revelation of "the mystery of his will, according to his good pleasure that he purposed in Christ" (Eph 1:9). God's plans involve union with Christ. Paul says that God planned to achieve in a timely fashion his goal of bringing "everything together in Christ, both things in heaven and things on earth in him" (Eph 1:10). The repetition of "in him" reinforces the idea of union with Christ. And the addition of "both things in heaven and things on earth" leaves no doubt as to the cosmic dimensions of God's plan.

Regeneration

All aspects of the application of salvation are individual and corporate. Only a few of them are also cosmic, including regeneration. Jesus addresses Nicodemus: "Truly I tell you, unless someone is born again, he cannot see the kingdom of God" (John 3:3; cf. v. 5).

Most references to regeneration are corporate, though such references do not exclude the individual:

> When the kindness of God our Savior and his love for mankind appeared, he saved us—not by works of righteousness that we had done, but according to his mercy—through the washing of regeneration and renewal by the Holy Spirit. (Titus 3:4–5)

> God, who is rich in mercy, because of his great love that he had for us, made us alive with Christ even though we were dead in trespasses. (Eph 2:4–5)

> Blessed be the God and Father of our Lord Jesus Christ. Because of his great mercy he has given us new birth into a living hope through the resurrection of Jesus Christ from the dead. (1 Pet 1:3)

> You have been born again—not of perishable seed but of imperishable—through the living and enduring word of God. (v. 23)

Jesus uses the word "regeneration" once to refer to cosmic renewal: "Truly I tell you, in the renewal [or "regeneration"] of all things, when the Son of Man sits on his glorious throne, you who have followed me will also sit on twelve thrones, judging the twelve tribes of Israel" (Matt 19:28).

Calling

Paul uses "calling" to speak of God's summoning individuals to himself in salvation:

> When God, who from my mother's womb set me apart and called me by his grace, was pleased to reveal his Son in me, so that I could

preach him among the Gentiles, I did not immediately consult with anyone. (Gal 1:15–16)[10]

Let each of you remain in the situation in which he was called. . . . Brothers and sisters, each person is to remain with God in the situation in which he was called. (1 Cor 7:20, 24)

Usually, however, NT writers use "calling" corporately of the church:

"The promise is for you and for your children, and for all who are far off, as many as the Lord our God will call." (Acts 2:39)

Those he predestined, he also called; and those he called, he also justified; and those he justified, he also glorified. (Rom 8:30)

Let the peace of Christ, to which you were also called in one body, rule your hearts. And be thankful. (Col 3:15)

The God of all grace, who called you to his eternal glory in Christ, will himself restore, establish, strengthen, and support you after you have suffered a little while. (1 Pet 5:10)

"Calling" and "call" are used of individual and communal salvation, but not of cosmic salvation.

Conversion

New Testament authors speak of the conversion of individuals and groups. Conversion consists of repentance (turning from sin) and faith (turning to Christ). These are distinguishable but inseparable. Repentance and faith are both initial and lifelong. We will deal only with the former here.

Initial repentance is both individual and communal, and this makes sense since one can scarcely have communal repentance apart from individual repentance. Jesus says, "I have not come to call the righteous, but sinners to repentance" (Luke 5:32). Peter reinforces Jesus's words: "The Lord does

---

[10] Although Paul's calling here could be synonymous with God's setting him apart from birth, we agree with Moo that it refers to God's revealing his Son to Paul on the Damascus Road; Douglas J. Moo, *Galatians*, BECNT (Grand Rapids: Baker Academic, 2013), 104.

not delay his promise, as some understand delay, but is patient with you, not wanting any to perish but all to come to repentance" (2 Pet 3:9). Luke tells us that repentance is also corporate: "When they heard this they became silent. And they glorified God, saying, 'So then, God has given repentance resulting in life even to the Gentiles'" (Acts 11:18). Paul speaks of the same reality: "The Lord's servant must not quarrel, but must be gentle to everyone, able to teach, and patient, instructing his opponents with gentleness. Perhaps God will grant them repentance leading them to the knowledge of the truth" (2 Tim 2:24–25).

Initial faith is both individual and corporate too. John invites individuals to trust Jesus: "God loved the world in this way: He gave his one and only Son, so that everyone who believes in him will not perish" (John 3:16). Paul recalls Timothy's conversion: "I recall your sincere faith that first lived in your grandmother Lois and in your mother Eunice and now, I am convinced, is in you also" (2 Tim 1:5).

Faith is also communal, for Jesus preaches to the Jews, "I told you that you will die in your sins. For if you do not believe that I am he, you will die in your sins" (John 8:24). Paul combines individual and corporate faith when he tells the Philippian jailer, "Believe on the Lord Jesus, and you will be saved—you and your household" (Acts 16:31). Paul famously teaches, "You are saved by grace through faith, and this is not from yourselves; it is God's gift" (Eph 2:8).

Both initial repentance and faith are individual and corporate. Neither is cosmic.

Justification

Scripture speaks of justification in individual and corporate terms. Paul expresses the need for justification in the same terms. He tells of individuals lacking righteousness: "There is no one righteous, not even one. There is no one who understands; there is no one who seeks God" (Rom 3:10–11). Paul is emphatic: "No one will be justified in his sight by the works of the law, because the knowledge of sin comes through the law" (v. 20).

God meets the needs of unsaved individuals with his grace: "I am not ashamed of the gospel, because it is the power of God for salvation to everyone who believes, first to the Jew, and also to the Greek. For in it the righteousness of God is revealed from faith to faith, just as it is written: 'The righteous will live by faith'" (Rom 1:16–17). Again and again Paul teaches that God declares righteous individuals who believe in Christ:

> The righteousness of God is through faith in Jesus Christ to all who believe, since there is no distinction. . . . God presented him to demonstrate his righteousness at the present time, so that he would be just and justify the one who has faith in Jesus. (Rom 3:22, 26)

> We conclude that a person is justified by faith apart from the works of the law. Or is God the God of Jews only? Is he not the God of Gentiles too? Yes, of Gentiles too, since there is one God who will justify the circumcised by faith and the uncircumcised through faith. (vv. 28–30)

> To the one who does not work, but believes on him who justifies the ungodly, his faith is credited for righteousness. (4:5)

More often the apostle views justification in communal terms. Believers "are justified freely by his grace through the redemption that is in Christ Jesus" (Rom 3:24). Paul denies that justification is by law-keeping. Instead, it is by faith as individual believers or as a church: "A person is not justified by the works of the law but by faith in Jesus Christ, even we ourselves have believed in Christ Jesus. This was so that we might be justified by faith in Christ and not by the works of the law, because by the works of the law no human being will be justified" (Gal 2:16). Paul reminds Titus that God "poured out his Spirit on us abundantly through Jesus Christ our Savior so that, having been justified by his grace, we may become heirs with the hope of eternal life" (Titus 3:6–7).

Justification by faith is presented in individual and corporate terms, but never in cosmic ones.

Adoption

Regarded as the warmest aspect of the application of salvation, adoption is God the Father's work of placing slaves of sin into his family as his beloved children. Writing to churches, Paul addresses the corporate aspect of adoption. At least once, however, he writes of adoption in the singular: "You are no longer a slave but a son, and if a son, then God has made you an heir" (Gal 4:7). God adopts individuals who trust Christ as their Redeemer and who constitute the church.

Almost always Paul appeals to the communal aspect of adoption, and he does so with regard to the Trinity. The Father planned to adopt his people: "He predestined us to be adopted as sons through Jesus Christ for himself, according to the good pleasure of his will" (Eph 1:5). The Son came to redeem slaves to sin so that we might become the sons of God: "When the time came to completion, God sent his Son, born of a woman, born under the law, to redeem those under the law, so that we might receive adoption as sons" (Gal 4:4–5). The Holy Spirit enables us to believe and assures us within of adoption: "You received the Spirit of adoption, by whom we cry out, '*Abba*, Father!' The Spirit himself testifies together with our spirits that we are God's children" (Rom 8:15–16).

Already we are God's children by faith in his Son: "Through faith you are all sons of God in Christ Jesus" (Gal 3:26). But our sonship is not yet fully revealed: "We ourselves who have the Spirit as the firstfruits—we also groan within ourselves, eagerly waiting for adoption, the redemption of our bodies" (Rom 8:23).

As with most aspects of the application of salvation, adoption is corporate, and singular, and never cosmic.

Sanctification

As we have seen, sanctification portrays salvation in terms of holiness. God sets his people apart from sin to holiness once and for all in definitive or initial sanctification. He works actual holiness into their lives in progressive sanctification. And he will perfect his people in final sanctification when Jesus returns. As is true of the other aspects of salvation, sanctification is both individual and communal.

God sanctifies individuals. Jesus proclaims, "If anyone loves me, he will keep my word. My Father will love him, and we will come to him and make our home with him" (John 14:23). Paul exhorts the Thessalonian church, "This is God's will, your sanctification: that you keep away from sexual immorality, that each of you knows how to control his own body in holiness and honor, not with lustful passions, like the Gentiles, who don't know God"

(1 Thess 4:3–5). The author to the Hebrews also shows concern for individual sanctification: "Pursue peace with everyone, and holiness—without it no one will see the Lord. Make sure that no one falls short of the grace of God" (Heb 12:14–15). John writes to Gaius, "Dear friend, do not imitate what is evil, but what is good" (3 John 11).

Although Scripture includes many references to individual sanctification, these are outnumbered by those referring to corporate sanctification. Jesus in the Sermon on the Mount teaches, "Blessed are those who hunger and thirst for righteousness, for they will be filled. . . . For I tell you, unless your righteousness surpasses that of the scribes and Pharisees, you will never get into the kingdom of heaven" (Matt 5:6, 20).

The Father, Son, and Spirit promote progressive sanctification. God the Father disciplines us "so that we can share his holiness" (Heb 12:10). The Son of God "loved the church" and died "to make her holy" (Eph 5:25–26). Paul urges thanksgiving to God for electing the Thessalonians "for salvation through sanctification by the Spirit and through belief in the truth" (2 Thess 2:13).

Peter promotes holiness of life: "As the one who called you is holy, you also are to be holy in all your conduct; for it is written, 'Be holy, because I am holy'" (1 Pet 1:15–16). He shares the impact the *eschaton* should have on God's people: "Since [the heavens and earth] are to be dissolved in this way, it is clear what sort of people you should be in holy conduct and godliness" (2 Pet 3:11).

God's work of sanctification concerns individuals and the church, but there is no clear mention of cosmic sanctification (though see Rev 21:27 and the upcoming section on glorification).

Preservation

God keeps his people both as individuals and as the church. Jesus spoke most frequently of the Father and himself as preserving their people for final salvation. He also spoke, less frequently, of the preservation of individuals: "This is the will of my Father: that everyone who sees the Son and believes in him will have eternal life, and I will raise him up on the last day" (John 6:40). Paul wrote often of God's keeping the church until the day of redemption. However, he wrote also of his own God-given confidence: "For this gospel

I was appointed a herald, apostle, and teacher, and that is why I suffer these things. But I am not ashamed, because I know whom I have believed and am persuaded that he is able to guard what has been entrusted to me until that day" (2 Tim 1:11–12). First John emphasizes believers' responsibility but also teaches God's preservation of them: "We know that everyone who has been born of God does not sin, but the one who is born of God keeps him, and the evil one does not touch him" (1 John 5:18).

Jesus and his apostles also taught that God's preservation is communal. Jesus said of his sheep, "I give them eternal life, and they will never perish. No one will snatch them out of my hand. My Father, who has given them to me, is greater than all. No one is able to snatch them out of the Father's hand" (John 10:28–29). As Paul puts it, "There is now no condemnation for those in Christ Jesus" (Rom 8:1). Paul promises the Corinthian church, "He will also strengthen you to the end, so that you will be blameless in the day of our Lord Jesus Christ. God is faithful; you were called by him into fellowship with his Son, Jesus Christ our Lord" (1 Cor 1:8–9). He also admonishes, "Don't grieve God's Holy Spirit. You were sealed by him for the day of redemption" (Eph 4:30). Again God promises through Paul, "If, while we were enemies, we were reconciled to God through the death of his Son, then how much more, having been reconciled, will we be saved by his life" (Rom 5:10).

Preservation is both individual and corporate but not cosmic.

Eternal Life and Glorification

Eternal life and glorification constitute the consummation of salvation for individuals, Christ's church, and even the cosmos. When his disciples question the sacrifices they have made to follow Jesus, he explains, "Truly I tell you, there is no one who has left a house, wife or brothers or sisters, parents or children because of the kingdom of God, who will not receive many times more at this time, and eternal life in the age to come" (Luke 18:29–30). John frequently promises eternal life for individual believers: "God loved the world in this way: He gave his one and only Son, so that everyone who believes in him will not perish but have eternal life" (John 3:16; cf. v. 36; 5:24). Paul's trust is in God: "The Lord will rescue me from every evil work and bring me safely into his heavenly kingdom. To him be the glory for ever and ever! Amen" (2 Tim 4:18).

Jesus makes communal promises of eternal life too: "Do not be amazed at this, because a time is coming when all who are in the graves will hear his voice and come out—those who have done good things, to the resurrection of life, but those who have done wicked things, to the resurrection of condemnation" (John 5:28–29). Paul's promises of eternal life and glory are chiefly communal:

> [Believers] are heirs of God and coheirs with Christ—if indeed we suffer with him so that we may also be glorified with him. (Rom 8:17)

> When Christ, who is your life, appears, then you also will appear with him in glory. (Col 3:4)

> [Christians await] the blessed hope, the appearing of the glory of our great God and Savior, Jesus Christ. (Titus 2:13)

Paul also teaches that the cosmos will participate in the glorification of believers. First, he says the saints' present sufferings will fade away in light of their future glory (Rom 8:18). Then he tells of the personified cosmos' longing for the final salvation of God's children (v. 19). This entails "the creation itself" being "set free from its bondage to corruption and obtain[ing] the freedom of the glory of the children of God" (v. 21 ESV).

The glory of God permeates the new heavens and new earth, as John sees:

> [The angel] then carried me away in the Spirit to a great, high mountain and showed me the holy city, Jerusalem, coming down out of heaven from God, arrayed with God's glory. Her radiance was like a precious jewel, like a jasper stone, clear as crystal. . . . The city does not need the sun or the moon to shine on it, because the glory of God illuminates it, and its lamp is the Lamb. (Rev 21:10–11, 23)

Conclusion

We have seen that salvation in its many expressions is always individual and corporate and sometimes cosmic. To summarize:

- Election is individual and corporate.
- Union with Christ is individual, corporate, and cosmic.

- Regeneration is individual, corporate, and cosmic.
- Calling is individual and corporate.
- Conversion is individual and corporate.
- Justification is individual and corporate.
- Adoption is individual and corporate.
- Sanctification is individual and corporate.
- Preservation is individual and corporate.
- Eternal life/glorification is individual, corporate, and cosmic.

The OT and NT tell primarily a corporate story, tracing God's dealings with Israel and the church, respectively. The biblical writers therefore portray salvation primarily in corporate terms. But this communal emphasis does not nullify individual responsibility, individual culpability, or the need for saving grace. Accordingly, Abraham, who "believed the Lord, [who] credited it to him as righteousness" (Gen 15:6), is a model of individual salvation by grace through faith in the NT (Rom 4:1–5; Gal 3:5–7; Heb 6:11–15; 11:8–10).

We found that three aspects of salvation include a cosmic element: union with Christ, regeneration, and glory.

Union: God's goal for the cosmos is 'to bring everything together in Christ, both things in heaven and things on earth in him'" (Eph 1:10).

Regeneration: "Truly I tell you, in the renewal [lit. "regeneration"] of all things, when the Son of Man sits on his glorious throne, you who have followed me will also sit on twelve thrones, judging the twelve tribes of Israel" (Matt 19:28).

Glory: The consummation involves "the creation itself" being "set free from its bondage to corruption" to "obtain the freedom of the glory of the children of God" (Rom 8:21 ESV). Moreover, the new Jerusalem, which comes down from heaven, will be "arrayed with God's glory" (Rev 21:11).

Although Scripture makes only three specific connections between aspects of the application of salvation and the cosmos, it also contains other hints along these lines. Paul indirectly connects salvation and election, for the same plan of God that in broad terms will unite "everything together in Christ, both things in heaven and things on earth in him" (Eph 1:10) includes our predestination (v. 11).

Paul hints at a link between adoption and the cosmos, for before he speaks of our final "adoption, the redemption of our bodies" (Rom 8:23) he portrays the creation as hoping to share in the "glorious freedom of God's children" (v. 21).

Peter suggests that God will sanctify the cosmos. He predicts the coming of the day of the Lord, when "The heavens will pass away with a loud noise, the elements will burn and be dissolved, and the earth and the works on it will be disclosed" (2 Pet 3:10). The text is difficult, but most likely Peter is teaching the means whereby the truth of verse 13 will be attained: "Based on his promise, we wait for new heavens and a new earth, where righteousness dwells." The difficult phrase "will be disclosed" speaks of "a smelting process from which the world will emerge purified" by fire.[11]

Salvation and God's Sovereignty and Human Responsibility

In ways we cannot fully understand, Scripture teaches both God's absolute sovereignty and genuine human responsibility. We see this in Joseph's brothers' wickedly selling him into slavery and God's overruling their evil for good (Gen 45:4–8; 50:20). We see it in God's sovereignly using wicked Assyria to punish wicked Israel, then promising to judge Assyria for its sins (Isa 10:5–19). Above all we see it in evil men's crucifying the holy Son of God and unwittingly fulfilling God's foreordained plan to save his people, even all who believe in Christ (Acts 2:22–24; 4:27–28).

Divine sovereignty and human responsibility are evident in each of the ten aspects of salvation we have studied.

Election

God's sovereignty shines in his election of his people. Paul teaches that God elected his people "before the foundation of the world" and that we were

---

[11] Thomas R. Schreiner, *1, 2 Peter, Jude*, NAC (Nashville: B&H, 2003), 387, quoting A. Wolters, "Worldview and Textual Criticism in 2 Peter 3:10," *WTJ* 49 (1987): 408.

predestined . . . "according to the plan of the one who works out everything in agreement with the purpose of his will" (Eph 1:4, 5, 11). Paul reminds Timothy that God "has saved us and called us with a holy calling, not according to our works, but according to his own purpose and grace, which was given to us in Christ Jesus before time began" (2 Tim 1:9). Emphatically Paul affirms the absolute divine prerogative in choosing and rejecting his creatures:

> Has the potter no right over the clay, to make from the same lump one piece of pottery for honor and another for dishonor? And what if God, wanting to display his wrath and to make his power known, endured with much patience objects of wrath prepared for destruction? And what if he did this to make known the riches of his glory on objects of mercy that he prepared beforehand for glory? (Rom 9:21–23)

Scripture teaches God's sovereignty in salvation, as we have seen. However, that is not the whole story, for Scripture also teaches the genuine responsibility of human beings before a holy God. Although predestinarian notes are sounded in a few judgment passages (Matt 7:23; Rev 20:14), their emphasis is overwhelmingly on failed human responsibility. God sends people to hell for their sinful actions (Matt 25:41–46; Mark 9:42; Jude 13; Rev 14:9; 20:12–13). Scripture teaches both divine control and human freedom, and so should we.

Union with Christ

God's sovereignty and humans' responsibility are evident in the theme of union with Christ. God sovereignly unites people to his Son for salvation. Paul teaches this in two passages in which he ties union with Christ to God's plan to choose people for salvation before creation:

> He chose us *in him*, before the foundation of the world, to be holy and blameless in love before him. (Eph 1:4, emphasis added)

> He has saved us and called us with a holy calling, not according to our works, but according to his own purpose and grace, which was given to us *in Christ Jesus* before time began. (2 Tim 1:9, emphasis added)

God elected a people for himself and planned to unite them to Christ. However, they are only actually joined to Christ when they believe in him for salvation (Gal 3:26–27; Eph 2:1–10). Union involves both divine sovereignty and human responsibility.

Regeneration

The Trinity's sovereignty stands behind the new birth. God the Father planned regeneration: "By his own choice, [the Father] gave us birth by the word of truth so that we would be a kind of firstfruits of his creatures" (Jas 1:18). The Father is the ultimate cause of the new birth. The Son's resurrection provides the power for regeneration, for the Father "has given us new birth into a living hope through the resurrection of Jesus Christ from the dead" (1 Pet 1:3). The Holy Spirit actually causes believers to be born again: "The wind blows where it pleases, and you hear its sound, but you don't know where it comes from or where it is going. So it is with everyone born of the Spirit" (John 3:8). Jesus compares the effects of the Spirit to those of the wind. As the mysterious wind blows where it will and we can only observe its effect, so it is with the Spirit. He is free, and we know he has "blown" by his effecting the new birth in those who were spiritually dead.

Regeneration is wholly God's work as he gives us new life. Those who are born of God believe in Christ (John 1:12–13; 3:1–18), which occurs through the gospel. We have been "born again—not of perishable seed but of imperishable—through the living and enduring word of God" (1 Pet 1:22–23).

Calling

God summons people to faith through the external and internal calls. He intends for the external or gospel call to go to everyone. God desires the salvation of the lost and calls them to believe in his Son for salvation (Isa 45:22; John 6:40; Acts 17:30–31; Rom 10:8–17). Through the gospel call God also issues a transformative call. In Pisidian Antioch, after rejection by the Jews, Paul and Barnabas turn to preach the word of God to the Gentiles in fulfillment of OT prediction (Isa 49:6). Luke records the response: "When the Gentiles heard this, they rejoiced and honored the word of the Lord, and all who had been appointed to eternal life believed" (Acts 13:48). God's sovereign election combines with his sovereign call to bring Gentiles to saving faith in Christ.

We see the same result in Lydia's conversion. Paul and his partners join women gathered by the river in Philippi for prayer. All the women hear the gospel call, the way of salvation. God grants at least one an effective call: "A God-fearing woman named Lydia, a dealer in purple cloth from the city of Thyatira, was listening. The Lord opened her heart to respond to what Paul was saying" (Acts 16:14).

There is a dynamic interplay between divine sovereignty and human responsibility that we cannot fully comprehend. God's effective call is sovereign: "Those he predestined, he also called; and those he called, he also justified; and those he justified, he also glorified" (Rom 8:30). At the same time, God commands people to believe and be saved. Paul and Silas gave God's command to the Philippian jailer: "'Believe in the Lord Jesus, and you will be saved—you and your household.' And they spoke the word of the Lord to him along with everyone in his house" (Acts 16:31–32). Further, God justly blames those who refuse to believe the gospel:

> The returning Christ will take "vengeance with flaming fire on those who don't know God and on those who don't obey the gospel of our Lord Jesus" (2 Thess 1:8).

> Paul laments that his fellow Israelites were "ignorant of the righteousness of God and attempted to establish their own righteousness[;] they have not submitted to God's righteousness. For Christ is the end of the law for righteousness to everyone who believes" (Rom 10:3–4).

And God entreats and pleads for all to come to him and to be saved. But to Israel he says, "All day long I have held out my hands to a disobedient and defiant people" (Rom 10:17). And, Jesus has said, "Come to me, all of you who are weary and burdened, and I will give you rest. Take up my yoke and learn from me, because I am lowly and humble in heart, and you will find rest for your souls" (Matt 11:28–29).

God uses the gospel call as his means to draw sinners to himself:

We ought to thank God always for you, brothers and sisters loved by the Lord, because from the beginning God has chosen you for salvation through sanctification by the Spirit and through belief in the truth. He called you to this through our gospel, so that you might obtain the glory of our Lord Jesus Christ. (2 Thess 2:13–14)

Conversion

Conversion is the aspect of salvation focusing on turning from sin to Christ (Acts 20:21; 1 Thess 1:9). When we think of conversion, we think of humans' responsibility to repent and believe, and this is correct. But, as is true of every other aspect of salvation, God is sovereign in conversion. He gives the gifts of initial saving repentance and faith. When Peter summarizes how God has used him to reach Cornelius and his family with the gospel, the leaders in Jerusalem praise God: "So then, God has given repentance resulting in life even to the Gentiles" (Acts 11:18). Among Paul's instructions to younger pastor Timothy are these words: "The Lord's servant must not quarrel, but must be gentle to everyone, able to teach, and patient, instructing his opponents with gentleness. Perhaps God will grant them repentance leading them to the knowledge of the truth" (2 Tim 2:24–25).

God also gives saving faith. After showing that "coming" to him means "believing" in him (John 6:35), Jesus says, "No one can come to me unless the Father who sent me draws him, and I will raise him up on the last day" (v. 44). As we have noted a number of times, Acts 13:48 depicts faith as the consequence of God's election: "All who had been appointed to eternal life believed." Condemning idolatry, Paul asserts, "No one can say, 'Jesus is Lord,' except by the Holy Spirit" (1 Cor 12:3). Ciampa and Rosner explain, "The declaration 'Jesus is Lord' is the most fundamental of all Christian statements of faith."[12]

God is sovereign in conversion, and human beings are responsible. Jesus declares, "Repent, because the kingdom of heaven has come near," and "I have not come to call the righteous, but sinners to repentance" (Matt 4:17; Luke 5:32). After his resurrection Jesus predicts the apostles' mission: "Repentance

---

[12] Roy E. Ciampa and Brian S. Rosner, *The First Letter to the Corinthians*, PNTC (Grand Rapids: Eerdmans, 2010), 566.

for forgiveness of sins [will] be proclaimed in [my] name to all the nations, beginning at Jerusalem" (Luke 24:46–47; cf. 2 Pet 3:9).

Faith is human beings' responsibility, as Jesus shows when he warns his hearers, "If you do not believe that I am he, you will die in your sins" (John 8:24). Paul gives faith a prominent place when stating his thematic statement for Romans: "I am not ashamed of the gospel, because it is the power of God for salvation to everyone who believes, first to the Jew, and also to the Greek. For in it the righteousness of God is revealed from faith to faith, just as it is written: 'The righteous will live by faith'" (Rom 1:16–17; cf. Gal 2:16). Paul insists that salvation is by God's grace through the instrumentality of faith (Eph 2:8; cf. Acts 16:31).

By now we are not surprised to find the divine sovereignty/human responsibility tension evident in conversion too.

Justification

It is common knowledge that justification is by God's grace and received in faith. Doubtless the human response is vital, and it might seem to be paramount. In truth both God's sovereign grace and believers' faith are involved, and we must not neglect God's role. In fact, exploring his role establishes our faith, for two reasons.

First, God's grace makes justification possible, for an absence of grace makes justification impossible. Paul is concise: believers "are justified freely by his grace through the redemption that is in Christ Jesus" (Rom 3:24). The apostle waxes eloquent to Titus: God "poured out his Spirit on us abundantly through Jesus Christ our Savior so that, having been justified by his grace, we may become heirs with the hope of eternal life" (Titus 3:6–7).

Second, God's role includes the work of Christ. Simply put, if Christ did not die for us, we would not be justified. Jesus's atoning work both propitiated God and procured righteousness for us. God forgave OT saints in prospect of making full atonement in the cross of Christ: "God put forward [Christ] as a propitiation . . . because in his divine forbearance he had passed over former sins. It was to show his righteousness at the present time, so that he might be just and the justifier of the one who has faith in Jesus" (Rom 3:25–26 ESV). Christ also died so that through his "one righteous act there is justification leading to life for everyone" who believes (5:18).

The Father's grace and Christ's atonement are the foundation stones of justification. Nevertheless, we play an important role, for we are not justified until we believe in Christ as Lord and Savior. Paul frequently teaches that faith is the means of justification. Already in his thematic statement for Romans he says three times that salvation is by faith (Rom 1:16–17). Many times he highlights the fact that salvation is received by faith, not law-keeping (e.g., 3:27–31; Gal 2:20).

God's sovereignty is evident in justification, for his grace and Christ's saving work are indispensable. But justification has objective and subjective sides, and we must exercise faith to be justified. Paul teaches that God is active even in our faith (John 6:44; 1 Cor 12:3), but this does not nullify our responsibility to believe. Here once more divine rule and human responsibility intertwine, and, if we follow the contours of Scripture, we will respect that relationship.

Adoption

Adoption, like justification, is a legal picture of salvation applied, and as such the two have many things in common. Adoption, like justification, is by God's grace through faith in the Redeemer. Adoption puts the spotlight on the Trinity's sovereign love. Paul ties together the Father's election and adoption: "In love he predestined us for adoption to himself as sons through Jesus Christ, according to the purpose of his will, to the praise of his glorious grace, with which he has blessed us in the Beloved" (Eph 1:4–6 ESV). John exclaims, "See what great love the Father has given us that we should be called God's children—and we are!" (1 John 3:1).

Further, our adoption depends entirely on the Redeemer's atoning work on our behalf. Paul writes, "God sent his Son, born of a woman, born under the law, to redeem those under the law, so that we might receive adoption as sons" (Gal 4:4–5). How does Christ accomplish this redemption? Paul tells us in the previous chapter: "Christ redeemed us from the curse of the law by becoming a curse for us" (3:13). The Son of God endured the penalty of the law so that we law-breakers might go free.

The Holy Spirit too participates in our adoption, for he empowers us to believe in Christ: "You did not receive a spirit of slavery to fall back into fear. Instead, you received the Spirit of adoption, by whom we cry out,

'*Abba*, Father!'" (Rom 8:15). The Spirit enables us to cry out to the Father for salvation.

The Father, Son, and Spirit, then, play sovereign roles in our adoption, namely, those of predestination, redemption, and heart-opening, respectively. As with the other doctrines we have studied, human beings play a role also. In this case we believe in Christ the Redeemer to be adopted. After revealing that most people rejected Christ at his first advent, John writes, "But to all who did receive him, he gave them the right to be children of God, to those who believe in his name" (John 1:12). Paul is terse: "Through faith you are all sons of God in Christ Jesus" (Gal 3:26). We are not surprised to learn that God is sovereign and we are responsible in adoption.

Sanctification

The Father, Son, and Holy Spirit are supreme in sanctification. The Father chooses us for ultimate sanctification: "He chose us in him, before the foundation of the world, to be holy and blameless in love before him" (Eph 1:4). Moreover, unlike "human fathers," who "disciplined us for a short time based on what seemed good to them," our heavenly Father "does it for our benefit, so that we can share his holiness" (Heb 12:9–10). The Son loved us and died for us "to make [the church] holy, cleansing her with the washing of water by the word" (Eph 5:25–26). And he will succeed in presenting the church to himself in final sanctification "in splendor, without spot or wrinkle or anything like that, but holy and blameless" (v. 27).

The Spirit joins the Father and Son in promoting our sanctification. Peter wrote his first epistle to believers scattered throughout "Pontus, Galatia, Cappadocia, Asia, and Bithynia," those who were "chosen according to the foreknowledge of God the Father, in the sanctification of the Spirit, for obedience to Jesus Christ and for sprinkling with his blood" (1:1–2 ESV). Peter here mentions the Father's foreloving (foreknowing) his people and the Spirit's setting them apart for definitive sanctification, which results in their obeying the gospel[13] and being cleansed by Christ's death. The three Trinitarian persons, then, work together to make believers holy.

---

[13] Like Paul, Peter sometimes refers to faith as obedience and unbelief as disobedience. See 1 Pet 1:22; 3:1, 20; 4:17.

It is God's will that we play an important role in our sanctification. God takes the lead, but we must follow. In regeneration God gives us the obedient hearts he promised in the new covenant (Jer 31:33), and we must apply those hearts to holiness. Paul speaks for all believers when he writes,

> Not that I have already obtained this or am already perfect, but I press on to make it my own, because Christ Jesus has made me his own. Brothers, I do not consider that I have made it my own. But one thing I do: forgetting what lies behind and straining forward to what lies ahead, I press on toward the goal for the prize of the upward call of God in Christ Jesus. (Phil 3:12–14)

Paul presses on and strains to reach maturity in Christ, and of course we must do the same. The apostle preaches Christ and disciples believers, with their maturity his goal: "We proclaim him, warning and teaching everyone with all wisdom, so that we may present everyone mature in Christ. I labor for this, striving with his strength that works powerfully in me" (Col 1:28–29). Paul's Christian life is not an effort to "let go and let God." Rather, he labors and strives, but all this is according to the internal strength given by God's Spirit. A justly famous text on the Christian life is Phil 2:12–13, in which Paul exhorts the Philippians to "work out" their "salvation with fear and trembling" (v. 12). He then speaks of the power needed to fulfill his command: "For it is God who is working in you both to will and to work according to his good purpose" (v. 13).

God is the Lord of our sanctification, yet Christians are active, not passive. Once more we observe the dynamic interplay between God's absolute control and genuine human responsiveness to his Word. We work hard, struggle, and strive, but our confidence is not in our will or holiness but in him who promised, "When [Christ] appears, we will be like him because we will see him as he is" (1 John 3:2).

Preservation

God's preservation of his people and their perseverance is a classic example of the tension between divine sovereignty and human responsibility. The biblical basis for preservation is wide and deep. The Trinity keeps believers saved, including the Father (John 6:38–40; 10:29; Rom 8:1, 28–39), the Son (John 6:37–40; 10:28–29; 17:9, 11, 15, 24; 1 John 5:18), and the Holy Spirit (2 Cor 1:21–22; Eph 1:13–14; 4:30). Scripture portrays God's attributes in action, preserving the people of God. This is true for God's sovereignty (Rom 8:28–30), justice (vv. 33–34), power (John 10:28), faithfulness (1 Cor 1:8–9; 1 Thess 5:23–24; 2 Thess 3:3; Heb 6:17–18), and love (Rom 8:35–39). Scripture also bases God's preservation of believers on the work of Christ. This includes his crucifixion (5:19; 8:1–4), resurrection (5:10; Heb 7:23–25), intercession (Luke 22:32–34; John 17:24; Rom 8:34; Heb 7:25), and second coming (John 14:2–3; 1 Pet 1:13).

God sovereignly preserves his saints, but at the same time Scripture teaches that they must persevere to the end to be saved. This is true in broad, general terms (Matt 24:13; Acts 14:21–22; Heb 10:36; Rev 14:12). It is also true in three specific areas: believers must persevere in faith (Col 1:21–23; Heb 12:1–4) love (John 13:34–35; 15:12; Titus 3:4–7; 1 Pet 1:22; 1 John 4:7–8, 20), and holiness (Eph 2:8–10; Heb 12:14; 1 John 2:3–5; 3:6–10).

Although we cannot perfectly coordinate God's sovereign preservation and the necessity of believers to persevere, Scripture provides guidelines. God's keeping us is the ultimate reason we keep on keeping on: "[The antichrists] went out from us, but they did not belong to us; for if they had belonged to us, they would have remained with us. However, they went out so that it might be made clear that none of them belongs to us" (1 John 2:19). Genuine believers persevere and do not apostatize. If the antichrists had been genuine believers, they would have persevered. Scripture also teaches that one way to recognize God's saints is by their perseverance (Luke 8:11–15; 2 Pet 1:3–11; 1 John 2:3–6). We thus can make some progress in correlating preservation and perseverance, though we cannot do so perfectly. Mystery remains, as it always does when the infinite meets the finite.

Eternal Life and Glorification

The OT says a little about eternal life (Dan 12:2) and believers' final glory (Ps 73:23–26), but the NT explodes these themes that magnify God's gracious reign and humans' responsibility to believe. Eternal life is a gift of God to his people:

Jesus answered, "If you knew the gift of God, and who is saying to you, 'Give me a drink,' you would ask him, and he would give you living water." (John 4:10)

[Jesus said,] "I give them eternal life, and they will never perish. No one will snatch them out of my hand." (v. 10:28)

The wages of sin is death, but the gift of God is eternal life in Christ Jesus our Lord. (Rom 6:23)

God also sovereignly gives glory to his people. As the divine potter he will pour out "the riches of his glory on objects of mercy that he prepared beforehand for glory" (Rom 9:23). Although this world's rulers regard God's wisdom as folly, the apostles "speak God's hidden wisdom in a mystery, a wisdom God predestined before the ages for our glory" (1 Cor 2:7). God's ultimate goal for us is the glorification of our beings, including our bodies. This too displays his rule. We await the returning Lord Jesus from heaven; when he appears, "He will transform the body of our humble condition into the likeness of his glorious body, by the power that enables him to subject everything to himself" (Phil 3:21).

In light of the magnificent display of divine grace in saving us from beginning to end, we might be tempted to downplay human responsibility. To do so would be wrong, however, for Scripture repeatedly calls sinners to faith in Christ for salvation (John 3:16; Acts 4:12; Rom 10:17). Jesus spoke of eternal life as the reward for anyone who left all for his sake and the gospel's (Mark 10:29–30). We are God's children and heirs, "If indeed we suffer with him so that we may also be glorified with him" (Rom 8:17). Genuine believers are identifiable, for "The one who sows to his flesh will reap destruction from the flesh, but the one who sows to the Spirit will reap eternal life from the Spirit" (Gal 6:8). Salvation is all of God, but those who name the name of Christ must "take hold of eternal life" (1 Tim 6:12, 19).

In sum: as with every aspect of salvation, the divine sovereignty/human responsibility paradox is evident in the realm of eternal life and glorification too.

Salvation and the "Already" and the "Not Yet"

A powerful biblical theme that permeates both Testaments is the "already" and the "not yet." Already God has fulfilled his promises, but not yet has he done so in finality and fullness. We see this in the OT themes of creation and exodus. The Bible's story begins, "In the beginning God created the heavens and the earth" (Gen 1:1). Isaiah predicts, "I will create new heavens and a new earth; the past events will not be remembered or come to mind" (Isa 65:17). Exodus 12–15 describe the exodus of the Israelites from Egyptian bondage. Isaiah employs exodus terminology to predict a new exodus (Isa 43:16–21; 51:9–11).

The "already/not yet" theme spreads throughout the NT. It is evident in each of the ten doctrinal aspects of salvation we have studied.

Election

God chose his people for salvation "before the foundation of the world" (Eph 1:4) and "before time began" (2 Tim 1:9; cf. Rev 13:8; 17:8). We are not to probe God's eternal counsels to determine someone's election. Instead, Paul shows us the way: "We know, brothers and sisters loved by God, that he has chosen you, because our gospel did not come to you in word only, but also in power, in the Holy Spirit, and with full assurance" (1 Thess 1:4–5). "Already" believers know their election because God has brought them to faith in Christ. This is why Paul addresses the Colossians as he does: "As God's chosen ones, holy and dearly loved, put on compassion, kindness, humility, gentleness, and patience, bearing with one another and forgiving one another if anyone has a grievance against another. Just as the Lord has forgiven you, so you are also to forgive" (Col 3:12–13). Because election is already, biblical writers refer to individuals (Rufus, Rom 16:13) and churches (2 Thess 2:13; 2 John 1, 13) as "chosen" or "elect." The people on the side of the Lamb are "called, chosen, and faithful" (Rev 17:14).

God chose us before creation, and election is manifested in time and space when those chosen trust Christ (cf. Acts 13:48), but the full effects of election are future. Paul puts election in the context of the plan of God: "Those he foreknew he also predestined. . . . And those he predestined, he also called; and those he called, he also justified; and those he justified, he also glorified" (Rom 8:29–30). God's loving his people beforehand (foreknowledge) and choosing them guarantees their ultimate glorification, which is still future. Paul affirms, "God did not appoint us to wrath, but to obtain salvation through our Lord Jesus Christ, who died for us, so that whether we are awake or asleep, we may live together with him" (1 Thess 5:9–10). Later, Paul tells why he perseveres in gospel ministry: "This is why I endure all things for the elect: so that they also may obtain salvation, which is in Christ Jesus, with eternal glory" (2 Tim 2:10).

Therefore, although election "already" took place before creation and is not repeated, its effects occur in history, and its full manifestation is "not yet"; it awaits Christ's second advent.

Union with Christ

God planned to unite his people to Christ in salvation before creation (Eph 1:4; 2 Tim 1:9), and thus their union was certain to occur. Actual union, however, occurs in time and space when the Spirit draws believers to Christ: "We were all baptized by one Spirit into one body—whether Jews or Greeks, whether slaves or free—and we were all given one Spirit to drink" (1 Cor 12:13). Actual union occurs by God's grace through believers' faith in Christ: "Through faith you are all sons of God in Christ Jesus" (Gal 3:26). Paul celebrates his faith-union with Christ: "I have been crucified with Christ, and I no longer live, but Christ lives in me. The life I now live in the body, I live by faith in the Son of God, who loved me and gave himself for me" (v. 2:20; cf. Phil 3:8–9).

Already God's people have been joined to Christ by faith in him. Not yet do we experience the full results of this union. God has joined Christians to his Son's death and resurrection. Therefore, "We suffer with him so that we may also be glorified with him" (Rom 8:17). We died with Christ, were raised with him, sat down with him in heaven, and even come again with him in a sense: "If you have been raised with Christ, seek the things above, where Christ is, seated at the right hand of God. . . . For you died, and your life is hidden with Christ in God. When Christ, who is your life, appears, then you also will appear with him in glory" (Col 3:1, 3–4). Final union involves glory. In the end God will "bring everything together in Christ, both things in heaven and things on earth in him" (Eph 1:10). One aspect of this is that "in the coming ages [God will] display the immeasurable riches of his grace through his kindness to us in Christ Jesus" (2:7). Our glorification is in Christ: "Just as in Adam all die, so also in Christ all will be made alive" (1 Cor 15:22).

Wayne Grudem's summary bears repeating:

> Union with Christ has its source in the election of God the Father before the foundation of the world and has its fruition in the glorification of the sons of God. The perspective of God's people is not narrow; it is broad and it is long. It is not confined to space and time; it has the expanse of eternity. Its orbit has two foci, one the electing love of God the Father in the counsels of eternity; the other glorification with Christ in the manifestation of his glory. The former has no beginning; the latter has no end.[14]

Regeneration

Now we are born again. This is the testimony of Paul, James, Peter, and John. Paul writes, "God, who is rich in mercy, because of his great love that he had for us, made us alive with Christ even though we were dead in trespasses" (Eph 2:4–5; cf. Titus 3:4–5). James adds, "By his own choice, [the Father] gave us birth by the word of truth so that we would be a kind of firstfruits of his creatures" (Jas 1:18). Peter joins the chorus: "Blessed be the God and Father of our Lord Jesus Christ. Because of his great mercy he has given us new birth through the resurrection of Jesus Christ from the dead" (1 Pet 1:3). And John agrees: "Everyone who believes that Jesus is the Christ has been born of God" (1 John 5:1).

Regeneration is already, but it is also not yet. Jesus proclaims, "This is the will of my Father: that everyone who sees the Son and believes in him will have eternal life, and I will raise him up on the last day" (John 6:40). Paul assures the Romans, "He who raised Christ from the dead will also bring your mortal bodies to life" (Rom 8:11). In his resurrection chapter the apostle predicts,

---

[14] Wayne Grudem, "Union with Christ," Monergism, https://www.monergism.com/union-christ-wayne-grudem, accessed March 14, 2022.

Flesh and blood cannot inherit the kingdom of God, nor can corruption inherit incorruption. Listen, I am telling you a mystery: We will not all fall asleep, but we will all be changed, in a moment, in the twinkling of an eye, at the last trumpet. For the trumpet will sound, and the dead will be raised incorruptible, and we will be changed. For this corruptible body must be clothed with incorruptibility, and this mortal body must be clothed with immortality. (1 Cor 15:50–53)

Calling

Calling is usually already but is also not yet in at least one case. God uses the gospel call to summon us savingly to himself. Paul places calling among other aspects of salvation: "Those he predestined, he also called; and those he called, he also justified; and those he justified, he also glorified" (Rom 8:30). Paul urges the Colossians, "Let the peace of Christ, to which you were also called in one body, rule your hearts. And be thankful" (Col 3:15). Paul connects election, sanctification, faith, calling, and glory, with only the last being yet future: "From the beginning God has chosen you for salvation through sanctification by the Spirit and through belief in the truth. He called you to this through our gospel, so that you might obtain the glory of our Lord Jesus Christ" (2 Thess 2:13–14). Peter, encouraging suffering Christians to persevere, likewise speaks of calling in the past tense while pointing to the future: "The God of all grace, who called you to his eternal glory in Christ, will himself restore, establish, strengthen, and support you after you have suffered a little while" (1 Pet 5:10).

In his message of the sheep and the goats Jesus speaks of his final calling of his people without using the words "call" or "calling": "Then the King will say to those on his right, 'Come, you who are blessed by my Father; inherit the kingdom prepared for you from the foundation of the world'" (Matt 25:34).

Conversion

Conversion belongs to this age, not the age to come. Therefore it is always already. We have repented and believed the gospel and continue to do both in the Christian life. But the time will come when our sins will be gone and faith will become sight. John the Baptist and Jesus call sinners to repent (Matt 3:1–2; 4:17). Christians rejoice to hear reports of Gentiles' turning from sin to Christ: "When they heard this they became silent. And they glorified God, saying, 'So then, God has given repentance resulting in life even to the Gentiles'" (Acts 11:18). Paul instructs Timothy to teach the truth patiently and gently, asking God to grant opponents "repentance leading them to the knowledge of the truth" (2 Tim 2:25).

John makes plain the necessity of unbelievers to trust Christ: "God did not send his Son into the world to condemn the world, but to save the world through him. Anyone who believes in him is not condemned, but anyone who does not believe is already condemned" (John 3:17–18). Jesus warns the Jews, "If you do not believe that I am he, you will die in your sins" (8:24). Paul is clear: "Faith comes from what is heard, and what is heard comes through the message about Christ" (Rom 10:17). Paul contrasts the present and intermediate states:

> We are always confident and know that while we are at home in the body we are away from the Lord. For we walk by faith, not by sight. In fact, we are confident, and we would prefer to be away from the body and at home with the Lord. Therefore, whether we are at home or away, we make it our aim to be pleasing to him. For we must all appear before the judgment seat of Christ, so that each may be repaid for what he has done in the body, whether good or evil. (2 Cor 5:6–10)

There will be no more need for repentance or faith in the eternal state of the new earth. As resurrected saints we will dwell in the "holy city" (Rev 21:10), concerning which John says, "Nothing unclean will ever enter it, nor anyone who does what is detestable or false, but only those written in the Lamb's book of life" (v. 27). All sin will be a thing of the past, and repentance will be unnecessary for totally sanctified beings—us!

Neither will there be a need for faith on the new earth, for "The throne of God and of the Lamb will be in the city, and his servants will worship him. They will see his face, and his name will be on their foreheads" (Rev 22:3–4). We will not need faith, for we will have sight of God.

Justification

Justification is both already and not yet. God justifies us now in prospect of his final verdict: "Since we have been justified by faith, we have peace with God through our Lord Jesus Christ" (Rom 5:1). God the Father declares believers righteous based on the work of Christ, who "was delivered up for our trespasses and raised for our justification" (Rom 4:25). Jesus's atoning death is both a "propitiation" (3:25–26 ESV) and "one rightness act" (5:18). Therefore, all who believe "are justified freely by [God's] grace through the redemption that is in Christ Jesus" (Rom 3:24).

Certainly, the missionary Paul's emphasis is on justification now. He speaks against merit theology and calls people to trust Christ for present justification. But at least three biblical passages teach a future justification on the last day. While speaking of how words reveal what is in the heart, Jesus warns, "I tell you that on the day of judgment people will have to account for every careless word they speak. For by your words you will be acquitted, and by your words you will be condemned" (Matt 12:36–37). At the Last Judgment God will vindicate all whom he freely declared righteous by grace through faith and who produced good fruit as a result. And he will condemn all those who were never justified and whose works showed it.

Twice Paul, the great preacher of free justification in the already, teaches that justification is also not yet. Contrasting the two Adams, he declares, "Just as through one man's disobedience the many were made sinners, so also through the one man's obedience the many will be made righteous" (Rom 5:19). That is, God will acquit his people on the last day, justifying all who believed in Christ and whose lives were transformed as a result. Paul teaches the same thing in Galatians. After condemning those who seek "to be justified by the law" (Gal 5:4) he announces, "We eagerly await through the Spirit, by faith, the hope of righteousness. For in Christ Jesus neither circumcision nor uncircumcision accomplishes anything; what matters is faith working through love" (vv. 5–6). Here forensic righteousness, justification, is a part of the Christian hope—that is, it is yet future. Commenting on this text, Doug Moo helps us:

> A future element of forensic righteousness is not incompatible with what Paul teaches about righteousness elsewhere. And there are

good reasons for thinking that the word [righteousness] here does indicate the content of Christian hope. . . . If righteousness refers to a future dimension of justification, then Paul affirms quite clearly that faith is the means not only of entering into relationship with God, but also of maintaining that relationship and of confirming that relationship on the day of judgment.[15]

Adoption

Like the other aspects of salvation, adoption is already and not yet. By God's grace through faith in his Son, we are God's children in the present. Paul asserts, "You received the Spirit of adoption, by whom we cry out, '*Abba*, Father!' The Spirit himself testifies together with our spirit that we are God's children" (Rom 8:15–16). God sent his Son to redeem lawbreakers "so that we might receive adoption as sons. And because you are sons, God sent the Spirit of his Son into our hearts, crying, '*Abba*, Father!'" (Gal 4:4–6).

John provides a transition: "Dear friends, we are God's children now, and what we will be has not yet been revealed" (1 John 3:2). Indeed, "Through faith [we] are all sons of God in Christ Jesus" (Gal 3:26). However, the full revelation of our sonship awaits the resurrection: "We ourselves who have the Spirit as the firstfruits—we also groan within ourselves, eagerly waiting for adoption, the redemption of our bodies" (Rom 8:23). God has made us his heirs—he has promised us an inheritance, which is future:

> Whatever you do, do it from the heart, as something done for the Lord and not for people, knowing that you will receive the reward of an inheritance from the Lord. You serve the Lord Christ. (Col 3:23–24)

> He poured out his Spirit on us abundantly through Jesus Christ our Savior so that, having been justified by his grace, we may become heirs with the hope of eternal life. (Titus 3:6–7)

---

[15] Douglas J. Moo, *Galatians*, ECNT (Grand Rapids: Baker Academic, 2013), 328–29.

He is the mediator of a new covenant, so that those who are called might receive the promise of the eternal inheritance. (Heb 9:15)

God and Father . . . has given us new birth . . . into an inheritance that is imperishable, undefiled, and unfading, kept in heaven for you. (1 Pet 1:3–4)

Sanctification

By this time it is no surprise to learn that sanctification is both already and not yet. In fact, our major heads for this doctrine were *initial* (definitive), *progressive* (Christian), and *final* sanctification. The first two heads represent sanctification past and present, while the third points to sanctification future. God planned our sanctification before time (Eph 1:4) and sanctifies his people through Christ's atonement (John 17:19; Eph 5:25–26).

Believers are active in progressive sanctification (Phil 3:12–14; 2 Thess 2:13). Jesus enjoins, "Blessed are those who hunger and thirst for righteousness" (Matt 5:6). Sanctification is now, and sometimes it is difficult, as Paul explains: "This is God's will, your sanctification: that you keep away from sexual immorality" (1 Thess 4:3; 1 Pet 1:15–16). Hebrews urges professed believers to "Pursue . . . holiness—without it no one will see the Lord" (Heb 12:14–15; cf. 3 John 11).

Sanctification is also not yet. Christ loved his church and gave himself to death on the cross for it. His purpose? "To make her holy, cleansing her with the washing of water by the word" (Eph 5:26). Will he succeed with such halting, wayward people? Indeed—he will not fail "to present the church to himself in splendor, without spot or wrinkle or anything like that, but holy and blameless" (v. 27). The apostle describes his ministry to the Gentiles in priestly terms, for he serves "as a priest of the gospel of God. God's purpose is that the Gentiles may be an acceptable offering, sanctified by the Holy Spirit" (Rom 15:16).

Paul's wish-prayer for the Thessalonians points to Christians' future, entire sanctification, which depends ultimately on the faithfulness of God: "Now may the God of peace himself sanctify you completely. And may your whole spirit, soul, and body be kept sound and blameless at the coming of our Lord Jesus Christ. He who calls you is faithful; he will do it" (1 Thess 5:23–24).

Preservation

Preservation and its corollary, perseverance, belong to this age, not the age to come. By definition, therefore, they are already and not yet. God keeps his people saved until the end, and therefore genuine believers persevere until the end (1 John 2:19). However, although these truths are ensconced in the already, they point toward the not yet, as Jesus teaches:

> "I have come down from heaven, not to do my own will, but the will of him who sent me. This is the will of him who sent me: that I should lose none of those he has given me but should raise them up on the last day. For this is the will of my Father: that everyone who sees the Son and believes in him will have eternal life, and I will raise him up on the last day." (John 6:38–40)

> "I give them eternal life, and they will never perish. No one will snatch them out of my hand. My Father, who has given them to me, is greater than all. No one is able to snatch them out of the Father's hand." (John 10:28–29)

Jesus came to accomplish the mission the Father gave him: to save believers and keep them until Jesus raises them from the dead. In John 10 Jesus expands on what preservation entails: he gives his people eternal life and categorically says they will never perish. Rather, he and the Father will protect them.

In various ways Paul teaches the same thing. He begins a familiar chapter thus: "Therefore, there is now no condemnation for those in Christ Jesus" (Rom 8:1). Moo correctly interprets "condemnation" in relation to the already and the not yet:

> The judicial flavor of the word "condemnation" strongly suggests that Paul is here thinking only of the believer's deliverance from the penalty that sin exacts. Like "death," a parallel term (cf. 5:16 and 17; 5:18 and 21; and 8:1 and 6), "condemnation" designates the state of "lostness," of estrangement from God that, apart from Christ, every person will experience for eternity.[16]

---

[16] Moo, *The Epistle to the Romans*, 472–73 (see chap. 2, n. 62).

The Holy Spirit is a divine guarantee (in the already) of salvation (in the not yet). As both the seal (Eph 1:13; 4:30) and down payment, he ensures our salvation "for the day of redemption" (v. 30). Paul has confidence: "I am not ashamed, because I know whom I have believed and am persuaded that he is able to guard what has been entrusted to me until that day" (2 Tim 1:12). Again, "The Lord will rescue me from every evil work and will bring me safely into his heavenly kingdom" (4:18).

Believers in Christ must persevere to the end to be saved (Heb 10:36; Rev 14:12), continuing specifically in faith (Heb 12:1–4), love (Titus 3:4–7), and holiness (Heb 12:14). God's preservation of his saints and their perseverance by their very nature belong to the already. They, in terms of divine sovereignty and human responsibility, respectively, point to the not yet when Christ will return, raise, and glorify his people for eternal life on the new earth.

Eternal Life and Glorification

"Already"

We commonly think of eternal life and eternal glory as being our future inheritance. This is true, but they are also present realities. Eternal life is primarily already in John's Gospel. Jesus tells the Samaritan woman, "If you knew the gift of God, and who is saying to you, 'Give me a drink,' you would ask him, and he would give you living water" (John 4:10). It is difficult to decide if "living water" refers to the Holy Spirit or to the eternal life he brings. Either way, Jesus promises eternal life in the present, even to a Samaritan woman.

Jesus contrasts the two eternal destinies: "The one who believes in the Son has eternal life, but the one who rejects the Son will not see life; instead, the wrath of God remains on him" (John 3:36). In John, Jesus refers often to the present dimension of eternal life: "Truly I tell you, anyone who hears my word and believes him who sent me has eternal life and will not come under judgment but has passed from death to life" (5:24; cf. 10:28). Again, "This is eternal life: that they may know you, the only true God, and the one you have sent—Jesus Christ" (John 17:3). John does the same in his first epistle: "Everyone who hates his brother or sister is a murderer, and you know that no murderer has eternal life residing in him" (1 John 3:15). Although Paul speaks of eternal life chiefly in the not yet, he twice tells Timothy to "take hold of eternal life" now (1 Tim 6:12, 19).

Glory refers primarily to future salvation, but Paul says that the Holy Spirit is transforming believers in glory now: "We all, with unveiled faces, are looking as in a mirror at the glory of the Lord and are being transformed into the same image from glory to glory; this is from the Lord who is the Spirit" (2 Cor 3:18).

"Not Yet"

Eternal life and glorification are largely not yet. Jesus promised "eternal life in the age to come" to those who sacrificed to follow him (Luke 18:30). Though John usually speaks of realized eschatology (the already), he sometimes speaks of consistent eschatology (the not yet): "A time is coming when all who are in the graves will hear his voice and come out—those who have done good things, to the resurrection of life" (John 5:28–29).

Paul uses "eternal life" most often of the age to come:

Paul, a servant of God and an apostle of Jesus Christ, for the faith of God's elect and their knowledge of the truth that leads to godliness, in the hope of eternal life that God, who cannot lie, promised before time began. (Titus 1:1–2)

He poured out his Spirit on us abundantly through Jesus Christ our Savior so that, having been justified by his grace, we may become heirs with the hope of eternal life. (Titus 3:6–7)

You, dear friends, as you build yourselves up in your most holy faith, praying in the Holy Spirit, keep yourselves in the love of God, waiting expectantly for the mercy of our Lord Jesus Christ for eternal life. (Jude 20–21)

Overwhelmingly, when NT writers speaks of "glory" in salvation they refer to the future. Paul wants the Thessalonians "to walk worthy of God, who calls [them] into his own kingdom and glory" (1 Thess 2:12). As a result, [the church] will "obtain the glory of our Lord Jesus Christ" (2 Thess 2:14). Union with Christ means suffering with him now and glory with him later

(Rom 8:17), for, "When Christ, who is your life, appears, then you also will appear with him in glory" (Col 3:4). Our hope is the resurrection, when God will raise our bodies "in glory" (1 Cor 15:43). The all-powerful Christ "will transform the body of our humble condition into the likeness of his glorious body" (Phil 3:21).

God will share his glory with all his people and with his creation. "The creation itself will also be set free from its bondage to corruption and obtain the freedom of the glory of the children of God" (Rom 8:21 ESV). God's glory will illuminate the new Jerusalem (Rev 21:23). Truly, his glory will fill the new heavens and new earth, as John saw with "the holy city, Jerusalem, coming down out of heaven from God, arrayed with God's glory. Her radiance was like a precious jewel, like a jasper stone, clear as crystal. . . . The city does not need the sun or the moon to shine on it, because the glory of God illuminates it, and its lamp is the Lamb" (vv. 10–11, 23).

How can struggling sinners, as we all are at times, make it to the eternal kingdom? Peter offers encouragement: "The God of all grace, who called you to his eternal glory in Christ, will himself restore, establish, strengthen, and support you after you have suffered a little while" (1 Pet 5:10). And all this is "to the praise of [God's] glorious grace" (Eph 1:6).

Salvation and the Kingdom of God

The kingdom of God is a grand and keynote biblical theme that connects the Testaments. Ecuadorian evangelical missiologist René Padilla summarizes salient aspects of the kingdom:

> The kingdom of God is God's dynamic power made visible through concrete signs pointing to Jesus as the Messiah. It is a new reality that has entered into the flow of history and affects human life not only morally and spiritually but physically and psychologically, materially and socially. In anticipation of the eschatological consummation at the end time, it has been inaugurated in the person and work of Christ. . . . The completion of God's purpose still lies in the future, but a foretaste of the eschaton is already possible. . . . The New Testament presents the church as the community of the kingdom in which Jesus is acknowledged as Lord of the universe

and through which, in anticipation of the end, the kingdom is concretely manifested in history.[17]

We will investigate ten salvific themes in relation to the kingdom.

Election

Although often overlooked, Scripture ties together election and the kingdom. James condemns the sin of partiality because his readers were favoring the rich and neglecting the poor: "Listen, my dear brothers and sisters: Didn't God choose the poor in this world to be rich in faith and heirs of the kingdom that he has promised to those who love him?" (Jas 2:5). Contrary to James's readers actions, God has favored the poor by including them among those chosen for salvation. James wants his readers to acknowledge that their partiality is sinful (v. 4) and to repent. He plays on words by teaching that God's election makes the poor "rich in faith and heirs."

What will those whom God chose, including poor believers, inherit? "The kingdom that [God] has promised to those who love him." Jesus put the kingdom, or reign, of God in the center of his message. Moo unlocks James's message:

> NT writers followed Jesus' lead, often using language of "inheriting the kingdom" to describe this final establishment of God's kingly power in the lives of his people (1 Cor 6:9, 10: 15:10; Gal 5:21; Eph 5:5). Christians, however poor in material possessions they may be, possess spiritual wealth presently and anticipate greater blessings in the future. It is from this spiritual vantage-point, not the material, that Christians should judge others.[18]

Peter also links election and the kingdom. After listing godly qualities that should characterize believers' lives and make them useful to and fruitful for God, Peter instructs his readers, "Therefore, brothers and sisters, make every effort to confirm your calling and election, because if you do these

---

[17] René Padilla, *Mission between the Times: Essays on the Kingdom of God* (Grand Rapids: Eerdmans, 1985), 189–90.

[18] Douglas J. Moo, *The Letter of James*, PNTC (Grand Rapids: Eerdmans, 2000), 106.

things you will never stumble" (2 Pet 1:10). Pursuing Christian virtues will help the readers confirm for themselves that God has chosen them for salvation and brought them to that salvation through the gospel. Peter sets forth the end of such a lifestyle: "In this way, entry into the eternal kingdom of our Lord and Savior Jesus Christ will be richly provided for you" (vv. 10–11). The apostle wants his readers to seek the Lord with all their hearts. If they do, their lives will show it, they will have great assurance, and God will gladly welcome them into his eternal kingdom.

Union with Christ

Paul in Colossians connects union with Christ and the kingdom of God. After sharing the content of his prayers for the Christians in Colossae, he declares that the Father "has rescued us from the domain of darkness and transferred us into the kingdom of the Son he loves. In him we have redemption, the forgiveness of sins" (Col 1:13–14). Our gracious Father has transferred us between realms. From the domain of darkness he has brought us to the kingdom of his beloved Son. We are citizens of God's eternal kingdom now, and greater joys await. God has united us to his Son in redemption—deliverance from bondage to Satan and self—that entails God's forgiveness of all our sins. F. F. Bruce captures Paul's thought: "Those who have been introduced into this new realm enjoy forthwith the principal benefits won for them by its ruler. In him they receive their redemption, with the forgiveness of sins—in him, because it is only as those who share the risen life of Christ that they have made effective in them what he has done for them."[19]

Regeneration

Jesus, Paul, and John tie together the new life of regeneration and the kingdom of God. Jesus surprises Nicodemus when, in response to his comment about Jesus's signs, Jesus says, "Truly I tell you, unless someone is born again, he cannot see the kingdom of God" (John 3:3). Jesus teaches that no matter what credentials or lifestyle Jews bring with them, they need God's radical

---

[19] F. F. Bruce, *The Epistles to the Colossians, to Philemon, and to the Ephesians,* NICNT (Grand Rapids: Eerdmans, 1984), 52–53.

transformation predicted by the OT in order to see or enter God's kingdom (cf. Ezek 36:25–26). We all need the new birth that comes from above—from God himself—to enter God's saving reign.

Paul also connects regeneration and God's kingdom. After frankly considering the catastrophic results that would follow if Christ were not raised from the dead, Paul affirms, "But as it is, Christ has been raised from the dead, the firstfruits of those who have fallen asleep" (1 Cor 15:20). When Paul labels Jesus "the firstfruits," he means that Jesus's resurrection will be the cause of his people's being raised to life. Paul then juxtaposes the two Adams:

> Since death came through a man, the resurrection of the dead also comes through a man. For just as in Adam all die, so also in Christ all will be made alive. But each in his own order: Christ, the firstfruits; afterward, at his coming, those who belong to Christ. Then comes the end, when he hands over the kingdom to God the Father, when he abolishes all rule and all authority and power. (1 Cor 15:21–24)

Adam's original sin brought physical and spiritual death to humankind. Christ's (death and) resurrection brings eternal life to his people. This eternal life means regeneration now and resurrection to life in the age to come. Christ dies and rises in service to the kingdom, which will be fully revealed only at his return, when he completes his role as Mediator, turning everything over to his Father.

When John contemplates the new Jerusalem, he combines images of the kingdom of God and of new life as well:

> He showed me the river of the water of life, clear as crystal, flowing from the throne of God and of the Lamb down the middle of the city's main street. The tree of life was on each side of the river, bearing twelve kinds of fruit, producing its fruit every month. The leaves of the tree are for healing the nations, and there will no longer be any curse. The throne of God and of the Lamb will be in the city, and his servants will worship him. (Rev 22:1–3)

In this vision John sees the thrones of "God and of the Lamb" at the beginning and the end of the passage. He also sees pictures of eternal life:

"the river of the water of life," flowing from the thrones of the Father and Son, and "the tree of life." Plainly John portrays the final dimension of God's reign with his emphasis on the thrones of God and the Lamb. John combines this with eternal life, as Beale shows: "The 'living waters' coming from God and the Lamb represent eternal life because the presence of God imparts life to all those able to enter into intimate communion with him (so 22:17)."[20] Further, God's kingdom promotes eternal life and banishes the curse, as again Beale notes: "There will be no form of curse in the new Jerusalem because God's consummate, ruling presence will fill the city: 'the throne of God and of the Lamb will be in it.'"[21]

Calling

Jesus, Paul, and Peter tie calling to the kingdom of God. He doesn't use the word "call," but King Jesus predicts his future calling of God's people to receive their inheritance in the final kingdom of God: "Then the King will say to those on his right, 'Come, you who are blessed by my Father; inherit the kingdom prepared for you from the foundation of the world'" (Matt 25:34). This involves "eternal life," in contrast to the "eternal punishment" the unsaved will receive (v. 46).

Paul wants the Thessalonian Christians to live for God now in light of his future calling them into the final manifestation of God's kingdom and glory: "As you know, like a father with his own children, we encouraged, comforted, and implored each one of you to walk worthy of God, who calls you into his own kingdom and glory" (1 Thess 2:11–12).

Peter urges his readers to strengthen their certainty of salvation by pursuing Christian virtues he has just listed: "Therefore, brothers and sisters, make every effort to confirm your calling and election, because if you do these things you will never stumble. For in this way, entry into the eternal kingdom of our Lord and Savior Jesus Christ will be richly provided for you" (2 Pet 1:10–11). Living for God with our whole hearts confirms experientially the fact that God brought us to faith in Christ (called us). This in turn

---

[20] G. K. Beale, *The Book of Revelation*, NIGTC (Grand Rapids: Eerdmans, 1999), 1107.

[21] Beale, *The Book of Revelation*, 1113.

is how we learn that the Father chose us, for he draws to faith in his Son those given him by the Father (John 6:37–40). The result of God's choosing and calling us, and our resultant living for him, is his richly welcoming us into Christ's eternal kingdom.

Conversion

As we have shown, conversion consists of repentance, turning from sin, and faith, turning to Christ offered in the gospel. The NT shows both aspects of conversion occurring in the context of the preaching of the kingdom of God. John the Baptist and Jesus link their calls to repentance with the coming of the kingdom in Jesus's ministry:

> In those days John the Baptist came, preaching in the wilderness of Judea and saying, "Repent, because the kingdom of heaven has come near!" (Matt 3:1–2)

> From then on Jesus began to preach, "Repent, because the kingdom of heaven has come near." (4:17)

Jesus Christ is the great royal son of David (2 Sam 7:12–16) and messianic king foretold by Isaiah (Isa 9:6–7). John the Baptist pointed to Jesus as the one coming after him who would inaugurate the kingdom in its NT expression. Jesus, like John, preached repentance, but, unlike John, Jesus himself brought the kingdom in his teaching, healing, exorcisms, and other miracles. At the same time, Jesus predicted a greater appearance of the kingdom at Pentecost, when he would pour out the Spirit on the church. When he did so, Peter preached a powerful message of repentance, and many were converted. Jesus also foretold that the greatest coming of the kingdom would accompany his second advent.

When Paul was imprisoned in Rome, he also joined a message of conversion with the kingdom of God. As Luke describes, "Many came to him at his lodging. From dawn to dusk he expounded and testified about the kingdom of God. He tried to persuade them about Jesus from both the Law of Moses and the Prophets. Some were persuaded by what he said, but others did not believe" (Acts 28:23–24). Luke emphasizes faith as the response to Paul's proclamation of the gospel while imprisoned.

Justification

Paul unites the kingdom and justification when he treats the two Adams in Romans 5. Although Rom 5:12–21 is the *textus classicus* for original sin, in its context it even more presents Christ's atonement as the ground of free justification to everyone who believes. Kingdom language permeates the passage; Paul speaks of the *reign* of death (vv. 14, 17) and sin (v. 21). This language serves as a contrasting background for the apostle's main message of believers' reigning in life (v. 17) and of grace's reign in righteousness (v. 12). Paul's kingdom language in turn sets the stage for his contrast between Adam's "one trespass" bringing "condemnation" and Christ's "one righteous act" bringing "justification leading to life" (v. 18). Paul juxtaposes Adam's primal "disobedience" that made people sinners and Christ's "obedience" that will make his people "righteous" (v. 19). Thus, in Paul's famous text on the two Adams he deals with justification in the context of God's kingdom.

Adoption

The theme of the kingdom of God so pervades the Scriptures that it intersects with most pictures of salvation, including adoption. We observe this in the teaching of King Jesus, as he speaks of his returning in glory to "sit on his glorious throne" and to separate the sheep from the goats (Matt 25:31). He will eternally bless his people when he welcomes them by saying, "Come, you who are blessed by my Father; *inherit the kingdom* prepared for you from the foundation of the world" (v. 34). Jesus's words "inherit the kingdom" arrest our attention by mixing two metaphors, one familial and one royal. King Jesus has a kingdom, and here he calls his own into the full revelation of that kingdom. As he does so, he tells them to enter into their inheritance, which is the privilege of the sons and daughters of God, who has adopted them into his family.

In Scripture's last book John presents the new heaven and the new earth. In this context he hears "a loud voice from the throne" of God, announcing his comforting presence with his people (Rev 21:3): "Then the one seated on the throne said, 'Look, I am making everything new,'" and he proclaims it done (vv. 5–6). Then God promises, "I will freely give to the thirsty from the spring of the water of life. The one who conquers will inherit these things, and I will be his God, and he will be my son" (vv. 6–7). Here, as the King ushering in the end, God speaks as the Father, acknowledging his adopted children and promising them a rich inheritance in his kingdom.

God the King who rules his people is also God the Father who loves those he has graciously adopted into his family. For all eternity he will be their King and their Father, and they will be his subjects and his beloved children.

Sanctification

Both Testaments coordinate the kingdom of God and sanctification. In a vision Daniel sees God, "the Ancient of Days," sitting on his awesome throne in heaven with myriads of angels as attendants, judging and destroying the earthly kingdoms opposing him (Dan 7:9–12). Daniel's main message is clear: "The Most High is the reigning king in heaven and earth."[22] Then Daniel sees "one like a son of man . . . coming with the clouds of heaven" who approaches the Ancient of Days and receives a universal and eternal kingdom in which all people will serve him (vv. 13–14). Alongside this kingdom language are references to God's people. Six times they are called "the holy ones" or "saints" (vv. 18, 21, 22 [2x], 25, 27). The Most High will prevail over all earthly kingdoms and deliver his holy ones, and they will reign with him forever (vv. 15–27).

After Jesus tells the parable of the weeds in the field, his disciples ask him to explain it to them (Matt 13:36). He identifies the sower of good seed as the Son of Man, the field as the world, the good seed as the children of God's kingdom, the weeds as children of the devil, and the enemy who sowed them as the devil (vv. 37–39). Jesus then applies the imagery of the weeds being gathered and burned to the fate of the lost: "The Son of Man will send out his angels, and they will gather from his kingdom all who cause sin and those guilty of lawlessness. They will throw them into the blazing furnace where there will be weeping and gnashing of teeth" (vv. 41–42).

Far different will be the fate of the saved: "Then the righteous will shine like the sun in their Father's kingdom" (v. 43). Jesus, alluding to Dan 12:3 LXX, is not teaching merit theology, that "the righteous" earn God's favor.

---

[22] Joyce G. Baldwin, *Daniel*, TOTC (Leicester, ENG: InterVarsity, 1978), 137.

Rather, "the righteous" are the godly, saved freely by his grace, though that
is not stated here. Jesus contrasts them with "those guilty of lawlessness" (v.
41). Carson helps: "These righteous people . . . once the light of the world,
now radiate perfections and experience bliss in the consummation of their
hopes."[23] Having lived holy lives by God's grace, they will reflect the glory of
God in "their Father's kingdom" (v. 43).

Paul too links the kingdom of God and sanctification. Christians in
Rome disagree strongly concerning clean and unclean foods and the observance of holy days. Paul urges both "strong" and "weak" believers to promote
unity among themselves. They are not to judge one another but to be careful
not to cause one another to sin (Rom 14:13). They are not to overemphasize matters of minor importance, for "The kingdom of God is not eating
and drinking, but righteousness, peace, and joy in the Holy Spirit" (v. 17).
Although he speaks often of forensic righteousness in Romans, the context indicates that here Paul speaks of moral righteousness or holiness. He
teaches that the most important things in God's kingdom are not our views
on debatable matters but the holiness, unity, and joy that the Spirit instills.

Preservation

Jesus instructs his disciples that they are not to follow the mores of the
"kings of the Gentiles," who "lord it over" their subjects. Instead, those in
Jesus's kingdom are to follow the example of Jesus, who said, "I am among
you as the one who serves" (Luke 22:27). He promises them the blessings of his future kingdom: "I bestow on you a kingdom, just as my Father
bestowed one on me, so that you may eat and drink at my table in my
kingdom. And you will sit on thrones judging the twelve tribes of Israel"
(vv. 29–30). Then Jesus promises to pray for Peter, that his faith would not
completely fail upon attack by Satan (vv. 31–32). Peter denies this would
ever happen (v. 33). Then Jesus predicts that Peter will deny him three times
(v. 34). In a context dealing with the future kingdom of God, Jesus predicts
that Peter will persevere in his faith, "even after wavering terribly. Why
did he succeed? Not because of the greatness of his dedication to Christ.

---

[23] D. A. Carson, "Matthew," in *The Expositor's Bible Commentary* (Grand Rapids:
Zondervan, 1984), 327.

He persevered because his Lord preserved him by praying for him."[24] Mercifully, the glorified Christ in his role of heavenly King does the same today for his struggling people.

Paul also teaches God's preservation of his saints in the context of the kingdom. After affirming Christ's deity and his kingship "over every ruler and authority" (Col 2:10), he tells how God regenerated and forgave all who believe in Jesus (v. 13). Paul's next words depict God's preservation of his people in Christ's cross: "He erased the certificate of debt, with its obligations, that was against us and opposed to us, and has taken it away by nailing it to the cross. He disarmed the rulers and authorities and disgraced them publicly; he triumphed over them in him" (vv. 14–15). In his atonement Christ paid the sin-debt we could not pay, and he paid it in full. On that basis "[God] forgave us all our trespasses" (v. 13). The apostle's words in verse 15 form an inclusion with those in verse 10: Christ the victorious King has vanquished the evil spiritual powers. Believers will persevere to the end and be saved because God preserves them. And one important basis for preservation is the saving work of King Jesus.

Approaching death, Paul personally testifies to God's keeping him saved for entrance "into his heavenly kingdom" (2 Tim 4:18). In closing personal remarks in his second letter to Timothy, the apostle asks him to come and minister to him. Paul's tone is mixed, speaking of friends and enemies. He reports that at the beginning of legal proceedings he was alone. Paul's confidence, however, in this life and the next is not in human support but in the Lord's. God has strengthened him, enabling him to preach the gospel. Before giving God praise, he ends on a triumphant note: "The Lord will rescue me from every evil deed and bring me safely into his heavenly kingdom. To him be the glory for ever and ever! Amen" (2 Tim 4:18). Yarbrough underlines God's preservation of his apostle: "Paul expects death soon. . . . Even in death the believer is not separated from Christ (Rom 8:35–37). . . . 'Will bring me safely' refers to Christ's work of redemption that ensures the believers' arrival in his 'heavenly kingdom,' that is, in heaven."[25]

---

[24] Peterson, *Our Secure Salvation*, 30 (see chap. 9, n. 174).

[25] Robert W. Yarbrough, *The Letters to Timothy and Titus*, PNTC (Grand Rapids: Eerdmans, 2018), 455–56.

Eternal Life and Glorification

Scripture coordinates the themes of eternal life and glory with the kingdom of God. We see this in the Gospels, at least once in Paul, and in Revelation. As we have observed, Jesus, speaking in royal language, promises eternal blessings to those whose dedication to him involves sacrifice:

> "Truly I tell you, in the renewal of all things, when the Son of Man sits on his glorious throne, you who have followed me will also sit on twelve thrones, judging the twelve tribes of Israel. And everyone who has left houses or brothers or sisters or father or mother or children or fields because of my name will receive a hundred times more and will inherit eternal life." (Matt 19:28–29)

In addition, returning King Jesus, after separating believers and unbelievers, will welcome the former: "Come, you who are blessed by my Father; inherit the kingdom prepared for you from the foundation of the world" (Matt 25:34). And at the end of the same discourse Jesus promises them "eternal life" (v. 46).

Paul urges the Thessalonians to pursue sanctification by reminding them that God has called them "into his own kingdom and glory" (1 Thess 2:12). Although Paul does not speak of the kingdom of God as often as Jesus does, he here combines "kingdom" with a favorite theme, "glory," in the space of three words.

Revelation also combines royal language with pictures of final salvation. Jesus promises every overcomer in the church of Laodicea, "To the one who conquers I will give the right to sit with me on my throne, just as I also conquered and sat down with my Father on his throne" (Rev 3:21). Jesus thus promises admission to the final installment of the kingdom of God to those who "conquer" the opposition of the world. Later John speaks of those cleansed by Christ's atonement:

> They are before the throne of God, and they serve him day and night in his temple. The one seated on the throne will shelter them: They will no longer hunger; they will no longer thirst; the sun will no longer strike them, nor will any scorching heat. For the Lamb

who is at the center of the throne will shepherd them; he will guide them to springs of the waters of life, and God will wipe away every tear from their eyes. (Rev 7:15–17)

John thus combines kingdom language with images of God's final deliverance of his people, including their access to "springs of the waters of life." Further, Revelation fittingly links God's final reign with the worship of his people:

"The kingdom of the world has become the kingdom of our Lord and of his Christ, and he will reign forever and ever."

The twenty-four elders, who were seated before God on their thrones, fell facedown and worshiped God, saying, "We give you thanks, Lord God, the Almighty, who is and who was, because you have taken your great power and have begun to reign. The nations were angry, but your wrath has come. The time has come for the dead to be judged and to give the reward to your servants the prophets, to the saints, and to those who fear your name, both small and great." (Rev 11:15–18)

Salvation and Covenant

This is a significant biblical theme, as the following verses bear witness:

"I will make a new covenant with the house of Israel and with the house of Judah." (Jer 31:31)

"This cup is the new covenant in my blood, which is poured out for you." (Luke 22:20)

He has made us competent to be ministers of a new covenant. (2 Cor 3:6)

He is the mediator of a new covenant. (Heb 9:15)

Given the intertwining of biblical themes, we are not surprised to find that the prominent theme of covenant connects with all ten of our soteriological aspects, from election to eternal life and glory.

Election

God chose Abraham, an idolator, ultimately to reach all nations with salvation. God entered into a covenant with him and instructed him to leave Ur in the Chaldees and go to a new and distant land. God promised to make Abraham into a great nation, to bless him, to make his name great, and to make him a blessing to others (Gen 12:1–2). God promised, "I will bless those who bless you, I will curse anyone who treats you with contempt, and all the peoples on earth will be blessed through you" (v. 3). This is the Abrahamic covenant, and it is fulfilled, as Paul explains, when Gentiles believe in Jesus:

> You know, then, that those who have faith, these are Abraham's sons. Now the Scripture saw in advance that God would justify the Gentiles by faith and proclaimed the gospel ahead of time to Abraham, saying, "All the nations will be blessed through you." Consequently, those who have faith are blessed with Abraham, who had faith. (Gal 3:7–9)

God's election of Abraham and his descendants pertains to all his spiritual descendants, all who believe in Jesus. Whether Jews or Gentiles, all Christians are Abraham's children. Remarkably, God's election of Abraham also still pertains to all his blood descendants, ethnic Israel. Paul explicates the anomalous situation of first-century unbelieving Israelites. Writing predominantly to Gentile Christians, he says, "Regarding the gospel, [the Jews] are enemies for your advantage, but regarding election, they are loved because of the patriarchs, since God's gracious gifts and calling are irrevocable" (Rom 11:28–29). Because God chose Abraham, Isaac, and Jacob and made them his covenant people, God loves their descendants, even in their unbelief. At the same time, the Jews oppose God and reject the gospel of Christ.

We thus see how the Abrahamic/new covenant concerns God's election of his people.

Union with Christ

Paul teaches that God's "blessing of Abraham" comes "to the Gentiles by Christ Jesus" (Gal 3:14) in fulfillment of the Abrahamic covenant. The promise of this covenant has to do with Christ and precedes the law of Moses by

430 years (v. 17). The promise is for Jews and Greeks who believe in Jesus and therefore "are all one in Christ Jesus," that is, in union with him (v. 28). And all those in union with him belong to him and as such "are Abraham's seed, heirs according to the promise" (v. 29). In this way Paul links membership in the Abrahamic covenant and faith union with Christ.

Regeneration

Paul's strongest new-covenant passage contrasts it favorably with the Mosaic covenant (2 Cor 3:6–11). Paul expresses strong confidence not in himself but "through Christ before God" (v. 4). Therefore, he finds his adequacy in the same place (v. 5). He then explicates, "He has made us competent to be ministers of a new covenant, not of the letter, but of the Spirit. For the letter kills, but the Spirit gives life" (v. 6). This is his first contrast of the Mosaic and new covenants. The former is characterized as being "of the letter," the demands of the law epitomized by the Ten Commandments. The Mosaic covenant "kills" because the Israelites could not keep its demands. By contrast, the new covenant is characterized by the Spirit, not the letter, and it results in "life," not death. Morgan and Peterson elucidate these contrasts: "The 'letter' and the 'Spirit', then, stand for two different covenants with different descriptions, demands and results. The law's letter 'kills'; it 'slays' the disobedient, as Paul has painfully learned (Rom 7:10–11). The Spirit 'gives life' in regeneration in this age and in resurrection to life in the age to come."[26]

The writer to the Hebrews also links the covenant with regeneration. Hebrews 8 consists largely of a quotation of Jeremiah's new-covenant passage (Jer 31:31–34). The writer quotes Jer 31:31, where God says that he will make a "new covenant" (Heb 8:8).

Although Hebrews does not explicitly mention regeneration, it implies it in these words: "I will put my laws into their minds and write them on their hearts. I will be their God, and they will be my people. And each person will not teach his fellow citizen, and each his brother or sister, saying, 'Know the Lord,' because they will all know me, from the least to the greatest of them" (vv. 10–11). F. F. Bruce interprets:

---

[26] Christopher W. Morgan and Robert A. Peterson, *The Glory of God and Paul: Texts, Themes, and Theology* (Downers Grove: IVP, 2022), 104.

The implanting of God's law in their hearts means much more than their committing of it to memory. . . . Jeremiah's words imply the receiving of a new heart by the people. . . . What was needed was a new nature, a heart liberated from its bondage to sin, a heart which not only spontaneously knew and loved the will of God but had the power to do it. The new covenant was a new one because it could impart this new heart.[27]

Calling

Paul ties calling to covenant in a passage discussed above under election: "Regarding the gospel, they [the Jews] are enemies for your [the Gentiles'] advantage, but regarding election, they are loved because of the patriarchs, since God's gracious gifts and calling are irrevocable" (Rom 11:28–29). In the last clause Paul tells why he is confident God is not finished with ethnic Israelites: God does not withdraw his "gracious gifts and calling"; they are "irrevocable."

Schreiner helps us understand Paul's message: "As usual in Paul (cf. 8:28, 30; 9:12), κλῆσις (*klēsis*, calling) denotes God's effective call to salvation, and here reflects on the call of Abraham and Israel. . . . The word ἀμεταμέλητα (*ametamelēta*, irrevocable) is a legal term (cf. 2 Cor. 7:10) indicating the unbreakable nature of God's gifts and calling."[28]

Immediately before this text, discussing the future of ethnic Israel, Paul writes, "The Deliverer will come from Zion; he will turn godlessness away from Jacob. And this will be my covenant with them when I take away their sins" (Rom 11:26–27 LXX, quoting Isa 59:20–21). The "covenant" referred to is the new covenant, and hence Paul combines the new covenant that takes away sins and God's calling of Israel.

In the writer to the Hebrews' only perfect passive use of the verb "called"[29] he unites the idea of calling with the new covenant in Christ

---

[27] F. F. Bruce, *The Epistle to the Hebrews*, NICNT (Grand Rapids: Eerdmans, 1964), 172–73.

[28] Schreiner, *Romans*, 626 (see chap. 6, n. 129).

[29] In fact, "It occurs nowhere else in the epistles; cf. Mt. 22:3, 4, 8; Rev. 19:9"; Paul Ellingworth, *The Epistle to the Hebrews*, NIGTC (Grand Rapids: Eerdmans, 1993), 462.

(Heb 9:15). Christ's sacrifice of himself is superior to OT animal sacrifices, for his blood, unlike theirs, "obtained eternal redemption" (v. 12). In addition, his atonement purifies believers' consciences before God, enabling them to serve him (vv. 13–14).

This sets the stage for verse 15: "Therefore, he is the mediator of a new covenant, so that those who are called might receive the promise of the eternal inheritance, because a death has taken place for redemption from the transgressions committed under the first covenant." Christ is the sole mediator of the new covenant, and his atonement alone brings the "eternal inheritance" to believers. The words with which this verse ends

> are nothing short of astonishing. . . . It was Christ, the Mediator of the new covenant, whose sacrifice redeemed Old Testament saints "from the transgressions committed under the first covenant" (Heb. 9:15). This means that Christ's atoning sacrifice not only saves all who come after him and trust him as Lord and Savior, but it also saves all who came before him and believed the gospel communicated through the sacrifices.[30]

Who benefits from this monumental sacrifice of Christ? He, "the mediator of a new covenant," died for sinners "so that those who are called might receive the promise of the eternal inheritance" (v. 15). Those whom God effectively calls to himself in salvation receive the benefits of Christ's great work, are redeemed, and become God's heirs.

Thus in at least two places NT writers speak of God's calling in the context of the new covenant.

Conversion

The NT combines each of these three doctrines—conversion, repentance, and faith—with the new covenant. Toward the end of Paul's most extensive new-covenant text, he likens the hardened hearts of the Israelites to whom Moses ministered to the veiled hearts of his fellow Jews who have not believed in Christ (2 Cor 3:13–15). Thankfully, Christ removes this veil: "Yet

---

[30] Robert A. Peterson, *Salvation Accomplished by the Son: The Work of Christ* (Wheaton: Crossway, 2012), 530.

still today, whenever Moses is read, a veil lies over their hearts, but whenever a person turns to the Lord, the veil is removed" (vv. 15–16). Turning to the Lord here means conversion, as Barnett shows:

> What does [Paul] mean by "turn"? The exact phrase "turn to the Lord" occurs many times in the OT (e.g., Deut 4:30; 2 Chron 24:19; 30:9; Isa 19:22) to portray Israel's return in penitence to her God. Within the NT this and similar expressions denoted Christian conversion, a turning to the Lord Jesus (1 Thess 1:9; Acts 9:35; 11:21; 14:15; 15:19; 26:20; 1 Pet 2:25; cf. Gal 4:9). "Turn to the Lord" here means conversion, to the Lord Jesus Christ.[31]

When people turn to Christ, as he is offered in the gospel, they become new-covenant believers.

Luke also ties together the new covenant and evangelical repentance. Peter proclaims that Jesus is the prophet whom Moses predicted would come (Acts 3:21–24). Peter then declares his hearers' allegiance to the Abrahamic/new covenant: "You are the sons of the prophets and of the covenant that God made with your ancestors, saying to Abraham, 'And all the families of the earth will be blessed through your offspring'" (v. 25). After Jesus died on the cross for our sins, "God raised up his servant and sent him first to you to bless you by turning each of you from your evil ways" (v. 26). Peter thus places his hearers in a covenantal context and then calls them to repentance so that they might receive the blessings God promised to Abraham.

Paul asserts that faith in Christ fulfills the Abrahamic covenant, bringing blessing to believers. "Christ redeemed us from the curse of the law by becoming a curse for us" (Gal 3:13). What was God's purpose in Christ's atonement? "That the blessing of Abraham would come to the Gentiles by Christ Jesus, so that we could receive the promised Spirit through faith" (v. 14). Notice that people access the Abrahamic promise through faith.

Hebrews also links the covenant to faith. Unlike the Levitical priests, who held their offices because of genealogy, Christ was appointed a priest

---

[31] Paul Barnett, *The Second Epistle to the Corinthians*, NICNT (Grand Rapids: Eerdmans, 1997), 199.

by God's swearing "You are a priest forever" (Heb 7:21, citing Ps 110:4). The writer explicates the significance in redemptive history of God's doing so: "Because of this oath, Jesus has also become the guarantee of a better covenant" (v. 22). The Levitical priests were numerous because, as one died, another took his place. Christ's priesthood is superior because as the crucified and risen One "He holds his priesthood permanently" (v. 24). The writer then applies this truth to the gospel: "Therefore, he is able to save completely those who come to God through him, since he always lives to intercede for them" (v. 25).

Thus we see that, as redemptive history unfolds, the Abrahamic/new covenant is joined to conversion and its components, repentance and faith.

Justification

The OT background for justification is impressive. When God entered into covenant with Abraham, Abraham believed God's Word and was justified: "Abram believed the LORD, and he credited it to him as righteousness" (Gen 15:6; cf. citations in Rom 4:3; Gal 3:6; Jas 2:23). After the covenant-cutting ceremony the words are explicit: "On that day the LORD made a covenant with Abram" (Gen 15:18).

The answer to the Westminster Shorter Catechism's question 33 ("What is justification?") is "Justification is an act of God's free grace, wherein he pardons all our sins, and accepts as righteous in his sight, only for the righteousness of Christ imputed to us, and received by faith alone." That is, justification involves the imputation of righteousness and the non-imputation of sin. The last promise of Jeremiah's new covenant prediction is "I will forgive their iniquity and never again remember their sin" (Jer 31:34; cf. Heb 8:12; 10:17).

At the Last Supper Jesus ratified the new covenant Jeremiah had predicted: "Then he took a cup, and after giving thanks, he gave it to them and said, 'Drink from it, all of you. For this is my blood of the covenant, which is poured out for many for the forgiveness of sins'" (Matt 26:27–28). Jesus thereby includes forgiveness in the new covenant.

Paul connects justification and the new covenant when he contrasts its ministry with that of the old covenant: "If the ministry that brought condemnation had glory, the ministry that brings righteousness overflows with even more glory" (2 Cor 3:9). "Condemnation" and "righteousness" have forensic meaning here because Paul juxtaposes them, as Harris explains: "δικαιοσύνη here is a relational rather than an ethical term, denoting a right standing before God, given by God (as in Rom 1:17; 3:21–22; 10:3; Phil 3:9), the status of being 'in the right' before the court of heaven. God's approval, not his condemnation, rests on those who are 'in Christ.'"[32] Once again, Scripture links the new covenant and justification.

It is the same when the author to the Hebrews ties the new covenant with God's promise: "I will forgive their wrongdoing, and I will never again remember their sins" (Heb 8:12).

Adoption

Like the other soteriological themes, adoption appears in conjunction with the covenant. The Judaizers had accused Paul of teaching false doctrine by repudiating the Mosaic Law. Paul responded by stressing the continuity between the Abrahamic and new covenants: "The law, which came 430 years later, does not invalidate a covenant previously established by God and thus cancel the promise. For if the inheritance is based on the law, it is no longer based on the promise; but God has graciously given it to Abraham through the promise" (Gal 3:17–18). The Judaizers erred when they regarded the law as God's main covenant. It is not; it is subordinate to the Abrahamic covenant that in Christ has become the new covenant.

Paul interprets God's promise to Abraham's "seed" in two ways. First, the "seed" is Christ: "The promises were spoken to Abraham and to his seed. He does not say 'and to seeds,' as though referring to many, but referring to one, and to your seed, who is Christ" (v. 16).

Second, toward the end of the passage Paul teaches that all believers in Christ are also to be regarded as Abraham's seed: "If you belong to Christ, then you are Abraham's seed, heirs according to the promise" (v. 29).

In between Paul's individual and corporate expositions of Abraham's "seed," he says the new covenant has eclipsed the Mosaic covenant and that therefore believers "are all sons of God in Christ Jesus" (26). Here Paul combines the covenant with faith in Christ.

---

[32] Harris, *The Second Epistle to the Corinthians*, 287–88.

Sanctification

Both Testaments speak of sanctification in the context of the covenant. After appearing to Abraham previously, God did so again and said, "I am God Almighty. Live in my presence and be blameless. I will set up my covenant between me and you, and I will multiply you greatly" (Gen 17:1–2). God thereby confirmed the covenant he had made with Abraham "to be [his] God and the God of [his] offspring after [him]" (v. 7). The ceremony of Genesis 15 made it clear that the covenant was monergistic in origin. Here we learn that it was also bilateral, for, after God's grace claimed Abraham for himself, God expected Abraham to live for him in holiness.

When Abraham was poised to sacrifice Isaac, God stayed his hand and said, "Abraham, Abraham! . . . Do not lay a hand on the boy or do anything to him. For now I know that you fear God, since you have not withheld your only son from me" (Gen 22:11–12). The covenant is indeed bilateral, and Abraham must love, fear, and obey God all his days.

God struck Zechariah mute for disbelieving that God would give him and Elizabeth a son. When the baby was born, his mother said his name was to be John, and to everyone's amazement Zechariah agreed! God enabled him to speak, and he immediately burst into praise of God, who "has visited and provided redemption for his people" (Luke 1:68). The birth of John the Baptist, the forerunner of the Messiah Jesus, was cause for rejoicing. Zechariah praised God for remembering the Abrahamic covenant (vv. 70–73). He added the purpose of God's gracious intervention: that his people "would serve him without fear in holiness and righteousness in his presence all [their] days" (vv. 74–75). Again, covenant and sanctification are joined.

We observe the same phenomenon at the Lord's Supper. Paul recounts to the Corinthians Jesus's institution of the Supper and adds words of correction. Paul rebukes the Corinthians for violating the horizontal dimension of union with Christ—union with other believers. The wealthy were feasting while the poor at the table with them had little to eat at the meal. As a result, God was disciplining the rich with sickness, illness, and even death for their sins (1 Cor 11:30). Paul enjoins the Corinthians to examine themselves and partake of the Supper in faith (vv. 27–29). The Supper is one of God's instruments of sanctification. And if the Corinthians heed Paul's correction, they will be spared God's temporal judgments.

Preservation

Paul quotes Jesus's words, "This cup is the new covenant in my blood" (1 Cor 11:25). Then Paul tells how God has visited many of the Corinthian believers with temporal judgments for their abuses at the Lord's table (v. 30). Ironically, Paul's words of judgment assure the errant Corinthians that God will keep them saved, even if he brings upon them such temporal punishments: "If we were properly judging ourselves, we would not be judged, but when we are judged by the Lord, we are disciplined, so that we may not be condemned with the world" (vv. 31–32). In this new-covenant text, then, Paul affirms God's preservation of his saints.

Hebrews' five warning passages are well-known. Not as well-known are the strong preservation passages in Heb 6:17–20 and 7:23–25.[33] In the latter text the writer affirms that Jesus, our great high priest, is "the guarantee of a better covenant" (v. 22). In this context the writer affirms Jesus's resurrection and its implication for his priesthood and the security of God's people: "Because he remains forever, he holds his priesthood permanently. Therefore, he is able to save completely those who come to God through him, since he always lives to intercede for them" (vv. 24–25). One aspect of the new and better covenant is God's declaration that Jesus will preserve his people for final salvation.

Hebrews extols Christ's magnificent and efficacious sacrifice and the resultant safety of his people: "By one offering he has perfected forever those who are sanctified" (Heb 10:14). Next the writer quotes Jeremiah's new-covenant passage: "This is the covenant I will make with them after those days, the Lord says, I will put my laws on their hearts and write them on their minds, and I will never again remember their sins and their lawless acts" (vv. 16–17). Twice Hebrews proclaims preservation, for Christ "has perfected forever" his people (v. 14) and promises to "never again remember their sins." The new covenant embraces eternal security.

---

[33] See Christopher Wade Cowan, "'Confident of Better Things': Assurance of Salvation in the Letter to the Hebrews," Ph.D. diss., The Southern Baptist Theological Seminary, 2012.

Eternal Life and Glorification

At his institution of the Lord's Supper, Jesus—after calling the cup "my blood of the covenant" (Matt 26:28)—says, "I tell you, I will not drink from this fruit of the vine from now on until that day when I drink it new with you in my Father's kingdom" (v. 29). Here, after speaking of the new covenant, Jesus pictures final salvation as sharing wine with his people in his Father's kingdom.

In Paul's version of the institution of the Supper, Jesus labels the cup "the new covenant in my blood" (1 Cor 11:25), then Paul adds an eschatological note: "As often as you eat this bread and drink the cup, you proclaim the Lord's death until he comes" (v. 26). Here Scripture connects the new covenant and Jesus's return, which Scripture teaches initiates final salvation.

Hebrews also links the new covenant and eternal life. After extolling Christ's blood, which secured "eternal redemption" (9:12) the writer announces, "He is the mediator of a new covenant, so that those who are called might receive the promise of the eternal inheritance" (v. 15). At the end of the same chapter Hebrews asserts that Christ "will appear a second time, not to bear sin, but to bring salvation to those who are waiting for him" (v. 28).

Matthew, Paul, and Hebrews thus tether the new covenant to the final kingdom of God, Jesus's return, and the salvation he will bring. These pictures overlap with eternal life and glorification.

Conclusion

This chapter has investigated the interface between the ten aspects of salvation treated in separate chapters and six key biblical-theological themes. As a result, we see how election, union, regeneration, calling, conversion, justification, adoption, sanctification, preservation, and eternal life and glorification crisscross these themes:

- Salvation and the Trinity
- Salvation as individual, corporate, and cosmic
- Salvation and God's sovereignty and human responsibility
- Salvation and the "already" and "not yet"

- Salvation and the kingdom of God
- Salvation and covenant

This points to the interdependence and coherence of biblical teaching, viewed in terms either of discrete systematic doctrines or of their place in biblical theology. We next turn our attention to the ways in which the doctrines of salvation impact the Christian life.

Salvation and the Christian Life

12

We examined ten aspects of salvation from both exegetical and systematic perspectives. Then we harmonized those doctrines under the biblical-theological themes of salvation and the Trinity; salvation as individual, corporate, and cosmic; God's sovereignty and human responsibility; the "already" and the "not yet"; the kingdom of God; and covenant. Now we explore how these ten doctrines function and what they contribute to our understanding and practice of the Christian life: union with Christ, election, regeneration, calling, conversion, justification, adoption, sanctification, perseverance, and eternal life and glorification.

Our Election

We Praise God

Both Testaments affirm that the sole author of election is God (Deut 14:2; Eph 1:4). He chooses individuals for salvation (Acts 13:48; Rom 9:15, 18) who corporately constitute the church. Election is based on God's love (Deut 7:7–8; Rom 9:16; 2 Tim 1:9) and will (Eph 1:11; Rom 9:11–13). God's foreknowledge is not mere precognition but refers to his setting his covenantal affection on his people (Rom 8:29; 11:2). God chose people in eternity past with a view to eternity future. Election confirms that salvation is by grace alone, giving all the glory to God alone. What is the result of all this for God's people? Paul answers loudly and clearly:

Blessed is the God and Father of our Lord Jesus Christ, who has blessed us with every spiritual blessing in the heavens in Christ. For he chose us in him, before the foundation of the world, to be holy and blameless in love before him. He predestined us to be adopted as sons through Jesus Christ for himself, according to the good pleasure of his will, to the praise of his glorious grace that he lavished on us in the Beloved One. (Eph 1:3–6)

In him we have also received an inheritance, because we were predestined according to the plan of the one who works out everything in agreement with the purpose of his will, so that we who had already put our hope in Christ might bring praise to his glory. (vv. 11–12)

Paul's answer in a word is *praise*, as Mariam Kamel explains: "When we encounter the love of God as revealed in his very character, adoration and doxology should be our response."[1] Believers, who are "brothers and sisters loved by the Lord, because from the beginning God has chosen [them] for salvation" (2 Thess 2:13), bless God the Father for choosing them before creation (v. 3). They praise the "good pleasure of his will" and "his glorious grace" for predestining them to be his loved children (vv. 5–6). They exult in the "praise of his glory" for such a rich salvation in Christ (v. 12). Baugh captures Paul's spirit:

Paul recounts three times in 1:3–14 how God's incredible redemption, revealed and accomplished in Christ, redounds "for the praise of the glory of his grace" (v. 6) and "for praise of his glory" (vv. 12, 14). For this reason, Paul not only recounts these as facts, but he is here *praising* the glory of his grace in benediction form: "Blessed (be) the God and Father of our Lord Jesus Christ. . . ." Here doctrine and practice meet in sweet fellowship of grateful praise.[2]

---

[1] Mariam J. Kamel, "How Does God's Love Inspire Social Justice?" in *The Love of God*, ed. Christopher W. Morgan, Theology in Community (Wheaton: Crossway, 2016), 211.

[2] S. M. Baugh, *Ephesians*, Evangelical Exegetical Commentary (Bellingham, WA: Lexham, 2016), 101–2.

We Embrace Our Mission

It is important to see doctrines in relationship to and in proportion with one another. So let's reflect on the past chapters and ask, why are we saved? We have seen that the Bible gives many reasons (beginning with the more ultimate reasons):

- Because God deserves to be praised.
- Because God loves us.
- Because God planned to save us.
- Because Jesus died for us.
- Because we heard the gospel.
- Because the Holy Spirit convicted us of sin and drew us to faith.
- Because we trusted Christ.

Our salvation is tied to God's glory, God's love, God's plan, Christ's death, the Spirit's work, the gospel message, and our faith in Christ. Our faith does not save us; God saves us through Christ. But our faith receives what God has done for us in Christ. We are never the source, ground, or cause of our salvation; God is. He is the Savior; we are the saved. He is the Redeemer; we are the redeemed. But salvation is by grace through faith, so we trust, we believe, we have faith, we repent (Eph 2:8–9).

We also learned that salvation comes through hearing "the word of truth, the gospel of your salvation" (Eph 1:13). This means that anyone speaking of election without speaking of missions fails to do justice to the Bible. In Gen 12:1–3 God chooses Abraham, promising, "I will make you into a great nation, I will bless you, I will make your name great." And God commissions him: "You will be a blessing. . . . and all the peoples on earth will be blessed through you." Abraham is chosen for the glory of God, for salvation, and for the sake of mission.

In Exod 19:5–6 God states his choice of Israel. They are his covenant people—his treasured possession, his kingdom of priests, his holy nation. The particularity is striking: out of all the nations, you are mine, God says. Even more striking is that God's particularity is for the sake of universality: out of all the nations, you are mine; *and* the whole earth is mine, so you will be for me a kingdom of priests and a holy nation. God is on a mission to save, and he plans to reach the nations through his chosen people. They will witness to him and his ways through their distinctiveness as his holy nation. And they will witness to him through their proclamation as a kingdom of priests, "bringing the knowledge of God to the nations, and bringing the nations to the means of atonement with God."[3]

Paul writes similarly in Romans 9–10. We ought to notice how he begins and ends this incredibly complex treatment on salvation history, Israel, the church, divine election, and human responsibility. He begins this theological discourse by stating his intense and unceasing burden for the salvation of his people, the Jews. He so longs for their salvation that he seems willing to go to hell in order for them to be saved, if that were actually possible (9:1–5). Then, after his hefty theological arguments about election and salvation history, Paul underlines his deep desire and prayer for the conversion of the Jews. He then reminds that "Everyone who calls on the name of the Lord will be saved" (10:13). But how will others call on Jesus without believing in Jesus? How will they believe without hearing the gospel? And how will they hear without someone telling them? Paul then reiterates the necessity of the gospel: faith comes through hearing, and hearing through the word of God, the gospel (vv. 14–17).[4] In the "Manila Manifesto" global church leaders captured our mission: "We affirm that God is calling the whole church to take the whole gospel to the whole world. So we determine to proclaim it faithfully, urgently, and sacrificially until he comes."[5]

Our Union with Christ

We Find True Community

It is amazing that the Persons of the Trinity indwell one another (*perichoresis*). The Father is in the Son (John 14:10; 17:23), the Son is in the Father

---

[3] Christopher J. H. Wright, *The Mission of God: Unlocking the Bible's Grand Narrative* (Downers Grove: IVP Academic, 2006), 331. Wright also helped us overall on Genesis 12 and Exodus 19.

[4] See J. I. Packer, *Evangelism and the Sovereignty of God* (Downers Grove: InterVarsity, 1973).

[5] The Manila Manifesto, Lausanne Movement website, accessed June 24, 2019, https://www.lausanne.org/content/manifesto/the-manila-manifesto.

(14:20), and the Father and Son are in one another (10:38; 14:10–11, 20; 17:2). Even more amazing is the Scripture's teaching that the Father indwells us (two times), the Son indwells us (six times), and the Holy Spirit indwells us (eight times). The Trinity indwells us!

More amazing still is the fact that we indwell the Trinitarian persons. We are in the Son (John 6:56; 14:20; 15:4–5). We are in the Father and the Son (17:20–21; 1 Thess 1:1; 2 Thess 1:1). It is important to clarify that all this is relational and covenantal, not ontological. The Bible maintains the Creator/creature distinction. God will always be our God, and we will always be his creatures. Further, the three Trinitarian persons indwell one another eternally by nature; that it what it means to be the Trinity. By contrast, their indwelling us and our indwelling them begins at conversion by God's grace through faith in the Son of God.

Further, not only are we personally in Christ, but so are all true believers. This means we are also united with one another (Eph 2:11–22; 3:3–6). Being in Christ, therefore, enables us to live in community with our Triune God and with one another! What a massive privilege it is to be the church, as How Chuang Chua of Singapore highlights:

> The church is the worldwide people of God, the community of those who have been redeemed by the work of Jesus Christ. The church transcends ethnic, cultural, and racial lines, being comprised of all those who have repented of their sin and trusted in Christ alone for their salvation. The church is the single most important institution on earth, the organism through which God advances his kingdom. . . . Indeed, the essential identity of the church as communal and relational is rooted in the eternal and blessed community of the Godhead. . . . While the church is created through the redemptive work of the triune God, it finds diverse expressions in different contexts in the form of local congregations. . . . The ultimate goal of the church is nothing less than the glory of God, expressed from every corner of the globe.[6]

---

[6] How Chuang Chua, "The Importance of the Global Church," in *ESV Global Study Bible* (Wheaton: Crossway, 2012), 1863–64.

We Discover Our Identity

Union with Christ defines us as God's people. Like "all the saints in Christ
Jesus who are in Philippi" (Phil 1:1), we too are "saints in Christ Jesus."
We are among the people who participate in Jesus's story. We died with
Christ (Rom 6:3–8), were raised with him (vv. 4–8), ascended with him
(Eph 2:6), and even will come again with him (Rom 8:19; Col 3:4). Union
with Christ brings us into an intimate relationship with him, likened to
the most intimate of human relationships—that between husband and wife
(1 Cor 6:15–17).

Even more, Ephesians reminds us of our identity in Christ. We are not
outsiders but included and chosen in Christ. We are not slaves but adopted
in Christ. We are the people of God, the body of Christ, the temple of
the Spirit.

Union also defines our identity permanently, for God sealed us "in"
Christ (Eph 1:13) "for the day of redemption" (4:30). Union thus tells us
who we are, those formerly separated from Christ and salvation and now
joined to him spiritually forever. Being "in Christ" motivates us to live for the
Father who planned our union with his Son, for him who died and arose so
that we would be united to him, and for the Spirit who effected union with
the Son. As Kenyan theologian James H. O. Kombo notes,

> While the Bible recognizes and ultimately rejoices in racial distinc-
> tion (Rev. 5:9–10; 7:9–10), it also teaches the equality of all peoples
> regardless of race or ethnicity (Eph. 2:14–18). In Christ, there is only
> one people, one nation, one "tribe" . . . (Gal. 3:28–29). . . . Identity in
> Christ supersedes all other identities. Moreover, all people are cre-
> ated in the image of God (Gen. 1:26–27; 9:6). And so, as we learn to
> resist the exaltation of ourselves or our ethnicity that our sin nature
> promotes, we can joyfully exult in the wonder of being included in
> the one nation that the Christian gospel produces—the "tribe" of
> Christ (Eph. 4:3–7).[7]

---

[7] James H. O. Kombo, "Social Ethics," in *ESV Global Study Bible* (Wheaton:
Crossway, 2012), 1903–4.

Our Regeneration

We Worship Our Triune God

Jesus defines regeneration as spiritual resurrection: "Truly I tell you, anyone who hears my word and believes him who sent me has eternal life and will not come under judgment but has passed from death to life" (John 5:24). Paul regards regeneration as a powerful illustration of grace: "God, who is rich in mercy, because of his great love that he had for us, made us alive with Christ even though we were dead in trespasses. You are saved by grace!" (Eph 2:4–5). The Trinity participates in the regeneration of believers, who constitute the church. The Father planned our regeneration (1 Pet 1:3), the resurrection of the Son empowers it (v. 3), and the Spirit effects it (John 3:8). Peter speaks for all believers when he prefaces his treatment of regeneration thus: "Blessed be the God and Father of our Lord Jesus Christ" (1 Pet 1:3).

We Bear Fruit

Regeneration, God's giving new life to the spiritually dead (Titus 3:5–6), is supernatural (John 3:8), is instantaneous (5:24), and leads to lifelong faith (1 John 5:1). It fulfills God's promise to circumcise people's hearts so they "will love him with all [their] heart and all [their] soul" (Deut 30:6). "The Spirit gives life" (2 Cor 3:6) and enables those born again to "show sincere brotherly love for each other, from a pure heart" and to "love one another constantly" (1 Pet 1:22–23).

First John accents the effects of regeneration on the Christian life. John's letter affirms that regeneration produces faith, holiness, and love. John offers a rhetorical question: "Who is the one who conquers the world but the one who believes that Jesus is the Son of God?" (1 John 5:5). He points to the source of saving faith: "Everyone who believes that Jesus is the Christ has been born of God (v. 1). Genuine faith in Jesus is the result of regeneration.

Holiness too is the result of the new birth, for Christ came to abolish sin:

> You know that he was revealed so that he might take away sins, and there is no sin in him. Everyone who remains in him does not sin; everyone who sins has not seen him or known him. (1 John 3:5–6)

The Son of God was revealed for this purpose: to destroy the devil's works. Everyone who has been born of God does not sin, because his seed remains in him; he is not able to sin, because he has been born of God. (vv. 8–9)

Indeed, regeneration produces godliness: "We know that everyone who has been born of God does not sin, but the one who is born of God keeps him, and the evil one does not touch him" (5:18). This is not sinless perfection (1:8, 10), for the Christian life involves confession of sin (v. 9), but it does mean walking "in the light, as . . . the blood of Jesus his Son cleanses us from all sin" (v. 7).

Regeneration's new life also manifests itself in love in the church, as John explains: "Dear friends, let us love one another, because love is from God, and everyone who loves has been born of God and knows God" (1 John 4:7). Genuine love assures believers that they "have passed from death to life" (3:14), but "Everyone who hates his brother or sister is a murderer, and you know that no murderer has eternal life residing in him" (v. 15).

We Share the Gospel

The Holy Spirit is God's agent in regeneration (John 3:8; Titus 3:5–6). And the Spirit uses the gospel to give new life: believers "have been born again—not of perishable seed but of imperishable—through the living and enduring word of God" (1 Pet 1:23; cf. Jas 1:18). This emboldens those who know the Lord to share the good news with those who don't know the Lord, for the Spirit working through the Word brings new life.

We Have Hope

Jesus's "one righteous act" of dying on the cross brings new life: Just as Adam's primal sin brought "condemnation for everyone, so also through [Christ's] one righteous act there is justification leading to life for everyone" (Rom 5:18). Jesus's resurrection along with his cross offer great hope: "Blessed be the God and Father of our Lord Jesus Christ. Because of his great mercy he has given us new birth into a living hope through the resurrection of Jesus Christ from the dead and into an inheritance that is imperishable, undefiled, and unfading, kept in heaven for you" (1 Pet 1:3–4). Because Jesus is alive, believers have new life now and God's promise of resurrection unto eternal life at Jesus's return (1 Cor 15:20–22).

Our Calling

We Are Confident in the Gospel

The gospel call is necessary for salvation (Rom 10:8–17), so we must promote it by praying, supporting missionaries, and witnessing. God uses the universal gospel to invite people to faith in Jesus. He also issues his performative call that brings people to salvation. If the church is faithful, all will hear the gospel call, in keeping with the spirit of God's prophets in both Testaments:

> "Turn to me and be saved, all the ends of the earth. For I am God, and there is no other." (Isa 45:22)

> The Lord . . . is patient with you, not wanting any to perish but all to come to repentance. (2 Pet 3:9)

Luke shows how calling promotes evangelism. In Philippi Paul, Silas, and Timothy sat down by a river to share the gospel with women gathered there, one of whom was "a God-fearing woman named Lydia" (Acts 16:14). As Paul gave the gospel call, God effectively called her to salvation: "The Lord opened her heart to respond to what Paul was saying" and she believed the gospel and was baptized along with her household (vv. 14–15). This is a model for us today. Prayerfully we share the gospel with those whom God brings into our lives. Our confidence rests in God's effectively calling some of them to himself, as he did Lydia. In the same way, God promised Paul when he was in Corinth that he had "many people in this city" (18:10). This promise encouraged Paul to keep evangelizing for another year and a half (v. 11), and the preaching of the gospel led to many conversions.

We Enjoy Real Change

Scripture underscores our identity by revealing short- and long-term results of God's calling people to himself to become members of his church. God wills that his call produces commendable lives now that reflect unity (Eph 4:1), freedom (Gal 5:13), harmony (Col 3:15), holiness (1 Thess 4:7), and faithfulness amidst suffering (1 Pet 2:21). God promises long-term results too: believers' obtaining an "eternal inheritance" (Heb 9:15) and the "glory of our Lord Jesus Christ" (2 Thess 2:14). By God's grace we will not fail to attain this grand inheritance and glory, because he will "restore, establish, strengthen, and support" us to the end (1 Pet 5:10).

Our Conversion

We Accept That Our Conversion May Differ from Others

Conversion is God's turning people from sin (repentance) to Christ (faith). Repentance and faith are necessary for salvation, inseparable, and not identical. Scripture records different styles of conversion, including Paul's exciting one (Acts 9:5) and Timothy's quiet one (2 Tim 1:5; 3:15). The significant thing is not whether a conversion is exciting or quiet but that it is real. Costa Rican scholar Orlando Costas also reminds us of the occurrence of group conversions:

> The concept of multi-individual decisions gives a sociological orientation to the experience of conversion because it affirms that conversion, which depends on a personal act of faith in Christ, can take place in a group setting, where all the members of a given group (family, clan, tribe or mutual interest group) participate in a similar experience with Christ after considering it together and deciding to turn to Christ at the same time.[8]

Whether exciting or quiet, individual or group, our conversion is one important way to portray what it means to be Christian. It is to say that we are the people who have turned from the realm of sin to that of the Father, Son, and Holy Spirit.

---

[8] Timothy C. Tennent, *Theology in the Context of World Christianity* (Grand Rapids: Zondervan, 2007), 99, citing Orlando Costas, *The Church and Its Mission: A Shattering Critique from the Third World* (Wheaton: Tyndale, 1974), 128.

Anthony Hoekema affirms that all conversions involve intellect, emotion, and volition and that one of these elements may predominate. He cites the intellectual conversion of C. S. Lewis, the emotional conversion of John Bunyan, and the volitional conversion of Augustine,[9] though, of course, every conversion has all three elements to some extent. Once again, we learn that no type of conversion is normative. The important thing is that by God's grace we have turned from sin to embrace Christ as he is offered in the gospel.

We Repent, Initially and As a Way of Life

Both repentance and faith are initial and ongoing. Initial repentance, also called evangelical repentance, occurs once and for all when someone turns from one's sins to Christ. We saw that repentance is relational and personal and that ongoing repentance, also called Christian repentance, is the result of initial repentance. It means turning from sin again and again and turning to Christ as an integral part of the Christian life. As Christians walk with Christ, they do not deny their sins but confess them daily: "If we say, 'We have no sin,' we are deceiving ourselves, and the truth is not in us. If we confess our sins, he is faithful and righteous to forgive us our sins and to cleanse us from all unrighteousness. If we say, 'We have not sinned,' we make him a liar, and his word is not in us" (1 John 1:8–10). Even when we are not conscious of sin, "The blood of Jesus his Son cleanses us from all sin" (v. 7).

We Have Faith, Initially and As a Way of Life

Faith too is initial and lifelong. Initial faith is trust in Christ as Lord and Savior as he is offered to us in the gospel (John 3:16; Gal 2:16). Faith is only as good as its object, and Paul describes the genuine object of saving faith: "Faith comes from what is heard, and what is heard comes through the message about Christ" (Rom 10:17). Our faith saves because we put our trust in the God who raises the dead, in Jesus Christ and him crucified.

---

[9] Hoekema, *Saved by Grace*, 117–20 (see chap. 3, n. 78).

We distinguish initial saving faith from lifelong Christian faith. Lifelong faith is a vital aspect of the Christian life, for daily "We walk by faith, not by sight" (2 Cor 5:7). Paul is our model, for he testified, "The life I now live in the body, I live by faith in the Son of God, who loved me and gave himself for me" (Gal 2:20). Our heart's desire should be for our faith to increase (2 Cor 10:15) and even to "flourish" (2 Thess 1:3).

Our Justification

We Glorify Our Triune God

Amazingly, the three persons of the Trinity all play roles in our justification. The Father serves as the judge who "justifies the ungodly" (Rom 4:5). The Son dies in our place and rises again as the basis of our justification (4:25). His death averts God's wrath from us (3:25–26) and obtains rightness for us (5:18–19). The Holy Spirit enables our faith, that we might believe and be justified (1 Cor 6:11). We as believing individuals constitute the church that "Christ loved" and for whom he "gave himself" (Eph 5:25).

Justification glorifies God's character. In Christ's death God maintains his moral integrity and justifies the ungodly. This is possible because in the cross God revealed both his grace and his righteousness as nothing else ever could (Rom 3:25–26). In response we glorify such a righteous and gracious God.

We Live Forgiven and Free

Justification identifies us as the people whom God declares righteous when we believe in Jesus as Lord and Savior. A holy God, who knows our sins better than we ever will, justifies us in his Son. He imputes Christ's righteousness to us (Rom 4:3; 5:19; 2 Cor 5:21). Consequently, God accepts us forever in his Son, which brings us many benefits.

First, free justification brings the forgiveness of sins to everyone who believes in Jesus. When he instituted the Lord's Supper for the Christian community, Jesus said of the cup, "This is my blood of the covenant, which is poured out for many for the forgiveness of sins" (Matt 26:28). Quoting Psalm 32, Paul equates the positive imputation of righteousness with the non-imputation of sin: "David also speaks of the blessing of the person to whom God credits righteousness apart from works: 'Blessed are those whose lawless acts are forgiven and whose sins are covered. Blessed is the person the Lord will never charge with sin'" (Rom 4:6–8).

Second, justification by grace through faith in Christ liberates us from everything the law could not (Gal 2:16). We are free from bondage to legalism, though Paul cautions against abusing our freedom:

> For freedom, Christ set us free. Stand firm, then, and don't submit again to a yoke of slavery. (Gal 5:1)

> You were called to be free, brothers and sisters; only don't use this freedom as an opportunity for the flesh, but serve one another through love. (v. 13)

As a result, justification brings great confidence of final salvation. When we turn from our own efforts to earn God's favor and instead trust Christ as our substitute, he "the righteous one" will "make many to be accounted righteous," for "he shall bear their iniquities" (Isa 53:11 ESV). As a result, we know that our sins are forgiven, as Calvin eloquently explains:

> If we ask in what way the conscience can be made quiet before God, we shall find the only way to be that unmerited righteousness be conferred upon us as a gift from God. . . . Consequently, the inheritance arises from faith in order to establish the promise according to grace. . . . We must come to the sacrifice by which God has been appeased. . . . In short, we must seek peace for ourselves solely in the anguish of Christ our Redeemer.[10]

This confidence and freedom enable us to stop trying to satisfy God with good works and instead invest ourselves in loving God and loving others, which essentially coincide. Luther put it penetratingly: "God does not need our good works, but our neighbor does."[11] Michael Horton ably captures

---

[10] John Calvin, *Institutes of the Christian Religion*, ed. John T. McNeill, trans. Ford Lewis Battles, 2 vols. (Philadelphia: Westminster, 1960), 3.13.3, 4 (1.765–67).

[11] Gustaf Wingren, *Luther on Vocation*, trans. Carl C. Rasmussen (Philadelphia: Muhlenberg Press, 1957; repr., Evansville, IN: Ballast, 2004), 2.

Luther's point: "God descends to serve humanity through our vocations, so instead of seeing good works as our works for God, they are now to be seen as God's work for our neighbor, which God performs through us. . . . When we are overwhelmed by the superabundance of God's gracious gift, we express our gratitude in horizontal works of love and service to the neighbor."[12]

Our Adoption

We Marvel at God's Love

God freed us, once slaves to sin and self (Gal 4:3, 7), and invited us into his family as sons (John 1:12). If we seek the ultimate reasons for our adoption, Paul supplies them: God adopted us "in love" and "according to the purpose of his will" (Eph 1:5 ESV). All this results in the "praise of his glorious grace that he lavished on us in the Beloved One" (v. 6).

We Delight in Being God's Children

The Trinitarian persons all participated in our adoption. The Father "predestined us to be adopted as sons" (Eph 1:5), "We have redemption through [the Son's] blood" (v. 7), and the "Spirit of adoption" enabled us to "cry out, '*Abba,* Father!'" (Rom 8:15). Astonishingly, the Father adopts us by grace through faith in his Son, and as a result we belong to our Father, and he to us! Our identity in Christ (Gal 3:26) is now as sons and daughters of the living God (4:4–5): "I will be a Father to you, and you will be sons and daughters to me, says the Lord Almighty" (2 Cor 6:18). All believers "have access in one Spirit to the Father" and are "members of God's household" in the church (Eph 2:18–19).

Packer vividly depicts what adoption means for the Christian life:

Do I know my own real identity? I am a child of God. God is my Father, heaven is my home, every day is one day nearer. My Saviour

---

[12] Michael S. Horton, *People and Place: A Covenant Ecclesiology* (Louisville: Westminster John Knox, 2008), 304. Note also Edwards, *Charity and Its Fruits,* 97: "God makes men the instruments of doing good to others. . . . Yea, He makes them like Himself, the great Fountain of all good, who is forever pouring down His blessings on mankind."

is my brother, every Christian is my brother too. Say it over and over to yourself first thing in the morning, last thing at night, . . . and ask that you may be enabled to live as one who knows it is all utterly and completely true. For this is the Christian's secret of—a happy life?—yes, certainly, but we have something both higher and profounder to say. This is the Christian's secret of a *Christian* life, and of a *God-honouring* life.[13]

We Belong to God's Family

Adoption entails responsibilities. First, although adoption means future glory, it also means present suffering: If "we suffer with him," we also will "be glorified with him" (Rom 8:17). Second, we submit to our heavenly Father's discipline, for "The Lord disciplines the one he loves" (Heb 12:6). He does this "for our benefit, so that we can share his holiness" (v. 10). Though we were formerly slaves, Christ redeems us with his blood and the Father adopts us, and as a result we enjoy the freedom of God's children (Gal 5:1, 13).

Adoption also brings great benefits, including assurance of salvation. The same Spirit of sonship who enables us to call God "Father" (Rom 8:15) also "himself testifies together with our spirit that we are God's children" (v. 16). Belonging to God's family carries great hope:

"Dear friends, we are God's children now, and what we will be has not yet been revealed. We know that when he appears, we will be like him because we will see him as he is" (1 John 3:2).

God adopts us as sons and heirs (Gal 4:7), "heirs of God and coheirs with Christ" (Rom 8:17). As a result we rejoice in our current sonship and long for its final manifestation (v. 23).

Our Sanctification

We Grow in Holiness

As with all aspects of the application of salvation, sanctification occurs in union with Christ (Rom 6:4, 6). The Trinity performs sanctification. The

---

[13] J. I. Packer, *Knowing God*, 20th anniversary edition (Downers Grove: InterVarsity, 1993), 207–8.

Father disciplines us to make us holy (Heb 12:9–10). The Son "loved the church and gave himself for her to make her holy" (Eph 5:25–26). The Holy Spirit also plays a pivotal role and is most associated with our sanctification: "From the beginning God has chosen you for salvation through sanctification by the Spirit and through belief in the truth" (2 Thess 2:13).

In initial sanctification the Holy Spirit sets us apart from sin to God and holiness, identifying us as saints (1 Cor 1:2). In final sanctification the Spirit will perfect us in holiness (1 John 3:2). The Spirit also energizes progressive sanctification, our growth in holiness, in which we take part (Phil 2:12–13; Col 1:29). The Spirit's power enables us to "remain" in Christ and bear fruit (John 15:4). Progressive sanctification pertains to both individuals and the church (1 Thess 4:3–7; Heb 4:1, 11, 16). God wants his saints to obey him and to strive for holiness (Eph 4:20–32; 1 Thess 4:3–7).

We Progress amidst Tensions

Various tensions mark progressive sanctification. First, we need both theological and practical knowledge to grow in holiness. We grow in God's Word and through life together with others, suffering, and other experiences (Jas 1:2–25). Second, sanctification embraces divine and human effort. God alone is holy (Isa 48:17) and sovereign (45:7; 1 Tim 6:15). Our holiness is his gift (2 Pet 1:3). His prior grace prompts our love and obedience. As we rely on the Holy Spirit and struggle against sin, he produces fruit in our lives and beyond (Gal 5:16, 22–23).

Third, sanctification involves repentance, daily turning from sin to holiness (Titus 2:11–12). This involves negative and positive aspects. We put off pride and put on love (Eph 4:20–32). Fourth, sanctification encompasses what God has done (the "already") and what he will yet do (the "not yet"). We have already been definitively sanctified as God's saints. But we will fight against sin until we go to Christ or he comes for us. We long for the entire sanctification that God promises, and we are confident that God "who calls [us] is faithful; he will do it" (1 Thess 5:24).

Fifth, sanctification takes place within the biblical tension between statements of fact concerning God's grace (the "indicative") and his orders for the Christian life (the "imperative"). The indicative of Christ's saving work is the foundation upon which we build the Christian life. However, we are active and not passive as we seek to grow in grace and holiness. We respond to God's imperatives and dedicate ourselves to him from the heart. Sixth, our pursuit of sanctification includes victories and defeats. With Paul we sometimes cry out in frustration (Rom 7:24). Yet we rejoice in the overcoming grace of God that does not give up on us (Col 1:29), for "We are more than conquerors through him who loved us" (Rom 8:37).

Because we live in the "not yet" of final salvation, we unavoidably live with the tensions of progressive sanctification. We must face them directly, acknowledging our weakness and our need for God's power to live the Christian life. We need the Scriptures and prayer, and we need the church, the people of God who love and support us. We need by God's grace to follow the example of Jesus, as Kamel reminds us: "The model of Jesus shapes a holy people into his humble likeness, people who *know* God and live according to the Spirit in their midst, and therefore love what and who God loves."[14] We need to serve God and others. With Paul we seek to "hold true" to what "we have attained" in Christ (Phil 3:16). God has accepted us, and as a result he is ours and we are his. Nevertheless, again with Paul we confess, "Not that I have already obtained this or am already perfect, but I press on to make it my own, because Christ Jesus has made me his own. Brothers, I do not consider that I have made it my own. But one thing I do: forgetting what lies behind and straining forward to what lies ahead, I press on toward the goal for the prize of the upward call of God in Christ Jesus" (vv. 12–14).

Our Preservation

We Enjoy Assurance

God saves us and keeps us until the end. Each person of the Trinity has acted on our behalf. The Father chose and keeps us (John 6:38–40; 10:28–29; Rom 8:1; 1 Cor 11:31–32). The Son saved us by his death and resurrection and preserves us (John 6:37, 39, 40, 44; 10:28–30; 17:9, 11, 12, 15, 24; 1 John 5:18). The Spirit is the Father's seal (2 Cor 1:22; Eph 1:13; 4:30), guaranteeing our salvation until the final "day of redemption" (v. 4:30).

---

[14] Kamel, "How Does God's Love Inspire Social Justice," 226.

God secures the preservation of his people through his divine attributes of sovereignty (Rom 8:28–30), justice (vv. 33–34), love (vv. 35–39), power (John 10:28), and faithfulness (1 Cor 1:8–9; 1 Thess 5:23–24). Christ's saving deeds assure us of final salvation: his cross (Rom 5:19), resurrection (Heb 7:23–25), intercession (v. 25), and second coming (John 14:2–3). God's saving and keeping us makes us who we are: his people "called, loved by God the Father and kept for Jesus Christ" (Jude 1).

The Trinity's work in saving us and keeping us is the ground of our assurance. The means of assurance are threefold: the promises of God's Word (John 10:28; Rom 8:1; Heb 7:24–25), the internal witness of the Holy Spirit (Rom 5:1–5; 8:16; 1 John 5:6–10), and believers' spiritual growth (Luke 8:11–15; 2 Pet 1:3–9; 1 John 2:3–6). Paul combines all three means of assurance in Rom 5:1–10.

We Persevere by Grace

True believers persevere to the end in faith (John 6:66–69; Col 1:19–23), holiness (Matt 5:8; Heb 12:14), and love (Matt 22:37–39; John 15:12; 1 Pet 1:22). God's preservation of us ensures our perseverance in faith (1 Cor 1:4–9; 1 Thess 5:23–24). Our perseverance confirms his preservation of us (Matt 7:16–23; John 15:1–8). Scripture identifies believers as those who conquer/overcome (Rom 8:28–39; 1 John 5:5; Rev 2:7, 11).

We Heed Warnings against Apostasy

Scripture warns the people of God against the danger of apostasy, of abandoning the Christian faith (Matt 24:9–10; 1 Tim 4:1; Heb 3:12). One of God's means of keeping his people saved and urging them to persevere is these warnings of apostasy. First John 2:18–19 integrates perseverance and apostasy and assures us that true believers do not apostatize.

The writer to the Hebrews impressively coordinates preservation, perseverance, assurance, and apostasy. After giving an exhortation to persevere (6:1–3), he then sounds the alarm against apostasy (vv. 4–6) before assuring the majority of his readers that they are saved (vv. 7–10). He follows an exhortation to persevere, given to bolster assurance (vv. 11–12), with a strong passage on preservation (vv. 13–20).

Our Eternal Life and Glorification

We Rejoice in Our Restoration

We were created in the image of God to worship and display God, but we all refused to acknowledge God's glory and instead sought our own glory. Through this we forfeited the glory God intended for us as his image-bearers. By his grace and through union with Christ, the perfect image, however, God saves us, restoring us as full image-bearers to participate in and reflect the glory we longed for the whole time. Thus, we are recipients of glory, are undergoing transformation through glory, and will be sharers of glory. Our salvation is not merely from sin but is also unto glory. We who exchanged the glory of God for idols, we who rebelled against God's glory, have been, are being, and will be completely transformed by the very glory we despised and rejected (Rom 1:18–31; 3:23; 8:28–30; 9:23; 2 Cor 3:18). Let's rejoice "in the hope of the glory of God" (Rom 5:2).

We Bear Christ's Image

The image of God, in which we were created (Gen 1:26–27), still exists in our being. Its function was tarnished in the fall but is gradually restored in Christ (Col 3:9–10; Eph 4:22–24). Amazingly, we are being transformed from glory to glory, as Paul expresses: "We all, with unveiled faces, are looking as in a mirror at the glory of the Lord and are being transformed into the same image from glory to glory; this is from the Lord who is the Spirit" (2 Cor 3:18). The image will be perfected when Christ, the true image (2 Cor 4:4; Col 1:15), powerfully conforms us to his image in resurrection: "He will transform the body of our humble condition into the likeness of his glorious body, by the power that enables him to subject everything to himself" (Phil 3:21). Ferguson points out, "The image and image-bearers are one in Spirit to the end, so that when Christ appears in glory image-bearers are one with him in that glory (Col 3:4). We are raised in Christ, with Christ, by Christ, to be like Christ."[15] In the meantime we know "Christ in [us], the hope of glory" (Col 1:27).

---

[15] Sinclair B. Ferguson, *The Holy Spirit*, CCT (Downers Grove: InterVarsity, 1996), 251.

We Get Ready for Christ's Return

Paul speaks of how God's grace teaches believers to live for God in the present while they look to the future with hope infused with joy (Titus 2:11–13). The NT says much about last things but never loses sight of the most important thing: the return of Christ. The OT pointed to the future "day of the Lord," when he would right wrongs and punish evildoers (Mal 4:1–6). The NT still speaks of that day (2 Pet 3:10) and even sharpens its focus, sometimes calling it the "day of our Lord Jesus" (2 Cor 1:14; cf. 1 Cor 1:8; Phil 1:6, 10; 2:16), when his glory will be universally magnified.

Most important for the Christian life is how Jesus's return will affect us. Jesus urges spiritual readiness for those who know him:

> "This is why you are also to be ready, because the Son of Man is coming at an hour you do not expect." (Matt 24:44)

> "Watch! Be alert! For you don't know when the time is coming. . . . And what I say to you, I say to everyone: Be alert!" (Mark 13:33, 37)

> "Be alert at all times, praying that you may have strength to escape all these things that are going to take place and to stand before the Son of Man." (Luke 21:36)

Our spiritual readiness concerns our encouragement (1 Thess 4:18), holiness (1 John 3:3), and joy (Titus 2:13).

We Suffer with the End in View

Paul encourages, "I consider that the sufferings of this present time are not worth comparing with the glory that is going to be revealed to us" (Rom 8:18). God will produce "for us an absolutely incomparable eternal weight of glory" (2 Cor 4:17). As believers we are a microcosm of the final redemption of the cosmos, the macrocosm: "The creation itself will also be set free from the bondage of corruption into the glorious freedom of God's children" (Rom 8:21). God will fulfill his purposes for his creation by delivering it from the curse (Rev 22:3) and perfecting us (1 Thess 5:23) and it (2 Pet 3:13). Ferguson puts it well: "The consummation of this glorification awaits the eschaton and the Spirit's ministry in the resurrection. Here, too, the pattern of his working is: as in Christ, so in believers and, by implication, in the universe."[16]

We Wait in Hope of Final Salvation

As Adam in the fall brought death, so Christ in his resurrection brings life (1 Cor 15:21–22). Correcting the Corinthians' faulty understanding that resurrection meant the resuscitation of decaying corpses, Paul teaches that God will change our present bodies into resurrection bodies that are incorruptible, strong, and glorious (vv. 42–44). In fact, the all-powerful Christ will transform our current bodies into resurrection bodies equipped for eternal life on the new earth (Phil 3:20–21).

Christ's work of reconciliation (Col 1:19–20) and redemption will deliver the whole creation. Christ's work results in deliverance for "the creation itself" alongside "God's children" (Rom 8:21). This means our ultimate hope is not a disembodied existence in heaven but a resurrected existence on the new earth. The former is our intermediate hope at death, when we will be "away from the body and at home with the Lord" (2 Cor 5:8). The latter, predicted in the OT (Isa 65:17–25) and expanded upon by Jesus (Matt 19:28) and his apostles (2 Pet 3:13), will be "absolutely incomparable" (2 Cor 4:17).

God will finish what he started. Once and for all God's victory will be consummated. God's judgment will be final, sin will be vanquished, justice will prevail, holiness will predominate, God's glory will be unobstructed, and the kingdom will be realized. God's eternal plan of cosmic reconciliation in Christ will be actualized, and God will be "all in all." The people of God will bear God's image perfectly, serving him, reigning with him, encountering him directly, and worshipping him (Rev 22:1–5). God will receive the worship he is due, and we will be blessed beyond description, finally living to the fullest the realities of being created in his image.

This is the grand finale of the biblical story. And this is our story as well. Not only is all of history headed to this; so are we. No wonder Paul writes, "From him and through him and to him are all things. To him be the glory forever. Amen" (Rom 11:36).

---

[16] Ferguson, *The Holy Spirit*, 249.

13

Salvation and the Glory of God

In Eph 1:3–14 Paul praises the Triune God for our salvation: the Father has chosen us, the Son has redeemed us, and the Spirit is our seal. These blessings of salvation are comprehensive: we have "every spiritual blessing," which includes being chosen, adopted, redeemed, forgiven, reconciled, given an inheritance, sealed, and more (from other passages we could add being called, made alive, justified, sanctified, kept, and glorified). God has accomplished all of this through the saving work of Christ and has applied it through our union with Christ. And at key intervals Paul explicitly incorporates a refrain:

- to the praise of his glorious grace (v. 6)
- praise to his glory (v. 12)
- to the praise of his glory (v. 14)

Paul's point is unmistakable: *the ultimate end of our salvation is not our salvation*, as important as that is. God chose us, adopted us, redeemed us, united us, gave us an inheritance, and sealed us *to the praise of his glory* (vv. 6, 12, 14).

Paul is emphatic: God's glory is his ultimate end.[1] But what does this mean? Ephesians discloses two aspects of this. First, God acts unto the praise of his glory, or to the praise of the glory of his grace. Thus, God's

---

[1] God's glory is the goal of creation; the exodus; Israel; Jesus's ministry, life, death, resurrection, and reign; our salvation; the church; the consummation; and all of salvation history. See Jonathan Edwards, "The End for Which God Created the World," in *God's Passion for His Glory*, ed. John Piper (Wheaton: Crossway, 1998), 125–36.

glory as his ultimate end means that God acts unto the reception of worship and praise of his creation, especially his people. Second, God acts to display himself throughout creation. He displays his love, mercy, grace, kindness, creative work, and wisdom (2:4–10; 3:8–10). God's glory as his ultimate end also means that God acts to display himself, and as he displays himself he communicates his greatness and fullness. That, in and of itself, glorifies him. So, according to Ephesians, God's glory as his ultimate end means that he acts to display himself and communicate his greatness, and that he acts to receive worship.

So let's consider how the glory of God relates to salvation as well as interrelated theological topics.

The Relationship between God's Glory and Salvation

Glory characterizes each person of the Trinity. Paul tells of the "glorious Father" (Eph 1:17), calls Jesus the "Lord of glory" (1 Cor 2:8), and connects the Spirit and glory (1 Cor 15:44; 2 Cor 3:18). Honor and glory fill Paul's doxologies, which praise the "glory of the blessed God" (1 Tim 1:11):

> Now to the King eternal, immortal, invisible, the only God, be honor and glory forever and ever. Amen. (1 Tim 1:17)

> He is the blessed and only Sovereign, the King of kings, and the Lord of lords, who alone is immortal and who lives in unapproachable light, whom no one has seen or can see, to him be honor and eternal power. Amen. (v. 6:15–16)

God's glory is also both intrinsic (internal) and extrinsic (revealed). God's extrinsic glory is the revelation of his intrinsic fullness. Paul, for instance, tethers the extrinsic exhibition of God's glory to a number of his attributes:

- righteousness and justice (Rom 3:21–26; 2 Cor 3:9; 2 Thess 1:8–9)
- power (Rom 6:4, 22; Eph 3:14–21)
- sovereignty (1 Cor 2:7; 2 Cor 4:6; Gal 1:4–5; Eph 1:11–12)
- holiness (Titus 2:11–14)
- wisdom (Rom 16:27; Eph 3:10–11)
- love and grace (Eph 1:6, 12, 14)
- patience and mercy (Rom 9:22–23)

The glorious God glorifies himself through our salvation. In the macro sense, our salvation is unto his glory (Eph 1:3–14). Our salvation broadly conceived also displays and magnifies his sovereignty (Gal 1:4–5), wisdom (Rom 16:25–27), and love and grace (Eph 2:1–10). In more particular aspects of our salvation God glorifies himself too. For example, God's saving us displays his patience and mercy in our election (Rom 9:22–23), his sovereignty in our calling (2 Cor 4:1–6), his love and grace in our new life (Eph 2:4–7), his righteousness and justice in our justification (Rom 3:21–26), and his power and holiness in our sanctification (Eph 3:20–21; Titus 2:11–14).

Humanity

Salvation is for humans, and humans are created in God's image to display God's glory and to give God glory through love, worship, and service. God created us directly and personally, and we experience the Creator-creature distinction. He is our Maker, who created us in his image. As such he distinguishes us from himself, animals, and all creation. Being made in God's image concerns who we are: specially created persons who can know God. It speaks of what we do: serve God's purposes, one another, and his creation. It concerns our relationships: with God, ourselves, others, and creation. Our identity as humans is further clarified as we learn that God has made us as holistic, unified persons with immaterial (our souls) and material parts (our bodies). Fundamentally, God has created us for his glory: to worship, love, delight in, serve, and reflect him. As we will see, sin disrupts this, while salvation restores it.

Sin

Salvation is from sin, and sin is failure to glorify God: "All have sinned and fall short of the glory of God" (Rom 3:23). Despite God's displaying his glory in his creation of the world (Ps 19:1–6) and humanity (Rom 2:14–15), all have refused to give God the glory he deserves: "They did not glorify him as God or show gratitude" (v. 1:21). Humans did not forfeit the image of God in the fall, but it was distorted, so that they glorified themselves or other idols instead of the glorious Creator: "Their thinking became worthless, and their senseless hearts were darkened. Claiming to be wise, they became fools and exchanged the glory of the immortal God for images resembling mortal man, birds, four-footed animals, and reptiles" (vv. 21–23).

So sin is exchanging the glory of the immortal God for idols (Rom 1:23; cf. Ps 106:20; Jer 2:11–12). Sin is falling short of God's glory (Rom 3:23), and sin dishonors his name (2:24). There is troubling irony here: as human beings we refused to acknowledge God's glory and sought our own glory instead. We thereby forfeited the glory God intended for us as his image-bearers. We find ourselves unable to escape sin's dominion, and we stand desperately in need of God's help. Wonderfully, God sent his Son to save us from our sinful condition initially, then gradually, then finally restoring us completely to what God had created us to be: spiritually alive to him and conformed to the image of Christ, reflecting and serving God through serving others and his creation.

Christ's Person

Salvation is through Christ, the image and glory of God. Christ is the second Adam, who by his "one righteous act," his becoming obedient to death on the cross, brings justification and eternal life to all who trust him as Savior (Rom 5:18–19). Gaffin notes, "The gospel-glory of 'Christ, who is the image of God' (2 Cor 4:4), is specifically the glory he possesses as the 'heavenly' image bearer," who has risen and ascended.[2] Further, those previously blinded by Satan see the light of the gospel and believe in the glorious Christ: "God who said, 'Let light shine out of darkness,' has shone in our hearts to give the light of the knowledge of God's glory in the face of Jesus Christ" (v. 6).

Paul often ties together Christ's person and God's glory. Paul uses a confession of faith to proclaim the Son of God's incarnation through to his ascension, when he was "taken up in glory": "He was manifested in the flesh, vindicated in the Spirit, seen by angels, preached among the nations, believed on in the world, taken up in glory" (1 Tim 3:16).

---

[2] Richard B. Gaffin, "The Glory of God in Paul's Epistles," in *The Glory of God*, ed. Christopher W. Morgan and Robert A. Peterson, Theology in Community (Wheaton: Crossway, 2010), 137–38.

Jesus is the glorious Lord whose return will be characterized by glory. Paul asserts Christ's deity: the rulers of this age, though professing to be wise, acted foolishly when they "crucified the Lord of glory" (1 Cor 2:8). Christians look to the future with hope and joy because they await "the blessed hope, the appearing of the glory of our great God and Savior, Jesus Christ" (Titus 2:13).

Paul epitomizes the revelation of God's mystery in Col 1:27: "God wanted to make known among the Gentiles the glorious wealth of this mystery, which is Christ in you, the hope of glory." Christ's indwelling his people gives them a sure hope of future glory in the final dimension of the kingdom of God. After dying on the cross, Christ was raised and became the "firstfruits of those who have fallen asleep" (1 Cor 15:20, 22), whose resurrection secures theirs. He is the second Adam, who brings life where our first father brought death: "Just as in Adam all die, so also in Christ shall all be made alive" (v. 22).

Christ's Work

Salvation is through Christ's saving work, and his saving work stresses glory. Paul paints six pictures of Christ's saving accomplishment. Each discloses God's glory, leads to ultimate glory for believers, and gives rise to eternal glory to God. Paul's first picture portrays propitiation. Christ propitiated the Father by paying the penalty that sinners deserved and could not pay—God's wrath (1 John 4:10). God displayed his glory by demonstrating his righteousness in Christ's death (Rom 3:25). God did this "so that he would be just and justify the one who has faith in Jesus" (v. 26). As a result, all boasting in merit salvation is silenced (vv. 27–31) and instead God's people glory in Christ's cross (Gal 6:14).

Paul's second picture depicts reconciliation (Rom 5:10). Jesus died in the place of estranged people to make peace between God and them and between them and God. Reconciliation puts the spotlight on God's grace and advances his glory. Christ's cross also reconciles people previously estranged from one another (Eph 2:13–22). In fact, Christ's saving work reconciles "everything to himself, whether things on earth or things in heaven, by making peace through his blood, shed on the cross" (Col 1:20), and this should not be interpreted to say everyone is saved. Instead, it means that everything in the universe is set right and that those who are enemies of God are pacified and their power is removed.

Paul's third picture portrays redemption. Christ died an accursed death on a cross (Gal 3:13) to free slaves to sin. As a result, they are adopted as God's free children (4:5, 7; 5:1) and their sins are forgiven (Col 1:14). God has sealed believers with the Holy Spirit "for the day of redemption" (Eph 4:30), and they await their final "adoption, the redemption of [their] bodies" (Rom 8:23)—that is, glorification, the "glory that is to going to be revealed to us" (v. 18).

Paul's fourth picture depicts a sacrifice. Humans are spiritually unclean before God and need to be purified. To meet that need Christ voluntarily became a sacrifice: "Christ also loved us and gave himself for us, a sacrificial and fragrant offering to God" (Eph 5:2). Christ's saving death glorifies God as it pleases him and demonstrates his righteousness. As a result, Jesus, the Lamb, deserves honor and glory because he "loves us and has set us free from our sins by his blood" (Rev 1:5).

Paul's fifth picture portrays a great victory. We face many powerful foes, including the devil, demons, the world, death, and hell. God sent a mighty champion, Jesus Christ, who overcame our enemies by his death and resurrection. God was glorified when he "disarmed the rulers and authorities and disgraced them publicly; he triumphed over them in" Christ (Col 2:15). But he has not yet thrown these foes into the lake of fire, but that day is coming. Already Christ has been exalted and glorified (Eph 1:21), but not yet has he come "in his glory and that of the Father and the holy angels" (Luke 9:26).

Paul's sixth picture depicts sanctification: "Christ loved the church and gave himself for her to make her holy, cleansing her with the washing of water by the word" (Eph 5:25–26). In definitive sanctification God has made believers saints, in progressive sanctification he works ongoing holiness into them, and in future sanctification he will perfect them in holiness at Christ's return. Christ died "to present the church to himself in splendor, without spot or wrinkle or anything like that, but holy and blameless" (v. 27). Therefore we are not surprised that the announcement of the wedding supper of the Lamb shouts out to the glory of God:

Hallelujah, because our Lord God, the Almighty, reigns!
Let us be glad, rejoice, and give him glory,
because the marriage of the Lamb has come,
and his bride has prepared herself. (Rev 19:6–7)

Paul speaks of reconciliation, though his words pertain to all six pictures of Christ's saving work: "We also boast in God through our Lord Jesus Christ, through whom we have now received this reconciliation" (Rom 5:11).

The Holy Spirit

Christ's work accomplishes our salvation, and the Holy Spirit applies it to us. Note how Paul ties the Holy Spirit to God's glory. First, he glorifies the Father, Son, and Spirit as God's seal on believers: "In him you also were sealed with the promised Holy Spirit" (Eph 1:13). The Father is the sealer (2 Cor 1:21–22), he seals believers in union with Christ, and God's seal is the Holy Spirit. The Father assures his people of final salvation when he seals them with the "Spirit of God . . . for the day of redemption" (Eph 4:30 ESV).

Second, Paul unites worship in the Spirit and glorying in Christ. The Judaizers boast in the rite of circumcision, but Paul asserts, "We are the circumcision, the ones who worship by the Spirit of God, boast in Christ Jesus, and do not put confidence in the flesh" (Phil 3:3).

Third, as we have seen, astonishingly Paul also regards glorification as the present work of the Spirit. We behold the Lord's glory, and he transforms us into his "image from glory to glory" (2 Cor 3:18). Who performs this work in believers? Paul explains: "This is from the Lord who is the Spirit" (v. 18).

The New Covenant

Salvation is connected to covenant, and glory is highlighted as a central feature of the new covenant. The new covenant far surpasses the old covenant in glory (2 Cor 3:4–18). The old covenant had glory, because God graciously chose Israel out of all nations (Exod 20:2; Deut 7:6–8). In grace God said to Israel, "You will be my own possession out of all the peoples, although the whole earth is mine, and you will be my kingdom of priests and my holy nation" (Exod 19:5–6). In grace God gave the old covenant to be the core of biblical ethics (Deut 5:6–21).

The face of Moses, the mediator of the old covenant, shone with glory as he returned from God's presence. But the glory of the new covenant far exceeds that of Moses (2 Cor 3:7). Paul calls the old covenant "the ministry that brought death" (v. 7) and "the ministry that brings condemnation" (v. 9) because the Ten Commandments denounced Israel's covenant-breaking. By contrast "the Spirit gives life" (v. 6), fulfils OT predictions, and causes new covenant believers to be born again, prompting them to obey God. The new covenant of the Spirit "overflows with even more glory" (v. 9). The old covenant had glory, but in comparison with the new covenant's glory the old covenant had none! "In fact, what had been glorious is not glorious now by comparison because of the glory that surpasses it" (v. 10).

Election

In Paul's two most extensive passages on election he connects election to God's glory. In Romans 9 Paul states, "The Scripture tells Pharaoh, I raised you up for this reason so that I may display my power in you and that my name may be proclaimed in the whole earth" (Rom 9:17). Paul again combines election and glory: God "did this to make known the riches of his glory on objects of mercy that he prepared beforehand for glory" (v. 23). God chose humans for "glory" (salvation) with the intention of manifesting the "riches of his glory."

In Eph 1:3–14 Paul links election to God's glory. After the apostle speaks of the Father's choosing us in Christ before creation for sanctification (v. 4) and predestinating us to adoption (v. 5), he offers praise to God for "his glorious grace that he lavished on us in the Beloved One" (v. 6). That God chose us unto salvation humbles us and glorifies God.

Grace and Faith

After praising the Trinitarian persons for salvation—the Father for election, the Son for redemption, and the Spirit as God's seal of salvation (Eph 1:3–4)—Paul exults in the "praise of his glorious grace" (v. 6). In the next chapter Paul tells of God's "mercy," "great love," "grace," and "kindness" in salvation (2:4–7). Then he communicates God's ultimate purpose in salvation: "so that in the coming ages he might display the immeasurable riches of his grace through his kindness to us in Christ Jesus" (v. 7).

Salvation in Scripture is always by grace through faith. Faith gives glory to God because it humbly rests in Christ alone for salvation. It refuses to trust in human pedigree or performance: "Because we know that a person is not justified by the works of the law but by faith in Jesus Christ, even we ourselves have believed in Christ Jesus. This was so that we might be justified by faith in Christ and not by the works of the law" (Gal 2:16).

True believers glorify God when they "worship by the Spirit of God, boast in Christ Jesus, and do not put confidence in the flesh" (Phil 3:3). Abraham is our example of faith, for when he believed he "gave glory to God" (Rom 4:20–21), believing that God was faithful to fulfill his promises. Paul too is worthy of emulation, for he preached, "As for me, I will never boast about anything except the cross of our Lord Jesus Christ. The world has been crucified to me through the cross, and I to the world" (Gal 6:14).

Union with Christ

God unites believers to Christ, and as a result his saving benefits become theirs. God gets glory to himself by exalting his Son as the fount of all spiritual blessings (Eph 1:3–14). Those united to Christ participate in his story: they die with him and are raised with him. This means they "suffer with him so that [they] may also be glorified with him" (Rom 8:17). Union with Christ pertains to individuals (Eph 2:1–10), the church (vv. 11–22), and the cosmos (1:9–10), all to his glory.

Tracing the image of God through Scripture gives insight into God's glory. As those created in his image and likeness, Adam and Eve reflected his glory. However, they forfeited this glory in the fall, and as a result the image was tarnished. God begins the process of restoring the image when he joins believers to Christ. God will perfectly repair his marred image in mankind when he raises his people from the dead, transforming their mortal bodies into incorruptible and glorious ones. Only then will God display his glory fully in believers, who will shine with the "light of the knowledge of God's glory in the face of Jesus Christ" (2 Cor 4:6).

Justification

Salvation viewed as justification brings glory to God by publicly manifesting his love and justice in Christ's cross. The basis of justification is Christ's atoning death, the supreme demonstration of God's love. Paul extols Christ's love, saying that it "surpasses knowledge" (Eph 3:19). He shows its superiority to even sacrificial human love: "Rarely will someone die for a just person—though for a good person perhaps someone might even dare to die. But God proves his own love for us in that while we were still sinners, Christ died for us" (Rom 5:7–8). John defines love not as human love reaching up but as God's love reaching down: "In this is love, not that we have loved God but that he loved us and sent his Son to be the propitiation for our sins" (1 John 4:10 ESV).

The text just cited proves that God's love is preeminently displayed in propitiation. Propitiation consists in the Son of God bearing God's wrath on the cross, taking the penalty our sins deserved. The main propitiation passage is Rom 3:25–26, which speaks of how "God put forward [Christ] as a propitiation by his blood, to be received by faith. This was to show God's righteousness, because in his divine forbearance he had passed over former sins. It was to show his righteousness at the present time, so that he might be just and the justifier of the one who has faith in Jesus" (ESV). God is able to deliver utter rebels without compromising his own moral integrity because his Son propitiated his justice. In justifying guilty sinners who believe in Jesus, God magnifies his grace and justice.

Adoption

Adoption is a work of God's free grace whereby he takes slaves of sin and puts them into his family as his beloved sons and daughters. Adoption, like justification, glorifies God because it is based on God's grace and received by believing in Jesus the Redeemer. We all were cursed because we had broken God's law (Gal 3:10). Wonderfully, "Christ redeemed us from the curse of the law by becoming a curse for us, because it is written, 'Cursed is everyone who is hung on a tree.' The purpose was that the blessing of Abraham would come to the Gentiles by Christ Jesus, so that we could receive the promised Spirit through faith" (vv. 13–14). Consequently, everyone who trusts Christ as Redeemer is "no longer a slave but a son, and if a son, then . . . an heir"

(4:7). God the Father is glorified in turning slaves into sons. The unique Son of God is glorified when the redeemed worship him as Redeemer (Rev 5:9). The "Spirit of adoption" is glorified when he enables believers to cry out, '*Abba*, Father!'" (Rom 8:15). The Father promises his adopted children a glorious inheritance. Indeed, he shares his glory with them, for he will bring "many sons and daughters to glory" (Heb 2:10).

Sanctification

Sanctification in its three tenses—past, present, and future—brings glory to God. Initial sanctification took place in the past and glorifies God because it makes saints out of sinners. Paul links election, initial sanctification, and glory:

> We ought to thank God always for you, brothers and sisters loved by the Lord, because from the beginning God has chosen you for salvation through sanctification by the Spirit and through belief in the truth. He called you to this through our gospel, so that you might obtain the glory of our Lord Jesus Christ. (2 Thess 2:13–14)

Progressive sanctification also glorifies God. Peter brings holy living and God's glory together in one context:

> Since Christ suffered in the flesh, arm yourselves also with the same understanding—because the one who suffers in the flesh is finished with sin—in order to live the remaining time in the flesh no longer for human desires, but for God's will. . . . If anyone serves, let it be from the strength God provides, so that God may be glorified through Jesus Christ in everything. To him be the glory and the power forever and ever. Amen. (1 Pet 4:1–2, 11)

Future sanctification will glorify God because it perfects God's saints in holiness. Paul sets a high standard when he exhorts husbands to love their wives "just as Christ loved the church and gave himself for her to make her holy, cleansing her with the washing of water by the word. He did this to present the church to himself in splendor, without spot or wrinkle or anything like that, but holy and blameless" (Eph 5:25–27). On that day we will be glorious, presented to Christ, and complete in him.

Although there is struggle in the Christian life, God assures us that because of the Holy Spirit's presence and power we will obtain final victory. Sinclair Ferguson sums up the Spirit's role:

> The mark we were created to reach, but have missed, was glory. We have sinned and failed to attain that destiny. Against this background, the task of the Spirit may be stated simply: to bring us to glory, to create glory within us, and to glorify us together with Christ. The startling significance of this might be plainer if we expressed it thus: the Spirit is given to glorify us; not just to 'add' glory as a crown to what we are, but actually to transform the very constitution of our being so that we become glorious. In the New Testament, this glorification is seen to begin already in the present order, in believers. Through the Spirit they are already being changed from glory to glory, as they gaze on/reflect the face of the Lord (2 Cor 3:17–18). But the consummation of this glorification awaits the eschaton and the Spirit's ministry in the resurrection.[3]

Preservation

God delivers us by grace, keeps us by grace, and will bring us into his heavenly kingdom in the same way. Romans 8 begins with a message of no condemnation and ends with a message of no separation.

> There is now no condemnation for those in Christ Jesus, because the law of the Spirit of life in Christ Jesus has set you free from the law of sin and death. (vv. 1–2)

> Who can separate us from the love of Christ? Can affliction or distress or persecution or famine or nakedness or danger or sword? As it is written: "Because of you we are being put to death all day long; we are counted as sheep to be slaughtered." No, in all these things we are more than conquerors through him who loved us. For I am persuaded that neither death nor life, nor angels nor rulers, nor

---

[3] Sinclair B. Ferguson, *The Holy Spirit*, CCT (Downers Grove: InterVarsity, 1996), 249–50.

things present nor things to come, nor powers, nor height nor depth, nor any other created thing will be able to separate us from the love of God that is in Christ Jesus our Lord. (vv. 35–39)

In many other places Paul teaches that God will preserve us for final salvation. Here is one more: "I am sure of this, that he who began a good work in you will bring it to completion at the day of Christ Jesus" (Phil 1:6).

Sometimes, when teaching God's preservation of his people, the apostle cannot help but launch into praise. Such is the case in 2 Tim 4:18: "The Lord will rescue me from every evil deed and bring me safely into his heavenly kingdom. To him be the glory for ever and ever! Amen."

The Church

God has many purposes for his church, but the highest one involves his glory. He glorifies himself by bringing Jews and Gentiles together in Christ to "create in himself one new man from the two" (Eph 2:15). Jews and Gentiles hated each other, and Paul lists spiritual shortcomings of the latter, including their separation from Christ and God (vv. 11–12). But Paul shares wonderful news with Gentiles: "Now in Christ Jesus, you who were far away have been brought near by the blood of Christ" (v. 13). Christ is the Reconciler, the peace-maker, who reconciled "both [groups] to God in one body through the cross" (v. 16).

Changing imagery, Paul speaks of God's constituting the church from Jews and Gentiles as constructing a building. In Jesus, the cornerstone, "The whole building, being put together, grows into a holy temple in the Lord" (v. 21), where the Spirit dwells. The Trinitarian persons all play roles, for "Through [Christ] we both have access in one Spirit to the Father" (v. 18). Jews and Gentiles united into one new humanity testify loudly to God's larger purposes. Astonishingly, it is God's will "that God's multi-faceted wisdom may now be made known through the church to the rulers and authorities in the heavens" (3:10). The church preaches Christ not only to humans in the gospel but also to the entire cosmos through the visible display of unity. God creates the church to display his greatness, and as he does so he glorifies himself. Paul proclaims, "Now to him who is able to do above and beyond all that we ask or think according to the power that works in us—to him be glory in the church and in Christ Jesus to all generations, forever and ever. Amen" (vv. 20–21).

Ministry

Scripture links God's glory to various forms of ministry, including missions and preaching. This is evident in the letters of Paul and Peter and in Revelation. God's glory gleams at the beginning and end of Paul's most famous epistle. Romans starts with God's giving Paul apostleship and accompanying power to proclaim the gospel among Gentiles "to bring about the obedience of faith for the sake of [Christ's] name" (Rom 1:5–6). Paul preached for many reasons, but the paramount reason was to promote the glory of the Father and the Son. The doxology that closes Romans sets forth the grand goal of all Christian ministry: "To the only wise God, through Jesus Christ—to him be the glory forever! Amen" (v. 16:27).

The act of preaching the gospel displays God's glory, for the Holy Spirit illumines "the light of the gospel of the glory of Christ, who is the image of God" (2 Cor 4:4). When Paul and his partners preach Christ as Lord, they place their confidence for results in the Creator, "who said, 'Let light shine out of darkness,'" and now "has shone in our hearts to give the light of the knowledge of God's glory in the face of Jesus Christ" (v. 6). This is a key aspect of the Spirit's ministry in the new covenant, which far outstrips the old covenant in glory (v. 3:8–10).

Paul's preaching eschewed rhetorical eloquence and showmanship, focusing instead on the crucified Christ (1 Cor 2:1–2). Paul resisted the orator's temptation to gain glory for himself and deliberately put the spotlight on Christ, "so that no one may boast in [God's] presence" (1:29).[4] Paul shared Jeremiah's goal: "As it is written: 'Let the one who boasts, boast in the Lord'" (v. 31, quoting Jer 9:24).

Peter too connects Christian service and God's glory. He views the Christian life as a stewardship of God's grace in which he entrusts believers with spiritual gifts: "Just as each one has received a gift, use it to serve others, as good stewards of the varied grace of God" (1 Pet 4:10). Peter here shares

---

[4] Roy E. Ciampa and Brian Rosner, *The First Letter to the Corinthians*, PNTC (Grand Rapids: Eerdmans, 2010), 86, 112.

a goal of God's people exercising their gifts: service to others. Paul shares a similar goal: "A manifestation of the Spirit is given to each person for the common good" (1 Cor 12:7).

Both apostles aspire for a higher goal, however. Paul is confident that "The Lord will rescue me from every evil work and will bring me safely into his heavenly kingdom. To him be the glory forever and ever! Amen" (2 Tim 4:18). Peter cites two examples of believers' using spiritual gifts and then points to the ultimate goal: "If anyone speaks, let it be as one who speaks God's words; if anyone serves, let it be from the strength God provides, so that God may be glorified through Jesus Christ in everything. To him be the glory and the power forever and ever. Amen" (1 Pet 4:11).

The book of Revelation speaks often of the servants of God, from beginning to end. The very first verse of the book reads: "The revelation of Jesus Christ that God gave him to show his servants what must soon take place. He made it known by sending his angel to his servant John" (Rev 1:1). In the last chapter John writes, "These words are faithful and true. The Lord, the God of the spirits of the prophets, has sent his angel to show his servants what must soon take place" (22:6). Verses throughout the book speak of God's servants.[5] Revelation tells of people's serving God: "For this reason they are before the throne of God, and they serve him day and night in his temple. The one seated on the throne will shelter them" (7:15). God summons his servants to give him glory for his judgment on Babylon, symbolic of the world's idolatrous system: "A voice came from the throne, saying, 'Praise our God, all his servants, and the ones who fear him, both small and great!'" (19:5). This worship describes an important occupation of God's people in the new earth: "There will no longer be any curse. The throne of God and of the Lamb will be in the city, and his servants will worship him" (22:3). Worshipping the Trinity means giving him the glory he is due. And this is exactly what his servants do.

The Future

Many aspects of eschatology bring glory to the One who alone deserves it and is guiding all history toward its intended outcome.

---

[5] God's servants are also mentioned in Rev 2:20; 6:11; 7:3; 10:7; 11:18; 19:2; 22:5.

Christ's Return

Christ's return is an important aspect of his saving work, and the focus of the second coming is squarely on "the revelation of the Lord Jesus from heaven" (2 Thess 1:7). Although Jesus's first coming was as a baby in a manger over which hung the shadow of the cross (Luke 2:34–35), in his second coming "the Son of Man comes in his glory, and all the angels with him, then he will sit on his glorious throne" (Matt 25:31). Christ's return will mean relief for persecuted Christians but condemnation for unbelievers. Paul writes concerning sinners and saints, respectively, "They will pay the penalty of eternal destruction from the Lord's presence and from his glorious strength on that day when he comes to be glorified by his saints and to be marveled at by all those who have believed" (2 Thess 1:9–10).

The first coming of Christ has changed everything, including the OT day of the Lord, which has now become "the day of our Lord Jesus Christ" (1 Cor 1:8). That day will publish Christ's glory. In fact, this is the most important truth pertaining to the Last Judgment. As weighty as eternal punishment and eternal bliss are, there is something even more important. The Trinity in that day will be glorified in the punishment of the lost and the deliverance of the saved:

> "The kingdom of the world has become the kingdom of our Lord and of his Christ, and he will reign forever and ever."
>
> The twenty-four elders, who were seated before God on their thrones, fell facedown and worshiped God, saying, "We give you thanks, Lord God, the Almighty, who is and who was, because you have taken your great power and have begun to reign. The nations were angry, but your wrath has come. The time has come for the dead to be judged and to give the reward to your servants the prophets, to the saints, and to those who fear your name, both small and great." (Rev 11:15–18)

The Resurrection

Our salvation is connected to the final resurrection, which is also linked to glory. While the OT spoke a little of the future resurrection (Isa 25:8; 26:19; Dan 12:2), the NT says a lot. This is because Jesus was raised from the dead, and his resurrection guarantees that of believers: "Because I live, you will live too" (John 14:19). Paul includes Jesus's resurrection in his summary of the gospel in 1 Cor 15:3–4. The apostle presents the risen Christ in two important roles. As the second Adam, he gives all his people eternal life now in regeneration and eternal life in resurrection on the last day: "Just as in Adam all die, so also in Christ all will be made alive" (v. 22). As the firstfruits, Jesus is the first person to experience the resurrection of the last day, and his resurrection secures ours: "Christ has been raised from the dead, the firstfruits of those who have fallen asleep" (v. 20).

The Corinthians wrongly imagined that resurrection from the dead meant the resuscitation of decaying corpses. Paul corrects this error by teaching that God will transform our present bodies into resurrection bodies. He gives an example of God's changing "bodies" (material forms) into different forms when God brings various plants from their corresponding seeds. Paul shows that God gives appropriate bodies to people, animals, birds, and fish (1 Cor 15:39). Even heavenly bodies differ from one another in glory (vv. 40–41). In light of the variety of bodies in God's creation and their varieties in glory, we cannot assume that our future bodies will be like rotting corpses.

To the contrary, our new bodies will be incredibly new, strong, and glorious. Paul revisits his plant analogy to praise the newness of our resurrection bodies: "So it is with the resurrection of the dead: Sown in corruption, raised in incorruption; sown in dishonor, raised in glory; sown in weakness, raised in power; sown a natural body, raised a spiritual body. If there is a natural body, there is also a spiritual body" (1 Cor 15:42–44).

Paul teaches that rather than creating new bodies for us *ex nihilo*, the Trinity will transform our present bodies into resurrection bodies: "If the Spirit of him who raised Jesus from the dead lives in you, then he who raised Christ from the dead will also bring your mortal bodies to life through his Spirit who lives in you" (Rom 8:11). Here the Father and Holy Spirit are active in our resurrection. Christ will be active too: "We eagerly wait for a Savior from [heaven], the Lord Jesus Christ. He will transform the body of our humble condition into the likeness of his glorious body, by the power that enables him to subject everything to himself" (Phil 3:20–21). The omnipotent Christ will change our current bodies into resurrection bodies equipped for everlasting life on the new earth.

Hell

We can also understand salvation by what we are saved from—sin (as we considered previously) and hell. The *summum bonum* of the universe is the glory of God, and he will be glorified in the fate of every human being, both sinner and saint. In 2 Thess 1:5–10 Paul teaches that "God's righteous judgment" will be revealed on the last day (cf. Rom 2:5). Then will occur "the revelation of the Lord Jesus from heaven with his powerful angels" (2 Thess 1:7). There will be great glory, for, "When the Son of Man comes in his glory, and all the angels with him, then he will sit on his glorious throne" (Matt 25:31). Christ will display his glory in giving relief to his persecuted people and repaying "with affliction those who afflict" them (2 Thess 1:6–7). Christ will take "vengeance with flaming fire on those who don't know God and on those who don't obey the gospel of our Lord Jesus" (v. 8). God will glorify his holiness and justice in his work of judgment when the lost "will pay the penalty of eternal destruction from the Lord's presence and from his glorious strength" (v. 9). On that same day he will "be glorified by his saints and . . . marveled at by all those who have believed" (v. 10).

Hell highlights three main images, which all appear in 2 Thessalonians 1. Punishment describes hell. As we've seen, the lost "will suffer . . . punishment" (2 Thess 1:9 ESV). In "righteous judgment" (v. 5) almighty God will justly inflict "eternal punishment" on them (Matt 25:46).

Destruction also describes hell. People who don't know the Lord "will pay the penalty of eternal destruction" (2 Thess 1:9). Annihilationism claims that this refers to irremediable extinction of being. But Paul uses the same word for "eternal" (*aiōnios*) to specify endlessness: in Rom 6:23 of "eternal life," in 16:26 of "the eternal God," and in 2 Thess 2:16 of "eternal encouragement." Further, as Beale shows, Paul draws the phrase "takes vengeance with flaming fire" from the only place it occurs in the OT, Isa 66:15, where the words are followed by a reference to eternal punishment: "Their worm will never die, their fire will never go out" (Isa 66:24)—words Jesus uses to portray eternal conscious punishment.[6] "Eternal destruction" involves utter ruin, the loss of everything God made for us to enjoy, forever.

---

[6] G. K. Beale, *1–2 Thessalonians*, IVPNTC (Downers Grove: InterVarsity, 2003), 189.

Separation describes hell too. Paul speaks of "eternal destruction from the Lord's presence and from his glorious strength" (2 Thess 1:9). The lost will be banished forever from God's presence of grace and glory. Fee shows that Paul cites Isa 2 from the LXX to indicate persons' being cut off from God's presence. Here it is separation from Christ's presence, and it lasts forever.[7]

Paul's words in Acts 24:15 draw a stark contrast between the two destinies of humans: "There will be a resurrection, both of the righteous and the unrighteous." Hell glorifies God's justice and involves resurrected people's suffering eternal punishment, ruin, and banishment from God's grace and glory. Heaven glorifies God's grace and involves resurrected people's eternally enjoying God's glorious presence on the new earth.

Heaven

The consummation of salvation is also spoken of in terms of glory. This is true of believers as a microcosm of God's creation and of the creation itself as the macrocosm. Paul describes the ultimate deliverance of God's people as "glory":

> [God] did this to make known the riches of his glory on objects of mercy that he prepared beforehand for glory. (Rom 9:23)

> Our momentary light affliction is producing for us an absolutely incomparable eternal weight of glory. (2 Cor 4:17)

> God wanted to make known among the Gentiles the glorious wealth of this mystery, which is Christ in you, the hope of glory. (Col 1:27)

> When Christ, who is your life, appears, then you also will appear with him in glory. (Col 3:4)

> God . . . calls you into his own kingdom and glory. (1 Thess 2:12)

> He called you to this through our gospel, so that you might obtain the glory of our Lord Jesus Christ. (2 Thess 2:14)

---

[7] Gordon D. Fee, *The First and Second Letters to the Thessalonians*, NICNT (Grand Rapids: Eerdmans, 2009), 259.

I endure all things for the elect: so that they also may obtain salvation, which is in Christ Jesus, with eternal glory. (2 Tim 2:10)

In Romans 8 Paul tells how both the microcosm, God's people, and the macrocosm, his creation, will shine with glory. Present sufferings cannot compare with the overwhelming glory to be revealed to Christians (v. 18) when they are glorified (vv. 17, 30). Christ's saving work delivers both the church and the creation: "The creation eagerly waits with anticipation for God's sons to be revealed. For the creation was subjected to futility—not willingly, but because of him who subjected it—in the hope that the creation itself will also be set free from the bondage to decay into the glorious freedom of God's children" (vv. 19–21).

Scripture's last two chapters describe the new heaven and earth, resplendent in glory. The "bride, the wife of the Lamb" is "the holy city, Jerusalem, coming down out of heaven from God, arrayed with God's glory. Her radiance [is] like a precious jewel, like a jasper stone, clear as crystal" (Rev 21:9–11). This description, like that of "gold" and "pearls" (in vv. 18–21), represents "the divine glory of the new cosmos, because God brought about her redemption and not she herself."[8]

Furthermore, the holy city will lack tabernacle and temple, which will be unnecessary. "The Lord God the Almighty and the Lamb are its temple. The city does not need the sun or the moon to shine on it, because the glory of God illuminates it, and its lamp is the Lamb" (vv. 22–23). In that day salvation will cover the earth, for "The nations will walk by its light, and the kings of the earth will bring their glory into it. . . . They will bring the glory and honor of the nations into it" (vv. 24, 26).

Synthesis

The Father has planned our salvation, the Son has accomplished it for us, and the Holy Spirit has applied it to us. This salvation is complete: we have "every spiritual blessing" (Eph 1:3). These blessings are comprehensive: God chooses, calls, makes alive, converts, justifies, adopts, sanctifies, preserves, and

---

[8] G. K. Beale, *The Book of Revelation*, NIGTC (Grand Rapids: Eerdmans, 1999), 1064.

glorifies us. God has accomplished all this for us through the saving work of Christ, and he has applied it to us through our union with Christ. And the ultimate end of our salvation is not our salvation but the glory of God, as the refrain in Ephesians highlights: to the praise of his glorious grace (Eph 1:6); praise to his glory (1:12); and to the praise of his glory (1:14).

That God saves us for his glory means at least two things. First, God acts to display himself, and as he displays himself he communicates his greatness and fullness. That in and of itself glorifies him (Eph 2:4–10; 3:8–12). Second, God acts to elicit love and praise from his creation, especially his people (Eph 1:3–14).

We should note a related pitfall: that God acts with his glory as his ultimate end does not imply that other ends are excluded. Those ends remain important and should not be marginalized. The Bible teaches that the ultimate end of our salvation is God's glory, and it puts forward additional goals. God's love as a motive for saving us is also set forth powerfully and regularly. For example, Eph 1:4–6 is instructive:

> In love he predestined us for adoption to himself as sons through Jesus Christ, according to the purpose of his will, to the praise of his glorious grace, with which he has blessed us in the Beloved. (ESV)

Notice also Eph 2:4–7:

> God, who is rich in mercy, because of his great love that he had for us, made us alive with Christ even though we were dead in trespasses. You are saved by grace! He also raised us up with him and seated us with him in the heavens in Christ Jesus, so that in the coming ages he might display the immeasurable riches of his grace through his kindness to us in Christ Jesus.

In the same Ephesians passages that underline that God acts unto his glory, we also see that God acts out of a genuine love for us. So our conviction that God acts with glory as his ultimate end must be linked to our recognition that God acts out of love for our good.

Other passages highlight this as well. John 3:16 states, "God loved the world in this way: he gave . . ." (see 1 John 4:9–10). Titus 3:4–7 ties our salvation to God's mercy. Rom 8:28 also makes it clear that redemptive history is, in large part, for the good of God's people.

Exodus is also noteworthy. Why does God redeem his people from slavery in Egypt? One might quickly reply, "for his glory." Certainly God redeems his people from slavery to glorify himself. But other concerns also play a part. Exodus presents God's reasons for deliverance in a multifaceted way: love for his oppressed people (3–4); faithfulness to the covenant promises made to Abraham, Isaac, and Jacob (3:15; 4:5; 6:8; 32:13; 34:6); so that Israel would serve Yahweh (4:23; 6:5); so that the people would know that he is Yahweh (6:7; 10:2; 13:1); to give the Promised Land (6:8); so that the Egyptians would know that he is Yahweh (5:2; 7:5; 14:3–4,15–18); so that Pharaoh would know Yahweh as incomparable (7:17; 8:10–18); to display God's power (9:16); so that his name might be proclaimed in all the earth (9:16); to pass down a heritage to the children (10:1–2); so that God's wonders might be multiplied (11:9); to receive glory over Pharaoh and his army (14:3–18); and for Israel's sake (18:8). So God delivers his people out of love, covenant faithfulness, and jealousy. He does so for his glory, for Israel's good, for judgment on Egypt, and for the continuance of his covenant people.

Realizing these multiple ends does not detract from an emphasis on God's glory but actually spotlights it. Indeed, in the exodus God displays his love, covenant faithfulness, jealously, providence, and power through his wonders, salvation, and judgment. And as we saw previously, in our salvation God displays his love, grace, holiness, righteousness, justice, wisdom, power, sovereignty, mercy, and patience. As God communicates himself, he glorifies himself.

Understanding this truth is significant as it helps us address a common question concerning God's glory: If God seeks his own glory above all things, does this mean he is selfish? After all, if we as humans seek our own glory, we are deemed selfish. The standard answer is that God is the ultimate being and the highest end, and we are not. It is good to seek the highest end, so God is right to make himself his own ultimate end. If we make ourselves the highest end, we act wrongly because we treat ourselves as the highest end when we are not. That argument is valid and substantial. But it omits something massively important: God's genuine desire for the good of his creatures.

God's love and his glory are united. It is important to stress that God saves us out of love, displays his kindness toward us for all eternity, and is glorified by putting his greatness, goodness, and fullness on display. As God displays himself, he glorifies himself. In this way God is self-giving and self-exalting. He gives himself to us and acts on our behalf, which simultaneously meets our needs and demonstrates his sufficiency.[9] Through it all he saves us for our good and, ultimately, for his glory.

---

[9] For more on how God's self-giving and self-exalting cohere, especially in the mutual glorification of the persons of the Trinity, see Christopher W. Morgan, "Toward a Theology of the Glory of God," in *The Glory of God*, ed. Christopher W. Morgan and Robert A. Peterson, Theology in Community 2 (Wheaton: Crossway, 2010), 175–87.

BIBLIOGRAPHY

Allison, Gregg R. *Sojourners and Strangers: The Doctrine of the Church*. FET. Wheaton, IL: Crossway, 2012.

Allison, Gregg R., and Andreas J Köstenberger. *The Holy Spirit*. TPG. Edited by David S. Dockery, Nathan A. Finn, and Christopher W. Morgan. Nashville: B&H Academic, 2020.

Althaus, Paul. *The Theology of Martin Luther*. Philadelphia: Fortress, 1966.

Anderson, Garwood P. *Paul's New Perspective: Charting a Soteriological Journey*. Downers Grove, IL: IVP Connect, 2016.

Anselm. *Basic Writings: Proslogium; Monologium; Gaunilon's on Behalf of the Fool; Cur Deus Homo*. trans. S. N. Deane. Second edition. La Salle, IL: Open Court, 1962.

Augustine. "The Confessions of St. Augustine." In *The Confessions and Letters of St. Augustine, with a Sketch of His Life and Work*, edited by Philip Schaff, 45–207. Grand Rapids: Eerdmans, 1986.

Aulén, Gustaf. *Christus Victor: An Historical Study of the Three Main Types of the Idea of the Atonement*. Translated by A. G. Hebert. New York: Macmillan, 1931, 1969.

Barber, Dan C., and Robert A. Peterson. *Life Everlasting: The Unfolding Story of Heaven*. EBT. Phillipsburg, NJ: P&R, 2012.

Barnes, Phil, Christopher Chanda, Tapiwa Ngwira, and Bento Simaoi. *Introduction to Missiology*. ATS. Niamey, Niger: Eleaf Resources, 2021.

Bavinck, Herman. *Reformed Dogmatics*. Vol. 3, *Sin and Salvation in Christ*. Edited by John Bolt. Translated by John Vriend. Grand Rapids: Baker, 2006.

Bayer, Hans F. *A Theology of Mark: The Dynamic between Christology and Authentic Discipleship*. EBT. Phillipsburg, NJ: P&R, 2012.

Berkhof, Louis. *Systematic Theology*. Grand Rapids: Eerdmans, 1939; reprint, 1996.

Berkouwer, G. C. *Faith and Justification*. Studies in Dogmatics. Grand Rapids: Eerdmans, 1954.

———. *Faith and Sanctification*. Studies in Dogmatics. Grand Rapids: Eerdmans, 1952.

Billings, J. Todd. *Union with Christ: Reframing Theology and Ministry for the Church*. Grand Rapids: Baker Academic, 2011.

Bird, Michael F. *Evangelical Theology: A Biblical and Systematic Introduction*. Grand Rapids: Zondervan, 2013.

Blocher, Henri. "Agnus Victor: The Atonement as Victory and Vicarious Punishment." In *What Does It Mean to Be Saved? Broadening Evangelical Horizons of Salvation*, edited by John G. Stackhouse, Jr., 67–91. Grand Rapids: Baker, 2002.

———. "Biblical Metaphors and the Doctrine of the Atonement." *Journal of the Evangelical Theological Society* 47, no. 4 (December, 2004): 639–40.

Bray, Gerald. *The Doctrine of God*. CCT. Downers Grove, IL: InterVarsity, 1993.

Burger, Hans. *Being in Christ: A Biblical and Systematic Investigation in a Reformed Perspective*. Eugene, OR: Wipf and Stock, 2009.

Burke, Trevor. *Adopted into God's Family: Exploring a Pauline Metaphor*. NSBT 22. Downers Grove, IL: Inter Varsity, 2006.

———. *The Message of Sonship: At Home in God's Household*. The Bible Speaks Today: Bible Themes Series. Downers Grove, IL: InterVarsity, 2011.

Calvin, John. *Institutes of the Christian Religion*. Edited by John T. McNeill. Translated by Ford Lewis Battles. Two volumes. Philadelphia: Westminster, 1960.

Campbell, Constantine R. *Paul and Union with Christ*. Grand Rapids: Zondervan, 2012.

Carson, D. A. "Atonement in Romans 3:21–26." In *The Glory of the Atonement: Biblical, Theological, and Practical Perspectives*, edited by Charles E. Hill and Frank A. James III, 119–39. Downers Grove, IL: InterVarsity, 2004.

———. *The Difficult Doctrine of the Love of God*. Wheaton, IL: Crossway, 2000.

———. *Divine Sovereignty and Human Responsibility: Biblical Perspectives in Tension*. Eugene, OR: Wipf and Stock, 2002.

———. *How Long, O Lord? Reflections on Suffering and Evil*. Grand Rapids: Baker, 1990.

———, ed. *Right with God: Justification in the Bible and the World*. Eugene, OR: Wipf and Stock, 2002.

Carson, D. A., Peter O'Brien, and Mark A. Seifrid, eds., *Justification and Variegated Nomism: Volume 1: The Complexities of Second-Temple Judaism*. Grand Rapids: Baker, 2001.

Carson, D. A., Peter O'Brien, and Mark A. Seifrid, eds., *Justification and Variegated Nomism: Volume 2: The Paradoxes of Paul*. Grand Rapids: Baker, 2004.

Chapell, Bryan. *Holiness by Grace: Delighting in the Joy that Is Our Strength*. Wheaton, IL: Crossway, 2001.

Chute, Anthony L., Christopher W. Morgan, and Robert A. Peterson, eds. *Why We Belong: Evangelical Unity and Denominational Diversity*. Wheaton, IL: Crossway, 2013.

Clowney, Edmund P. *The Church*. CCT. Downers Grove, IL: InterVarsity, 1995.

Cole, Graham A. *God the Peacemaker: How Atonement Brings Shalom*. NSBT 25. Downers Grove, IL: InterVarsity, 2009.

————. *He Who Gives Life: The Doctrine of the Holy Spirit.* FET. Wheaton, IL: Crossway, 2007.

Demarest, Bruce A. *The Cross and Salvation: The Doctrine of Salvation.* FET. Wheaton, IL: Crossway, 1997.

Dockery, David S., and Christopher W. Morgan, eds. *Christian Higher Education: Faith, Teaching, and Learning in the Evangelical Tradition.* Wheaton, IL: Crossway, 2018.

Dunn, James D. G. *The New Perspective on Paul.* Grand Rapids: Eerdmans, 2005.

————. *The New Perspective on Paul.* Revised edition. *WUNT,* vol. 185. Grand Rapids: Eerdmans, 2008.

————. *The Theology of Paul the Apostle.* Grand Rapids: Eerdmans, 1998.

————. *Paul and the Mosaic Law.* Grand Rapids: Eerdmans, 2001.

————, and Alan M. Suggate. *The Justice of God: A Fresh Look at the Old Doctrine of Justification by Faith.* Grand Rapids: Eerdmans, 1994.

Easley, Kendell H., and Christopher W. Morgan, eds. *The Community of Jesus: A Theology of the Church.* Nashville: B&H Academic, 2013.

Edwards, Jonathan. *Charity and Its Fruits.* Carlisle, PA: Banner of Truth, 1969.

————. *Freedom of the Will.* The Works of Jonathan Edwards, vol. 1. Edited by Paul Ramsey. New Haven, CT: Yale University Press, 1957.

————. *Religious Affections.* The Works of Jonathan Edwards, vol. 2. Edited by John H. Smith and Harry S. Stout. New Haven, CT: Yale University Press, 1959.

————. *Writings on the Trinity, Grace, and Faith.* The Works of Jonathan Edwards, vol. 21. Edited by Sang Hyun Lee. New Haven: Yale University Press, 2003.

Eilers, Kent, and Kyle Strobel. *Sanctified by Grace: A Theology of the Christian Life.* New York: Bloomsbury T&T Clark, 2014.

Erickson, Millard J. *Christian Theology*. Second edition. Grand Rapids: Baker, 1998.

Evans, William B. *Imputation and Impartation: Union with Christ in American Reformed Theology*. Studies in Christian History and Thought. Eugene, OR: Wipf & Stock, 2009.

Fee, Gordon. *God's Empowering Presence: The Holy Spirit in the Letters of Paul*. Peabody, MA: Hendrickson, 1994.

———. *Pauline Christology: An Exegetical-Theological Study*. Peabody, MA: Hendrickson, 2007.

Feinberg, John. *No One Like Him: The Doctrine of God*. FET. Wheaton, IL: Crossway, 2001.

Ferguson, Sinclair B. *Children of the Living God*. Carlisle, PA: Banner of Truth, 1989.

———. "Christus Victor et Propitiator: The Death of Christ, Substitute and Conqueror." In *For the Fame of God's Name: Essays in Honor of John Piper*, edited by Sam Storms and Justin Taylor, 171–89. Wheaton, IL: Crossway, 2010.

———. *The Holy Spirit*. CCT. Downers Grove, IL: InterVarsity, 1996.

Frame, John M. *The Doctrine of God: A Theology of Lordship*. Phillipsburg, NJ: P&R, 2002.

———. *Systematic Theology: An Introduction to Christian Belief*. Phillipsburg, NJ: P&R, 2013.

Gaffin, Richard B., Jr. *By Faith, Not by Sight: Paul and the Order of Salvation*. Second edition. Phillipsburg, NJ: P&R, 2013.

———. *Resurrection and Redemption*. Second edition. Phillipsburg, NJ: P&R, 1987.

———. "Union with Christ: Some Biblical and Theological Reflections." In *Always Reforming: Explorations in Systematic Theology*, edited by A. T. B. McGowan, 271–88. Downers Grove, IL: IVP Academic, 2006.

Garner, David B. *Sons in the Son: The Riches and Reach of Adoption in Christ.* Phillipsburg, NJ: P&R, 2016.

Gonet, Christina. *The Narrative of Salvation in Anselm of Canterbury's* Cur Deus Homo: *Extracting and Explicating the Story Embedded in the Text.* PhD diss, Gateway Seminary, 2022.

Green, Bradley G. *Covenant and Commandment: Works, Obedience, and Faithfulness in the Christian Life.* NSBT 33. Downers Grove, IL: InterVarsity, 2014.

Grudem, Wayne. *Systematic Theology.* Grand Rapids: MI: Zondervan, 1994.

Hill, Charles E., and Frank A. James III, eds. *The Glory of the Atonement: Biblical, Theological, and Practical Perspectives.* Downers Grove, IL: InterVarsity, 2004.

Hoekema, Anthony E. *The Bible and the Future.* Grand Rapids: Eerdmans, 1979.

———. *Created in God's Image.* Grand Rapids: Eerdmans, 1986.

———. *Saved by Grace.* Grand Rapids: Eerdmans, 1989.

Horton, Michael S. *The Christian Faith: A Systematic Theology for Pilgrims on the Way.* Grand Rapids: Zondervan, 2011.

———. *Covenant and Salvation: Union with Christ.* Louisville: Westminster John Knox, 2007.

Hughes, Philip Edgcumbe. *The True Image: The Origin and Destiny of Man in Christ.* Grand Rapids: Eerdmans, 1989.

Hurtado, Larry W. *Lord Jesus Christ: Devotion to Jesus in Earliest Christianity.* Grand Rapids: Eerdmans, 2003.

Johnson, Marcus Peter. *One with Christ: An Evangelical Theology of Salvation.* Wheaton, IL: Crossway, 2013.

Kapic, Kelly M., ed. *Sanctification: Explorations in Theology and Practice.* Downers Grove, IL: IVP Academic, 2014.

Kelly, J. N. D. *Early Christian Doctrines.* Revised edition. San Francisco: Harper and Row, 1978.

Kim, Seyoon. *The Origin of Paul's Gospel*. Grand Rapids: Eerdmans, 1981.

———. *Paul and the New Perspective: Second Thoughts on the Origin of Paul's Gospel*. Grand Rapids: Eerdmans, 2002.

Köstenberger, Andreas J. *A Theology of John's Gospel and Letters*. Biblical Theology of the New Testament. Grand Rapids: Zondervan, 2009.

Kruse, Colin G. *Paul, the Law, and Justification*. Peabody, MA: Hendrickson, 1997.

Ladd, George E. *The Presence of the Future: The Eschatology of Biblical Realism*. Grand Rapids: Eerdmans, 1974.

———. *A Theology of the New Testament*. Grand Rapids: Eerdmans, 1974.

Letham, Robert. *The Holy Trinity: In Scripture, History, Theology, and Worship*. Phillipsburg, NJ: P&R, 2004.

———. *Union with Christ: In Scripture, History, and Theology*. Phillipsburg, NJ: P&R, 2011.

———. *The Work of Christ*. CCT. Downers Grove, IL: InterVarsity, 1993.

Lints, Richard. *The Fabric of Theology: A Prolegomenon to Evangelical Theology*. Grand Rapids: Eerdmans, 1993.

Luther, Martin. *The Bondage of the Will*. Translated by J. I. Packer, and O. R. Johnston. Old Tappan, NJ: Revell, 1957.

Macleod, Donald. *The Person of Christ*. CCT. Downers Grove, IL: InterVarsity, 1998.

Marshall, I. Howard. *Aspects of the Atonement: Cross and Resurrection in the Reconciling of God and Humanity*. London: Paternoster, 2007.

———. *Jesus the Saviour: Studies in New Testament Theology*. Downers Grove, IL: InterVarsity, 1990.

———. *New Testament Theology*. Downers Grove, IL/Leicester, UK: IVP and Apollos, 2004.

———. "Soteriology in Hebrews." In *The Epistle to the Hebrews and Christian Theology*, edited by Richard Bauckham, Daniel R. Driver, Trevor A.

Hart, and Nathan MacDonald, 253–80. Grand Rapids: Eerdmans, 2009.

———. "The Theology of the Atonement." In *The Atonement Debate: Papers from the London Symposium on the Theology of Atonement*, edited by Derek Tidball, David Hilborn, and Justin Thacker, 49–68. Grand Rapids: Zondervan, 2008.

Martin, D. B. *Slavery as Salvation: The Metaphor of Slavery in Pauline Christianity*. New Haven: Yale University Press, 1990.

Martin, Ralph P. *Reconciliation: A Study of Paul's Theology*. Atlanta: John Knox, 1981.

McDonald, H. D. *The New Testament Concept of Atonement*. Grand Rapids: Baker, 1994.

McGowan, A. T. B. "The Atonement as Penal Substitution." In *Always Reforming: Explorations in Systematic Theology*, edited by A. T. B. McGowan, 183–210. Downers Grove, IL: InterVarsity, 2006.

McGrath, Alister E. *Iustitia Dei: A History of the Christian Doctrine of Justification*. New York: Cambridge University Press, 1986.

McKnight, Scot. *The Apostle Paul and the Christian Life: Ethical and Missional Implications of the New Perspective*. Grand Rapids: Baker Academic, 2016.

McKnight, Scot, and B. J. Oropeza, eds. *Perspectives on Paul: Five Views*. Grand Rapids: Baker Academic, 2020.

Morgan, Christopher W. *A Theology of James: Wisdom for God's People*. EBT. Phillipsburg, NJ: P&R, 2010.

Morgan, Christopher W., ed. *Biblical Spirituality*. Theology in Community. Wheaton, IL: Crossway, 2019.

———. *The Love of God*. Theology in Community. Wheaton, IL: Crossway, 2016.

Morgan, Christopher W., and B. Dale Ellenburg. *James: Wisdom for the Community*. Focus on the Bible Commentaries. Fearn, UK: Christian Focus, 2008.

Morgan, Christopher W., Matthew Y. Emerson, and R. Lucas Stamps, eds. *Baptists and the Christian Tradition: Towards an Evangelical Baptist Catholicity*. Nashville: B&H Academic, 2020.

Morgan, Christopher W., with Robert A. Peterson. *Christian Theology: The Biblical Story and Our Faith*. Nashville: B&H Academic, 2020.

Morgan, Christopher W., and Robert A. Peterson. *A Concise Dictionary of Theological Terms*. Nashville: B&H Academic, 2020.

———. *The Glory of God and Paul*. NSBT 58. Edited by D. A. Carson. Downers Grove, IL: Intervarsity, 2022.

———. *What Is Hell?* Basics of the Faith. Phillipsburg, NJ: P&R, 2000.

Morgan, Christopher W., and Robert A. Peterson, eds. *The Deity of Christ*. Theology in Community. Wheaton, IL: Crossway, 2011.

———. *Faith Comes by Hearing: A Response to Inclusivism*. Downers Grove, IL: InterVarsity, 2008.

———. *Fallen: A Theology of Sin*. Theology in Community. Wheaton, IL: Crossway, 2013.

———. *The Glory of God*. Theology in Community. Wheaton, IL: Crossway, 2010.

———. *Heaven*. Theology in Community. Wheaton, IL: Crossway, 2014.

———. *Hell under Fire*. Grand Rapids: Zondervan, 2004.

———. *Is Hell for Real?* Grand Rapids: Zondervan, 2001.

———. *The Kingdom of God*. Theology in Community. Wheaton, IL: Crossway, 2012.

———. *Suffering and the Goodness of God*. Theology in Community. Wheaton, IL: Crossway, 2008.

Morris, Leon. *The Apostolic Preaching of the Cross*. Third edition. Grand Rapids: Eerdmans, 1965.

———. *The Atonement: Its Meaning and Significance*. Leicester, UK: InterVarsity, 1983.

————. *The Cross in the New Testament.* Grand Rapids: Eerdmans, 1965.

Murray, John. *The Atonement.* Philadelphia: Presbyterian and Reformed, 1962.

————. *Redemption Accomplished and Applied.* Grand Rapids: Eerdmans 1955.

Owen, John. *Overcoming Sin and Temptation.* Edited by Kelly Kapic and Justin Taylor. Wheaton, IL: Crossway, 2006.

Packer, James I. *Evangelism and the Sovereignty of God.* Chicago: InterVarsity, 1961.

————. *Keep in Step with the Spirit.* Grand Rapids: Revell, 1984.

————. *Knowing God.* Downers Grove, IL: InterVarsity, 1993.

————. *A Quest for Godliness: The Puritan Vision of the Christian Life.* Wheaton, IL: Crossway, 1990.

————. *Rediscovering Holiness: Know the Fullness of Life with God.* Ventura, CA: Regal, 2009.

————. "What Did the Cross Achieve? The Logic of Penal Substitution." *Tyndale Bulletin* 25 (1974): 3–45.

Peterson, David. *Possessed by God: A New Testament Theology of Sanctification and Holiness.* NSBT 1. Downers Grove, IL: InterVarsity, 1995.

————. *Transformed by God: New Covenant Life and Ministry.* Downers Grove, IL: IVP Academic, 2012.

Peterson, David, ed. *Where Wrath and Mercy Meet: Proclaiming the Atonement Today.* Carlisle, UK: Paternoster, 2001.

Peterson, Robert A. *Adopted by God.* Phillipsburg, NJ: P&R, 2001.

————. *The Assurance of Salvation: Biblical Hope for Our Struggles.* Grand Rapids: Zondervan, 2019.

————. *Calvin and the Atonement.* Fearn, UK: Mentor, 1999.

————. *Election and Free Will.* EBT. Phillipsburg, NJ: P&R, 2001.

————. *Life Everlasting: The Unfolding Story of Heaven.* EBT. Phillipsburg, NJ: P&R, 2012.

———. *Getting to Know John's Gospel: A Fresh Look at Its Main Ideas.* Phillipsburg, NJ: P&R, 1989.

———. *Our Secure Salvation: Perseverance and Apostasy.* EBT. Phillipsburg, NJ: P&R, 2005.

———. *Salvation Accomplished by the Son: The Work of Christ.* Wheaton, IL: Crossway, 2012.

———. *Salvation Applied by the Spirit: Union with Christ.* Wheaton, IL: Crossway, 2014.

Peterson, Robert A., and Michael D. Williams. *Why I Am Not an Arminian.* Downers Grove, IL: InterVarsity, 2004.

Pinnock, Clark H., ed. *Grace Unlimited.* Minneapolis: Bethany House, 1975.

Piper, John. *Counted Righteous in Christ: Should We Abandon the Imputation of Christ's Righteousness?* Wheaton, IL: Crossway, 2002.

———. *The Future of Justification: A Response to N. T. Wright.* Wheaton, IL: Crossway, 2007.

Quarles, Charles L. *A Theology of Matthew: Jesus Revealed as Deliverer, King, and Incarnate Creator.* EBT. Phillipsburg, NJ: P&R, 2013.

Reeves, Michael. *Delighting in the Trinity: An Introduction to the Christian Faith.* Downers Grove, IL: IVP Academic, 2012.

Ridderbos, Herman. *Paul: An Outline of His Theology.* Translated by John Richard de Witt. Grand Rapids: Eerdmans, 1975.

Rodgers, Kevin. *Introduction to the Series.* ATS. Niamey, Niger: Eleaf Resources, 2021.

Rosner, Brian S. *Paul and the Law: Keeping the Commandments of God.* NSBT 31. Downers Grove, IL: InterVarsity, 2013.

Rusch, William G., and George A. Lindbeck, eds. *Justification and the Future of the Ecumenical Movement: The Joint Declaration on the Doctrine of Justification.* Unitas Books. Collegeville, MN: Liturgical Press, 2003.

Ryle, J. C. *Holiness: Its Nature, Hindrances, Difficulties, and Roots.* London: William Hunt & Co., 1889.

Sanders, E. P. *Paul and Palestinian Judaism: A Comparison in Patterns of Religion.* London: SCM, 1977.

Sanders, Fred. *The Triune God.* New Studies in Dogmatics. Edited by Michael Allen and Scott R. Swain. Grand Rapids: Zondervan, 2016.

Schreiner, Thomas R. *1, 2 Peter, Jude.* New American Commentary 37. Nashville: Broadman and Holman, 2003.

———, *40 Questions about Christians and Biblical Law.* 40 Questions & Answers. Grand Rapids: Kregel Academic, 2010.

———. *Commentary on Hebrews.* Evangelical Biblical Theology Commentary. Bellingham, WA: Lexham, 2021.

———. *Covenant and God's Purpose for the World.* Short Studies in Biblical Theology. Wheaton, IL: Crossway, 2017.

———. *Faith Alone: The Doctrine of Justification.* Grand Rapids: Zondervan, 2015.

———. *Galatians.* Zondervan Exegetical Commentary on the New Testament. Grand Rapids: Zondervan, 2010.

———. *Handbook on Acts and Paul's Letters.* Handbooks on the New Testament. Grand Rapids: Baker Academic, 2019.

———. *Interpreting the Pauline Epistles.* Second edition. Grand Rapids: Baker Academic, 2011.

———. *The Joy of Hearing: A Theology of the Book of Revelation.* Wheaton, IL: Crossway, 2021.

———. *The King in His Beauty: A Biblical Theology of the Old and New Testaments.* Grand Rapids: Baker Academic, 2113.

———. *The Law and Its Fulfillment: A Pauline Theology of Law.* Grand Rapids: Baker, 1993.

———. *Magnifying God in Christ: A Summary of New Testament Theology.* Grand Rapids: Baker Academic, 2010.

———. *New Testament Theology: Magnifying God in Christ.* Grand Rapids: Baker, 2008.

———. *Paul: Apostle of God's Glory.* Downers Grove, IL: IVP Academic, 2001.

———. *Romans.* Baker Exegetical Commentary on the New Testament. Grand Rapids: Baker Academic, 1998.

———. *Run to Win the Prize: Perseverance in the New Testament.* Wheaton, IL: Crossway, 2010.

———. *Spiritual Gifts: What They Are and Why They Matter.* Nashville: B&H, 2018.

Schreiner, Thomas R., and Ardel B. Caneday. *The Race Set Before Us: A Biblical Theology of Perseverance & Assurance.* Grand Rapids: Baker Academic, 2013.

Schreiner, Thomas R., Luke Timothy Johnson, Douglas A. Campbell, and Mark D. Nanos. *Four Views on the Apostle Paul.* Grand Rapids: Zondervan, 2012.

Schreiner, Thomas R., and Bruce A. Ware, eds. *Still Sovereign: Contemporary Perspectives on Election, Foreknowledge, and Grace.* Grand Rapids: Baker Academic, 2000.

Seifrid, Mark A. *Christ, Our Righteousness: Paul's Theology of Justification.* NSBT 9. Downers Grove, IL: InterVarsity, 2000.

Stott, John R. W. *The Cross of Christ.* Downers Grove, IL: InterVarsity, 1986.

Stuhlmacher, Peter. *Revisiting Paul's Doctrine of Justification: A Challenge to the New Perspective.* Downers Grove, IL: InterVarsity, 2001.

Tankersley, Lee. "The Courtroom and the Created Order: How Penal Substitution Brings about New Creation." PhD diss., Southern Baptist Theological Seminary, 2010.

Wellum, Stephen J. *God the Son Incarnate: The Doctrine of Christ.* FET. Wheaton, IL: Crossway, 2016.

Vanhoozer, Kevin J. *The Drama of Doctrine: A Canonical Linguistic Approach to Christian Theology*. Louisville: Westminster John Knox, 2005.

Vos, Geerhardus. *The Pauline Eschatology*. Grand Rapids: Baker, 1979 (orig. 1930).

Waltke, Bruce K. *An Old Testament Theology*. Grand Rapids: Zondervan, 2007.

Waters, Guy Prentiss. *Justification and the New Perspectives on Paul: A Review and Response*. Phillipsburg, NJ: P&R, 2004.

Westerholm, Stephen. *Perspectives Old and New on Paul: The "Lutheran" Paul and His Critics*. Grand Rapids: Eerdmans, 2003.

Williams, Michael D. *Far as the Curse Is Found: The Covenant Story of Redemption*. Phillipsburg, NJ: P&R, 2005.

Wright, N. T. *Justification: God's Plan & Paul's Vision*. Downers Grove, IL: IVP Academic, 2009.

———. *Paul and His Recent Interpreters: Some Contemporary Debates*. London: SPCK, 2015.

———. *What Saint Paul Really Said: Was Paul of Tarsus the Real Founder of Christianity?* Grand Rapids: Eerdmans, 1997.

Yoakum, Trevor, and Sylvain Allaboe. *The Doctrine of God*. ATS. Niamey, Niger: Eleaf Resources, 2021.

NAME INDEX

SUBJECT INDEX

A

Abba, 217–18, 302
Abel, 10, 134, 160
Abraham, 10, 18, 27, 43–46, 72–73, 80, 86, 91, 134–35, 166, 168, 172, 178, 182, 199–200, 210, 286–87, 363, 398, 403, 405, 439
access, 35, 336, 402, 443
activism, 250
Adam, 8–9, 17–18, 28–29, 65, 70, 120, 123, 168, 192, 196, 199, 287, 320
Adam Christology, 25–26, 174, 192, 287, 329, 380, 389, 392
adoption, 1, 14, 31, 41, 55, 191, 203, 205, 209–20, 302, 344, 349–50, 358–59, 364, 370–71, 381–82, 392–93, 404, 422–23, 436, 440–41
affliction, 161, 306, 335, 448
already/not yet, 4, 32, 213, 220, 258–59, 283, 314, 333, 375–86, 424
annihilationism, 448
antichrist, 314, 373
apostasy, 15, 265–68, 273–74, 279, 287, 306–8, 313–15, 373, 426
apostles, 13, 31, 49, 107, 129, 368
appointment, 47, 53, 78, 85, 171, 353
Arminianism, 69–70, 72, 80
Arminians, 62–63, 70

Arminius, Jacob, 68–69
assurance, 99, 138, 185, 264–65, 268, 279, 300–306, 311–12, 316, 331, 388, 423, 425–26
Assyria, 207, 364
atonement, 33, 39, 92, 164, 169, 195–96, 216, 299, 369–70, 392, 395–96, 401
    limited, 70
    universal, 70
attributes of God, 127, 171, 283–87, 373, 426, 432
Augustine, 63–66, 68
authority, 7–8, 52, 77, 188, 210

B

baptism, 19, 25, 30, 93, 114, 117–18, 124, 187, 231–32, 253
Barnabas, 53, 85, 131, 366
Belgic Confession, 71
belief, 1, 5, 18, 52, 69–71, 85, 103–4, 116, 135, 137–38, 144, 210, 217, 271, 324–26, 333, 349–50, 370, 395
Beza, Theodore, 68
body, 9, 213, 253, 337–38, 341, 352, 374, 429, 447
bondage of the will, 66
book of life, 14, 62–63, 75
born again, 1, 111, 113–15, 125, 215, 348, 366

SCRIPTURE INDEX

481